Micro-Distilleries in the U.S. and Canada

3rd Edition

David J. Reimer Sr.

Micro-Distilleries in the U.S. and Canada, Third Edition

Cover Design by: Jerry F. Cavill Jr.

Website: www.microdistillerybooks.com
Email: david@microdistillerybooks.com, sales@microdistillerybooks.com
Facebook: Micro Distilleries, Micro-Distilleries in the U.S. and Canada
Twitter: @djreimersr, @microdbooks
Pinterest: MicroD Books

Printed in the United States of America
April 2013

Print ISBN: 978-0-9852599-3-8

eBook ISBN: 978-0-9852599-4-5

Published by:

Crave Press

www.cravepress.com

Acknowledgements

I would like to thank everyone at the distilleries that took the time to talk with me and had the patience to answer all my questions. It was their expertise, enthusiasm, and cooperation that helped to steer me in the right direction to make this third edition possible.

I would be remiss if I didn't thank Christina Steffy, Jerry F. Cavill Jr., and Enchanted Acres Photography by Roxanne Richardson for helping to bring all of this together again.

Front Cover

Row 1
Prairie Organic Vodka - Phillips Distilling Company, MN
Velocipede Vodka - Elm City Distillery LLC, CT
Luminous Vodka - Door County Distillery, WI
Cathead Vodka - Cathead Distillery LLC, MS
Plantation Vodka - Thirteenth Colony Distilleries, GA
Koenig Potato Vodka - Koenig Distillery, ID
WebFoot Vodka - 4 Spirits Distillery, OR
Smugglers' Notch Rum - Smugglers' Notch Distillery, VT
Maui Reserve Gold Rum - Haleakala Distilleries, HI
Whistling Andy Hibiscus-Coconut Rum - Whistling Andy, MT
Toulouse Red Absinthe Rouge - Atelier Vie, LA

Row 2
Devil's Share Bourbon - Ballast Point Spirits, CA
Dark Horse Distillery Reserve Bourbon - Dark Horse Distillery, KS
Wigle Organic Rye Whiskey - Pittsburgh Distilling Co., PA
Willett Straight Bourbon Whiskey - Willett Distillery, KY
Fireside Bourbon - Mile High Spirits LLC, CO
Baby Blue Whisky - Balcones Distillery, TX
Thirteen Corners Whiskey - Wishkah River Distillery, WA
Catdaddy Spiced Moonshine - Piedmont Distillers, NC

Row 3
(left)
Eight Bells Rum - New England Distilling, ME
Owney's NYC Rum - The Noble Experiment NYC, NY
Spring Mill Straight Bourbon - Heartland Distillers, IN

Row 3
(right upper)
Canadian Rye Vodka - 66 Gilead Distillery, ON Canada
Cinco ~ Five Star Vodka - Azar Distillery, TX
Widow Jane Bourbon Whiskey - Cacao Prieto LLC, NY
Industry City Distillery Batch No. 3 - Industry City Distillery Inc., NY
Real Russian Vodka - Premier Distillery LLC, IL

Row 3
(right lower)
Watershed Distillery Four Peel Gin - Watershed Distillery, OH
Schramm Organic Gin - Pemberton Distillery Inc., BC Canada
RE:FIND Gin - RE:FIND Distillery, CA
Roundhouse Gin - Roundhouse Sprits, CO

Row 4
Spike Vodka - Spink Distillery, TX

Back Cover
Down Time Single Malt Whiskey - Deerhammer Distilling Co., CO
Bowen's Whiskey - Bowen's Spirits Inc., CA
Oola Waitsburg Bourbon Whiskey - Oola Distillery, WA

Preface

A micro-distillery, often referred to as an "Artisan" "boutique" or "craft" distillery, is a small distillery producing premium spirits in small batches. While this term is most commonly used in the United States, micro-distilleries exist all over the world; however this book concentrates on the distilleries in the U.S. and Canada.

For a trade that dates back to the 1600s in America, it has taken a long time to recover from Prohibition. For the first time since the days of Al Capone, small distilleries are being reestablished. It was during Prohibition in the United States that most small distilleries were forced out of business, leaving only the mega-distilleries to resume operation when Prohibition was repealed. However, within the last decade, the number of micro-distilleries in the United States and Canada has rocketed from a couple dozen to more than a couple hundred. This number represents not only stand-alone distilleries, but also includes many micro-breweries and small wineries that established distilleries within their brewing or winemaking operations. The west coast of the U.S. has experienced the highest number of micro-distillery openings as these are states with more relaxed legislation.

Today's micro-distillery trend is a long way from where it was before Prohibition. After the repeal of the eighteenth amendment, what remained of the country's liquor industry was consolidated into a few large companies. While these mammoths substantially profited from Prohibition, they also greatly lowered consumer expectations. At the time, America's large but then underground drinking population wasn't fussy, and many drinkers believed they were getting the real deal from bootleggers or speakeasy bartenders, who often rebottled homemade gin or whiskey and sold it as top-shelf liquor.

Despite the recession, people with a passion for hand crafted sprits are opening micro-distilleries. And, contrary to myths about the foolishness of starting a business in a downturn, many are holding their own financially and finding audiences for their award winning, hand-crafted superior spirits.

While micro-distilleries represent a less than 5% of the overall spirits market, micro-distillers appeal to individuals who appreciate quality over mass production.

Peaden Brothers Distillery

Main Street
Fairhope, AL 36532
251-583-5660

Owners / Operators:
Trey Peaden, Co-owner
Tyler Peaden, Co-owner
Robert Ellis, Co-owner / International Sales

Email: info@peadenbrothersdistillery.com
Website: www.peadenbrothersdistillery.com
Facebook: Peaden Brothers Distillery
Twitter: @peadenbrothers

Type: Micro-distillery under construction. Opening in 2013.

Hours of operation: TBA

Tours: Available after opening. Watch website.

Types of spirits produced: Flavored whiskeys, aged rums

Names of spirits:
• TBA

Best known for / most popular: TBA

Average bottle price: TBA

Distribution: U.S., Canada

Interesting facts:
The Peaden Brothers are third generation distillers of southern whiskey.

Alaska Distillery

1540 North Shoreline Drive
Wasilla, AK 99654
907-382-6250

Owners / Operators:
Toby Foster, CEO / President
Shawn Ansley, Owner
Scotti MacDonald, Owner
Winston Chelf, Owner

Email: toby@alaskadistillery.com
Website: www.alaskadistillery.com
Facebook: Alaska Distillery
Twitter: @AK_Distillery

Type: Micro-distillery. Opened in 2007.

Hours of operation:
Monday through Friday, 8:00am to 5:00pm

Tours: Tours are available

Types of spirits produced: Gin, vodka

Names of spirits:
- Permafrost Alaska Vodka
- Permafrost Alaska Gin
- Alaska Distillery Gin
- Alaska Distillery Smoked Salmon Vodka
- Alaska Distillery Red Raspberry Vodka
- Alaska Distillery High Bush Cranberry Vodka
- Alaska Distillery Low Bush Blueberry Vodka
- Alaska Distillery Birch Syrup Vodka
- Alaska Distillery Wild Blackberry Vodka
- Alaska Distillery Rhubarb Vodka
- Frostbite Alaska Vodka
- Purgatory Hemp Seed Vodka
- Bear Creek Alaska Whiskey

Best known for / most popular: Alaska Distillery Smoked Salmon Vodka

Average bottle price: $24.99 to $37.99

Distribution: AK, AZ, CA, CO, GA, IL, IN, KY, MT, TN, TX, WA; Canada AB, BC

Interesting facts: Alaska Distillery is Alaska's first distillery

Bare Distillery

6310 A Street
Anchorage, AK 99518
907-561-2100

Owners / Operators:
Kyle T. Ryan, President / Founder
Jeremy Loyer, VP / Founder

Email: vodka@truulipeak.com
Website: www.truulipeak.com
Facebook: Truuli Peak Vodka
Twitter: @TruuliPeakVodka
Blog: Truuli Peak Vodka Blog
YouTube: Hot Mixology, Truuli Peak Vodka

Type: Micro-distillery. Opened in 2011.

Hours of operation: Daily, 9:00am to 5:00pm

Tours: Available by appointment

Types of spirits produced: Vodka

Names of spirits:
• Truuli Peak Vodka

Best known for / most popular: Truuli Peak Vodka

Average bottle price: $39.99

Distribution: AK

Interesting facts:
• Truuli Peak Vodka is named after the highest elevation in the Kenai Mountain range, situated just outside of Anchorage. Rising at 6,612 feet above sea level, Truuli Peak is a majestic summit within the pristine Alaskan environment. The word Truuli is the ancient Alaska native term for the Kenai Mountain Range.
• Truuli Peak Vodka is made from local barley, honey and Eklutna glacier water.

Arizona High Spirits Distillery

h i g h s p i r t s

4366 E. Huntington Drive, Bldg. 2
Flagstaff, AZ 86004
928-853-1021

Owners / Operators:
Dana Kanzler, Managing Partner / Head Distiller

Email: dskanzler@yahoo.com
Website: www.arizonahighspirits.com
Facebook: Mogollon Brewing Company
Twitter: @AZHighSpirits
YouTube: Arizona High Spirits

Type: Micro-distillery. Opened in 2006.

Hours of operation: Monday through Friday, 7:00am to 5:00pm

Tours: Available by appointment

Types of spirits produced: Vodka, gin, rum, whisky

Names of spirits:
- Prickly Pear Vodka
- Chili Vodka
- American Vodka
- Desert Dry Gin
- Pieces of Eight Spiced Rum
- Prickly Pear Liqueur
- Single Malt Mesquite Smoked Whisky

Best known for: Prickly Pear Vodka

Average bottle price: $20.00 to $30.00

Distribution: AZ, CA, NV, TX

Interesting facts: Arizona High Spirits is located at an elevation of 7,000 feet.

Desert Diamond Distillery

4875 N Olympic Drive
Kingman, AZ 86401
928-757-7611

Owners / Operators:
The Patt Family

Email: info@desertdiamonddistillery.com
Website: www.desertdiamonddistillery.com
Facebook: Desert Diamond Distillery
Twitter: @D3Spirits

Type: Micro-distillery. Opened in 2009.

Hours of operation:
Monday through Thursday, 10:00am to 5:00pm
Friday and Saturday, 10:00am to 6:00pm
Sunday by appointment only

Tours: Available by appointment

Types of spirits produced: Vodka, rum

Names of spirits:
- Desert Diamond Distillery Gold Miner Vodka
- Desert Diamond Distillery Gold Miner Rum
- Desert Diamond Distillery Gold Miner Agave Rum
- Desert Diamond Distillery Gold Miner Dark Rum
- Desert Diamond Distillery Gold Miner Barrel Reserve Rum

Best known for / most popular: Not provided

Average bottle price: Not provided

Distribution: AZ, NV

Rock Town Distillery Inc.

ROCK TOWN
DISTILLERY
LITTLE ROCK, ARKANSAS
www.rocktowndistillery.com

1216 East 6th Street
Little Rock, AR 72202
501-907-5244

Owners / Operators:
Phil Brandon, Owner

Email: phil@rocktowndistillery.com
Website: www.arkansaslightning.com
Facebook: Rock Town Distillery
Twitter: @rocktowndistill
Instagram: phil4100

Type: Micro-distillery. Opened in 2010.

Hours of operation:
Monday through Friday, 8:00am to 5:00pm

Tours:
Wednesday through Friday, 4:00pm
Saturday and Sunday, 1:30pm and 3:00pm
No reservation required

Types of spirits produced:
Vodka, gin, rum, bourbon, whiskey,
moonshine and flavored moonshines

Names of spirits:
- Brandon's Vodka
- Brandon's Gin
- Arkansas Lightning (Moonshine)
- Arkansas Young Bourbon Whiskey
- Arkansas Hickory Smoked Whiskey
- Riverboat Rum
- Apple Pie Arkansas Lightning
- Lightning Hot Cinnamon Arkansas Lightning

Best known for / most popular: Apple Pie Arkansas Lightning

Average bottle price: $29.99

Distribution: AR, FL, GA, IL, LA, MO, MS, OR, OK, PA, TN, TX

Interesting facts:
Rock Town Distillery is Arkansas' first legal distillery since prohibition.

1512 Spirits

Rohnert Park, CA 94928

Owners / Operators:
Salvatore P. Cimino, Owner / Master Distiller

Email: info@1512spirits.com
Website: www.1512spirits.com
Facebook: 1512 Spirits
Twitter: @1512Spirits

Type: Nano-distillery. Opened in 2011.

Hours of operation: Not provided

Tours: Not provided

Types of spirits produced: Whiskey, grappa, poitin

Names of spirits:
- 1512 Barbershop Rye Whiskey
- 1512 Spirits Aged 100% Rye Whiskey
- 1512 Spirits 2nd Chance Wheat Whiskey
- 1512 Spirits Signature Poitin
- 1512 Spirits Grappa
- 1512 Spirits Bourbon #1

Best known for / most popular:
1512 Spirits Aged 100% Rye Whiskey

Average bottle price: $115.00

Distribution: CA, NY; UK

Interesting facts: Smallest commercial distillery in CA.

American Craft Whiskey Distillery and **Greenway Distillers Inc.**

American Craft Whiskey Distillery (ACWD)
1110 Bel Arbres Road
Redwood Valley, CA 95470

Greenway Distiller Inc.
5000 Low Gap Road
Ukiah, CA 95482

Office address:
157 E. Gobbi Street
Ukiah, CA 95482

707-485-2941

Owners / Operators:
Crispin Cain, President / Distiller / Spirits Master
Tamar Kaye, Vice President

Email: acwd.1@netzero.net , crispin@greenwaydistillers.com
Website: www.craftdistillers.com
Facebook: Greenway Distillers, Inc.

Type: Micro-distillery. Opened in 2010.

Hours of operation: Monday through Friday, 6:00am to 5:00pm

Tours: Available by appointment

Types of spirits produced:
ACWD produces whiskey, GD produces absinthe and rose liqueur.

Names of spirits:
- Crispin's Rose Liqueur
- Germain-Robin Absinthe Superieure
- Low Gap Clear Whiskey

Best known for / most popular: Crispin's Rose Liqueur

Average bottle price: $45.00

Distribution: See www.caddellwilliams.com

Interesting facts: Not provided

Ballast Point Spirits

10051 Old Grove Road, Suite B1
San Diego, CA 92131
858-695-2739

Owners / Operators:
Jack White and Yuseff Cherney, Owners

Email: yuseff@ballastpoint.com
Website: www.ballastpoint.com
Facebook: Ballast Point Brewing & Spirits
Twitter: @BPbrewing

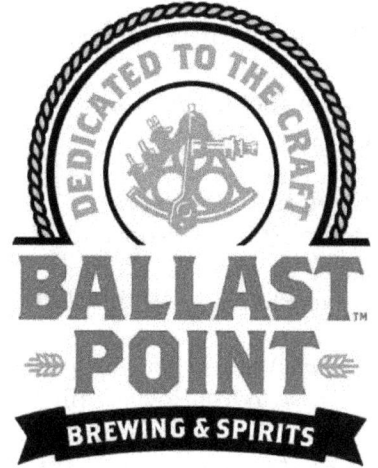

Type: Brewery / Micro-distillery. Opened in 2008.

Hours of operation:
Monday through Saturday, 11:00am to 9:00pm
Sunday, 11:00am to 7:00pm

Tours: Available
Monday through Saturday, 12:00pm, 2:00pm, and 5:00pm
Sundays, 12:00pm and 2:00pm

Types of spirits produced: Bourbon, gin, rum, vodka, whiskey

Names of spirits:
- Old Grove Gin
- Three Sheets Barrel Aged Rum
- Three Sheets White Rum
- Devil's Share Whiskey
- Devils' Share Bourbon
- Devil's Share Moonshine
- Fugu Vodka

Average bottle price:
$24.00 to $65.00

Distribution: CA

Interesting facts:
First licensed distillery in San Diego since Prohibition

Bowen's Spirits Inc.

Bakersfield, CA 93308
661-343-2041

Owners / Operators:
Wade Bowen, Proprietor / CEO
JoJo Bowen, VP Sales
Dave Plivelich, VP Marketing

Email: Wade@BowenSpirits.com
      JoJo@BowenSpirits.com
      Dave@BowenSpirits.com
Website: www.bowenspirits.com
Facebook: Bowen's Whiskey

Type: Micro-distillery. Opened in 2012.

Hours of operation: Not provided

Tours: Not provided

Types of spirits produced: Whiskey

Names of spirits:
• Bowen's Whiskey

Best known for / most popular: Bowen's Whiskey

Average bottle price: $38.99

Distribution: CA, DC, DE, IL, WY; Canada MB

Interesting facts:
Bakersfield is the home of country music's legendary Bakersfield sound created, most notably, by Buck Owen's and Merle Haggard.

10

Cal-Czech Distillery

1209 Hwy 49
Angels Camp, CA 95222
209-736-2990

Owners / Operators:
Rocky Cozzo, Owner / Distiller

Email: rocky@vodkamorava.com
Website: www.vodkamorava.com
Facebook: Cal-Czech Distillery
Twitter: @VodkaMorava

Type: Micro-distillery. Opened in 2012.

Hours of operation: Monday through Friday, 9:00am to 5:00pm

Tours: Available by appointment

Types of spirits produced: Vodka

Names of spirits:
• Vodka Morava

Best known for: Vodka Morava

Average bottle price: $30.00 to $40.00

Distribution: Available through distributors

Interesting facts: Techniques are inspired by Czech and Ukrainian distillers.

Charbay Winery & Distillery

4001 Spring Mountain Road
St. Helena, CA 94574
707-963-9327

Owners / Operators:
Miles and Susan Karakasevic, Owners
Miles Karakasevic, Grand Master Distiller
Susan Karakasevic, General Manager
Marko Karakasevic, Master Distiller
Charles Henning, Managing Director

Email: Susan Karakasevic: susan@charbay.com
     Marko Karakasevic: marko@charbay.com
     John Reagh, Tasting Room: visit@charbay.com
Website: www.charbay.com
Facebook: Charbay Winery & Distillery
Twitter: @Charbay
Blog: www.charbayblog.com

Type: Winery / Micro-distillery. Opened in 1983.

Hours of operation: Daily, 10:00am to 4:00pm

Tours: Available

Types of spirits produced: Whiskey, vodka, rum, grappa, brandy, liqueurs

Names of spirits:
* Charbay Black Walnut Liqueur
* Charbay Brandy No. 83 Folle Blanche
* Charbay Doubled & Twisted Light Whiskey
* Charbay Grappa di Marko
* Charbay Tahitian Vanilla Bean Rum
* Charbay Tequila Blanco
* Charbay Vodka
* Charbay Whiskey, Release II

Best known for / most popular: Charbay Vodka and Whiskey

Average bottle price: $38.00 to $350.00

Distribution: Nationwide in high end shops, restaurants, and clubs

Interesting facts:
* Charbay is family owned and operated by 12th and 13th generation distillers and winemakers.
* Charbay Whiskey, Release 5 won the 2013 Good Food Award

Cutler's Artisan Spirits

137 Anacapa Street, Ste. D
Santa Barbara, CA 93101
805-680-4009

Owners / Operators:
Ian Cutler, Owner / Head Distiller

Email: info@cutlersartisan.com
Website: www.cutlersartisan.com
Facebook: Cutler's Artisan Spirits

Type: Micro-distillery. Opening in 2013.

Hours of operation: Monday through Thursday, 1:00pm to 5:00pm
Saturday and Sunday, 10:00am to 5:00pm

Tours: Available by appointment

Types of spirits produced: Whiskey, vodka, gin, liqueurs

Names of spirits:
• TBA

Best known for / most popular: TBA

Average bottle price: TBA

Distribution: TBA

Interesting facts: Not provided

Distillery No. 209

Pier 50 Shed B, Mailbox 9
San Francisco, CA 94158
415-369-0209

DISTILLERY № 209

Owners / Operators:
Leslie Rudd, Founder
Samantha Rudd, Owner
Arne Hillesland, Ginerator
Joe Fairchild, COO

Email: Joe Fairchild: joe.fairchild@distillery209.com
Arne Hillesland: arne@distillery209.com
Website: www.distillery209.com, www.209gin.com
Facebook: Distillery No. 209
Twitter: @distillery209

Type: Micro-distillery. Opened in 2005.

Hours of operation: Not open to the public

Tours: Not available

Types of spirits produced: Gin, vodka

Names of spirits:
- No. 209 Gin
- No. 209 Kosher-for-Passover Gin
- No. 209 Kosher-for-Passover Vodka

Best known for: Basil Gimlet and Last Word

Average bottle price: $29.99 to $34.99

Distribution: 34 states and internationally

Interesting facts: Distillery No. 209 was the 209th registered distillery permitted in the United States. No. 209 Kosher-for-Passover Gin is the first and only known Passover certified gin in the world.

GIN
5XD

DISTILLERY № 209
SAN FRANCISCO

Essential Spirits Alambic Distilleries

144 A&B, South Whisman Road
Mountain View, CA 94041
650-962-0546

Owners / Operators:
Dave Classick Sr., Owner / Master Distiller
Andrea Mirenda, Owner / President
Dave Classick Jr., Distiller / ITO
Audrey Classick, Brand Ambassador

Email: service@essentialspirits.com
Website: www.essentialspirits.com
Facebook: Sgt. Classick Hawaiian Rum
Twitter: @SgtClassick

Type: Micro-distillery. Opened in 1998.

Hours of operation:
January to November – Monday through Friday, 10:00am to 7:00pm
December – Closed

Tours: Available

Types of spirits produced: Rum, gin, grappa, pear eau-de-vie, vodka

Names of spirits:
House Brands
* Sergeant Classick Hawaiian Rum (Silver and Gold)
* Classick Grappa di Cabernet - Stags Leap
* Classick Pure Pear Eau-de-Vie

Contract Brands
* DH Krahn Gin
* Hana Gin
* Ice Fox Vodka
* Island Rum (Silver and Gold)
* Hula Girl RTD Cocktails
* U4RIK Grape based Vodka
* Del Dotto Estates - Howell Mountain Grappa de Cabernet
* Vino Robles Grappa de Petite Syrah

Best known for / most popular:
Sgt. Classick Rumadillo (rum and tonic with fresh lime)

Average bottle price: $20.00 to $38.00

Distribution: CA, FL, NY, WA

15

Falcon Spirits LLC

3701 Collins Avenue 1 B & C
Richmond, CA 94806
510-234-3252

Owners / Operators:
Farid Dormishian, Owner / Operator

Email: faridd@falconspirits.com
Website: www.falconspirits.com
Facebook: Falcon Spirits
Twitter: @FalconSpirits

Type: Micro-distillery. Opened in 2011.

Hours of operation: Not provided

Tours: Not provided

Types of spirits produced: Gin

Names of spirits:
• Botanica Spiritvs

Best known for / most popular: Botanica Spiritvs

Average bottle price: Not provided

Distribution: Not provided

Interesting facts: Not provided

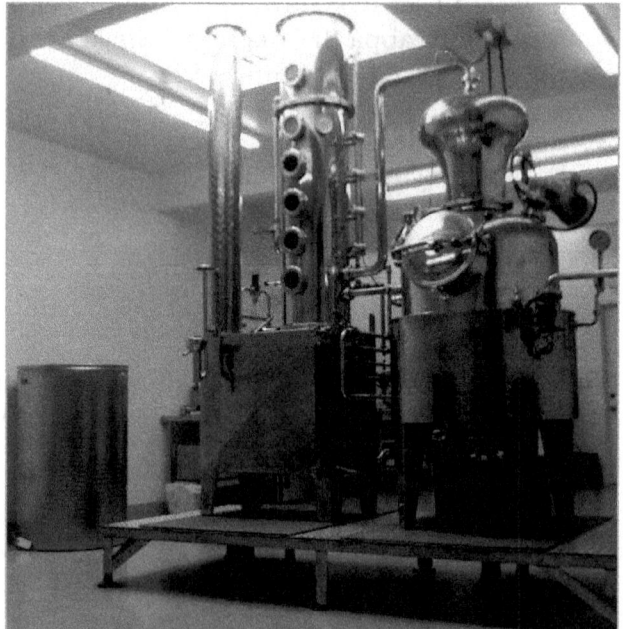

Fog's End Distillery

425 Alta Street, Bldg. #25
Gonzales, CA 93926

Owners / Operators:
Craig Pakish, Founder

Email: info@fogsenddistillery.com
Website: www.fogsenddistillery.com

Type: Micro-distillery. Opened in 2012.

Hours of operation: Not provided

Tours: Not provided

Types of spirits produced: Whiskey, moonshine, rye

Names of spirits:
- White Dog
- Monterey Rye
- California Moonshine
- Primo Aqua Ardiente

Best known for / most popular: California Moonshine

Average bottle price: Not provided

Distribution: CA

Interesting facts: Not provided

Germain-Robin

1110 Bel Arbres Road
Redwood Valley, CA 95470
707-468-7899

craft distillers®
pure, beautifully made spirits

Owners / Operators:
Ansley Coale, President
Joe Corley, Distiller

Email: alambic@pacific.net
Website: www.craftdistillers.com
Facebook: Craft Distillers

Type: Micro-distillery. Opened in 1982.

Hours of operation: Monday through Friday, 9:00am to 5:00pm

Tours: Not available

Types of spirits produced:
Absinthe, apple brandy, brandy, grappa, liqueurs

Names of spirits:
- Germain-Robin Brandy
- Germain-Robin Apple Brandy
- Germain-Robin Grappa
- Germain-Robin Créme de Poète Liqueur
- Germain-Robin Absinthe Superieure

Best known for: Grape Brandy

Average bottle price: $48.00 to $350.00

Distribution: Distillery and retail locations nationwide

Interesting facts: Hubert Germain-Robin was the first known distiller to use wines from world-class varietal grapes.

GreenBar Collective

Los Angeles, CA 90021
213-375-3668

Owners / Operators:
Melkon Khosrovian, Owner
Litty Mathew, Owner

Email: info@greenbar.biz
Website: www.greenbar.biz
Facebook: GreenBar
Twitter: @GreenBarDrinks

Type: Micro-distillery. Opened in 2004.

Hours of operation: Not provided

Tours: Not provided

Types of spirits produced: Gin, vodka, rum, whiskey, liqueur

Names of spirits:
- TRU Organic Gin
- TRU Organic Vodka
- CRUSOE Organic Rum
- FRUITLAB Organic Liqueur

Best known for / most popular: TRU Organic Gin

Average bottle price: Not provided

Distribution: Not provided

Interesting facts: All organic spirits

HelloCello
Prohibition Spirits

21877 8th Street East #4
Sonoma, CA 95476
707-721-6390

Owners / Operators:
Fred Groth, Founder / Distiller / Ambassador
Amy Groth, Founder / Distiller / Ambassador

Email: info@hellosonoma.com
Website: www.hellosonoma.com, www.prohibition-spirits.com
Facebook: HelloCello-Limoncello di Sonoma
Twitter: HelloSonoma

Type: Micro-distillery. Opened in 2009.

Hours of operation: Available by appointment

Tours: Available by appointment

Types of spirits produced: Vodka, rum, whiskey, liqueur

Names of spirits:
- Solano Vodka
- Sugar Daddy Light Rum
- Sugar Daddy Amber Rum
- Sugar Daddy Dark Rum
- Hooker's House Bourbon
- Hooker's House Rye
- Hooker's House General's Reserve
- Hooker's House Corn Whiskey
- Limoncello di Sonoma
- OrangeCello di Sonoma
- FigCello di Sonoma
- Nocino
- Chauvet Brandy

Best known for / most popular:
Hookers House Bourbon and Limoncello di Sonoma

Average bottle price: $32.00

Distribution: Not provided

Interesting facts: Not provided

High Roller Spirits

3133 Hull Road
Atwater, CA 95301
209-385-2966

Owners / Operators:
David Souza, Founder / Master Distiller
Sharon Ambrosia, Operations Manager

Email: david@highrollerspirits.com
Website: www.highrollerspirits.com
Facebook: High Roller Premium Vodka
Twitter: @HighRollerVodka

Type: Micro-distillery. Opened in 2011.

Hours of operation: Not provided

Tours: Not provided

Types of spirits produced: Vodka

Names of spirits:
• High Roller Premium Vodka

Best known for / most popular: High Roller Premium Vodka

Average bottle price: Not provided

Distribution: CA, NE, TN

Interesting facts:
Gluten free vodka made from sweet potatoes

Humboldt Distillery

735 10th Street
Fortuna, CA 95540
707-725-1700

Owners / Operators:
Abe Stevens, Owner/Distiller

Email: info@humboldtdistillery.com
Website: www.humboldtdistillery.com
Facebook: Humboldt Distillery

Type: Micro-distillery. Opening in 2013.

Hours of operation: Monday through Friday, 9:00am to 5:00pm

Tours: Check website for current schedule

Types of spirits produced: Vodka, rum

Names of spirits:
• Humboldt Distillery Vodka
• Humboldt Distillery Spiced Rum

Best known for / most popular: Not provided

Average bottle price: $20.00 to $29.00

Distribution: Northern CA

Interesting facts: Spirits are certified organic

22

Kill Devil Spirit Company

2766 Via Orange Way, Ste. O
San Diego, CA 91978

Owners / Operators:
Ray Digilio, Co-owner
Ankit Bhatt, Co-owner

Email: ray.dig@ardistillery.com
Website: www.killdevilspiritco.com
Facebook: Kill Devil Spirit Co.
Twitter: @ARdistillery

Type: Micro-distillery. Opened in 2011.

Hours of operation: Not provided

Tours: Not provided

Types of spirits produced: Vodka, whiskey

Names of spirits:
- Rx Vodka
- Ugly White Rye Whiskey

Best known for / most popular: Rx Vodka

Average bottle price: Not provided

Distribution: Not provided

Interesting facts: San Diego's first all craft micro-distillery

Lost Spirits Distillery

Monterey County, CA 93907

Owners / Operators:
Bryan Davis, Co-owner
Joanne David, Co-owner

Email: info@lostspirits.net
Website: www.lostspirits.net
Facebook: Lost Spirits Distillery
Twitter: @LostSpirits1

Type: Micro-distillery. First release in 2012.

Hours of operation: Available by appointment

Tours: Available by reservation. See website.

Types of spirits produced: Whiskey

Names of spirits:
- Leviathan American Peated Single Malt Whiskey
- Paradiso Peated American Single Malt Whiskey

Best known for / most popular:
Leviathan Peated American Single Malt Whiskey

Average bottle price: $55.00

Distribution: CA, DC, IL, NY, TN; Germany, Sweden, Denmark, UK

Interesting facts:
- Lost Spirits is best known for producing some of the world's most heavily peated whiskeys. What sets the distillery apart from other peated malt houses is the use of exotic and rare peat sources such as peat harvested from Canadian forests, California islands, and tropical climates.
- The distillery is also home to one of the only operational log and copper pot still left in the United States. Log and copper stills are made of oak tanks fitted with a copper neck.
- The entire distillery, including the equipment, was built by hand by the founders.

Napa Valley Distillery

225 Walnut Street
Napa, CA 94558
707-259-5411

Owners / Operators:
Arthur and Lusine Hartunian, Owners / Operators

Email: sales@napaspirits.com
Website: www.napaspirits.com
Facebook: Napa Valley Distillery
Twitter: @NapaVodka

Type: Micro-distillery. Opened in 2009.

Hours of operation: Daily, 10:00am to 6:00pm

Tours: Available

Types of spirits produced: Brandy, vodka, whiskey, liqueur

Names of spirits:
- Napa Vodka Vintage Reserve
- Barrel-Aged Cocktails
  Old Hollywood, Negroni, Mint Julep, East India, Manhattan
- Old Hollywood Gin
- Napa Valley Meyer Lemon Liqueur

Best known for: Japanese James Bond
Served at Iron Chef Morimoto's restaurant in Napa, CA

Average bottle price: $30.00

Distribution:
CA, NVM LA, WI, TN, FL, MD, DC, IL; Canada AB, QC

Interesting facts:
This is the world's first known "vintage vodka,"
handcrafted entirely from premium Napa Valley
Sauvignon Blanc from a single vintage and a single
Napa Valley Estate.

Old World Spirits LLC

121 Industrial Road, #3-4
Belmont, CA 94002
650-622-9222

Owners / Operators:
Davorin Kuchan, President

Email: info@oldworldspirits.com
Website: www.oldworldspirits.com
Facebook: Old World Spirits, LLC
Twitter: @oldworldspirits
YouTube: Old World Spirits Product Feature
Yelp: Old World Spirits
foursquare: OldWorldSpirits

Type: Micro-distillery. Opened in 2008.

Hours of operation: Monday through Saturday, 9:00am to 5:00pm

Tours: Available on the last Friday of the month and by appointment

Types of spirits produced: Whiskey, gin, absinthe, liqueurs, brandies, bitters

Names of spirits:
- Kuchan Eaux De Vie
  - Poire Williams
  - Indian Blood Peach
  - O'Henry Oak Aged Peach
- Kuchan Nocino Black Walnut Liqueur
- La Sorciere Absinthe Verte and Bleue
- Blade California Small Batch Gin
- Rusty Blade Barrel Aged Gin
- Kuchan Alambic Brandy
- Goldrun Rye Whiskey

Best known for: Blade Gin, Rusty Blade, La Sorciere Absinthe, Kuchan Nocino and Goldrun 100% Rye Whiskey

Average bottle price: $30.00 to $75.00

Distribution: CA, CO, ID, NV, OR, WA

Interesting facts: First known U.S. distillery to release "blanche" clear style absinthe and Rusty Blade Barrel Aged Gin

RE:FIND Distillery

2725 Adelaida Road
Paso Robles, CA 93446
805-239-9456

Owners / Operators:
Alex Villicana, Owner / Distiller
Monica Villicana, Owner

Email: alex@refinddistillery.com, monica@refinddistillery.com
Website: www.refinddistillery.com
Facebook: Re:Find Distillery
Twitter: @re_find

Type: Micro-distillery. Opened in 2012.

Hours of operation: Monday through Friday, 8:00am to 5:00pm

Tours: Daily, 11:00am to 5:00pm

Types of spirits produced: Vodka, gin, brandy

Names of spirits:
• RE:FIND Vodka
• RE:FIND Gin
• RE:FIND Neutral Brandy
• RE:FIND Botanical Brandy

Best known for / most popular: RE:FIND Gin

Average bottle price: $35.00 to $38.00

Distribution: CA

27

Saint James Spirits

5220 Fourth Street, Unit 17
Irwindale, CA 91701
626-856-6930

Owners / Operators:
James Busuttil, Owner

Email: sjspirits@earthlink.net
Website: www.saintjamesspirits.com

Type: Micro-distillery. Opened in 1995.

Hours of operation: Not provided

Tours: Not provided

Types of spirits produced: Brandy, rum, agave, grappa, whisky

Names of spirits:
- Mojo Vodka
- California Gold Agave
- Saint James Spirits Grappa
- Royale Hawaiian Pineapple Rum
- Saint James Spirits Pineapple Brandy
- Saint James Spirits Kirsch (Eau de Vie)
- Peregrine Rock – California Pure Malt Whisky

Best known for / most popular: Not provided

Average bottle price: Not provided

Distribution: CA

Interesting facts: Not provided

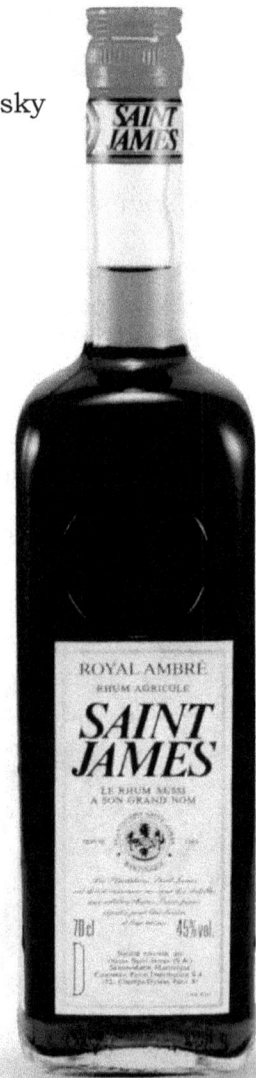

Spirit Works Distillery

6790 McKinley Street #100
Sebastopol, CA 95472
707-634-4793

Owners / Operators:
Ashby Marshall, Owner / Distiller
Timo Marshall, Owner / Distiller

Email: hello@spiritworksdistillery.com
Website: www.spiritworksdistillery.com
Facebook: Spirit Works Distillery

Type: Micro-distillery. Opened in 2013.

Hours of operation: Not provided

Tours: Available, call or email for information

Types of spirits produced: Gin, whiskey

Names of spirits:
- Spirit Works Gin
- Spirit Works Sloe Gin
- Spirit Works Wheat Whiskey
- Spirit Works Rye Whiskey

Best known for / most popular: Spirit Works Gin

Average bottle price: Not provided

Distribution: Not provided

Interesting facts: Not provided

St. George Spirits

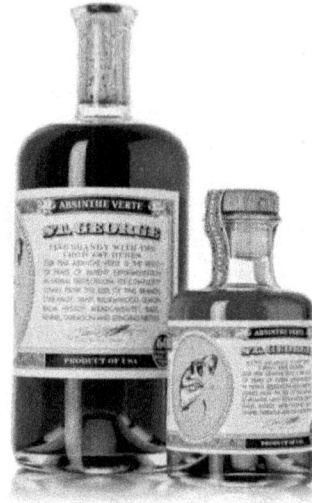

ST. GEORGE SPIRITS

2601 Monarch Street
Alameda, CA 94501
510-769-1601

Owners / Operators:
Lance Winters, Owner / Master Distiller

Email: info@stgeorgespirits.com
           tastingroom@stgeorgespirits.com
Website: www.stgeorgespirits.com
Facebook: St. George Spirits
Twitter: @StGeorgeSpirits
Flickr: St. George Spirits
YouTube: St. George Spirits
Yelp: St. George Spirits Alameda

Type: Micro-distillery. Opened in 1982.

Hours of operation: Tasting room and on-site store; Wednesday through Saturday, 12:00pm to 7:00pm; Sunday 12:00pm to 5:00pm.

Tours: Available Wednesday through Saturday, 1:00pm, 2:00pm, 3:00pm, 4:00pm, 5:00pm, 6:00pm; Sunday 1:00pm, 2:00pm, 3:00pm, 4:00pm

Types of spirits produced: Eaux de vie, fruit liqueurs, single malt whiskey, absinthe, rum, coffee liqueur, gin, bourbon

Names of spirits:
- St. George Brandy
- St. George Single Malt Whiskey
- St. George Absinthe Verte
- Agua Azul (agave spirit)
- Agua Libre Rum
- Breaking & Entering Bourbon
- St. George Botanivore Gin
- St. George Terroir Gin
- St. George Dry Rye Gin

Best known for / most popular:
St. George Absinthe Verte

Average bottle price: $20.00 to $80.00

Distribution: Nationwide, on-site store

Interesting facts: St. George Spirits is housed in a 65,000 square foot airplane hangar on the former Alameda Naval Air Station.

Stillwater Spirits

611 2nd Street
Petaluma, CA 94952
707-778-6041

Owners / Operators:
John Moylan, Co-owner
Donald Payne, Co-owner
Paddy Giffen Co-owner
Brendan Moylan, General Manager
Tim Welch, Distiller

Email: stillwaterspirits@gmail.com
Website: www.stillwaterspirits.com
Facebook: Stillwater Spirits & Moylan's Distilling

Type: Micro-distillery. Opened in 2004.

Hours of operation: Monday through Friday, 10:00am to 6:00pm

Tours: Not available

Types of spirits produced: Vodka, gin, rum, whisky, brandy

Names of spirits:
- Stillwater Spirits Gin
- Stillwater Spirits Vodka 80°
- Stillwater Spirits Vodka 100°
- Stillwater Spirits Asian Pear Brandy
- Stillwater Spirits Cabernet Sauvignon Grappa
- Moylan's Distilling Bourbon Cask Strength
- Moylan's Distilling Rye Whisky
- Moylan's Distilling Beer Schnapps
- Moylan's Distilling American Single Malt Whisky
- Moylan's Distilling American Single Malt Cask Strength
- Moylan's Distilling Cherry Wood Malt Cask Strength

Best known for / most popular: Stillwater Spirits Gin

Average bottle price: $30.00 to $60.00

Distribution: San Francisco CA area

Interesting facts: Not provided

Tahoe Moonshine Distillery Inc.

1611 Shop Street #4B
South Lake Tahoe, CA 96150
530-416-0313

Owners / Operators:
Jeffrey VanHee, Owner / Master Distiller

Email: jeffrey@tahoemoonshine.com
Website: www.tahoemoonshine.com
Facebook: Tahoe Moonshine Distillery

Type: Micro-distillery. Opened in 2010.

Hours of operation: Not provided

Tours: Not provided

Types of spirits produced: Whiskey, gin, rum, vodka, liqueur

Names of spirits:
- Stormin' Whiskey
- Jagged Peaks Gin
- California Dreamin' Rum
- Jug Dealer Rum
- Snowflake Vodka
- Dream Bean Coffee Liqueur
- VanHees' Mean Irish Cream
- Hot Stinkin' Garlic Vodka
- Peanut Butter Vodka

Best known for / most popular: Stormin' Whiskey

Average bottle price: $23.00

Distribution: CA, NV

Interesting facts: Not provided

Treasure Island Distillery

990 13th Street
San Francisco, CA 94130
415-935-7989

Owners / Operators:
Owned and operated by the William Smith family

Email: william@sfvodka.com
Website: www.sfvodka.com
Facebook: SFVodka
Twitter: @SFVodka

Type: Micro-distillery. Opened in 2009.

Hours of operation:
Monday through Saturday, 9:00am to 6:00pm

Tours: Not open to the public

Types of spirits produced:
Vodkas made from corn, grapes, and cane

Names of spirits:
• China Beach San Francisco Vodka
• Ocean Beach San Francisco Vodka
• Baker Beach San Francisco Vodka

Best known for: China Beach San Francisco Vodka

Average bottle price: $35.00

Distribution: San Francisco Bay Area

Interesting facts: Treasure Island Distillery operates out of the old Navy brig on Treasure Island in San Francisco. The space consists of the solitary confinement cells, intake and processing areas, the guard's room, the infirmary, and one of the two exercise yards.

Valley Spirits LLC

553 Mariposa Road, Ste. #1
Modesto, CA 95354
209-484-0311

Owners / Operators:
Lee Palleschi, Proprietor

Email: masterdistiller@drinkvalleyspirits.com
Website: www.drinkvalleyspirits.com
Facebook: Cold House Vodka
Twitter: @ColdHouseVodka

Type: Micro-distillery. Opened in 2010.

Hours of operation: 8:00am to 5:00pm

Tours: Available

Types of spirits produced: Vodka, moonshine, whiskey

Names of spirits:
- Cold House Vodka
- Moonshine Bandits Outlaw Moonshine
- Prohibition Spirits

Best known for / most popular: Cold House Vodka

Average bottle price: $24.00

Distribution: CA, NV

Interesting facts: Not provided

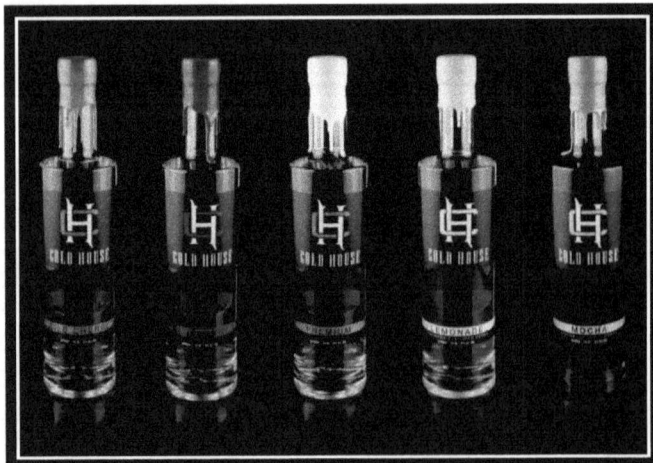

Ventura Limoncello Company

2646 Palma Drive, Ste. 160
Ventura, CA 93003
805-658-0881

Owners / Operators:
James Carling, President
Manuela Zaretti-Carling, Vice President

Email: General info: info@venturalimoncello.com
        James Carling: James@venturalimoncello.com
Website: www.venturalimoncello.com
Facebook: Ventura Limoncello
Twitter: @VLimoncello
YouTube: Ventura Limoncello Channel
LinkedIn: James Carling

Type: Micro-distillery. Opened in 2008.

Hours of operation:
Monday through Friday, 9:00am to 5:00pm

Tours: By appointment only

Types of spirits produced: Liqueur

Names of spirits:
- Ventura Limoncello Originale
- Ventura Limoncello Crema
- Ventura Orangecello Blood Orange

Best known for / most popular:
Ventura Limoncello Originale

Average bottle price: $16.00 to $28.00

Distribution: AK, AZ, CA, CT, HI, IL, MO, NJ, NV, NY, OR

Interesting facts:
- All citrus used is grown in Ventura County, CA.
- Awards - Ventura Limoncello Originale
  Gold Medal 2013, Spirit of the Americas
  Gold Medal 2011, 2008 SF World Spirits Competition
  Gold Medal 2011, MicroLiquor Awards
- Awards - Ventura Orangecello Blood Orange
  Double Gold Medal - Best in Class
  2011 San Francisco World Spirits Competition
- Awards - Ventura Limoncello Crema
  Gold Medal -- 2010 LA SIP Awards

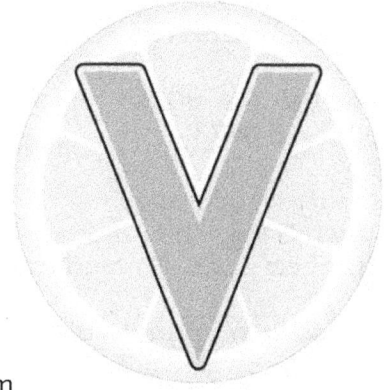

Altitude Spirits

Boulder, CO 80306
303-245-8773

Owners / Operators:
Mitch Baris, Co-founder
Matthew Baris, Co-founder

Email: info@altitudespirits.com
Website: www.vodka14.com, www.altitudespirits.com
Facebook: Vodka 14
Twitter: @Vodka14, @AltitudeSpirits

Type: Micro-distillery. Opened in 2005.

Hours of operation: Not provided

Tours: Not provided

Types of spirits produced: Vodka

Names of spirits:
• Vodka 14

Best known for / most popular: Not provided

Average bottle price: Not provided

Distribution: Not provided

Interesting facts: Organic vodka

Black Canyon Distillery

13710 Deere Court #B
Mead, CO 80504
720-204-1909

Owners / Operators:
Fred Lesnick, Co-owner / Master Distiller
Susan Lesnick, Co-owner / V.P. and Secretary
Chris Broadfoot, Co-owner / Director of Promotions
Jeannetta Broadfoot, Co-owner / Account Manager

Email: fred@blackcanyondistillery.com
Website: www.blackcanyondistillery.com
Facebook: Black Canyon Distillery

Type: Micro-distillery. Opened in 2011.

Hours of operation:
Wednesday through Friday, 9:00am to 5:00pm
Saturday, 8:00am to 4:00pm (call first)

Tours: Available by appointment

Types of spirits produced: Whiskey

Names of spirits:
- Black Canyon Sour Mash Corn Whiskey
- Black Canyon Rita

Best known for / most popular: Black Canyon Rita

Average bottle price: $25.00 to $28.00

Distribution: CO

Interesting facts: Not provided

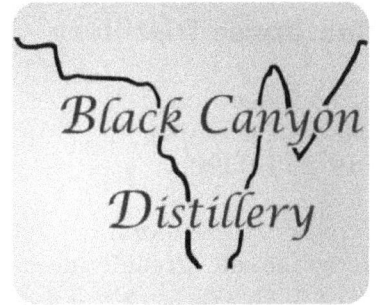

Boathouse Distillery

6573 Ridge Road
Salida, CO 81201
719-239-0390

Owners / Operators:
Jerry Mallett, President

Email: jmallett123@yahoo.com
Website: www.boathousedistillery.com

Type: Micro-distillery. Opening in 2013.

Hours of operation: 8:00am to 4:00pm

Tours: Not available

Types of spirits produced:
Single malt whiskey, bourbon, various vodkas

Names of spirits:
• Rocky Mountain Bourbon
• Boathouse Whiskey
• Boathouse Vodka

Best known for / most popular: Rocky Mountain Bourbon, Boathouse Whiskey

Average bottle price: $18.50 to $35.00

Distribution: CO

Interesting facts: TBA

38

Boulder Distillery

Clear Spirit Company Inc.

2500 47th Street, Unit 10
Boulder, CO 80301
303-442-1244

Owners / Operators:
Steve Viezbicke, Owner

Email: info@303vodka.com
Website: www.303vodka.com
Facebook: 303 Vodka – Boulder Distillery – Clear Spirit
Twitter: @303Vodka

Type: Micro-distillery. Opened in 2009.

Hours of operation:
Sunday through Tuesday, Closed
Wednesday through Saturday, 2:00pm to 10:00pm

Tours: Available

Types of spirits produced: Vodka, whiskey

Names of spirits:
- Viezbicke 303 Vodka
- Viezbicke 303 Whiskey

Best known for / most popular: Viezbicke 303 Vodka

Average bottle price: Not provided

Distribution: CO

Interesting facts: Boulder's first distillery since prohibition.

Breckenridge Distillery

1925 Airport Road
Breckenridge, CO 80424
970-547-9759

Owners / Operators:
Bryan Nolt, President
Jordan Via, Master Distiller
Jennifer Querbes, Director of Operations
Litch Polich, Head Brand Ambassador

Email: Bryan Nolt: bryan@breckenridgedistillery.com
           Jordan Via: jordan@breckenridgedistillery.com
           Jennifer Querbes: jen@breckenridgedistillery.com
           Litch Polich: litch@breckenridgedistillery.com
Website: www.breckenridgedistillery.com
Facebook: Breckenridge Distillery
Twitter: @breckdistillery

Type: Micro-Distillery. Opened in 2010.

Hours of operation:
Tasting Room, 11:00am to 9:00pm (closed Tuesday)
Distillery, 11:00am to 6:00pm (closed Monday)

Tours: Available

Types of spirits produced:
Vodka, bourbon, whiskey, rum, bitters

Names of spirits:
- Seasonal Spiced Bourbon
- Turin-Style Bitters
- Wild-Harvested Genepi Liqueur
- Dark Spiced Naval Rum
- Rocky Ford Watermelon Vodka

Best known for / most popular: Breckenridge Bourbon

Average bottle price: $30.00 to $40.00

Distribution: AL, AR, CA, CO, CT, FL, GA, IA, IL, MA, MO, MS, NC, ND, NE, NJ, NY, OK, RI, SD, TX, VA, WV

Interesting facts: World's highest distillery

Colorado Gold Distillery

1290 S. Grand Mesa Drive
Cedaredge, CO 81413
970-856-2600

Owners / Operators:
Tom and Pam Cooper, Owners

Email: coop2@sopris.net
Website: www.coloradogolddistillers.com
Facebook: Colorado Gold Distillery

Type: Micro-distillery. Opened in 2007.

Hours of operation: Monday through Saturday, 10:00am to 4:00pm

Tours: Available

Types of spirits produced:
Agave spirits, whiskey, gin, vodka, bourbon whiskey, brandy

Names of spirits:
- Colorado Gold Premium Gin
- Colorado Gold Premium Vodka
- Colorado Gold's Own Agave Spirits
- Colorado's Own Corn Whiskey
- Colorado Gold Straight Bourbon Whiskey

Best known for / most popular: Colorado Gold Premium Vodka

Average bottle price: $25.00 to $60.00

Distribution: AZ, CA, CT, LA, NM, OR, TX

Interesting facts: Not provided

Dancing Pines Distillery

1527 Taurus Court, #110
Loveland, CO 80537
970-635-3426

Owners / Operators:
Christopher McNay, Co-owner
Kristian Naslund, Co-owner
Kimberly Naslund, Co-owner

Email: info@dpdistillery.com
Website: www.dancingpinesdistillery.com
Facebook: Dancing Pines Distillery
Twitter: @DPDistillery

Type: Micro-distillery. Opened in 2010.

Hours of operation: Open to the public Saturdays, 1:00pm to 7:00pm

Tours: Saturdays at 2:00pm, 4:00pm, and 6:00pm by reservation

Types of spirits produced: Rum, whiskey, gin, liqueurs

Names of spirits:
• Dancing Pines Bourbon
• Dancing Pines Black Walnut Bourbon
• Dancing Pines Gin
• Dancing Pines Rum
• Dancing Pines Cask Rum
• Dancing Pines Spice Rum
• Dancing Pines Brulee Liqueur
• Dancing Pines Chai Liqueur
• Dancing Pines Cherry Tart Liqueur
• Dancing Pines Espresso Liqueur

Best known for: Dancing Pines Bourbon

Average bottle price: $30.00 to $50.00

Distribution: AZ, CA, CO, CT, DC, DE, FL,
 GA, ID, IL, LA, MA, MD, NJ, NV, NY, SC,
 VA, WA, WV, WY

Interesting facts: Not provided

Deerhammer Distilling Company

321 East Main Street
Buena Vista, CO 81211
719-395-9464

Owners / Operators:
Lenny Eckstein, Owner / Manager
Amy Eckstein, Owner / Barmaid

Email: info@deerhammer.com
Website: www.deerhammer.com
Facebook: Deerhammer Distilling Company
Twitter: @Deerhammer

Type: Micro-distillery. Opened in 2010.

Hours of operation:
Winter Hours
Thursday through Saturday, 4:00pm to 10:00pm

Summer Hours
Wednesday through Sunday, 2:00pm to 10:00pm

Tours: Available

Types of spirits produced: Whiskey, brandy, gin

Names of spirits:
- Whitewater Whiskey
- Down Time Single Malt Whiskey
- Buena Vista Brandy
- Bullwheel Gin

Best known for / most popular:
Whitewater Whiskey

Average bottle price: $38.00

Distribution: CO

Interesting facts: Deerhammer is located at 8,000 feet above sea level in the Arkansas River Valley — surrounded by the highest concentration of 14,000 foot peaks in the country.

Distillery 291

1647 S. Tejon Street
Colorado Springs, CO 80905
719-323-8010

Owners / Operators:
Michael Myers, Owner

Email: info@distillery291.com
Website: www.distillery291.com
Facebook: Distillery 291
Twitter: @distillery291

Type: Craft-distillery. Opened in 2011.

Hours of operation: Not provided

Tours: Not provided

Types of spirits produced: Whiskey

Names of spirits:
- 291 Colorado Whiskey Aspen Stave Finished (aged)
- 291 Fresh Colorado Whiskey (corn, unaged)
- 291 Colorado Rye Whiskey White Dog
- 291 American Whiskey

Best known for / most popular: Not provided

Average bottle price: Not provided

Distribution: Self/Distillery 291

Interesting facts:
- From grain to barrel to bottle in 339 square feet
- First craft distillery in Colorado Springs, CO

Downslope Distilling

6770 S. Dawson Circle
Centennial, CO 80122
303-693-4300

Owners / Operators:
Andrew Causey, Owner
Mitch Abate, Owner

Email: General info: spirits@downslopedistilling.com
      Media/Business: andy@downslopedistilling.com
      Technical/Product: mitch@downslopedistilling.com
Website: www.downslopedistilling.com
Facebook: Downslope Distilling
Twitter: @DownslopeDist

Type: Micro-distillery. Opened in 2009.

Hours of operation: Daily

Tours: Available Friday through Sunday, 12:00pm to 4:00pm.

Types of spirits produced: Vodka, rum, whiskey

Names of spirits:
- Downslope Cane Vodka
- Downslope Grain Vodka
- Downslope Pepper Vodka
- Downslope White Rum
- Downslope Gold Rum
- Downslope Spiced Rum
- Downslope Vanilla Rum
- Downslope Wine Barrel Aged Rum
- Downslope Double Diamond Whiskey
- Downslope Malt Whiskey

Best known for / most popular: Vodka from Maui cane, Vanilla Rum, Wine Barrel Aged Rum, Pepper Vodka, Double Diamond Whiskey

Average bottle price: $25.00 to $32.00

Distribution: CO, MA, NE, NJ, NM, OR, TX, WA

Interesting facts: The barrels used at Downslope originate from wineries. When they are retired from aging spirits, they house beer at local breweries.

Feisty Spirits

1708 E Lincoln Avenue, #1
Fort Collins, CO 80524
970-444-2FUN

Owners / Operators:
David Monahan, Co-founder
Jamison Gulden, Co-founder

Email: info@FeistySpirits.com
Website: www.FeistySpirits.com
Facebook: Feisty Spirits
Twitter: @FeistySpirits

Type: Micro-distillery. Opened in 2012.

Hours of operation: Check website

Tours: Check website

Types of spirits produced: Whiskey

Names of spirits:
- Feisty Spirits Blue Corn Bourbon
- Feisty Spirits Rye
- Feisty Spirits Elementals
  A line of single grain whiskeys

Best known for / most popular: Bourbon Whiskey

Average bottle price: $40.00

Distribution: CO

Interesting facts:
Made with organic grains and natural ingredients

Golden Moon Distillery
Maison De La Vie Ltd.

412 Violet Street
Golden, CO 80401
303-993-7174

Owners / Operators:
Stephen Gould, Co-proprietor / Distiller
Karen Knight, Co-proprietor

Email: s.gould@gouldgobal.com
Website: www.goldenmoondistillery.com
Facebook: Golden Moon Distillery
Twitter: @goldenmoondistillery

Type: Micro-distillery. Opened in 2008.

Hours of operation: Monday through Friday, 9:00am to 5:00pm

Tours: Available

Types of spirits produced: Gin, absinthe, grappa, apple jack, crème de violette, dry curacao and amer dit picon.

Names of spirits:
- Golden Moon Gin
- Redux Absinthe
- Redux Absinthe No.2
- Golden Moon Colorado Grappa
- Golden Moon Colorado Apple Jack
- Golden Moon Crème de Violette
- Golden Moon Dry Curacao
- Golden Moon Amer dit Picon

Best known for / most popular: Golden Moon Gin

Average bottle price: $27.00 to $86.00

Distribution: U.S.

47

Honey House Distillery

33633 Hwy 550, Ste. A
Durango, CO 81301
970-247-1474

Owners / Operators:
Kevin Culhane, Co-owner
Sheree Culhane, Co-owner
Danny Culhane, Co-owner
Adam Bergal, Co-owner

Email: kevin@honeyhousedistillery.com
Website: www.honeyhousedistillery.com
Facebook: Honey House Distillery

Type: Micro-distillery. Opened in 2013.

Hours of operation:
Memorial Day to Labor Day, 8:00am to 6:00pm
Labor Day to Memorial Day, 9:00am to 5:00pm

Tours: Available

Types of spirits produced: Rocky Mountain Honey infused Bourbon Whiskey

Names of spirits:
- Colorado Honey
- Wildflower Gin
- Hex Vodka

Best known for / most popular: Colorado Honey

Average bottle price: $35.00

Distribution: CO

Interesting facts:
Colorado Honey is made from fine bourbon whiskey infused with 100% pure Rocky Mountain Honey from Honeyville, a third generation family beekeeping business. Unlike most major brands of honey whiskey, Colorado Honey is made with pure honey, not honey liqueur.

Leopold Bros.

4950 Nome Street
Denver, CO 80239

Owners / Operators:
Todd Leopold, Co-owner
Scott Leopold, Co-owner

Email: sales@leopoldbros.com
Website: www.leopoldbros.com
Facebook: Leopold Bros.
Twitter: @LeopoldBros

Type: Micro-distillery. Opened in 1999.

Hours of operation: Not provided

Tours: Not provided

Types of spirits produced:
Vodka, gin, whiskey, liqueur, absinthe

Names of spirits:
- Silver Tree American Small Batch Vodka
- Leopold Bros. American Small Batch Gin
- Leopold Bros. American Small Batch Whiskey
- Leopold Bros. New York Apple Whiskey
- Leopold Bros. Rocky Mountain Blackberry Whiskey
- Leopold Bros. Rocky Mountain Peach Whiskey
- Leopold Bros. Georgia Peach Whiskey
- Leopold Bros. Rocky Mountain Blackberry Liqueur
- Leopold Bros. Michigan Tart Cherry Liqueur
- Leopold Bros. New England Cranberry Liqueur
- Leopold Bros. American Orange Liqueur
- Leopold Bros. Frenchpress Style American Coffee Liqueur
- Leopold Bros. Three Pins Alpine Herbal Liqueur
- Leopold Bros. Absinthe Verte

Best known for / most popular: Not provided

Average bottle price: Not provided

Distribution: AZ, CA, CO, DC, GA, ID, IL, NV, VA, WY

Interesting facts: Not provided

Mancos Valley Distillery

116 N. Main Street
Mancos, CO 81328
970-946-0229

Owners / Operators:
Ian James, Owner / Distiller

Email: info@mancosvalleydistillery.com
Website: www.mancosvalleydistillery.com
Facebook: Mancos Valley Distillery, LLC
Twitter: @MVDistillery

Type: Micro-distillery. Opened in 2010.

Hours of operation: Friday 5:00pm to 10:00pm; Saturday 4:00pm to 9:00pm

Tours: Not provided

Types of spirits produced: Rum, liqueur

Names of spirits:
• Ian's Alley Rum
• Ian's Alley Spiced Rum
• Colorado Coffee Liqueur

Best known for / most popular: Ian's Alley Rum

Average bottle price: Not provided

Distribution: CO

Interesting facts: Not provided

50

Mile High Spirits LLC

2920 Larimer Street
Denver, CO 80205
303-601-3499

Owners / Operators:
Joe Vonfeldt, Co-owners
Chase Campbell, Co-owners
Wyn Ferrell, Co-owners

Email: info@milehighspiritsllc.com
Website: www.milehighspiritsllc.com
Facebook: Mile High Spirits
Twitter: @MileHighSpirits

Type: Micro-distillery. Opened in 2012.

Hours of operation:
Monday through Friday, 4:00pm to 12:00am
Saturday and Sunday, 11:00am to 1:00pm
Sunday, 11:00am to 8:00pm

Tours: Not available

Types of spirits produced:
Vodka, whiskey, gin, rum

Names of spirits:
• Fireside Bourbon
• Elevate Vodka
• Peg Leg Rum
• Denver Dry Gin
• Distroya Liqueur

Best known for / most popular:
Fireside Bourbon and Elevate Vodka

Average bottle price: $19.00 to $30.00

Distribution: On-site

Interesting facts:
• Mile High Spirits is one of only a few distilleries in the world to use an all glass still for its distillation.
• Micro Liquor Awards 2012, Fireside, Gold in Flavor, Silver in Packaging.
• Micro Liquor Awards 2012, Elevate, Silver in flavor and Silver in packaging.
• Denver International Spirits Competition 2013, Silver Medal Fireside
• Denver International Spirits Competition 2013, Gold Medal Elevate

51

Montanya Distillers LLC

Distillery and Tasting Room:
130 Elk Avenue
Crested Butte, CO 81224

Silverton Tasting Room:
1314 Greene Street
Silverton, CO 81433

970-799-3206 or 800-975-6154

Owners / Operators:
Karen Hoskin, President / Co-Owner
Brice Hoskin, Vice President / Co-Owner

Email: info@montanyadistillers.com
Website: www.montanyadistillers.com
Facebook: Montanya Distillers
Twitter: @montanyarum
LinkedIn: Montanya Distillers
Yelp: Montanya Distillers
Trip Advisor: Montanya Distillers
Instagram: montanyarum
Pinterest: Montanya Rum

Type: Micro-distillery. Opened in 2008.

Hours of operation: Daily, 11:00am to 9:00pm

Tours: Available

Types of spirits produced: Light and dark rum

Names of spirits:
- Montanya Oro Rum
- Montanya Platino Rum

Average bottle price: $24.99 to $32.99

Distribution: Available in 38 states

Interesting facts: Montanya Distillers is one the few U.S. distilleries owned and operated by a woman, with a female distiller and a female general manager.

Mystic Mountain Distillery LLC

11505 Spring Valley Road
Larkspur, CO 80118
303-663-9375

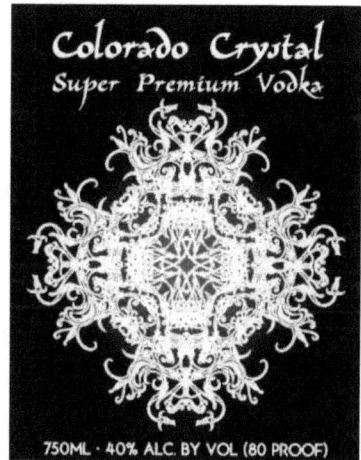

Owners / Operators:
Fred Linneman, General Manager

Email: info@mysticmtnspirits.com
Website: www.mysticmtnspirits.com
Facebook: Mystic Mountain Distillery

Type: Micro-distillery. Opened in 2005.

Hours of operation: 9:00am to 2:00pm

Tours: Not available

Types of spirits produced: Gin, moonshine, rum, tequila, vodka, whiskey

Names of spirits:
- Colorado Blue Vodka
- BOHICA Vodka
- Colorado Crystal Vodka
- Rocky Mountain Moonshine
- Colorado Fog Gin
- Blackjack Aces High Whiskey

Average bottle price: $20.00 to $25.00

Distribution:

Interesting facts: Not provided

Peach Street Distillers

144 South Kluge Avenue, Bldg. #2
Palisade, CO 81526
970-464-1128

Owners / Operators:
Rory Donovan, Owner

Email: info@peachstreetdistillers.com
Website: www.peachstreetdistillers.com
Facebook: Peach Street Distillers
Twitter: @PSDistillers

Type: Micro-distillery. Opened in 2005.

Hours of operation:
Monday through Thursday, 12:00pm to 10:00pm
Friday and Saturday, 12:00pm to 12:00am
Sunday, 10:00am to 10:00pm

Tours: Available May through September, Fridays 3:00pm

Types of spirits produced: Bourbon, vodka, gin, brandy, grappa, agave spirit

Names of spirits:
- Colorado Straight Bourbon
- Goat Artisan Vodka
- Jackelope Gin
- Jackelope and Jenny Gin
- Jack & Jenny Peach Brandy
- Jack & Jenny Pear Brandy
- Aged Peach Brandy
- Aged Pear Brandy
- Grappa of Gewurztraminer
- Grappa of Viognier
- Grappa Muscat
- Dagave Gold
- Dagave Extra
- Dagave Silver

Best known for / most popular:
Colorado Straight Bourbon

Average bottle price: $30.00 to $60.00

Distribution: CA, CO, IL, LA, NJ, NY, TX

Interesting facts: American Distillers Institute Distillery of the Year, 2012

Peak Spirits® Farm Distillery

26567 North Road
Hotchkills, CO 81419
970-361-4249

CapRock®

Owners / Operators:
Lance Hanson, Owner / Distiller

Email: lance@peakspirits.com
Website: www.peakspirits.com
Facebook: Peak Spirits
Twitter: @peakspirits

Type: Micro-distillery. Opened in 2005.

Hours of operation: Vary

Tours: Available by appointment

Types of spirits produced:
Gin, vodka, eaux de vie

Names of spirits:
- CapRock® Organic Gin
- CapRock® Organic Vodka
- CapRock® Organic Eaux de Vie
- CapRock® Biodynamic® Estate Grappa

Best known for / most popular: Gin

Average bottle price: $35.00

Distribution: CA, CO, DC, IL, MA, MD, RI, SC, VA

Interesting facts:
All products are 100% USDA-certified organic or Demeter-certified Biodynamic

Rocky Mountain Distilling Co.

6660 Delmonico Drive, Ste. D-223
Colorado Springs, CO 80919
970-306-6222

Owners / Operators:
Todd Ficken, Owner

Email: info@rockymountaindistilling.com
Website: www.rockymountindistilling.com
Foursquare: Rocky Mountain Distilling Co.

Type: Micro-distillery. Opening in 2013.

Hours of operation: Monday through Friday, 10:00am to 6:00pm

Tours: Available by appointment

Types of spirits produced: Vodka

Names of spirits:
• VR Vodka

Best known for / most popular: VR Vodka

Average bottle price: Not provided

Distribution: Not provided

Interesting facts: Not provided

Roundhouse Spirits

5311 Western Avenue, Ste. 180
Boulder, CO 80301
303-819-5598

Owners / Operators:
Charles (Ted) Palmer, Co-owner
Michael Belochi, Co-owner / Director of Sales

Email: info@roundhousespirits.com
Website: www.roundhousespirits.com
Facebook: Roundhouse Spirits
Twitter: @RndhouseSpirits

Type: Micro-distillery. Opened in 2008.

Hours of operation: Vary

Tours: Available

Types of spirits produced: Gin and liqueur

Names of spirits:
- Roundhouse Gin
- Imperial Barrel Aged Gin
- Corretto Coffee Liqueur

Best known for / most popular:
Roundhouse Gin as a sipping gin on the rocks

Average bottle price: $25.00 to $45.00

Distribution: CO, DC, IL, MD, NJ, NY

Interesting facts:
Roundhouse Spirits is the 6th licensed distillery in CO.

Spirit Hound Distillers

4196 Ute Highway
Lyons, CO 80540

Owners / Operators:
Matthew Rooney, Co-founder / President
Craig Engelhorn, Co-founder / Head Distiller
Neil Sullivan, Co-founder / VP Operations
Wayne Anderson, Co-founder / Business Development

Email: info@spirithounds.com
Website: www.spirithounddistillers.com
Facebook: Spirit Hound Distillers

Type: Micro-distillery. Opened in 2012.

Hours of operation: Vary

Tours: Available

Types of spirits produced: Whisky, gin, liqueur

Names of spirits:
- Spirit Hound Gin
- Mountain Bum Rum
- Richardo's Coffee Liqueur

Best known for: Spirit Hound Gin

Distribution: Boulder / Denver CO area

Interesting facts: First craft distillery in Lyons CO

Spring44 Distilling

505 West 66th Street
Loveland, CO 80538
970-445-0744

Owners / Operators:
Jeff Lindauer, Co-founder / CEO
Russ Wall, Co-founder / CMO
Jeff McPhie, Co-founder / COO
Robin Marisco, CFO
Rob Masters, Head Distiller
Ryan Jackson, Production Manager

Email: info@spring44.com
Website: www.spring44.com
Facebook: Spring44
Twitter: @Spring44spirits
YouTube: Spring44Distilling's Channel

Type: Craft-distillery. Opened in 2012.

Hours of operation: Friday, 4:00pm to 7:00pm; Saturday, 2:00pm to 7:00pm

Tours: Available

Types of spirits produced: Vodka, gin

Names of spirits:
- Spring44 Gin
- Spring44 Vodka
- Spring44 Honey Vodka
- Rob's Mountain Gin

Best known for / most popular: Spring44 Gin

Average bottle price: $25.00 to $30.00

Distribution: CO, FL, NJ, NY

Interesting facts:
Spring44 handcrafts 9,044 feet up in the Colorado Rockies.

Still Cellars
a distillery and arthouse.

1115 Colorado Avenue, Ste. C
Longmont, CO 80501
720-204-6064

Owners / Operators:
Jason R. Houston, Founder / Owner / Operator / Zymologist
Sadye Rose W., Founder / Owner / Operator / Arthouse Maven

Email: spirits@stillcellars.com
Website: www.stillcellars.com

Type: Micro-distillery. Opened in 2012.

Hours of operation:
Friday, 3:00pm to 8:00pm; Saturday 2:00pm to 7:00pm
Recommended to call in advance to confirm

Tours: Available by appointment

Types of spirits produced:
Single malt whiskey, vodka, apple spirits

Names of spirits:
- Still Cellars Vodka
- Still Cellars Whiskey Barley
- Still Cellars Apple Cinnamon
- Still Cellars Apple Ginger
- Still Cellars Apple Straightup

Best known for / most popular:
Apple spirits made from Colorado apples
and infused with spices

Average bottle price: $38.00 to $44.00

Distribution: CO

Interesting facts:
- Certified organic
- Tasting room is an arthouse featuring local artists

Stranahan's Colorado Whiskey Distillery

200 S. Kalamath Street
Denver, CO 80223
303-296-7440

Owners / Operators:
Proximo Distillers, LLC
Pete Macca, General Manager
Rob Dietrich, Head Distiller
Caley Shoemaker, Production Administrator
Kristin Forsch, Brand Ambassador

Email: info@stranahans.com
Website: www.stranahans.com
Facebook: Stranahans Colorado Whiskey
Twitter: @Stranahans

Type: Craft-distillery. Opened in 2004.

Hours of operation:
Distillery Operations, Daily
Gift Shop, Monday through Friday, 11:00am to 5:00pm
          Saturday, 10:00am to 5:00pm; Sunday, closed

Tours: Available. Register via website

Types of spirits produced: Whiskey

Names of spirits:
- Stranahan's Colorado Whiskey
- Snowflake

Best known for / most popular: Snowflake

Average bottle price: $60.00 to $99.00

Distribution: CO

Interesting facts:
- Stranahan's is the first legal distillery in Colorado.
- Bottles are filled and packaged by hand by distillery staff and volunteers.

Syntax Spirits LLC

625 3rd Street, Unit C
Greeley, CO 80631
970-352-5466 (hours and location)

Owners / Operators:
Heather Bean, Owner
Jeff Copeland, Owner

Email: General info: info@syntaxspirits.com
         Heather Bean: heather@syntaxspirits.com
         Jeff Copeland: jeff@syntaxspirits.com
Website: www.syntaxspirits.com
Facebook: Syntax Spirits Distillery
Twitter: @SyntaxSpirits

Type: Micro-distillery. Opened in 2010.

Hours of operation:
Wednesday and Thursday, 4:00pm to 9:00pm
Friday, 4:00pm to 11:00pm
Saturday, 12:00pm to 11:00pm; Sunday, 12:00pm to 6:00pm

Tours: Wednesday through Saturday 5:00pm and 7:00pm
Sunday by request (space/time permitting)

Types of spirits produced:
Vodka, rum, whisky, infused spirits, liqueurs

Names of spirits:
- Class V™ Vodka
- Powder™ White Rum
- White Cat™ Whiskey
- Big Cat™ Whisky
- Perky Pepper™ Pepper Flavored Vodka

Best known for: Class V™ Vodka, Powder™ White Rum

Average bottle price: $25.00 to $35.00

Distribution: CO

Interesting facts:
- One of only a small handful of distilleries in CO that makes all alcohol in-house, with no alcohol supplementation from outside sources.
- One of only a few woman owned-and-operated distilleries in the U.S.

Photo by: Jafe Parsons

Tesouro Distillery

105 South Sunset Street, Ste. A
Longmont, CO 80501
303-746-2819

Owners / Operators:
Greg Dubbe', Owner

Email: info@tesourodistillery.com
Website: www.tesourodistillery.com

Type: Micro-distillery. Opened in 2011.

Hours of operation: Vary

Tours: Vary

Types of spirits produced: Rum

Names of spirits:
• Tesouro Rum

Best known for / most popular: Tesouro Rum

Average bottle price: $30.00 to $35.00

Distribution: CO

Interesting facts: Not provided

Trail Town Still

240 Palomino Trail, Unit A
Ridgway, CO 81432
970-626-3060

Owners / Operators:
Joe Alaimo, General Manager / Distiller
Lynda Gegauff, Sommelier
Jessica Knepp, Sales Room Manager

Email: still@trailtownstill.com
Website: www.trailtownstill.com
Facebook: Trail Town Still
Twitter: @trailtownstill
YouTube: trailtownstill

Type: Micro-distillery. Opened in 2011.

Hours of operation:
Monday through Saturday, 4:00pm to 11:00pm

Tours: Available

Types of spirits produced: Gin, vodka, light whiskey, agave liquor, rum

Names of spirits:
- Trail Town Still Colorado Gin
- Trail Town Still Colorado Vodka
- Trail Town Still Coyote Light Whiskey
- Trail Town Still Colorado Agave Liquor Desert Water

Average bottle price: $38.00 to $54.00

Distribution: Not provided

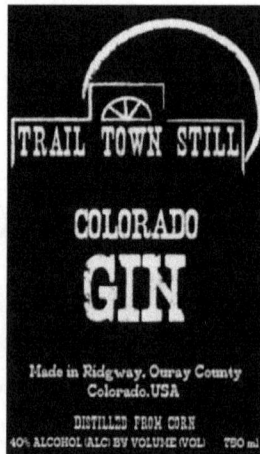

64

Wood's High Mountain Distillery

144 W 1st Street
Salida, CO 81201
719-207-4315

Owners / Operators:
P.T. Wood, Owner
Lee Wood, Owner

Email: info@woodsdistillery.com
Website: www.woodsdistillery.com
Facebook: Wood's High Mountain Distillery
Twitter: @WoodsDistillery

Type: Micro-distillery. Opened in 2012.

Hours of operation:
Tasting room – Daily, 4:00pm to 8:00pm

Tours: Available

Types of spirits produced: Gin, whiskey

Names of spirits:
- Treeline Gin
- Tenderfoot Whiskey

Best known for / most popular: Treeline Gin

Average bottle price: Not provided

Distribution: CO

Interesting facts:
- The still at WHMD was built in German around 1880.
- Wood's High Mountain Distillery is making "Treeline Barrel Rested" Gin. They refill their empty whiskey barrels and age their standard "treeline" gin in them for 2-6 months.

Woody Creek Distillers

60 Sunset Drive
Basalt, CO 81621
970-279-5110

Owners / Operators:
Mary Scanlan, CEO
Mark Kleckner, CFO / COO
Pat Scanlan, Founder / Partner
Amiee White Beazley, Director of Marketing

Email: Mark Kleckner: mark@woodycreekdistillers.com
        Amiee White Beazley: ami@woodycreekdistillers.com
Website: www.woodycreekdistillers.com
Facebook: WoodyCreekDistillers
Twitter: @WoodyCreekDisti
YouTube: WoodyCreekDistillers
Vimeo: Woody Creek Distillers
Flickr: WoodyCreekDistillers

Type: Craft-distillery. Opened in 2012.

Hours of operation:
Wednesday through Saturday, 12:00pm to 7:00pm

Tours: Available by appointment

Types of spirits produced:
Potato vodka, bourbon, whiskey, apple brandy, pear eau de vie, gin

Names of spirits:
- Woody Creek Distillers 100 % Colorado Potato Vodka
- Woody Creek Distillers Reserve Stobrawa Vodka
- Woody Creek Distillers Apple Brandy
- Woody Creek Distillers Pear Eau de Vie

Best known for / most popular: Woody Creek Distillers 100% Potato Vodka

Average bottle price: $35.00

Distribution: CO

Interesting facts:
Woody Creek Distillers is a seed to sip distillery.

Elm City Distillery LLC

53 Capital Drive
Wallingford, CT 06492
203-285-8830

Owners / Operators:
Eric Kotowski, Owner

Email: info@elmcitydistillery.com
Website: www.elmcitydistillery.com
Facebook: Elm City Distillery
Twitter: @ECDistillery

Type: Micro-distillery. Opened in 2010.

Hours of operation:
Monday through Friday, 9:00am to 5:00pm

Tours: Available by appointment

Types of spirits produced: Vodka, whiskey

Names of spirits:
* Velocipede Vodka
* Nine Square Rye

Best known for / most popular: Not provided

Average bottle price: $24.00

Distribution: CT

Interesting facts: Not provided

Onyx Spirits Company LLC

64D Oakland Avenue
East Hartford, CT 06108
860-550-1939

Owners / Operators:
Adam von Gootkin, Co-founder
Peter Kowalczyk, Co-founder

Email: contact@onyxspirits.com
Website: www.onyxspirits.com
Facebook: Onyx Spirits Company
Twitter: @OnyxSpirits
YouTube: OnyxSpirits's Channel

Type: Micro-distillery. Opened in 2011.

Hours of operation:
Monday through Friday, 9:00am to 6:00pm

Tours: Not available

Types of spirits produced:
New England Style Ultra-Premium American
Moonshine

Names of spirits:
- Onyx Moonshine
  (in .750ml, .375ml, and 1.75ml)

- Releasing soon:
  High proof Onyx Moonshine
  Barrel Aged Onyx Moonshine

Best known for: Onyx Moonshine

Average bottle price: $22.00 to $28.00

Distribution: CT, MA, RI
Purchase online: drinkbetter.com/onyx

Interesting facts:
Onyx Moonshine is the first legal moonshine to
be produced in New England since Prohibition.

ONYX SPIRITS CO

PRODUCERS OF FINE LIQUOR

MANCHESTER, CONNECTICUT

Westford Hill Distillers

196 Chatey Road
Ashford, CT 06278
860-429-0464

Owners / Operators:
Louis Chatey, Co-owner
Margaret Chatey, Co-owner

Email: info@westfordhill.com
Website: www.westfordhill.com
Facebook: Westford Hills Distillers

Type: Micro-distillery. Opened in 1997.

Hours of operation: Not provided

Tours: Not available

Types of spirits produced: Brandy, vodka

Names of spirits:
- Aged Apple Brandy
- Framboise Eau de vie
- Pear William Eau de vie
- Kirsch Eau de vie
- Fraise Eau de vie
- Poire Prisonniere
- Rime Organic Vodka

Best known for / most popular: Aged Apple Brandy

Average bottle price: $20.00

Distribution: CA, CT, MA, RI

Interesting facts: Not provided

Dogfish Head Craft Brewery

320 Rehoboth Avenue
Rehoboth Beach, DE 19971
302-226-BREW (2739)

Owners / Operators:
Sam Calagione, Founder / President
Alison Schrader, Off-Centered Distiller

Email: info@dogfish.com
Website: www.dogfish.com
Facebook: Dogfish Head Beer
Twitter: @dogfishbeer
YouTube: Dogfish Head
Google Plus: Dogfish Head Craft Brewery

Type: Micro-Distillery. Opened in 2002.

Hours of operation:
Sunday through Thursday, 12:00pm to 11:00pm
Friday and Saturday, 12:00pm to 1:00am

Tours: Not available

Types of spirits produced: Rum, vodka, gin

Names of spirits:
- Brown Honey Rum
- White Light Rum
- Wit Spiced Rhum
- Blue Hen Vodka
- Blue Hen Vodka Infusions

Best known for / most popular: Brown Honey Rum, Peanut Butter Vodka

Average bottle price: $25.00

Distribution: DE

Interesting facts: Not provided

Painted Stave Distillery

106 W. Commerce Street
Smyrna, DE 19977

Owners / Operators:
Mike Rasmussen, Co-owner
Ron Gomes Jr., Co-owner

Email: Mike Rasmussen:
mike@paintedstave.com
　　　　Ron Gomes Jr.: ron@paintedstave.com
Website: www.paindedstave.com
Facebook: Painted Stave

Type: Micro-distillery. Opening in 2013.

Hours of operation: TBA

Tours: TBA

Types of spirits produced: TBA

Names of spirits:
• TBA

Best known for / most popular: TBA

Average bottle price: TBA

Distribution: TBA

Interesting facts: First standalone distillery in Delaware

New Columbia Distillers

1832 Fenwick Street NE
Washington, DC 20002
202-733-1710

Owners / Operators:
John Uselton, Owner / Distiller
Michael Lowe, Owner / Distiller
Saul Mutchnick, VP of Sales

Email: cheers@greenhatgin.com
Website: www.greenhatgin.com
Facebook: New Columbia Distillers
Twitter: @dcdistillers

Type: Micro-distillery. Opened in 2012.

Hours of operation: Monday through Friday, 8:00am to 5:30pm

Tours: Available Saturday, 1:00pm to 4:00pm

Types of spirits produced: Gin, rye whiskey

Names of spirits:
• Green Hat Gin
• Green Hat Seasonal Gin

Best known for / most popular: Green Hat Gin

Average bottle price: $32.00 TO $36.00

Distribution: DC, MD, VA

Interesting facts:
First DC distillery since before Prohibition

Alchemist Distilleries Inc.

6468-6470 NW 77th Court
Miami, FL 33166
718-360-3123

Owners / Operators:
D.J. Noel, President

Email: djno@alchemistdistillery.com
Website: www.alchemistdistillery.com
Facebook: Alchemist Distilleries

Type: Micro-distillery. Opened in 2013.

Hours of operation: Vary

Tours: Available by appointment

Types of spirits produced: Whiskey, vodka, rum

Names of spirits:
- Alchemist Distillery Whiskey
- Alchemist Distillery Vodka
- Alchemist Distillery Rum

Best known for / most popular: Alchemist Distillery Whiskey

Average bottle price: $24.99 to $32.99

Distribution: FL

Interesting facts:
In addition to their core spirits, Alchemist Distilleries creates spirits using farm fresh produce. They buy seasonal, local produce from Florida farmers and craft unique spirits using these fresh ingredients. Like the produce, theses unique spirits are available only on a seasonal basis.

Cape Spirits Inc.

131 SW 3rd Place
Cape Coral, FL 33991

Owners / Operators:
JoAnn Elardo, President

Email: info@wickeddolphin.com
Website: www.wickeddolphin.com
Facebook: Wicked Dolphin
Twitter: @GettingWicked

Type: Micro-distillery. Opened in 2012.

Hours of operation: Monday through Friday, 9:00am to 5:00pm

Tours: Available Thursdays and Saturdays, 11:00am to 2:00pm

Types of spirits produced: Rum

Names of spirits:
• Wicked Dolphin Rum

Best known for / most popular: The Wicked Dolphin Punch

Average bottle price: $24.99

Distribution: Republic National Distributing Co.

Interesting facts: The first distillery in Lee County FL.

Drum Circle Distilling

2212 Industrial Boulevard
Sarasota, FL 34234
941-358-1900

Owners / Operators:
Troy Roberts, Founder / CEO / Distiller
Tom Clarke, Partner / COO
Ryan Adams, Partner

Email: info@drumcircledistilling.com
Website: www.drumcircledistilling.com
Facebook: Siesta Key Rum
Twitter: @SiestaKeyRum

Type: Micro-distillery. Opened in 2007.

Hours of operation: Not provided

Tours: Available by appointment

Types of spirits produced: Rum

Names of spirits:
• Siesta Key Spiced Rum
• Siesta Key Silver Rum
• Siesta Key Gold Rum

Best known for / most popular: Not provided

Average bottle price: Not provided

Distribution: AZ, CA, CT, DE, GA, MD, NJ, NV, TX, WA

Interesting facts: Not provided

Empire Winery & Distillery

11807 Little Road
New Port Richey, FL 34654
727-819-2821

Owners / Operators:
Henry Kasprow, Owner

Email: empirewinery@msn.com
Website: www.empirewineryanddistillery.com
Facebook: V6 Vodka

Type: Winery / Micro-distillery. Opened in 2002.

Hours of operation: Not provided

Tours: Not provided

Types of spirits produced: Vodka, grappa, mead, liqueur

Names of spirits:
- T & W V6 Rye Vodka
- T & W Grappa Di Muscatto
- T & W Royal Mead Honey Wine
- T & W Lemonela Liqueur
- T &W Limonela Liqueur
- T & W Orangela Liqueur

Best known for / most popular: Not provided

Average bottle price: Not provided

Distribution: Not provided

Interesting facts: Not provided

Fat Dog Spirits LLC

3212 North 40th Street
Tampa, FL 33605
813-503-5995

Owners / Operators:
Nick Carbone, Proprietor

Email: fatdogspirits@earthlink.net
Website: www.fatdogspirits.com
Facebook: Fat Dog Spirits

Type: Micro-distillery. Opened in 2004

Hours of operation: Vary

Tours: Available upon request.

Types of spirits produced: Absinthe verte, gin, vodka

Names of spirits:
- Nicholas Gin
- Touch Vodka-Original
- Touch Red Grapefruit Flavored Vodka
- Touch Key Lime Flavored Vodka
- Touch Valencia Orange Flavored Vodka
- Artemisia Superior Absinthe Verte

Best known for / most popular: Nicholas Gin

Average bottle price: $32.00 to $34.00

Distribution: FL, IL

Interesting facts: Fat Dog Distillery is the second U.S. distillery to be approved to make Artemisia Absinthe in over 100 years.

Fish Hawk Spirits LLC

16162 SW 44th Street
Ocala, FL 34481

Owners / Operators:
R. Matthew Bagdanovich, Managing Member
James M. Brady, Managing Member
A. Christian Howard, Managing Member

Email: fishhawk@fishhawkspirits.net
Website: www.fishhawkspirits.net
Facebook: Fish Hawk Spirits
Twitter: @FHspirits

Type: Micro-distillery. Opened in 2012.

Hours of operation: Not provided

Tours: Not provided

Types of spirits produced: Absinthe

Names of spirits:
- Absinthia Rubra
- Marion Black 106

Best known for / most popular: Not provided

Average bottle price: Not provided

Distribution: FL

Interesting facts: Not provided

78

Florida Farm Distillers

Umatilla, FL 32784
352-455-7232

Owners / Operators:
Dick & Marti Waters, Owners / Distillers

Email: whiskey@palmridgereserve.com
Website: www.palmridgereserve.com
Facebook: Palm Ridge Reserve
Twitter: @handmadewhiskey

Type: Micro-distillery. Opened in 2008.

Hours of operation: Vary

Tours: Not available

Types of spirits produced: Whiskey

Names of spirits:
• Palm Ridge Reserve

Best known for / most popular: Palm Ridge Reserve

Average bottle price: $50.00 to $60.00

Distribution: FL

Interesting facts: Not provided

PALM RIDGE
R E S E R V E ™

Handmade Micro Batch
Florida Whiskey

NJoy Spirits LLC

7237 Wild Buck Road
Weeki Wachee, FL 34613
352-592-9622

Owners / Operators:
Natalie Joy, Co-owner
Kevin S. Goff, Co-owner

Email: njoyspirits@att.net

Type: Micro-distillery. Opening in 2013.

Hours of operation: TBA

Tours: TBA

Types of spirits produced: Whiskey

Names of spirits:
• Wild Buck Whiskey

Best known for / most popular: Wild Buck Whiskey

Average bottle price: $49.99

Distribution: Not provided

Interesting facts: Not provided

WILD BUCK WHISKEY

WILD BUCK WHISKEY
AMERICAN RYE
PROUDLY MADE BY HAND
50% ALC. By Vol
(100 Proof)
750 ML

TAKE A STEP BACK TO AN AGE WHEN
WHISKEY WAS MADE ONE BATCH AT A
TIME ~ IN THE GREAT COUNTRY OF
AMERICA.
Made the old fashioned way in a hand
hammered copper still using only all natural
grains and filtered rainwater.
Wild Buck Whiskey is a great tasting
Whiskey, born and matured within the cypress
swamps of Old Florida.
Always bold and untamed as nature intended.

GOVERNMENT WARNING: (1) ACCORDING TO
THE SURGEON GENERAL, WOMEN SHOULD NOT
DRINK ALCOHOLIC BEVERAGES DURING
PREGNANCY BECAUSE OF THE RISK OF BIRTH
DEFECTS. (2) CONSUMPTION OF ALCOHOLIC
BEVERAGES IMPAIRS YOUR ABILITY TO DRIVE A
CAR OR OPERATE MACHINERY, AND MAY CAUSE
HEALTH PROBLEMS.
Produced And Bottled By
NJoy Spirits, LLC
Wild Buck Road
Weeki Wachee, Florida
www.njoyspirits.com

Rollins Distillery

5680 Gulf Breeze Pkwy., D-10
Gulf Breeze, FL 32563
850-503-1275

Owners / Operators:
Paul Rollins, Co-Owner / President / Master Distiller
Lamia Rollins, Co-Owner / Administrative Director
Patrick Rollins, Marketing Director

Email: info@rollinsdistillery.com
Website: www.rollinsdistillery.com, www.espritdekrewe.com
Facebook: Rollins Distillery
Twitter: @CraftyRams

Type: Craft-distillery. Opened in 2012.

Hours of operation: Daily, 8:00am to 5:00pm

Tours: Available

Types of spirits produced: Rum, vodka

Names of spirits:
- Esprit de Krewe™ Crystal Rum
- Esprit de Krewe™ Spiced Rum
- Esprit de Krewe™ Vodka

Best known for / most popular: Not provided

Average bottle price: Not provided

Distribution: Not provided

Interesting facts: First distillery in the Florida Panhandle

Spirits of the USA LLC

Jacksonville, FL 35522
866-795-5463

Owners / Operators:
Michael Gerard, Founder / CEO

Email: info@spiritsoftheusa.com
Website: www.spiritsoftheusa.com
Facebook: Spirits of the USA
Twitter: @SPIRITSUSA

Type: Craft-distillery. Opened in 2008.

Hours of operation: Not provided

Tours: Not provided

Types of spirits produced: Vodka, gin, rum

Names of spirits:
- Coyote Vodka
- Coyote Ice Peppermint Flavored Vodka
- Coyote Jalapeño Flavored Vodka
- Coyote Mango Flavored Vodka
- Black Window Gin
- Rattlesnake Tequila
- Rattlesnake Jalapeño Tequila
- Deadman's Mango Flavored Rum
- Deadman's Dark & Spice Rum
- Runner Energy Drink

Best known for / most popular: Not provided

Average bottle price: Not provided

Distribution: FL

Interesting facts: Not provided

The Florida Distillery

501 S. Falkenburg Road, Ste. C-6
Tampa, FL 33619
813-347-6565

Owners / Operators:
Lee Nelson, Co-owners
Pat O'Brian, Co-owner
Nefreteri Jacobsen, Operations Assistant

Email: info@floridadistillery.net
Website: www.cane-vodka.com
Facebook: The Florida Cane Distillery
Twitter: @FLVODKA
Instagram: CaneVodka
Pinterest: Cane Vodka

Type: Micro-distillery. Opened in 2012.

Hours of operation: Daily

Tours: Not available

Types of spirits produced: Vodka

Names of spirits:
- Cane Vodka
- Cane Vodka Gator Grape
- Cane Vodka Orlando Orange
- Cane Vodka Buccaneer Blueberry
- Cane Vodka Plant City Strawberry

Best known for / most popular: Cane Vodka

Average bottle price: $30.00

Distribution: FL

Interesting facts: Not provided

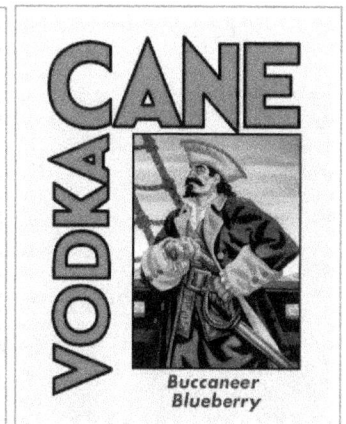

Dawsonville Moonshine Distillery
Free Spirits Distillery

415 Hwy. 53 East
Dawsonville, GA 30534
770-401-1211

Owners / Operators:
Cheryl Wood, Owner

Email: moonshiners@dawsonvillemoonshinedistillery.com
Website: www.dawsonvillemoonshinedistillery.com
Facebook: Dawsonville Moonshine Distillery
Twitter: @Moonshiners_

Type: Micro-distillery. Opened in 2012.

Hours of operation:
Monday through Saturday, 10:00am to 4:00pm
Sunday, 12:00pm to 4:00pm

Tours: Available

Types of spirits produced: Whiskey

Names of spirits:
• Dawsonville Moonshine Georgia Corn Whiskey

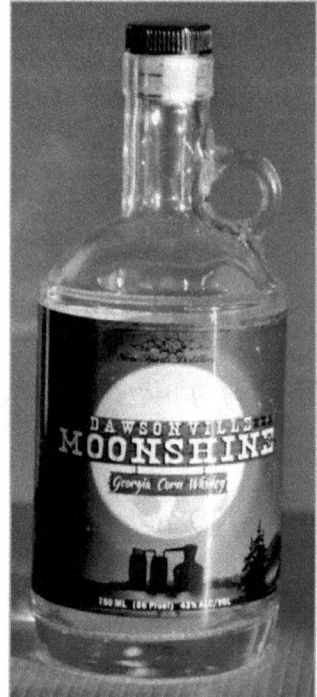

Best known for / most popular:
Dawsonville Moonshine Georgia Corn Whiskey

Average bottle price: $25.00

Distribution: GA

Interesting facts: The distillery is under the same room as the Georgia Racing Hall of Fame and city hall.

Georgia Distilling Company

121 Blandy Way
Milledgeville, GA 31061
478-453-1086

Owners / Operators:
Shawn Hall, Co-owner
Bill Mauldin, Co-owner

Email: info@georgiadistillingcompany.com
Website: www.georgiadistilling.com
Facebook: Georgia Distilling Company, Inc.
Twitter: @GeorgiaDistiCo, @GrandaddyMimms

Type: Micro-distillery. Opened in 2009.

Hours of operation: Not provided

Tours: Not available

Types of spirits produced: Moonshine, vodka, whiskey

Names of spirits:
- Georgia Vodka
- Bear Creek Sippin' Shine
- Grandaddy Mimm's Whiskey
- Tootsie's Apple Pie Whiskey
- Doc Holliday Rye Whiskey
- Copperhead Georgia Sour Mash

Best known for / most popular: Grandaddy Mimm's

Average bottle price: $20.00

Distribution: Not provided

Interesting facts: Not provided

85

Ivy Mountain Distillery LLC

1896 Dick's Hill Parkway
Mt. Airy, GA 30563

Owners / Operators:
Carlene Holder, Owner
Carlos Lovell, Master Distiller

Email: carlene@ivymountaindistillery.com
Website: www.ivymountaindistillery.com
Facebook: Ivy Mountain Distillery

Type: Micro-distillery. Opened in 2011.

Hours of operation: Not provided

Tours: Available first Tuesday, third Friday
of each month, 9:00am and 3:00pm

Types of spirits produced: Whiskey, brandy

Names of spirits:
• Ivy Mountain Georgia Sour Mash Whiskey™
• Ivy Mountain Georgia Sour Mash Spirits™
• Ivy Mountain Apple Brandy™
• Ivy Mountain Georgia Peach Brandy™

Best known for / most popular: Not provided

Average bottle price: $24.00

Distribution: Not provided
Eagle Rock Distributors (GA)
Southern Wine & Spirits (NC, SC, FL)

Interesting facts:
The master distiller is 85 years young.
The recipe belongs to his father and was used
to make illegal whiskey generations ago.

86

Richland Distilling Company

333 Broad Street
Richland, GA 31825
229-887-3537 / 941-545-4311

Owners / Operators:
Erik Vonk, Founder / Proprietor
Jay McCain, General Manager
Karin Vonk, Marketing and Public Relations

Email: cheers@richlandrum.com
Website: www.richlandrum.com
Facebook: Richland Distilling Company

Type: Artisan Rum Distillery. Opened in 2011.

Hours of operation:
Monday through Friday, 9:00am to 5:00pm

Tours: Available by appointment

Types of spirits produced: Rum

Names of spirits:
• Richland Rum
• Richland Rum – Vennebroeck Velvet Proprietor's Private Reserve

Best known for: Richland Rum

Average bottle price: $55.00

Distribution: GA, TN. Other states upon request.

Interesting facts:
• Richland Rum operates a 200 gallon copper-pot still hand made to order from Portugal.
• Superior aged Rum, artisan crafted from pure sugar cane syrup, copper pot distilled in small batches and patiently aged in American oak barrels.

Thirteenth Colony Distilleries

305 N. Dudley Street
Americus, GA 31709
229-924-3310

Owners / Operators:
Alton Darby, Chairman / CEO
Kent Cost, President
Gilbert S. Klemann MD, VP of Product Development
Lindsey Cotton, Marketing / Office Manager
Graham Arthur, Production and Facility Manager / Distiller
Elizabeth Warnock, Distillery Representative
Anna Payne, Office Administrator

Email: info@13colony.net
Website: www.13colony.net
Facebook: Southern Vodka
Twitter: @13thColony

Type: Micro-distillery. Opened in 2009.

Hours of operation: Not provided

Tours: Not provided

Types of spirits produced: Gin, vodka, whiskey

Names of spirits:
- Plantation Vodka
- Southern Gin
- Southern Vodka
- Southern Corn Whiskey

Best known for / most popular: Plantation Vodka

Average bottle price: Not provided

Distribution: AL, GA, LA, MS, NJ, WV, WY

Interesting facts: Not provided

Thirteenth Colony Distilleries
Southern Hand Crafted, Small Batch Spirits... made by friends, for friends

Haleakala Distillers

Kula, HI 96790

Owners / Operators:
Jim Sargent, Master Distiller
Leslie Sargent, Managing Director

Website: www.haleakaladistillers.com

Type: Micro-distillery. Opened in 2003.

Hours of operation: Vary

Tours: Not available

Types of spirits produced: Rum, liqueur

Names of spirits:
- Maui Dark Rum ™
- Maui Gold Rum
- Maui Platinum Rum,
- Maui Reserve Gold Rum ™
- Maui Pineapple Flavored Rum
- Maui Okolehao (made from Ti root)
- Braddah Kimo's Extreme 155 Proof Rum

Best known for: Maui Dark Rum ™

Average bottle price: $20.00 in Hawaii

Distribution: HI and a handful of liquor retailers on the U.S. mainland. Visit www.mauirum.biz for details.

Interesting facts: Not provided

Hawaii Sea Spirits LLC

4051 Omaopio Road
Kula, HI 96790
866-77-OCEAN

Owners / Operators:
Shay Smith, President / CEO
Kyle Smith, Production Director
Don Freytag, Chief Marketing Officer / Sales Director
Sye Vasquez, Board Member / Advisor
Craig Duvall, Board Member / Advisor

Email: Sales: sales@oceanvodka.com
        Shay Smith: shay@oceanvodka.com
        Kyle Smith: kyle@oceanvodka.com
        Don Freytag: don@oceanvodka.com
Website: www.oceanvodka.com
Facebook: Ocean Vodka
Twitter: @OceanVodka

Type: Craft-distillery. Opened in 2006.

Hours of operation: Monday through Friday, 9:00am to 5:00pm

Tours: Available, check website for reservation information

Types of spirits produced: Vodka

Names of spirits:
• Ocean Vodka

Best known for: Ocean Vodka

Average bottle price: $32.00

Distribution: U.S., Japan, Canada

Interesting facts:
• 100% Gluten Free
• Uses only 100% USDA Certified Organic sugar cane
• The only known vodka in the world made from organic sugar cane
• The only known spirit in the world made with deep ocean mineral water, sourced 3,000 feet below the Kona coast of the island of Hawaii.
• 100% solar powered
• New craft-distillery and organic farm located 1,000 feet above the ocean on the slopes of Mt. Haleakala in Kula, Maui.
• Give back to oceanic causes every year.

Island Distillers Inc.

220 Puuhale Road, #B3
Honolulu, HI 96819
808-492-4632

Owners / Operators:
Dave Flintstone, Owner

Email: dave@islanddistillers.com
Website: www.islanddistillers.com
Facebook: Hawaiian Vodka
YouTube: Hawaiianvodka's Channel

Type: Micro-distillery. Opened in 2009.

Hours of operation: Open daily, hours vary

Tours: Not available

Types of spirits produced: Vodka, moonshine

Names of spirits:
- Hawaiian Vodka
- Hawaiian Coconut Vodka
- Hawaiian Moonshine

Best known for: Hawaiian Moonshine

Average bottle price: $25.00 to $33.00

Distribution: Hawaii

Interesting facts:
Island Distillers is Honolulu's only licensed distillery.

Kōloa Rum Company

2-2741 Kaumualii Highway, Ste. C
Kalaheo, HI 96741
808-332-9333

Owners / Operators:
Bob Gunter, President / CEO
Alicia Iverson, CFO
Jeanne Toulon, Director of Public Relations
Rex Riddle, Hawaii State Sales Manager
Michael Riley, Operations Manager

Email: info@koloarum
Website: www.koloarum.com
Facebook: Koloa Rum Company
Twitter: @KoloaRumCompany
Pinterest: Koloa Rum Company

PREMIUM HAWAIIAN RUM

kaua'i · hawaii

Type: Micro-distillery. Opened in 2009.

Hours of operation: Vary. Visit website for tasting room and store hours

Tours: Not available

Types of spirits produced: Rum and related spirits products

Names of spirits:
- Kaua`i White
- Kaua`i Gold
- Kaua`i Dark Rum
- Kaua`i Spice Rum

Best known for: Kaua`i Dark Rum

Average bottle price: $29.95 to $32.95

Distribution: AZ, CA, GA, HI, IA, IL, MN, NV, OR, UT, WA, W; Western Canada

Interesting facts: The history of Hawaii's first sugar plantation lives within each bottle of Kōloa Rum. The rum is carefully handcrafted in single batches from Kaua`i grown raw crystal sugar from the west side of the island and from pure mountain rainwater that is captured and slowly filtered through layers of volcanic strata before finally reaching vast underground aquifers from Mt. Wai`ale`ale and the nearby mountain peaks and rainforests. It is distilled in a 1,210 gallon vintage copper-pot still that was manufactured in New England shortly after World War II.

44° North Vodka

134 N. 3300 E.
Rigby, ID 83442
206-649-3598

Owners / Operators:
Ken Wyatt, Co-Founder
Ron Zier, Co-Founder

Email: ken@44northvodka.com
Website: www.44northvodka.com
Facebook: 44° North Vodka
Twitter: @44NorthVodka

Type: Micro-distillery. Opened in 2004.

Hours of operation: Not provided

Tours: Not provided

Types of spirits produced: Vodka

Names of spirits:
- 44° North Magic Valley Vodka
- 44° North Rainier Cherry Vodka
- 44° North Mountain Huckleberry Vodka

Best known for / most popular: Not provided

Average bottle price: Not provided

Distribution: Nationwide

Interesting facts: Not provided

93

Bardenay Inc.

610 Grove Street
Boise, ID 83702
208-426-0538

Bardenay Eagle
155 E Riverside Drive
Eagle, ID 83616

Bardenay Coeur d'Alene
1710 W Riverstone Drive
Coeur d'Alene, ID 83814

Owners / Operators:
Kevin Settles, Owner

Email: info@bardenay.com
Website: www.bardenay.com
Facebook: Bardenay
Twitter: @Bardenay
UrbanSpoon: Bardenay
Yelp: Bardenay Restaurant & Distillery
Trip Advisor: Bardenay Restaurant & Distillery

Type: Micro-distillery. Opened in 2000.

Hours of operation: Vary

Tours: Available

Types of spirits produced: Gin, rum, vodka

Names of spirits:
- Bardenay Vodka
- Bardenay London Dry Gin
- Bardenay Small Batch Rum
- Ginger Spiced Rum
- Lemon Vodka

Best known for: Bardenay Vodka

Average bottle price: $10.00 to $20.00

Distribution: ID

Interesting facts: Bardenay Distillery is the nation's first restaurant distillery.

Grand Teton Distillery

1755 North Highway 33
Driggs, ID 83422
208-354-7263

Owners / Operators:
Lea Beckett, President
William Beckett, VP
John Boczar, VP / Master Distiller

Email: info@tetonvodka.com
Website: www.tetonvodka.com
Facebook: Grand Teton Vodka
Twitter: @TetonVodka
LinkedIn: Grand Teton Vodka

Type: Micro-distillery. Opened in 2012.

Hours of operation: Monday through Friday, 9:00am to 5:00pm

Tours: Available by appointment

Types of spirits produced: Vodka

Names of spirits:
• Grand Teton Vodka

Best known for / most popular: Grand Teton Vodka

Average bottle price: $18.95 to $21.95

Distribution: AR, ID, MT, OR, WY

Interesting facts:
• Won a Gold Medal, 94 Points from Beverage Testing Institute in Chicago in 2012, making Grand Teton Vodka the #1 ranked potato vodka in the world.
• Won a Double Gold Medal at the 2013 San Francisco Spirits Competition.

Koenig Distillery

20928 Grape Lane
Caldwell, ID 83607
208-455-8386

Owners / Operators:
Andrew Koenig, Owner / Master Distiller

Email: info@koenigdistilleryandwinery.com
Website: www.koenigdistilleryandwinery.com
Facebook: Koenig Distillery and Winery
Twitter: @DrinkKoenig

Type: Micro-distillery. Opened in 1999.

Hours of operation:
Tasting room: Friday through Sunday, 12:00pm to 5:00pm

Tours: Private tours are available.

Types of spirits produced: Vodka, grappa, brandy

Names of spirits:
- Koenig Potato Vodka
- Koenig Huckleberry Flavored Vodka
- Koenig Pear Brandy
- Koenig Apricot Brandy
- Koenig Cherry Brandy
- Koenig Plum Brandy
- Koenig Grappa

Best known for: Koenig Potato Vodka

Average bottle price: $19.95

Distribution: CA, ID, MT, OR, PA, WA

Interesting facts:
It takes more than 15 pounds of fresh fruit to make each bottle of brandy.

Few Spirits LLC

918 Chicago Avenue
Evanston, IL 60202
847-920-8628

Owners / Operators:
Paul Hletko, Founder

Email: info@fewspirits.com
Website: www.fewspirits.com
Facebook: Few Spirits
Twitter: @fewspirits
Blog: fewspirits.tumblr.com
Yelp: Few Spirits
LinkedIn: Few Spirits

Type: Micro-distillery. Opened in 2011.

Hours of operation:
Tours every Saturday, 2:00pm and 3:00pm

Tours: Available

Types of spirits produced: Gin, whiskey

Names of spirits:
- Few American Gin
- Few White Whiskey
- Few Bourbon
- Few Rye

Average bottle price: $35.00 to $80.00

Distribution: IL

Interesting facts: Few Spirits is the first legal alcohol ever produced in Evanston, Illinois.

Hum Spirits Company

676 N. LaSalle Drive, Unit 329
Chicago, IL 60654
312-735-1838

Owners / Operators:
Jennifer Piccione, Chief Executive Officer
Adam Seger, Chief Innovative Officer
Bryce Williford, Chief Financial Officer
Erin Ramsay, Social Media Coordinator / Executive Assistant

Email: info@humspirits.com
Website: www.humspirits.com
Facebook: The Hum Spirits Company
Twitter: @humspirits
YouTube: Hum Channel
Foursquare: Adam S.

Type: Micro-distillery. Opened in 2009.

Hours of operation: 9:00am to 6:00pm

Tours: Available

Types of spirits produced: Liqueur

Names of spirits:
• Hum Botanical Spirit

Best known for: Hum Botanical Spirit

Average bottle price: $36.00

Distribution: AZ, CA, DC, DE, FL, GA, ID, IL, LA, MD, MN, MT, NJ, NV, NY, TN, TX, WA, VA

Interesting facts: All ingredients for Hum are from California and it is produced at Pennsylvania Pure Distilleries in Glenshaw, Pennsylvania. Bottles used for samples and R&D are re-purposed into hummingbird feeders.

Koval Distillery

5121 N. Ravenswood Avenue
Chicago, IL 60640
312-878-7988

Owners / Operators:
Robert Birnecker, Owner / Master Distiller
Sonat Birnecker, Owner / President

Email: info@koval-distillery.com
Website: www.koval-distillery.com
Facebook: KOVAL Distillery
Twitter: @kovaldistillery

Type: Micro-distillery. Opened in 2008.

Hours of operation: Not provided

Tours: Available

Types of spirits produced:
Brandy, beer spirit, whiskey, liqueurs

Names of spirits: KOVAL Brand

Aged Whiskey:
- Rye
- Millet
- Oat
- Bourbon
- Four Grain
- Limited Edition Charred Barrel Wheat
- Limited Edition Charred Barrel Spelt
- Limited Edition Toasted Barrel Rye
- Limited Edition Toasted Barrel Wheat
- Limited Edition Toasted Barrel Oat
- Limited Edition Toasted Barrel Millet
- Limited Edition Toasted Barrel Spelt

Brandy:
- Pear Brandy (Williams)
- Apple Brandy

White Whiskey:
- White Rye
- Limited Edition White Wheat
- Limited Edition White Oat
- Limited Edition White Spelt
- Limited Edition White Millet

Liqueurs:
- Jasmine
- Coffee
- Rose Hip
- Ginger
- Orange Blossom
- Chrysanthemum & Honey
- Caraway

Beer spirit:
- Bierbrand

Average bottle price: $25.00 to $45.00

Distribution:
CA, DC, DE, FL, GA, IL, IN, KY, LA, MA, MD, MI, MO, NJ, NM, NY, RI, TN, WI

Interesting facts: Koval Distillery is the first boutique distillery located in Chicago since Prohibition.

Letherbee Distillers

1815 W. Berteau Avenue
Chicago, IL 60647

Owners / Operators:
Brenton Engel, Owner / Distiller

Email: brenton@letherbee.com
Website: www.letherbee.com
Facebook: Letherbee Distillers
Twitter: @letherbee

Type: Micro-distillery. Opened in 2012.

Hours of operation: Vary

Tours: Not available

Types of spirits produced:
Gin, absinthe, malört, herbal liquors and liqueurs, specialty seasonal spirits

Names of spirits:
*   Letherbee Gin
*   Absinthe Brun (Barrel-Aged)
*   Malört Liqueur
*   Autumnal Gin
*   Vernal Gin

Best known for: Letherbee Gin

Average bottle price: Affordable

Distribution: CA, IL

LETHERBEE DISTILLERS
CHICAGO ILLINOIS

Photo by Brian Guido

Mastermind Vodka

4262 State Route 162
Pontoon Beach, IL 62040
618-512-1039

Owners / Operators:
Carl Levering, President
Chris Egan, Brand Executive
Julie Martin, Controller
Travis McDonald, Asst. Distiller / Tour Coordinator

Email: info@mastermindvodka.com
Website: www.mastermindvodka.com
Facebook: Mastermind Vodka
Twitter: @MastermindVodka

Type: Micro-distillery. Opened in 2011.

Hours of operation:
Tuesday through Saturday, 10:00am to 9:00pm

Tours: Available

Types of spirits produced: Vodka, moonshine

Names of spirits:
- Mastermind Vodka
- LPR Moonshine

Best known for / most popular: Mastermind Vodka

Average bottle price: $27.00 to $35.00

Distribution: IL, MO

Interesting facts:
- 100% American

Mid-Oak Distillery

4704 W. 147th Street
Midlothian, IL 60445
708-925-9318

Owners / Operators:
Matthew Altman, President / Master Distillery
Dominic D'Ambrosio, Vice President of Marketing

Email: admin@cdvodka.com
Website: www.cdvodka.com
Facebook: Mid-Oak Distillery
            Mid-Oak Distillery Featuring CD Vodka

Type: Micro-distillery. Opened in 2012.

Hours of operation:
Tasting room - Wednesday through Saturday, 5:00pm to 10:00pm
                Sunday, 12:00pm to 5:00pm
Distillery operations - Monday and Tuesday

Tours: Available by appointment

Types of spirits produced: Vodka

Names of spirits:
• CD Vodka

Best known for / most popular:
CD Vodka

Average bottle price: $25.00

Distribution: IL, WI

Interesting facts: What's in a name?
The CD on the bottle's label symbolizes the reign of Russia's Catherine the Great in the late 1700s. Catherine allowed only the noble class of Russia to distill vodka in their homes; however, they were not allowed to sell it. With no commercial interest in producing vodka, the focus was on the spirit's quality and so only the most stringent methods of production were followed. Because of this, it is said that the finest vodka in the history of the world was made during Catalina Dynastii or, loosely translated, Catherine's Dynasty.

North Shore Distillery

28913 Herky Drive, Unit 308
Lake Bluff, IL 60044
847-574-2499

Owners / Operators:
Derek Kassebaum, Co-owner
Sonja Kassebaum, Co-owner

Email: tours@northshoredistillery.com
Website: www.northshoredistillery.com
Facebook: North Shore Distillery
Twitter: @NSDistillery

Type: Micro-distillery. Opened in 2004.

Hours of operation: Monday through Friday, 10:00am to 6:00pm

Tours: Available

Types of spirits produced: Vodka, absinthe, gin

Names of spirits:
- Distiller's Gin No. 6
- Distiller's Gin No. 11
- Sirène Absinthe Verte
- North Shore Vodka
- Aquavit Private Reserve
- Sol Chamomile Citrus Vodka

Best known for / most popular: Not provided

Average bottle price: Not provided

Distribution: CA, IA, IL, IN, KY, MN, MO, MT, PA, WI

Interesting facts: Not provided

Premiere Distillery LLC

Gurnee, IL 60031
847-662-4444

Owners / Operators:
Inna Feldman-Gerber, President
Gregory Feldman, Master Distiller

Email: info@premieredistillery.com
Website: www.premieredistillery.com
Facebook: Premiere Distillery
Twitter: @premieredistill
Pinterest: Inna Feldman-Gerber

Type: Micro-distillery. Opened in 2012.

Hours of operation: Vary

Tours: Not available

Types of spirits produced: Vodka

Names of spirits:
• Real Russian Vodka

Best known for / most popular: Real Russian Vodka

Average bottle price: $19.99

Distribution: IL, IN

Interesting facts:
• Third generation master distiller is from Russia
• Only known American vodka handcrafted by real Russians
• Heirloom family recipe that dates back to 1905
• Distilled 6 times from winter wheat
• Filtered 10 times through a proprietary filtration system designed by the master distiller
• Woman owned distillery

104

Quincy Street Distillery

39 E. Quincy Street
Riverside, IL 60546
708-870-5987

Owners / Operators:
Derrick C. Mancini, Owner

Email: manager@quincystreetdistillery.com
Website: www.quincystreetdistillery.com
Facebook: Quincy Street Distillery
Twitter: @QSDistillery

Type: Micro-distillery. Opened in 2012.

Hours of operation:
Friday, 4:00pm to 8:00pm; Saturday 2:00pm to 6:00pm

Tours: Available by appointment

Types of spirits produced:
Gin, whiskey, absinthe, aquavit, liqueur, eau de vie, vodka

Names of spirits:
- Water Tower White Lightning™ Unaged Illinois Corn Whiskey
- Old No. 176™ Gin
- Prairie Sunshine™ Wildflower Honey Spirit
- Prairie Moonshine™ Corn & Honey Spirit
- Bourbon Spring™ Young Rested Illinois Bourbon Whiskey

Best known for: Artisanal spirits crafted with creative historical interpretations

Average bottle price: $25.00 to $55.00

Distribution: IL

Interesting facts:
- The Riverside landmark water tower burned down "like a giant candle" on New Year's Eve one hundred years ago.
- Engine No. 176 was the first to be custom built for the Chicago, Burlington, & Quincy Railroad, and gives its name to our interpretation of prohibition-era "railroad" gin.
- Bourbon Spring is a historical site near the distillery where in 1834 the Cook County militia was formed with the election of Colonel Beaubien and celebrated with bourbon barrels in the spring.

Tailwinds Distilling Company

14912 S. Eastern Avenue, Unit 103
Plainfield, IL 60544
815-290-0786

Owners / Operators:
Toby Beall, Founder / Head Distiller
Brad Beall, Manager
Jillian Beall, Founder
Jamey Beall, Operator/ Manager/ Distiller

Email: info@tailwindsdistilling.com
Website: www.tailwindsdistilling.com
Facebook: Tailwinds Distilling
Twitter: @Tailwinds_Rum

Type: Micro-distillery. Opened in 2012.

Hours of operation:
Friday and Saturday, 12:00 to 8:00pm; Sunday, 12:00pm to 5:00pm

Tours: Available on Saturdays, 1:00pm and 3:00pm

Types of spirits produced: Rum, 100% blue agave spirit

Names of spirits:
• Taildragger White Rum
• Taildragger Amber Rum
• Midnight Caye Silver 100% Blue Agave Spirit
• Midnight Caye Rested 100% Blue Agave Spirit

Best known for / most popular: Taildragger Rum

Average bottle price: $27.00 to $40.00

Distribution: IL

Interesting facts: "Tailwinds" is a sendoff given to pilots...life is just easier with the wind at your back.

Heartland Distillers

9402 Uptown Drive, Ste. 1000
Indianapolis, IN 46256
800-417-0150

HEARTLAND DISTILLERS

Owners / Operators:
Stuart Hobson, Owner / Distiller

Email: stuart@heartlanddistillers.com
Websites: www.heartlanddistillers.com, www.springmillbourbon.com
www.indianavodka.com, www.indianainfusions.com
www.sorgrhum.com
Facebook: Heartland Distillers, Indiana Vodka, Indiana Infusions
Spring Mill Bourbon, Sorgrhum
Twitter: @Indiana_Vodka, @springmillbourb

Type: Micro-distillery. Opened in 2009.

Hours of operation: Closed to the public

Tours: Available by appointment

Types of spirits produced:
Gin, vodka, whiskey, sweet sorghum spirits, bourbon

Names of spirits:
- Heartland Distiller's Reserve Vodka
- Heartland Distiller's Reserve Bourbon
- Indiana Vodka
- Indiana Infusions
- Prohibition Gin
- Spring Mill Straight Bourbon Whiskey
  (90 proof and Cask Strength)
- Sorgrhum White – America's First Sweet Sorghum Spirit
- Sorgrhum Barrel Aged

Best known for: Indiana Vodka

Average bottle price: $17.00 to $25.00

Distribution: Glazers Wholesale, Southern Wine & Spirits

Interesting facts:
- Heartland Distillers is Indiana's first legal new distillery since Prohibition.
- Sorgrhum is produced from Amish harvested and pressed sorghum cane. The sorghum cane is pressed on a horse drawn press and then cooked into a syrup over open wood flames before fermentation and distillation.
- Spring Mill Bourbon is twice barreled in new charred oak and then bottled in ceramic stone bottles.

Huber's Starlight Distillery

19816 Huber Road
Starlight, IN 47106
812-923-9463

Owners / Operators:
Ted Huber, Co-owner
Greg Huber, Co-owner

Email: contactus@huberwinery.com
Website: www.starlightdistillery.com
Facebook: Huber's Orchard & Winery

Type: Winery / Micro-distillery.
Winery opened in 1978. Distillery opened in 2000.

Hours of operation: Daily, 12:00pm to 6:00pm

Tours: Available upon request

Types of spirits produced:
Brandy, grappa, ports, fruit infusions

Names of spirits:
- Starlight Distillery Grappa
- Starlight Distillery Brandy
- Starlight Distillery Apple Brandy
- Starlight Distillery Applejack Brandy
- Starlight Distillery Private Reserve Brandy

Best known for / most popular: Apple Brandy & Applejack

Average bottle price: $20.99 to $59.99

Distribution: IL, IN, KY, MO, OH

Interesting facts:
Huber's Starlight Distillery primarily uses fruits and grapes grown on their 600 acre estate that was founded in 1843 by their ancestors from Baden-Baden Germany.

Virtuoso Distillers LLC

4211 Grape Road
Mishawaka, IN 46545
574-876-4450

Owners / Operators:
Steve Ross, Owner

Email: steve@18vodka.com
Website: www.18vodka.com
Facebook: 18 Vodka
Twitter: @18Vodka

Type: Micro-distillery. Opened in 2008.

Hours of operation: Daily, 10:00am to 5:00pm

Tours: Available by appointment

Types of spirits produced: Vodka, whiskey, lemoncello

Names of spirits:
• 18 Vodka

Best known for: Vodka

Average bottle price: $23.00 to $28.00

Distribution: DC, IL, IN

Interesting facts: 18 Vodka is made from 100% rye.

Broadbent Distillery

6175 50th Avenue
Norwalk, IA 50211
515-981-0011

Owners / Operators:
E. John Broadbent, President

Email: ejab2@aol.com
Website: www.twojaysiowa.com
Facebook: Broadbent Distillery

Type: Micro-distillery. Opened in 2012.

Hours of operation: Vary

Tours: Available by appointment

Types of spirits produced: Whiskey, grappa

Names of spirits:
- Two Jays Corn Whiskey
- Two Jays Corn Whiskey Country Style
- Grappa

Best known for: Two Jays Iowa Corn Whiskey Country Style

Average bottle price: $16.00 to $35.00

Distribution: IA

Interesting facts: Broadbent Distillery is Iowa's fourth licensed micro-distillery since prohibition and the smallest legal one Iowa.

Two Jay's™

Iowa Corn WHISKEY
Country Style

Broadbent Distillery; Norwalk, Iowa 50211
40% ALC. BY VOL.   750 ML

Our small Micro Distillery originated out of the need to create a market for the family owned Grape Vineyard. Faced with not being able to sell its Grapes in 2009, the Broadbent Distillery was created on our family acreage nestled in rural Warren County, Iowa. The homemade Still was built and modern technology incorporated in the processes for making Grappa and Corn Whiskey using Iowa grown Fruit and Iowa grown Grains. Broadbent Distillery processes small batches only, while distilling its product two times in order to provide our customers with premium quality Spirits. While continued improvements are being made, we are dedicated to providing you with a quality flavor for your Spirits experience.

Cedar Ridge Distillery

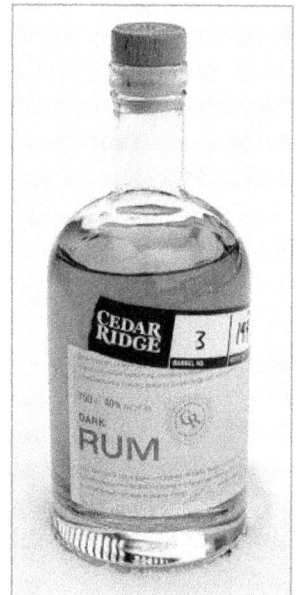

1441 Marak Road
Swisher, IA 52338
319-857-4300

Owners / Operators:
Jeff Quint, Owner

Email: info@crwine.com
Websites: www.crwine.com, www.clearheartspirits.com, www.crdistillery.com
Facebook: Cedar Ridge Winery & Distillery
Twitter: @CedarRidge4
Yelp: Cedar Ridge Vineyards, Winery and Distillery
YouTube: Cedar Ridge
Instagram: cedarridgevineyards

Type: Winery / Micro-distillery. Opened in 2005.

Hours of operation: Wednesday through Friday from 11:00am to 9:00pm
Saturday and Sunday from 11:00am to 5:00pm

Tours: Available upon request

Types of spirits produced:
Brandy, bourbon whiskey, gin, grappa, liqueur, rum, vodka

Names of spirits:
- ClearHeart Vodka
- ClearHeart Gin
- ClearHeart Light Rum
- Cedar Ridge Dark Rum
- Cedar Ridge Single Malt Whiskey
- Cedar Ridge Iowa Bourbon Whiskey
- Cedar Ridge Apple Brandy
- Cedar Ridge Grape Brandy
- Cedar Ridge Lemoncella (lemon liqueur)
- Cedar Ridge Lamponcella (raspberry liqueur)
- Cedar Ridge Grappa

Best known for: ClearHeart Vodka

Average bottle price: Not provided

Distribution: IA, IL, MO, NE

Interesting facts: Cedar Ridge Distillery is Iowa's first micro-distillery.

Mississippi River Distilling Company

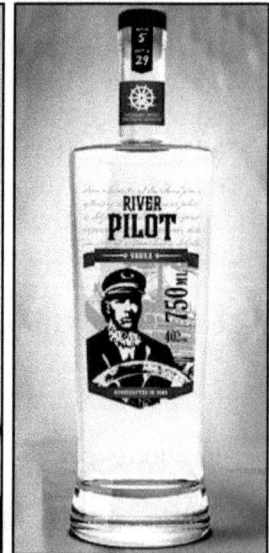

303 North Cody Road
LeClaire, IA 52753
563-484-4342

Owners / Operators:
Ryan and Garrett Burchett, Owners

Email: info@mrdistilling.com
Website: www.mrdistilling.com
Facebook: Mississippi River Distilling Company
Twitter: @mrivrdistilling
YouTube: Mississippi River Distilling
Pinterest: Mississippi River Distilling Company

Type: Micro-distillery. Opened in 2010.

Hours of operation:
Monday through Saturday, 10:00am to 5:00pm
Sunday 12:00pm to 5:00pm

Tours: Available

Types of spirits produced: Bourbon whiskey, gin, vodka

Names of spirits:
- River Pilot Vodka
- River Rose Gin
- River Baron Artisan Spirit
- Cody Road Bourbon Whiskey
- Cody Road Rye Whiskey

Best known for: River Pilot Vodka

Average bottle price: $25.00 to $30.00

Distribution:
IA, IL, MO, MN, NE, TX, WI

Interesting facts:
100% of the grain is sourced from
within 25 miles of the distillery.

MISSISSIPPI RIVER
DISTILLING COMPANY

112

Templeton Rye Distillery

209 East 3rd Street
Templeton, IA 51463
712-669-8793

Owners / Operators:
Kevin Boersma, Distillery Manager

Email: info@templetonrye.com
Website: www.templetonrye.com
Facebook: Templeton Rye
Twitter: @TempletonRye
YouTube: Templeton Rye Whiskey

Type: Micro-distillery. Opened in 2005.

Hours of operation: 8:00am to 5:00pm

Tours: Available

Types of spirits produced: Whiskey

Names of spirits:
• Templeton Rye Whiskey

Best known for / most popular: Templeton Rye

Average bottle price: $39.00

Distribution: CA, IA, IL, NY

Interesting facts: Templeton Rye was Al Capone's whiskey of choice.

Werner Distilling LLC

101 N. Hamburg Street
Holstein, IA 51025
712-368-2806

Owners / Operators:
Gregory and Karen Brunelle, Managers

Email: sales@wernerdistilling.com
Facebook: Werner Distilling

Type: Micro-distillery. Opened in 2102.

Hours of operation: Vary

Tours: Available by appointment

Types of spirits produced: Rum

Names of spirits:
- Holstein Rum
- Holstein Spiced Rum

Best known for / most popular: Holstein Rum

Average bottle price: $20.00 to $25.00

Distribution: IA

Interesting facts: Pictured on the label are Karen's grandfather and great-grandfather working the field on the family farm in 1931.

Dark Horse Distillery

11740 West 86th Terrace
Lenexa, KS 66214
913-492-3275

Owners / Operators:
Kris Hennessy, Owner

Email: info@dhdistillery.com
Website: www.dhdistillery.com
Facebook: Dark Horse Distillery
Twitter: @DHDistillery
Pinterest: Dark Horse Distillery

Type: Micro-distillery. Opened in 2010.

Hours of operation: Monday through Friday, 8:00am to 5:00pm

Tours: Available

Types of spirits produced: Whiskey, vodka

Names of spirits:
- Long Shot White Whiskey
- Dark Horse Distillery Reunion Rye Whiskey
- Dark Horse Distillery Reserve Bourbon Whiskey
- Rider Vodka

Best known for / most popular: Long Shot White Whiskey

Average bottle price: $18.00 to $42.00

Distribution: KS, MO

Interesting facts:
Not provided

Good Spirits Distilling

2019 E. Spruce Circle, #A
Olathe, KS 66062
913-397-8815

Owners / Operators:
Todd Bukaty, President
Ron Bailey, Vice President

Email: tbukaty@goodspiritsdistilling.com
Website: www.goodspiritsdistilling.com
Facebook: Clear10 Vodka
Twitter: @CLEAR10Vodka

Type: Micro-distillery. Opened in 2008.

Hours of operation: Daily, 9:00am to 5:00pm

Tours: Not available

Types of spirits produced: Vodka, triple sec, flavored vodka, private label

Names of spirits:
• Czar
• CLEAR10 Vodka
• Twister Vodka
• Aeroplano Vodka
• Tailgater's Vodka
• Miss Kitty's Velvet Vodka
• Dizzythree Expresso Vodka
• Dodge City Distillery Bourbon Whiskey

Best known for: Asian Mahito

Average bottle price: $20.00

Distribution: AR, KS, MO, OK

Interesting facts: CLEAR10 Vodka is gluten free

Barrel House Distilling Co.

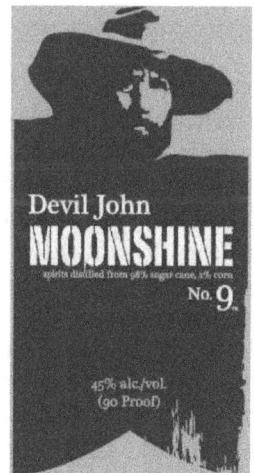

1200 Manchester Street
Lexington, KY 40504
859-259-0159

Owners / Operators:
Jeff Wiseman, Owner
Peter Wright, Owner
Frank Marino, Owner

Email: barrelhousedistillery@yahoo.com
Website: www.barrelhousedistillery.com, www.purebluevodka.com
Facebook: Barrel House Distilling Company
Twitter: @DevilJohnShine
Type: Micro-distillery. Opened in 2008.

Hours of operation: Vary

Tours: Available

Types of spirits produced: Moonshine, rum, vodka, whiskey

Names of spirits:
- Pure Blue Vodka
- Devil John Moonshine
- Kentucky Honey (rum)

Best known for: The Winchester and the KY Martini

Average bottle price: $20.00 to $25.00

Distribution: DC, IL, KY, MD, TN

Interesting facts:
Barrel House Distilling is spearheading stream and watershed cleanup in Kentucky as a service to its community.

E.H. Taylor, Jr. Old Fashioned Copper Distillery
Microstill is located at Buffalo Trace Distillery

113 Great Buffalo Trace
Frankfort, KY 40601
502-223-7641

Owners / Operators:
Buffalo Trace Distillery

Email: info@buffalotrace.com
Website: www.buffalotracedistillery.com
Facebook: Buffalo Trace Distillery
Twitter: @BuffaloTrace
YouTube: Buffalo Trace Distillery

Type: Micro-distillery. Opened in 2009.

Hours of operation:
Monday through Friday, 9:00am to 5:00pm
Saturday 10:00am to 5:00pm
Sunday April to October, 12:00pm to 5pm

Gift shop hours: Monday through Friday, 9:00am to 4:30pm
Saturday, 10:00am to 3:00pm

Tours: Four complimentary tours available. See website for details.

Types of spirits produced: Bourbon Whiskey

Names of spirits:
• E.H. Taylor, Jr. Straight Kentucky Bourbon Whiskey

Best known for: E.H. Taylor, Jr. Straight Kentucky Bourbon Whiskey

Average bottle price: Not provided

Distribution: Not provided

Interesting facts: Today, Buffalo Trace Distillery carries on Col. E. H. Taylor Jr's spirit of innovation through its E.H. Taylor Jr. Old Fashioned Copper Distillery, a microstill located on the grounds of Buffalo Trace Distillery. This microstill allows the distillery to conduct experiments on a smaller scale and has received many awards for its creations. The Experimental Collection, as the product line is called, has been responsible for such ground breaking experiments as unique mash bills, various types of wood, and barrel toasts. Currently there are more than 1500 experimental barrels of whiskey aging in the warehouses of Buffalo Trace Distillery.

Limestone Branch Distillery

1280 Veterans Memorial Highway
Lebanon, KY 40033
270-699-9004

Owners / Operators:
Steve Beam, Owner
Paul Beam, Owner

Email: steve@limestonebranch.com
Website: www.limestonebranch.com
Facebook: Limestone Branch Distillery
Twitter: @limestonebranch

Type: Micro-distillery. Opened in 2011.

Hours of operation:
Monday through Saturday, 10:00am to 5:00pm; Sunday 1:00pm to 5:00pm

Tours: Available

Types of spirits produced: Moonshine

Names of spirits:
- TJ Pottinger Sugar Shine
- TJ Pottinger Kentucky Whiskey
- Revenge

Best known for: TJ Pottinger Sugar Shine

Average bottle price: $17.50 to $30.00

Distribution: IN, KY

Interesting facts: Not provided

MB Roland Distillery

137 Barkers Mill Road
Pembroke, KY 42266
270-640-7744

Owners / Operators:
Paul Tomaszewski, Owner
Merry Beth (Roland) Tomaszewski, Owner

Email: info@mbrdistillery.com
Website: www.mbrdistillery.com
Facebook: MB Roland Distillery
Twitter: @MBRDistillery

Type: Micro-distillery. Opened in 2009.

Hours of operation: Tuesday through Saturday, 10:00am to 6:00pm

Tours: Available

Types of spirits produced:
Bourbon/whiskey, shine, flavored shines

Names of spirits:
• MBR Kentucky Bourbon Whiskey
• MBR Kentucky Black Patch Whiskey
• MBR Kentucky White Dog
• MBR Kentucky Black Dog
• MBR True Kentucky Shine
• MBR Kentucky Apple Pie
• MBR Kentucky Blueberry Shine
• MBR Kentucky Pink Lemonade
• MBR Kentucky Strawberry Shine
• MBR St. Elmo's Fire
• MBR Kentucky Mint Julep

Best known for / most popular:
Kentucky Bourbon Whiskey and Kentucky Black Dog

Average bottle price: $17.00 to $32.00

Distribution: DC, DE, GA, IL, IN, KY, MD, MI, MO, TN

Interesting facts: MB Roland Distillery was built on a former Amish dairy farm.

Old Pogue Distillery

716 W. 2nd Street
Maysville, KY 41056
317-697-5039

Owners / Operators:
Peter H. Pogue, President
Paul K. Pogue, Principal / Head Distiller
John P. Pogue, Sr., Principal / Supervisor Emeritus
John P. Pogue, Jr., Principal / Vice President of Sales and Marketing
Henry E. Pogue V, Principal / Vice President Facilities Management
Robert W. Pogue, Principal / Vice President of Corporate Compliance
John A. Pogue, Partner / Distiller

Email: info@oldpogue.com
Website: www.oldpogue.com
Facebook: Old Pogue Bourbon
Twitter: @OldPogueBourbon

Type: Micro-distillery. Opened in 2011.

Hours of operation: Monday through Friday, 10:00am to 4:30pm

Tours: Available by appointment

Types of spirits produced: Bourbon whiskey, rye whiskey

Names of spirits:
* Old Pogue "Master's Select" Kentucky Straight Bourbon
* Limestone Landing Single Malt Rye Un-aged Whiskey
* Old Maysville Club Rye Whiskey
* Five Fathers Pure Rye Whisky

Best known for/ most popular: Old Pogue

Average bottle price: $40.00 to $45.00

Distribution: U.S., Canada

Interesting facts: The original H.E. Pogue Distillery operated from 1876-1951 with 3 generations of Pogues serving as owners and distillers. The 5th, 6th, and now 7th generation of Pogues, original descendants of H.E. Pogue, have located their micro-distillery on the same property as the original distillery. The new distillery was started as a way to carry on the family tradition using all the original recipes from their forefathers.

121

Silver Trail Distillery

5402 Aurora Highway
Hardin, KY 42048
270-354-6209

Owners / Operators:
Spencer Balentine, Owner

Email: silvertraildistillery@gmail.com
Website: www.lblmoonshine.com
Facebook: Silver Trail Distillery

Type: Micro-distillery. Opened in 2011.

Hours of operation: Not provided

Tours: Not provided

Types of spirits produced: Moonshine

Names of spirits:
• LBL Most Wanted Moonshine

Best known for / most popular:
LBL Most Wanted Moonshine

Average bottle price: Not provided

Distribution: KY

Interesting facts: Not provided

Whiskey Thief Distilling Company

283 Crab Orchard Road
Graefenburg, KY 40601
970-447-8007

Owners / Operators:
Ross Caldwell, Co-owner / Distiller
Heather Caldwell, Co-owner

Email: ross@whiskeythief.us

Type: Micro-distillery. Opening in 2013.

Hours of operation: Daily, 9:00am to 5:00pm

Tours: Available by appointment

Types of spirits produced:
White dog, flavored white dog

Names of spirits:
• Foggy Dog Whiskey
• White Dog Whiskey

Best known for / most popular: Not provided

Average bottle price: $19.00 to $29.00

Distribution: KY, OH

Interesting facts:
• The "Still House" is built in the style of a Kentucky Tobacco barn.
• Bourbon recipe is used for all White Dog spirits.
• Plan to release an uncut, unfiltered aged in six or seven years.

Willett Distillery

1869 Loretto Road
Bardstown, KY 40004
502-348-0899

Owners / Operators:
Mr. Even Kulsveen, Executive Director

Email: visitorcenter@willettdistillery.com
Website: www.willettdistillery.com
Facebook: Willett Distillery
Twitter: @WillettWhiskey

Type: Micro-distillery. Opened in 1936.

Hours of operation: Gift shop
Monday through Friday, 9:00am to 4:30pm
Saturday, 10:00am to 3:30pm
Sunday, 12:00pm to 3:30 (April - December)

Tours: Available
Monday through Friday, 10:00am, 11:30am, 1:30pm, 3:00pm
Saturday, 10:00am, 11:30am, 1:00pm, 2:00pm
Sunday, 12:30pm, 2:00pm
(Sunday tours available April - December)

Types of spirits produced: Bourbon, rye whiskey

Names of spirits:
• Willett Pot Still Reserve Bourbon
• Willett Family Estate Bottled Bourbon
• Willett Family Estate Bottled Rye
• Rowan's Creek
• Noah's Mill
• Johnny Drum Private Stock

Best known for / most popular:
Willett Pot Still Reserve Bourbon

Average bottle price: $15.00 to $300.00

Distribution: AZ, CA, CO, CT, DE, DC, FL, GA, HI, IL, IN, KY, LA MD, MA, MN, MI*, MO, MT*, NV, NJ. NY, NC*, OR, PA, SC, TN, TX, VA*, WA, WI, WY*

(The asterisk denotes a state where they do not have a distributor, but still deliver product via special orders).

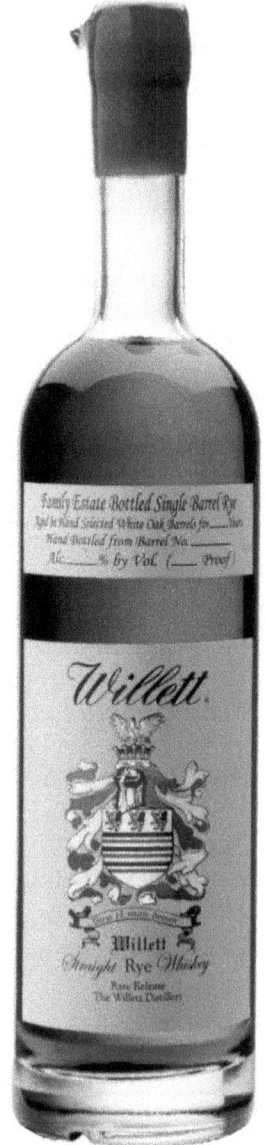

Atelier Vie

1001 S. Broad Street
New Orleans, LA 70125
504-813-4700

Owners / Operators:
Jedd Haas, President
Brennan Steele, Ambassador
Skylar Rosenbloom, Chief Bean Hunter
Jascha Jacobson, Distiller

Email: jedd@ateliervie.com
Website: www.ateliervie.com
Facebook: Atelier Vie, LLC
Twitter: @AtelierVie, @TolulouseRed, @Buck25Vodka
YouTube: Atelier Vie

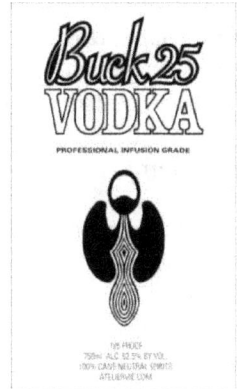

Type: Micro-distillery. Opened in 2012.

Hours of operation:
Monthly "Bottle Sales Hours" are announced on their website. Customer purchases are limited to 1 case every 30 days; no sales to licensed LA retailers.

Tours: Not available

Types of spirits produced: Vodka, abinsthe

Names of spirits:
- Buck 25 Vodka
- Toulouse Red Absinthe Rouge

Best known for / most popular: Toulouse Red Absinthe

Average bottle price: $30.00 to $60.00

Distribution: DC, New Orleans metro area, North Shore, and Baton Rouge

Interesting facts:
- Buck 25, a 125 proof "Professional Infusion Grade" Vodka, is a secret ingredient for chefs and bartenders.
- Toulouse Red is distilled with attention to both the classic methods of absinthe distillation and the innovations from more recent American absinthe trailblazing. Toulouse Red is bottled at the traditional 136 proof (68% ABV) and is produced from all natural ingredients. The classic method for serving absinthe, a dilution with ice water at ratios in the range of 3:1 to 5:1, produces a final drinking strength of about 23 to 34 proof (11.5% to 17% ABV) – about the strength of a strong wine. Toulouse Red is distilled in New Orleans from 100% natural ingredients.

Celebration Distillation

2815 Frenchmen Street
New Orleans, LA 70122
504-945-9400

Owners / Operators:
James Michalopoulos, Founder / Owner
Parker Schonekas, Operations Manager
Erick Leowko, Sales Manager
Jason Coleman, Marketing Manager

Email: info@oldneworleansrum.com
Website: www.oldneworleansrum.com
Facebook: Old New Orleans Rum
Myspace: Old New Orleans Rum
Twitter: @NewOrleansRum

Type: Micro-distillery. Opened in 1995.

Hours of operation:
Monday through Friday, 9:00am to 5:00pm
Saturday, 1:30pm to 5:00pm

Tours: Available

Types of spirits produced: Rum

Names of spirits:
- Old New Orleans Crystal Rum
- Old New Orleans Amber Rum
- Old New Orleans Cajun Spice Rum
- Old New Orleans 10 Year Rum
- Gingeroo – an Old New Orleans Rum Bottled Cocktail

Best known for: Cajun Spice Rum

Average bottle price: $17.00 to $21.00

Distribution: CA, FL, IL, LA, MI, MO, MS, NE, NC, NY, VA, WI

Interesting facts:
- Celebration Distillation is the oldest continuously licensed and operating rum distillery in the continental United States.
- Cajun Spice Rum has been the highest rated flavored rum four years in a row from 2007 to 2010 by the Beverage Testing Institute.
- In 2012 Celebration Distillation partnered with a local sugar cane mill to install a pump and pipeline to extract B-cut molasses from the milling process. Using the B-cut molasses has produced a more flavorful and fully integrated rum.

Donner-Peltier Distillers

1635 St. Patrick Highway
Thibodaux, LA 70301
985-446-0002

Owners / Operators:
Tom Donner, Co-owner
Elizabeth Donner, Co-owner
Henry M. Peltier, Co-owner
Jennifer N. Peltier, Co-owner
Connie Couchot, Distillery Manager

Email: conniecouchot@hotmail.com
Website: www.dp-distillers.com
Facebook: Donner-Peltier Distillers

Type: Micro-distillery. Opened in 2012.

Hours of operation:
Monday through Saturday, 12:00pm to 6:30pm

Tours: Available

Types of spirits produced: Vodka, rum

Names of spirits:
- Orysa Vodka
- Rougaroux Sugarshine
- Rougaroux Full Moon Dark Rum

Best known for / most popular: Not provided

Average bottle price: Not provided

Distribution: LA

Interesting facts: Not provided

Louisiana Spirits LLC

20909 South I-10 Frontage Road
Lacassine, LA 70650

Owners / Operators:
Tim Litel, Co-founder
Skip Cortese, Co-founder
Trey Litel, Co-founder

Email: info@laspirits.net
Website: www.laspirits.net, www.bayourum.com
Facebook: Louisiana Spirits, Bayou Rum
Twitter: @BayouRum

Type: Cicro-distillery. Opened in June 2013.

Hours of operation: Call for reservations

Tours: Available Tuesday through Sunday

Types of spirits produced: Rum

Names of spirits:
- Silver Bayou Rum
- Spiced Bayou Rum

Best known for / most popular: Bayou Rum

Average bottle price: TBA

Distribution: Republic National Distributing Co.

Interesting facts: Bayou Rum is handmade using 100% natural Louisiana cane sugar and molasses in a traditional pot still.

Rank Wildcat Spirits LLC

619 Bonin Road
Lafayette, LA 70508
337-257-3385

Owners / Operators:
David C. Meaux, Founder / Owner / Distiller
Cole G. LeBlanc, Founder / Owner / Distiller

Email: davidcmeaux@rankwildcat.com
            colegleblanc@rankwildcat.com
Website: www.rankwildcat.com
Facebook: Rank Wildcat Spirits, LLC
YouTube: Rank Wildcat Spirits, LLC

Type: Micro-distillery. Opened in 2011.

Hours of operation: Not open to the public

Tours: Not available

Types of spirits produced: Rum

Names of spirits:
* Sweet Crude Rum

Best known for / most popular: Sweet Crude Rum

Average bottle price: $21.00 to $24.00

Distribution: LA

Interesting facts:
Rank Wildcat Spirits, LLC is Acadiana's first micro-distillery and second licensed rum distillery to open in Louisiana. Additionally, Rank Wildcat Spirits is solely owned and operated by two Acadiana locals. They built everything from the ground up including their one-of-a-kind stainless steel and copper still they named Lulu.

Having no high-dollar investors, government aid or industrial professionals to grease the wheels, Rank Wildcat is truly a "grass roots" Acadiana project.

129

Maine Distilleries LLC

437 US Route 1
Freeport, ME 04032
207-865-4828

Owners / Operators:
Chris Dowe, Owner / CEO
Lee Thibodeau, Owner
Don Thibodeau, Owner
Bob Harkins, Owner

Email: info@coldrivervodka.com
Website: www.mainedistilleries.com
Facebook: Maine Distilleries
Twitter: @MaineSpirits

Type: Micro-distillery. Opened in 2005.

Hours of operation: Daily, 6:00am to 11:00pm

Tours: Available

Types of spirits produced: Vodka, gin

Names of spirits:
- Cold River Classic Vodka
- Cold River Blueberry Vodka
- Cold River Gin

Best known for / most popular: Cold River Classic Vodka

Average bottle price: $27.99 to $38.99

Distribution: ME, MA, RI, CT, NJ, DE, MD, DC, IN, CO, TN, GA, PA, NC, ID, MT, OR, WY, Great Britain, Ireland and the western provinces of Canada.

Interesting facts:
- Spirits are gluten free
- Spirits are certified Kosher

New England Distilling

26 Evergreen Drive, Unit B
Portland, ME 04103
207-878-9759

Owners / Operators:
Ned Wight, Owner / Distiller

Email: info@newenglanddistilling.com
Website: www.newenglanddistilling.com
Facebook: New England Distilling
Twitter: @NEDistilling

Type: Micro-distillery. Opened in 2012.

Hours of operation: Monday through Friday, 12:00pm to 5:00pm

Tours: Available Monday through Friday, 12:00pm to 5:00pm

Types of spirits produced: Gin, whiskey, rum

Names of spirits:
- Ingenium Gin
- Eight Bells Rum
- Whiskey (not yet named)

Best known for: Ingenium Gin

Average bottle price: Not provided

Distribution: ME, NY

Interesting facts:
Handcrafted on 150 years and six generations of family tradition

Northern Maine Distilling Company

66 Industrial Drive, Ste. J
Houlton, ME 04730
518-505-7243

Owners / Operators:
Scott Galbiati, Co-owner
Jessica Jewell, Co-owner

Email: scott@twenty2vodka.com
Website: www.twenty2vodka.com
Facebook: Twenty2
Twitter: @Twenty2Vodka
Pinterest: Scott @ Twenty2 Vodka
Tumblr: Twenty2vodka
Flickr: Twenty2Vodka

Type: Micro-distillery. Opened in 2010.

Hours of operation: Not provided

Tours: Not provided

Types of spirits produced: Vodka

Names of spirits:
• Twenty 2 True Micro Distilled Vodka

Best known for / most popular: Twenty 2 Vodka

Average bottle price: $26.99

Distribution: DC, ME, MD, NJ

Interesting facts: Not provided

Spirits of Maine Distillery

175 Chicken Mill Road
Gouldsboro, ME 04607
207-546-2408

Owners / Operators:
Robert and Kathe Bartlett, Owners

Email: info@bartlettwinery.com
Website: www.bartlettwinery.com
Facebook: Bartlett Maine Estate Winery

Type: Winery / Micro-distillery. Opened in 2007.

Hours of operation:
Open June to mid-October - Monday through Saturday, 10:00am to 5:00pm
Closed Sundays and holidays
Open by appointment after season

Tours: Not available

Types of spirits produced: Brandy, eau de vie, rum, geist

Names of spirits:
- Fine Apple Brandy
- Pear Eau de Vie
- Peach Eau de Vie
- Honey Eau de Vie
- Raspberry Geist
- Light Rum and Dark Rum

Best known for: Pear Eau de Vie

Average bottle price: $30.00 to $40.00

Distribution: ME

Interesting facts:
- Bartlett Maine Estate Winery became Maine's first licensed winery in 1982.
- Spirits of Maine Distillery became Maine's second distillery in 2007.

Sweetgrass Farm Winery & Distillery

347 Carroll Road
Union, ME 04862
207-785-3024

Owners / Operators:
Keith and Constance Bodine, Owners

Email: info@sweetgrasswinery.com
Website: www.sweetgrasswinery.com
          www.backrivergin.com
Facebook: Back River Gin
Twitter: @BackRiverGin

Type: Winery / Micro-distillery. Opened in 2005.

Hours of operation:
Daily, 11:00am to 5:00pm Mother's Day to December 31

Tours: Available

Types of spirits produced:
Gin, rum, apple brandy, whiskey, liqueurs, wines, vanilla extract, bitters

Names of spirits:
* Back River Gin
* Three Crow Rum
* Maple Smash Liqueur

Best known for: Back River Gin

Average bottle price: $21.49 to $34.49

Distribution: ME

Interesting facts: Not provided

134

Tree Spirits

152 Fairfield Street
Oakland, ME 04963
207-861-2723

Owners / Operators:
Bruce Olson, Co-owner
Karen Heck, Co-owner

Email: info@treespiritsofmaine.com
Website: www.treespiritsofmaine.com
Facebook: Tree Spirits

Type: Micro-distillery. Opened in 2009.

Hours of operation:
Friday, 3:30 to 5:30; Saturday, 12:00pm to 5:00pm

Tours: Available

Types of spirits produced: Applejack, liqueur

Names of spirits:
• Tree Spirits Applejack
• Tree Spirits Knotted Maple

Best known for / most popular: Not provided

Average bottle price: Not provided

Distribution: ME

Interesting facts: Not provided

hand crafted wine and distilled spirits

135

Blackwater Distilling Inc.

184 Log Canoe Circle
Stevensville, MD 21666
443-249-3123

Owners / Operators:
Christopher Cook, CEO
Jon Cook, COO
Mark Troxler, VP of Business Development
Jon Blair, Production Manager

Email: info@blackwaterdistilling.com
Website: www.blackwaterdistilling.com, www.sloopbetty.com
Facebook: Sloop Betty, Blackwater Distilling
Twitter: @sloopbetty
YouTube: Sloop Betty TV
LinkedIn: Sloop Betty Vodka

Type: Micro-distillery. Opened in 2010.

Hours of operation: Not provided

Tours: Not available

Types of spirits produced: Vodka

Names of spirits:
• Sloop Betty

Best known for: Sloop Betty

Average bottle price: $29.99

Distribution: DC, DE, MD

Interesting facts:
Blackwater Distilling is the first licensed distillery in MD in nearly 40 years.

Fiore Winery & Distillery

3026 Whiteford Road
Pylesville, MD 21132
410-879-4007, 410-452-0132

Owners / Operators:
Mike Fiore, Owner
Rose Fiore, Owner
Eric Fiore, Owner

Email: mike.fiore@fiorewinery.com
Website: www.fiorewinery.com
Facebook: Fiore Winery
Twitter: @FioreWinery

Type: Winery / Micro-distillery. Opened in 2009.

Hours of operation:
Monday through Saturday, 10:00am to 5:00pm; Sunday, 12:00pm to 5:00pm

Tours: Available

Types of spirits produced: Brandy, grappa, limoncello

Names of spirits:
• Fiore Grappa
• Fiore Limoncello

Best known for: Wine and grappa

Average bottle price: $15.00 to $25.00

Distribution: MD

Interesting facts: Not provided

137

Berkshire Mountain Distillers Inc.

Great Barrington, MA 01230
413-229-0219

Owners / Operators:
Chris Weld, Owner

Email: cweld@berkshiremountaindistillers.com
Website: www.berkshiremountaindistillers.com
Facebook: Berkshire Mountain Distillers
Twitter: @BerkshireMtDist

Type: Micro-distillery. Opened in 2007.

Hours of operation: Not open to the public

Tours: Not available.

Types of spirits produced: Vodka, gin, bourbon, corn whiskey, rum, bitters

Names of spirits:
- Greylock Gin
- Ethereal Gin
- Barrel Aged Ethereal Gin
- Ragged Mountain Rum
- Ice Glen Vodka
- Berkshire Bourbon
- New England Corn Whiskey
- Cocktail Kingdom Bitters

Best known for: Greylock Gin

Average bottle price: $25.99 to $45.99

Distribution: Available in more than 20 states

Interesting facts:
Berkshire Mountain Distillers is the Berkshire's first legal distillery since prohibition and located in a renovated 1950 hay barn that sits in the midst of an apple orchard.

138

Bully Boy Distillers

35 Cedric Street
Boston, MA 02119
617-442-6000

Owners / Operators:
Will Willis, Co-owner
Dave Willis, Co-owner

Email: info@bullyboydistillers.com
Website: www.bullyboydistillers.com
Facebook: Bully Boy Distillers
Twitter: @bullyboybooze
Blog: bullyboydistillers.blogspot.com

Type: Micro-distillery. Opened in 2010.

Hours of operation: Open for tours

Tours: Available by appointment

Types of spirits produced: Vodka, whiskey, rum

Names of spirits:
- Bully Boy Vodka
- Bully Boy Boston Rum
- Bully Boy Bully Boy White Rum
- Bully Boy White Whiskey
- Bully Boy American Straight Whiskey

Best known for / most popular: Bully Boy Boston Rum

Average bottle price: Not provided

Distribution: MA, NH, RI

Interesting facts:
The distillery is named after Bully
Boy, a favorite farm workhorse.

GrandTen Distilling

383 Dorchester Avenue
Boston, MA 02127
617-269-0497

Owners / Operators:
Spencer McMinn, Co-founder
Matthew Nuernberger, Co-founder

Email: info@grandten.com
Website: www.grandten.com
Facebook: GrandTen Distilling
Twitter: @GrandTen

Type: Micro-distillery. Opened in 2012.

Hours of operation: Not provided

Tours: Saturday, 12:00pm to 4:00pm or by appointment

Types of spirits produced: Rum, vodka, gin, liqueur

Names of spirits:
- Wire Works American Gin
- Wire Works Special Reserve Gin
- Fire Puncher Vodka
- Angelica - Botanical Liqueur
- Amandine - Barrel Aged Almond Liqueur
- Craneberry - Massachusetts Cranberry Liqueur

Best known for / most popular: Not provided

Average bottle price: $25.00 to $35.00

Distribution: MA, WA

Interesting facts: Not provided

140

Nashoba Valley Spirits Ltd.

100 Wattaquadoc Hill Road
Bolton, MA 01740
978-779-5521

Email: email@nashobawinery.com
Website: www.nashobawinery.com
Facebook: Nashoba Valley Winery
Twitter: @NashobaWinery

Type: Winery / Farmers-Distiller. Opened in 2003.

Hours of operation: Monday through Friday, 10:00 to 5:00pm

Tours: Available on weekends

Types of spirits produced: Vodka, brandies, eau de vie, cordials

Names of spirits:
- Foggy Bog Brandy
- Nashoba Vodka
- Cherry Eau de vie
- Vidal Grappa
- Raspberry Eau de vie
- Elephant Heart Plum-infused Brandy
- Silk Peach Brandy
- Apple Brandy
- Elderberry Brandy
- Baerenfang Fruit and Honey Blended Brandy
- Northern Comfort Brandy
- Johnny Hop Appl and Hop flower-infused Brandy
- Nashoba Single-malt Whiskey

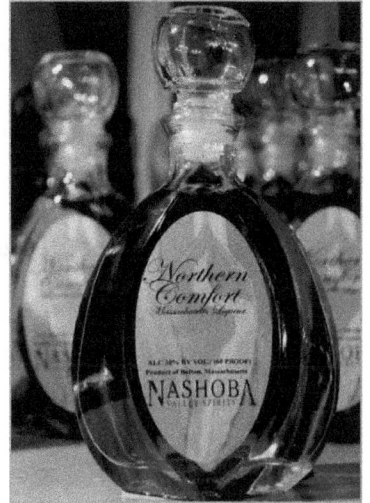

Best known for / most popular: Foggy Bog Brandy

Average bottle price: $21.00 to $26.00

Distribution: Not provided

Interesting facts: Not provided

Privateer Rum

28 Mitchell Road
Ipswich, MA 01938
978-356-0477

Owners / Operators:
Andrew Cabot, Owner

Email: info@privateerrum.com
Website: www.privateerrum.com
Facebook: Privateer Rum
Twitter: @PrivateerRum

Type: Micro-distillery. Opened in 2011.

Hours of operation: Not provided

Tours: Not provided

Types of spirits produced: Rum

Names of spirits:
- Privateer Silver Reserve Rum
- Privateer True American Rum

Best known for / most popular: Not provided

Average bottle price: Not provided

Distribution: MA

Interesting facts: Not provided

Ryan & Wood Inc.

15 Great Republic Drive
Gloucester, MA 01930
978-281-2282

Owners / Operators:
Bob Ryan and Dave Wood, Owners
Kathy Ryan and Maryann Wood, Owners

Email: Bob Ryan: bob@ryanandwood.com
             Kathy Ryan: kathy@ryanandwood.com
Website: www.ryanandwood.com
Facebook: Ryan & Wood Inc., Distilleries
Twitter: @ryanandwood

Type: Micro-distillery. Opened in 2006.

Hours of operation: Daily, 8:00am to 5:00pm

Tours: Available

Types of spirits produced: Gin, rum, vodka, whiskey

Names of spirits:
- Beauport Vodka
- Folly Cove Rum
- Knockabout Gin
- Ryan & Wood Straight Rye Whiskey
- Ryan & Wood Straight Wheat Whiskey

Best known for: Knockabout Gin

Average bottle price: $28.00

Distribution: MA

Interesting facts: Not provided

143

Triple Eight Distillery

5 Bartlett Farm Road
Nantucket, MA 02554
508-325-5929

Owners / Operators:
Jay Harman, Owner
Dean Long, Owner
Randy Hudson, Owner

Email: jay@ciscobrewers.com
Website: www.ciscobrewers.com/distillery
Facebook: Cisco Brewers Nantucket
Twitter: @ciscobrewers

Type: Micro-distillery. Opened in 2000.

Hours of operation: Daily, 10:00am to 7:00pm

Tours: Available by appointment

Types of spirits produced:
Gin, rum, notch single malt whisky, vodka

Names of spirits:
• Triple Eight Vodka
• Hurricane Rum
• Gale Force Gin
• Notch Single Malt Whisky

Best known for: Triple Eight Vodka

Average bottle price: Not provided

Distribution: CO, MA

Interesting facts:
One of the first micro-distilleries in Massachusetts

Turkey Shore Distilleries

23 Hayward Street, #8
Ipswich, MA 01938
978-356-0048

Owners / Operators:
Mat Perry, Co-founder
Evan Parker, Co-founder

Email: info@turkeyshoredistilleries.com
Website: www.turkeyshoredistilleries.com
Facebook: Turkey Shore Distilleries
Twitter: @OldIpswichRum

Type: Craft-distillery. Opened in 2010.

Hours of operation: Monday through Friday, 9:00am to 5:00pm

Tours: Available

Types of spirits produced: Rum

Names of spirits:
- Old Ipswich "White Cap" Rum
- Old Ipswich "Tavern Style" Rum
- Old Ipswich "Greenhead" Spiced Rum
- Old Ipswich "Golden Marsh" Spiced Rum

Best known for / most popular: Not provided

Average bottle price: Not provided

Distribution: MA

Interesting facts: Not provided

Artesian Distillers

955 Ken O Sha Industrial Park Drive SE
Grand Rapids, MI 49508
616-252-1700

Owners / Operators:
Amir Haririan, CEO
Leslie Haririan, Co-founder

Email: amir@artesiandistillers.com
Website: www.artesiandistillers.com
Facebook: Artesian Distillers
Twitter: @Adistillers

Type: Micro-distillery. Opened in 2009.

Hours of operation: Daily, 10:00am to 3:00pm

Tours: Available

Types of spirits produced: Rum, vodka, gin, bourbon whiskey

Names of spirits:
- 1492 Cristobal Rum
- Shipwreck Spiced Pirate Rhum
- RMD Vodka
- RMD Gin
- RMD Rum
- Glen Scotch Whisky
- Prohibition Edition Bourbon

Best known for / most popular: Not provided

Average bottle price: Not provided

Distribution: MI

Interesting facts: Not provided

Big Cedar Distilling Inc.

29130 Maystead Road
Sturgis, MI 49061
269-998-3610

Owners / Operators:
Dong Stanke, Co-owner
Tina Stanke, Co-owner

Email: doug@incentivevodka.com
Website: www.incentivevodka.com
Facebook: Incentive Vodka
Twitter: @BigCedarDistill

Type: Micro-distillery. Opened in 2009.

Hours of operation: Not provided

Tours: Not provided

Types of spirits produced: Vodka

Names of spirits:
• Incentive Vodka

Best known for / most popular: Incentive Vodka

Average bottle price: Not provided

Distribution: MI

Interesting facts: Incentive Vodka is gluten free

Chateau Chantal

15900 Rue de Vin
Traverse City, MI 49686
231-223-4110

Owners / Operators:
Robert Begin, Founder
James Krupka, CEO
Mark Johnson, Winemaker
Brian Hosmer, Winemaker

Email: wine@chateauchantal.com
      mjohnson@chateauchantal.com
Website: www.chateauchantal.com
Facebook: Chateau Chantal Winery
Twitter: @chateauchantal
Blog: chateauchantal.wordpress.com

Type: Winery / Micro-distillery. Opened in 2001.

Hours of operation:
June through August: Monday through Saturday, 11:00am to 9:00pm
September through October: Monday through Saturday, 11:00am to 7:00pm
November through mid-June: Monday through Saturday, 11:00am to 5:00pm
Sundays year round: 11:00am to 5:00pm
Closed: Thanksgiving, Christmas, New Year's, Easter

Tours: Tours available June through August

Types of spirits produced: Brandy, eau de vie

Names of spirits:
- Chateau Chantal Cherry Eau de Vie
- Chateau Chantal Pear Eau de Vie
- Chateau Chantal Plum Eau de Vie
- Chateau Chantal Brandy – "Cinq à Sept"
- Chateau Chantal Cerise
- Chateau Chantal Cerise Noir
- Chateau Chantal Entice

Best known for: Chateau Chantal Cerise

Average bottle price: $24.99 to $34.00

Distribution: IL, MI

Interesting facts: Not provided

Corey Lake Orchards

12147 Corey Lake Road
Three Rivers, MI 49093
269-244-5690

Owners / Operators:
Dayton Hubbard, Owner

Email: oreylakeorchards@gmail.com
Website: www.coreylakeorchards.com
Facebook: Corey Lake Orchards

Type: Micro-distillery. Opened in 1999.

Hours of operation: Open May through October, 8:00am to 6:00pm

Tours: Available Saturday afternoons and by appointment

Types of spirits produced: Brandy

Names of spirits:
- Hubbard's Apple Brandy
- Hubbard's Cherry Brandy
- Hubbard's Grape Brandy
- Hubbard's Peach Brandy
- Hubbard's Pear Brandy

Best known for: Hubbard's Apple Brandy

Average bottle price: $10.00 to $30.00

Distribution: Corey Lake Orchards

Interesting facts: All Hubbard's brandies are made from fruit grown on its farm.

Entente Spirits LLC

10983 Hills Road
Baroda, MI 49101
269-422-1617

Owners / Operators:
Moersch Family, Owners

Email: info@roundbarndistillery.com
Website: www.roundbarndistillery.com
Facebook: The Round Barn Winery
Twitter: @RoundBarnWinery
YouTube: Round Barn Winery

Type: Winery / Micro-distillery. Opened in 1999.

Hours of operation: Open year-round

Tours: Not available

Types of spirits produced: Bourbon, rum, vodka, brandy

Names of spirits:
• DiVine Bourbon
• DiVine Rum
• DiVine Vodka
• Other products are labeled under Round Barn

Best known for: DiVine Vodka

Average bottle price: $15.00 to 35.00

Distribution: IL, IN, MI

Interesting facts:
• Entente Sprits tasting rooms are located in turn of the century barns, including an Amish-built round barn.
• DiVine Vodka is made from grapes.

150

Grand Traverse Distillery

781 Industrial Circle, Ste. 5
Traverse City, MI 49696
231-947-8635

Owners / Operators:
Kent Rabish, Owner / Distiller
George Wertman, General Manager / Distiller

Email: kent@grandtraversedistillery.com
Website: www.grandtraversedistillery.com
Facebook: Grand Traverse Distillery

Type: Micro-distillery. Opened in 2007.

Hours of operation:
Thursday and Friday, 12:00pm to 5:00pm; Saturday, 11:00am to 4:00pm
Retail sales Monday through Friday, 11:00am to 5:00pm

Tours: Available

Types of spirits produced: Vodka, whiskey

Names of spirits:
- True North Vodka
- True North Cherry Flavored Vodka
- True North Chocolate Flavored Vodka
- Wheat Vodka
- Ole George Whiskey
- Bourbon Whiskey

Best known for: True North Vodka

Average bottle price: Not provided

Distribution: Not provided

Interesting facts:
Grand Traverse Distillery is northern Michigan's oldest micro-distillery.

Journeyman Distillery

109 Generations Drive
Three Oaks, MI 49128
269-820-2050

Owners / Operators:
Bill Welter, Founder
Nick Gurniewicz, Partner

Email: info@journeymandistillery.com
Website: www.journeymandistillery.com
Facebook: Journeyman Distillery
Twitter: @JourneymanDist
YouTube: JourneymanDistillery's Channel

Type: Micro-distillery. Opened in 2011.

Hours of operation: Vary by season

Tours: Available, register on website

Types of spirits produced:
White whiskey, wheat whiskey, rye whiskey,
vodka, gin, bourbon

Names of spirits:
- W.R. Whiskey (White Whiskey)
- Ravenswood Rye (Rye Whiskey)
- Buggy Whip Wheat (Wheat Whiskey)
- Red Arrow Vodka
- Road's End Rum
- Bilberry Black Heart's Gin
- Featherbone Bourbon
- Three Oaks Single Malt
- Michigan Spirit Whiskey

Best known for: W.R. Whiskey

Average bottle price: $19.99 to $49.99

Distribution: Only available at the distillery

Interesting facts: Certified organic by Midwest Organic Services Association.

New Holland Artisan Spirits

66 East 8th Street
Holland, MI 49423
616-355-6422

Owners / Operators:
Not provided

Email: info@newhollandbrew.com
Website: www.newhollandbrew.com
Facebook: New Holland Artisan Spirits
Twitter: @NHAS_Spirits

Type: Micro-distillery. Opened in 2005.

Hours of operation: Not provided

Tours: Available

Types of spirits produced: Bourbon, gin, whiskey, brandy

Names of spirits:
- Knickerbocker Gin
- Beer Barrel Bourbon
- Walleye Rye Whiskey
- Malthouse Whiskey
- Hatter Royale Hopquila
- Dutchess Vodka
- Dutchess Citrus Vodka
- Double Down Barley Whiskey
- Bill's Michigan Wheat Whiskey
- Zeppelin Bend Straight Whiskey
- Freshwater Superior Single Barrel Rum
- Freshwater Michigan Amber Rum
- Freshwater Huron White Rum

Best known for / most popular: Dutchess Vodka

Average bottle price: Not provided

Distribution: Not provided

Interesting facts: Not provided

Northern Latitudes Distillery

112 E. Philip Street, Ste. B
Lake Leelanau, MI 49653
231-256-2700

Owners / Operators:
Mark Moseler, Co-owner
Mandy Moseler, Co-owner

Email: info@nldistillery.com
Website: www.nldistillery.com
Facebook: Northern Latitudes Distillery
Twitter: @NLatitudes

Type: Micro-distillery. Opened in 2012.

Hours of operation:
Monday through Thursday, 11:00am to 6:00pm
Friday and Saturday, 11:00am to 8:00pm
Sunday, 12:00pm to 5:00pm

Tours: Available by appointment

Types of spirits produced: Gin, vodka, liqueur

Names of spirits:
- Jack Pine Gin
- Ice Dunes Vodka
- Deer Camp Vodka
- Limoncello di Leelanau Lemon Liqueur

Best known for / most popular: Jack Pine Gin

Average bottle price: Not provided

Distribution: Not provided

Interesting facts: First full service distillery in Leelanau County MI.

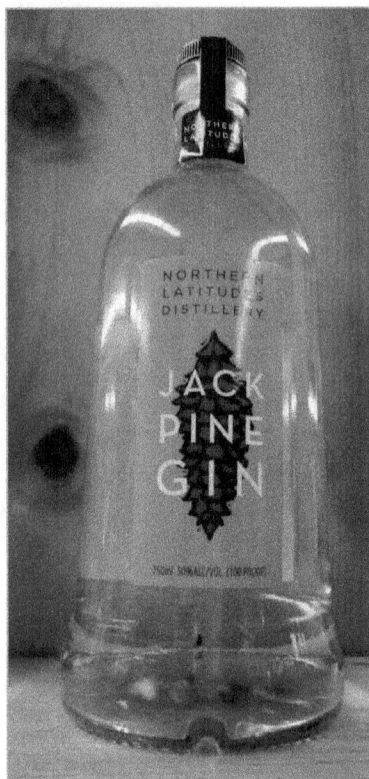

Northern United Brewing Company & Distilling

13512 Peninsula Drive
Traverse City, MI 49686
231-223-8700

Owners / Operators:
Mike Hall, Head Distiller
Michael Wooster, Manager
Josh Lentz, Supervisor
Kaleb Longworth, Assistant Distiller
Sam Maxbauer, Assistant Distiller
Charles Psenka, Sr., Chief Liaison

Email: jpbrewery.traverse@nubco.net
Website: www.civilizedspirits.com
Facebook: Civilized Spirits
Twitter: @DrinkCivilized

Type: Micro-distillery. Opened in 2010.

Hours of operation: As demand dictates

Tours: Available by appointment

Types of spirits produced:
Vodka, rum, gin, cherry spirit, agave, whiskies, apple spirit

Names of spirits:
- Civilized Vodka
- Civilized Sakura
- Civilized Whiskey
- Civilized White Dog
- Civilized Single Malt Whiskey
- Civilized Rum
- Civilized Gin

Best known for / most popular: Civilized Vodka

Average bottle price: $30.00 to $40.00

Distribution: MI

Interesting facts: Not provided

155

St. Julian Winery

716 S. Kalamazoo Street
Paw Paw, MI 49079
800-732-6002

Owners / Operators:
David Braganini, President
Larry Gilbert, Resident Distiller

Email: wines@stjulian.com
Website: www.stjulian.com
Facebook: St. Julian Winery
Twitter: @stjulianwinery
Pinterest: St. Julian Winery

Type: Winery / Micro-distillery. Opened in 2000.

Hours of operation:
Monday through Saturday, 9:00 am to 6:00pm
Sunday, noon to 5:00pm

Tours: Available

Types of spirits produced: Brandy, vodka

Names of spirits:
- A & G Brandy
- Grey Heron Vodka

Best known for / most popular: Grey Heron Vodka

Average bottle price: $34.99

Distribution: Michigan tasting locations in Paw Paw, Union Pier, Frankenmuth, and Dundee.

Interesting facts: Family owned and operated, St. Julian produces all of its wines and spirits from 100% Michigan grown fruit. A & G Brandy is aged in Michigan oak.

Two James Spirits

2445 Michigan Avenue
Detroit, MI 48216

Owners / Operators:
David Landrum, President
Peter Bailey, Vice President

Email: David Landrum, david@twojames.com
          Peter Bailey, peter@twojames.com
Website: www.twojames.com
Facebook: Two James Spirits
Twitter: @TwoJamesSpirits

Type: Micro-distillery. Opened in March 2012.

Hours of operation:
Tuesday through Thursday, 2:00pm to 8:00pm
Friday and Saturday, 2:00pm to 10:00pm; Sunday, 12:00pm to 4:00pm

Tours: Available by appointment

Types of spirits produced: Vodka, gin, bourbon, whiskey

Names of spirits:
- Two James Gin
- Two James Vodka
- Two James Bourbon
- Two James Rye Whiskey
- Two James "Reserve" Single Malt Whiskey

Average bottle price: $30.00 to $50.00

Distribution: Detroit, MI metro area.

Interesting facts: Two James is located in Corktown, Detroit's oldest neighborhood, and is the first licensed distillery in Detroit since Prohibition.

Ugly Dog Distillery LLC

14496 North Territorial Road
Chelsea, MI 48118
734-444-0433

Owners / Operators:
Jon Dyer, Owner

Email: jon@uglydogdistillery.com
Website: www.uglydogvodka.com
Facebook: Ugly Dog Distillery
Twitter: @UglyDogBooze, @UglyDogVodka

Type: Micro-distillery. Opened in 2010.

Hours of operation: Monday through Saturday, 10:00am to 6:00pm

Tours: Available by appointment

Types of spirits produced: Vodka, rum, gin

Names of spirits:
- Ugly Dog Gin
- Ugly Dog Rum
- Ugly Dog Vodka
- Ugly Dog Bacon Vodka
- Ugly Dog Raspberry Vodka
- Ugly Dog Whipped Cream Vodka

Best known for / most popular: Ugly Dog Vodka

Average bottle price: $16.98 to $19.97

Distribution: MI

Interesting facts:
- The Vodka is distilled from 100% Michigan grown wheat.
- The Rum is made from Florida grown sugar cane.

Uncle Don's Apple Pie Craft Distillery

805 N. Mitchell Street
Cadillac, MI 49601
231-779-6939

Owners / Operators:
Don "Uncle Don" Gondzar

Email: dgondzar@uncledonsapplepie.com
Website: www.uncledonsapplepie.com
Facebook: Uncle Don's Apple Pie, LLC
LinkedIn: Uncle Don's Apple Pie

Type: Craft-distillery. Opened in 2012.

Hours of operation:
Tuesday through Thursday, 12:00pm to 5:00pm
Friday and Saturday, 12:00pm to 6:00pm

Tours: Available

Types of spirits produced: Vodka, spirits

Names of spirits:
• Big Gun Vodka
• Uncle Don's Shining Spirits
• Uncle Don's Country Cocktails
  Old Fashion Apple, Fuzzy Peach, Black Cherry, Blueberry, Raspberry

Best known for / most popular: Not provided

Average bottle price: Not provided

Distribution: Not provided

Interesting facts: First craft distillery in Cadillac MI.

Valentine Distilling Company

161 Vester Street
Ferndale, MI 48220
248-629-9951

Owners / Operators:
Rifino Valentine, President / Founder

Email: info@valentinevodka.com
Website: www.valentinedistilling.com
Facebook: Valentine Vodka
Twitter: @valentinevodka

Type: Micro-distillery. Opened in 2007.

Hours of operation: Wednesday and Thursday, 4:30pm to 11:00,
Friday and Saturday, 4:30pm to 1:00pm; Sunday 12:00pm to 6:00pm

Tours: Available by appointment

Types of spirits produced:
Vodka, gin, barrel aged gin, whiskey

Names of spirits:
- Valentine Vodka
- Valentine White Blossom Elderflower Flavored Vodka
- Valentine Liberator Gin
- Valentine Woodward Limited Whiskey

Best known for / most popular: Vodka

Average bottle price: $30.00

Distribution: IL, MI, TN

Interesting facts: Valentine Distilling Co. is located in a refurbished building that once house a Packard Body Shop, built 1927

Remarks: "I have always believed in the quality of handmade, premium products. Whether it is jam made with fresh fruit on a small family farm or a pint from my favorite microbrewery, I've always appreciated the care and quality of ingredients that a small, local producer uses in their products. It is also a good feeling knowing that I'm not only getting a better product, but that my hard earned money is going to a true artisan rather than a faceless corporation in a far away country. So when I found myself craving a premium martini, with imported vodka being my only option, I made it my mission to create one of the world's best vodka, right here in the USA!"

Rifino Valentine, President and Founder, Valentine Distilling Co.

Panther Distillery

300 East Pike Street
Osakis, MN 56360
320-859-2256

Owners / Operators:
Adrian Panther, Owner
Brett Grinager, Master Distillery

Email: pantherdistillery@gmail.com
Website: www.pantherdistillery.com
Facebook: Panther Distillery

Type: Micro-distillery. Opened in 2011.

Hours of operation:
Monday through Saturday, 10:00am to 4:00pm

Tours: Available

Types of spirits produced: Whiskey, bourbon

Names of spirits:
- White Water Whiskey
- Spiked Apple Spirits

Best known for / most popular: White Water Whiskey

Average bottle price: $19.99

Distribution: MN, ND

Interesting facts: First legal whiskey distillery in MN

Phillips Distilling Company

500 Washington Avenue South
Minneapolis, MN 55415

Owners / Operators:
Phillips Distilling Company

Email: info@prairievodka.com
Website: www.prairievodka.com
Facebook: Prairie Organic Vodka
Twitter: @prairievodka

Type: Micro-distillery. Opened in 2008.

Hours of operation: Not provided

Tours: Not provided

Types of spirits produced: Vodka

Names of spirits:
• Prairie Organic Vodka

Best known for / most popular: Organic Vodka

Average bottle price: $19.99

Distribution: U.S. and Canada

Interesting facts:
• Oregon Tilth organic certification
• Certified Kosher
• Crafted with single vintage, Minnesota organic corn
• After the harvest, the corn is brought to the farmer-owned distillery in Benson, MN; a sustainable co-op that converts leftover corncobs into fuel and returns leftover distillers grains to local farmers for use as feed
• Food & Wine Magazine Best New Vodka, 2009
• Two time Double Gold Winner, San Francisco World Spirits Competition
• Wine Enthusiast Magazine: Buying Guide Rating 92

Cathead Distillery LLC
Bottle Tree Beverage Company

Gluckstadt, MS 39110
601-667-3038

Owners / Operators:
Austin Evans, Owner
Richard Patrick, Owner

Email: info@catheadvodka.com
Website: www.catheadvodka.com
Facebook: Cathead Vodka
Twitter: @CATHEADVodka

Type: Micro-distillery. Opened in 2010.

Hours of operation: Monday through Friday, 9:00am to 5:00pm

Tours: Available

Types of spirits produced:
Vodka, gin, moonshine, whiskey, liqueur

Names of spirits:
- Cathead Vodka
- Cathead Honeysuckle Vodka
- Gold Coast White Whiskey
- Gold Coast Bourbon
- Bristow Gin
- Hoodoo Chicory Liqueur

Best known for / most popular: Lazy Cat

Average bottle price: $19.99

Distribution:
AL, AR, CO, FL, GA, IN, LA, MS, SC, TN, VA

Interesting facts:
The first legal commercial distillery in MS

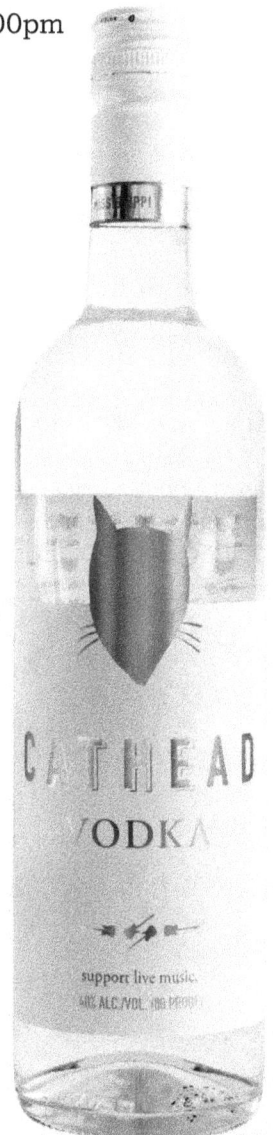

163

Copper Run Distillery

1901 Day Road
Walnut Shade, MO 65771
417-587-3456

Owners / Operators:
Jim Blansit, Owner / Master Distiller

Email: info@copperrundistillery.com
Website: www.copperrundistillery.com
Facebook: Copper Run Distillery
Foursquare: Copper Run Distillery
Yelp: Copper Run Distillery
Instagram: copperrundistillery

Type: Micro-distillery. Opened in 2009.

Hours of operation: Open Daily, 11:00am to 9:00pm

Tours: Available

Types of spirits produced: Moonshine, whiskey, rum

Names of spirits:
- Copper Run Moonshine
- Copper Run Spirit Whiskey
- Copper Run Gold Rum

Best known for / most popular: Copper Run Moonshine

Average bottle price: $30.00

Distribution: MO, ship to most states

Crown Valley Distilling Company

13326 State Route F
Ste. Genevieve, MO 63670
573-756-9700

Owners / Operators:
Joe and Loretta Scott, Owners
Bryan Siddle, Director of Operations

Email: Bryan Siddle: bsiddle@crownvalleywinery.com
Distiller: seckl@crownvalleywinery.com
Website: www.crownvalleybrewery.com
Facebook: Crown Valley Brewing and Distilling, Crown Valley Vodka
Twitter: @CrownValleyBrew
Blog: blog.crownvalleybrewery.com

Type: Brewery / Micro-distillery. Opened in 2009.

Hours of operation: Vary by season

Tours: Available

Types of spirits produced:
Whiskey, vodkas, absinthe, and flavored spirits

Names of spirits:
• Missouri Moonshine
• Crown Valley Vodka

Best known for / most popular:
Missouri Moonshine

Average bottle price: $30.00

Distribution: On-site, DE, IL, KY, MO, TN

Interesting facts:
Moonshine Facts

Moonshine Facts

• Moonshine has several different nicknames, such as white lightnin', corn liquor, corn squeezins', etc.

• "Bootleggers," are what they called the people that transport and sold moonshine. They got their name from colonial times when they would hide the bottles in their tall riding boots.

• After the Revolutionary War, the government needed money to pay for that war and started taxing liquors and spirits. Against those liquor taxes and the President, George Washington, called on the militia to quell the uprising and take the leaders into custody. This is known as, The Whiskey Rebellion.

Mad Buffalo Distillery

7616 Shawneetown Spur
Union, MO 63084
636-395-7418

Owners / Operators:
Chris Burnette, President / Head Distiller
William Cole Uphouse, VP of Operation
Jason Wink, VP of Production
Terry Burnette, Director of Quality Control
Elise Burnette, VP of Marketing
Josh Johnson, VP of Sales,
Robert Ralston, Director of Storage / Shipping
Matthew Schimmel, Director of Missouri Sales
Michael Owczarski, Director of Facilities

Email: info@madbuffalodistillery.com
Website: www.madbuffalodistillery.com
Facebook: Mad Buffalo Distillery
Twitter: @madbuffalobrew

Type: Brewery / Micro-distillery. Opened in 2012.

Hours of operation: Vary

Tours: Not available

Types of spirits produced: Whiskey

Names of spirits:
• Thunderbeast Storm Moonshine Corn Whiskey
• Thunderbeast Baby Buffalo Bourbon
• Thunderbeast Spirit Aged Corn Whiskey
• Thunderbeast Stampede Vodka
• Thunderbeast Prairie Gin

Best known for: Thunderbeast Storm Moonshine

Average bottle price: $28.00

Distribution: MO

Interesting facts: Made From 100% Missouri corn grown on site at their family farm. All products are made from ingredients grown, ground, malted, mashed, distilled, bottled and labeled on site in a true Ground to Glass process.

Pinckney Bend Distillery

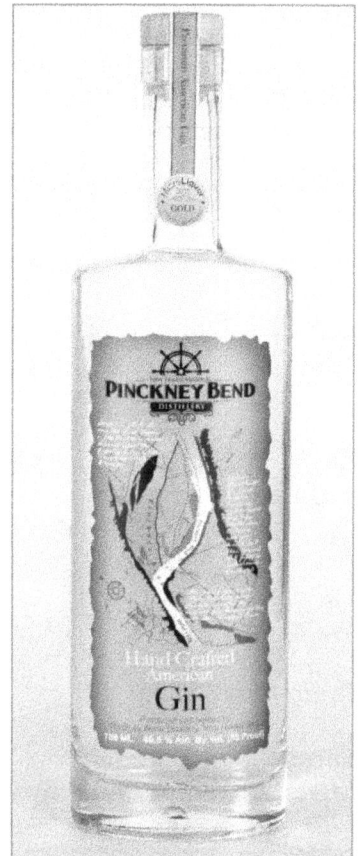

1101B Miller Street
New Haven, MO 63068
573-237-5559

Owners / Operators:
Jerome Meyer, President / CEO
Thomas Anderson, VP Production and Product Development
Ralph Haynes, VP Sales and Marketing

Email: ralph@pinckneybend.com
Website: www.pinckneybend.com
Facebook: Pinckney Bend Distillery
Twitter: @Pinckney_Bend, @ardentspirits

Type: Micro-distillery. Opened in 2011.

Hours of operation: Not open to the public

Tours: Not available

Types of spirits produced: Gin, vodka

Names of spirits:
- Pinckney Bend American Gin
- Pinckney Ben American Vodka

Best known for / most popular:
Pinckney Bend American Gin

Average bottle price: $26.00 to $29.00

Distribution: MO

Interesting facts:
Pinckney Bend was a navigational hazard well-known to generations Missouri River boatmen.

S. D. Strong Distilling

8500 NW River Park Road, #136A
Parkville, MO 64152
816-686-8269

Owners / Operators:
Steve Strong, President

Email: info@sdstrongdistilling.com
Website: www.sdstrongdistilling.com
Facebook: S.D. Strong Distilling
Twitter: @StillStrongMO
Instagram: sdstrongdistiller

Type: Micro-distillery. Opened in 2012.

Hours of operation: Not open to the public

Tours: Available by appointment

Types of spirits produced: Vodka, gin (coming soon), whiskey (coming soon)

Names of spirits:
• S.D. Strong Vodka

Best known for / most popular: S.D. Strong Vodka

Average bottle price: $19.99

Distribution: MO

Interesting facts:
The nation's first and only known micro-distillery located in a cave.

Square One Brewery and Distillery

1727 Park Avenue
St. Louis, MO 63104
314-231-2537

Owners / Operators:
Steve Neukomm, Owner

Email: steve@squareonebrewery.com
Website: www.squareonebrewery.com
Website: www.spiritsofstlouisdistillery.com
Facebook: Square One Brewery & Distillery
Twitter: @SquareOneBrews

Type: Brewery / Micro-distillery. Opened in 2008.

Hours of operation:
Monday through Saturday 11:00am to 1:30am, Sunday 10:00am to 12:00am

Tours: Available by appointment

Types of spirits produced: Agave blue, gin, liqueurs, rum, whiskey, vodka

Names of spirits:
Under the brand name "Spirits of St. Louis"
• JJ Neukomm American Malt Whiskey
• Vermont Night Whiskey Liqueur
• Midwest Spring Wheat Vodka
• Island Time Amber Rum
• Regatta Bay Gin
• Agave Blue

Average bottle price: $25.00 to $48.00

Distribution: MO

Interesting facts:
Square One was the first legal distillery in St. Louis since Prohibition.

St. Louis Distillery

755 Friedens Road, Ste. B
St. Charles, MO 63303
636-925-1577

Owners / Operators:
Bill Schroer, Owner / Distiller
Greg Deters, Owner / Distiller
Steve Herberholt, Owner / Distiller

Email: info@stldistillery.com
Website: www.cardinalsinvodka.com
Facebook: Cardinal Sin Vodka
Twitter: @CardinalSinVod

Type: Micro-distillery. Opened in 2012.

Hours of operation: Vary

Tours: Available by appointment

Types of spirits produced: Vodka

Names of spirits:
- Cardinal Sin Vodka

Best known for / most popular:
Cardinal Sin Vodka

Average bottle price: $27.99 to $29.99

Distribution: MO, IL

Interesting facts: Not provided

Cardinal
SIN
ARTISAN · VODKA
ST. LOUIS DISTILLERY

3-Time
Gold Medal
Winner

MicroLiquor
SPIRIT AWARDS

SIP AWARDS

90 Gold Medal Exceptional

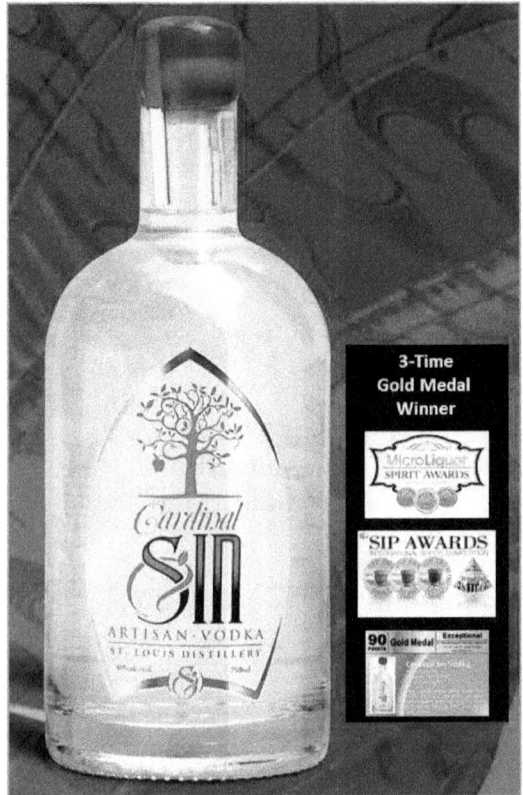

Steve   Bill   Greg

170

StilL 630

1000 S. 4th Street
St. Louis, MO 63104
314-513-2275

Owners / Operators:
David Weglarz, Owner / Distiller
Jim Schultz, Owner
Dyke Minix, Owner
Ben Pippenger, Owner

Email: distillery@still630.com
Website: www.still630.com
Facebook: StilL 630 Distillery
Twitter: @StilL630

Type: Micro-distillery. Opened in 2012.

Hours of operation: Monday through Sunday, 1:00pm to 6:30pm

Tours: Friday through Sunday at 1:00pm, 3:00pm, and 5:00pm

Types of spirits produced: Rum, whiskey, bourbon

Names of spirits:
- Sir Whisquila
- Bell Bourbon
- Barrel Master
- Expedition Rum
- American Whiskey
- RallyPoint Rye Whiskey
- Big Jake White Dog Whiskey
- S.S. Sorghum Whiskey

Best known for / most popular:
Rally Point Rye Whiskey, Sir Whisquila, and S.S. Sorghum Whiskey

Average bottle price: $28.00 to $35.00

Distribution: MO

Interesting facts:
- Located just south of Busch Stadium in downtown St. Louis

- The '630' in the name derives from the height and width of the Gateway Arch, which itself is a monument to the indomitable spirit of the frontiersmen and women.

Glacier Distilling Company

10237 Highway 2 E
Coram, MT 59913
406-387-9887

Owners / Operators:
Nicolas Lee, Distiller
Lauren Oscilowski, Assistant Distiller

Email: info@glacierdistilling.com
Website: www.glacierdistilling.com
Facebook: Glacier Distilling Company
Twitter: @GlacierWhiskey

Type: Micro-distillery. Opened in 2011.

Hours of operation: Vary by season

Tours: Available

Types of spirits produced:
Whiskey, brandy, liqueur

Names of spirits:
- Glacier Dew Rye Spirit
- North Fork Whiskey
- Bad Rock Rye
- Wheatfish Whiskey

Best known for / most popular: Glacier Dew

Average bottle price: $28.00 to $64.00

Distribution: MT

Interesting facts: The recipe for Glacier Dew was inspired by legendary moonshiner Josephine Doody who produced some renowned shine in Glacier Park back in the early 1900s.

GLACIER DISTILLING
The Whiskey Barn

PHOTO BY KELLEY CHRISTENSEN (2011)

Headframe Spirits

21 S. Montana
Butte, MT 59701
406-299-2886

Owners / Operators:
John McKee, Co-owner
Courtney McKee, Co-owner

Email: cheers@headframespirits.com
Website: www.headframespirits.com
Facebook: Headframe Spirits
Twitter: @HeadframeSpirit

Type: Micro-distillery. Opened in 2010.

Hours of operation:
Monday through Saturday, 10:00am to 8:00pm
Sunday, 12:00pm to 5:00pm

Tours: Available

Types of spirits produced: Gin, vodka, whiskey, liqueur

Names of spirits:
- Anselmo Gin
- High Ore Vodka
- Destroying Angel Whiskey
- Neversweat Bourbon Whiskey
- Orphan Girl Bourbon Cream Liqueur

Best known for / most popular: Anselmo Gin

Average bottle price: Not provided

Distribution: Not provided

Interesting facts: Not provided

173

Montgomery Distillery

129 West Front Street
Missoula, MT 59802
406-926-1725

Owners / Operators:
Ryan Montgomery, Co-founder
Jenny Montgomery, Co-founder
Tom Montgomery, Operations Manager
Chad Larrabee, Production Manager

Email: info@montgomerydistillery.com
Website: www.montgomerydistillery.com
Facebook: Montgomery Distillery
Twitter: @montstill

Type: Micro-distillery. Opened in 2011.

Hours of operation: Monday through Saturday, 12:00pm to 8:00pm

Tours: Available

Types of spirits produced: Gin, vodka, whiskey

Names of spirits:
- Whyte Laydie Gin
- Quicksilver Vodka

Best known for / most popular: Whyte Laydie Gin

Average bottle price: Not provided

Distribution: Not provided

Interesting facts: Not provided

RoughStock Distillery

81211 Gallatin Road, Ste. A
Bozeman, MT 59718

Owners / Operators:
Bryan Schulz, Co-owner
Kari Schulz, Co-owner

Website: www.montanawhiskey.com
Facebook: RoughStock Montana Whiskey

Type: Micro-distillery. Opened in 2008.

Hours of operation:
Monday through Friday, 11:00am to 6:00pm
Saturday, 11:00am to 3:00pm; Sunday, Closed

Tours: Available

Types of spirits produced: Whiskey

Names of spirits:
- RoughStock Montana Pure Malt Whiskey
- RoughStock Montana Black Label Whiskey
- RoughStock Montana Spring Wheat Whiskey
- RoughStock Montana Straight Rye Whiskey
- RoughStock Montana Sweet Corn Whiskey

Interesting facts: RoughStock Distillery is Montana's first legal distillery since Prohibition and the first to make whiskey in Montana in more than 100 years.

Swanson's Mountain View Apple Orchard and Distillery

1752 Mountain View Orchards Road
Corvallis, MT 59828
406-961-3434

Owners / Operators:
Swanson family

Email: mountain.view.orchards@gmail.com
Website: https://sites.google.com/site/mountainvieworchards
Facebook: Swanson's Mountain View Distillery

Type: Micro-distillery. Opened in 2011.

Hours of operation: Daily, 9:00am to 5:00pm

Tours: Available

Types of spirits produced: Honey spirit, brandy, cider

Names of spirits:
- Legendary Gold Honey Spirit
- Bitterroot Heritage Apple Brandy
- Harvest Legacy Dessert Cider

Best known for / most popular:
Legendary Gold Honey Spirit

Average bottle price: $8.00 to $30.00

Distribution: Not provided

Interesting facts: Not provided

The Montana Distillery
Flathead Distillers

Whitefish, MT

Owners / Operators:
Mark Hlebichuk, Co-owner
Sharie McDonald-Hlebichuk, Co-owner

Email: info@flatheadvodka.com
Website: www.themontanadistillery.com
Facebook: Flathead Vodka

Type: Micro-distillery. Opened in 2010.

Hours of operation: Not provided

Tours: Not provided

Types of spirits produced: Vodka

Names of spirits:
* Flathead Vodka
* Cherry Infused Flathead Vodka
* Coffee Infused Flathead Vodka

Best known for / most popular: Flathead Vodka

Average bottle price: $23.99

Distribution: Not provided

Interesting facts:
84 proof vodka, made from sugar beets

177

Trailhead Spirits
Bootleg Distillery Inc.

2314 Montana Avenue
Billings, MT 59101
406-969-1627

Owners / Operators:
Casey McGowan, President
Steffanie McGowan, Vice President

Email: casey@trailheadspirits.com, steffanie@trailheadspirits.com
Website: www.trailheadspirits.com
Facebook: Trailhead Spirits

Type: Micro-distillery. Opened in 2013.

Hours of operation:
Monday through Sunday, 12:00pm to 8:00pm
Cocktail service from 4:00pm to 8:00pm

Tours: Available

Types of spirits produced: Vodka, gin

Names of spirits:
- Great North Vodka
- Healy's Gin

Best known for / most popular: Great North Vodka

Average bottle price: $27.00

Distribution: MT

Interesting facts:
The wheat used is sourced from from the
McGowan family farms in Highwood, MT.

178

Vilya Spirits LLC
Formerly Ridge Distillery LLC

19 Artemisia Way
Kalispell, MT 59901
406-756-5964

Owners / Operators:
Joe and Julie Legate, Owner / Operators

Email: info@vilyaspirits.com
Website: www.vilyaspirits.com
Facebook: Vilya Spirits

Type: Micro-distillery. Opened in 2008.

Hours of operation: Not open to the public

Tours: Available by appointment

Types of spirits produced: Gin, absinthe

Names of spirits:
- Silvertip American Dry Gin
- Extrait d'Absinthe Verte
- Extrait d'Absinthe Blanche

Best known for / most popular: Absinthe

Average bottle price: $30.00 to $68.00

Distribution: AZ, CA, CT, DC, DE, FL, GA, IL, MD, MA, MT, NJ, NV, NY, RI, SC, TN, WA, WV

Interesting facts: The distillery is powered by hydroelectric energy.

Whistling Andy Distillery

8541 Mt. Hwy 35
Bigfork, MT 59911
406-837-2620

Owners / Operators:
Brian Anderson, Owner / Distiller
Mike Marchetti, Owner
Dana Marchetti, Bookeeping
Chandra Hodges, Operations
Lisa Cloutier, Outside Sales and Marketing

Email: brian@whistlingandy.com, marketing@whistlingandy.com
Website: www.whistlingandy.com
Facebook: Whistling Andy
Twitter: @WhistlingAndy

Type: Micro-distillery. Opened in 2010.

Hours of operation: Monday through Sunday, 12:00pm to 8:00pm

Tours: Available by appointment

Types of spirits produced: Rum, gin, whiskey, vodka, kirsch

Names of spirits:
- Whistling Andy Gin
- Whistling Andy Vodka
- Whistling Andy Silver Rum
- Whistling Andy Moonshine
- Whistling Andy Hopshnop
- Whistling Andy Harvest Select
- Whistling Andy Hibiscus-Coconut Rum

Best known for / most popular: Hibiscus Crush

Average bottle price: $24.00 to $48.00

Distribution: AZ, CA, IL, MO, MT, NV, OR; Canada

Interesting facts:
A veteran owned distillery, hires returning veterans.

Willie's Distillery

312 East Main Street
Ennis, MT 59729
406-682-4117

Owners / Operators:
Willie Blazer, Co-owner
Robin Blazer, Co-owner

Email: info@williesdistillery.com
Website: www.williesdistillery.com
Facebook: Willie's Distillery, Inc
Twitter: @mtmoonshine

Type: Micro-distillery. Opened in 2012.

Hours of operation: Daily with varied hours.
Normally 10:00am to 8:00pm (seasonal)

Tours: Available

Types of spirits produced:
Moonshine, whiskey, vodka, gin, liqueurs, brandy

Names of spirits:
• Bighorn Whiskey
• Snowcrest Vodka
• Montana Moonshine
• Montana Honey Moonshine
• Montana Wild Chokecherry Liqueur

Best known for: Montana Moonshine

Average bottle price: $20.00 to $40.00

Distribution: MT

Interesting facts:
• Located in a small cowboy town of 840
  people and around 11,000,000 trout.
• Just 200 yards from Blue Ribbon Fly-
  Fishing on the Madison River.

Cooper's Chase Distillery LLC

584 18th Road
West Point, NE 68788
402-380-0233

Owners / Operators:
Doug Throener, Owner

Email: info@cooperschase.com
Website: www.cooperschase.com
Facebook: Cooper's Chase Distillery

Type: Micro-distillery. Opened in 2009.

Hours of operation: Not provided

Tours: Not provided

Types of spirits produced: Vodka

Names of spirits:
• Chase Nebraska Vodka

Best known for / most popular: Chase Nebraska Vodka

Average bottle price: Not provided

Distribution: Not provided

Interesting facts: Not provided

Sòlas Distillery

11941 Centennial Road Suite #1
La Vista, NE 68128
402-763-8868

Owners / Operators:
Zac Triemert, Founder / President / Master Distiller
Jason Payne, Vice President
Holly Mulkins, Spirits Ambassador / VP of Sales & Marketing

Email: Zac Triemert: zac@solasdistillery.com
  Jason Payne: jason@solasdistillery.com
  Holly Mulkins: holly@solasdistillery.com
Website: www.solasdistillery.com
Facebook: Sòlas Distillery, Joss Vodka
Twitter: @SòlasDistillery

Type: Micro-distillery. Opened in 2009.

Hours of operation: Not provided

Tours: Available

Types of spirits produced: Vodka, rum, whisky

Names of spirits:
- Joss Vodka
- Chava Rum
- Sòlas Single Malt Whisky

Best known for / most popular: Joss Vodka

Average bottle price: $20.00 to $60.00

Distribution: NE

Interesting facts: Not provided

Churchill Vineyards and Distillery

1045 Dodge Lane
Fallon, NV 89406
775-423-4000

Owners / Operators:
Colby Frey, Owner / Winemaker / Distiller
Ashley Frey, Owner / Marketing

Email: info@churchillvineyards.com
          Ashley Frey: Ashley@churchillvineyards.com
          Colby Frey: Colby@churchillvineyards.com
Website: www.churchillvineyards.com
Facebook: Churchill Vineyards
Twitter: @churchillwines

Type: Winery / Micro-distillery. Opened in 2010.

Hours of operation: Open by appointment

Tours: Available by appointment

Types of spirits produced: Whiskey, vodka, brandy, grappa

Names of spirits:
- Nevada Vodka
- Nevada Brandy
- Nevada Single Malt Whiskey

Best known for / most popular: Churchill Vineyards Grappa and Coke

Average bottle price: $20.00 to $50.00

Distribution: NV

Interesting facts: Spirits grown, produced, and bottled on-site by fifth generation Nevada farmer, Colby Frey.

Las Vegas Distillery

7330 Eastgate Road, Ste. 100
Henderson, NV 89011
702-629-7534

Owners / Operators:
Katalin and George Rácz, Owners

Email: info@lasvegasdistillery.com
Website: www.lasvegasdistillery.com
Facebook: Las Vegas Distillery
Twitter: @VegasDistillery

Type: Micro-distillery. Opened in 2011.

Hours of operation: Not provided

Tours: Available

Types of spirits produced: Vodka, rumskey

Names of spirits:
- Nevada Vodka
- Seven Grain Vodka
- White Rumskey

Best known for / most popular: Nevada Vodka

Average bottle price: Not provided

Distribution: NV

Interesting facts:
Las Vegas Distillery is one of the first legal distilleries in the history of Nevada.

Flag Hill Winery & Distillery

297 North River Road
Lee, NH 03861
603-659-2949

Owners / Operators:
Frank W. Reinhold, Jr, Owner

Email: wine-info@flaghill.com
Website: www.flaghill.com
Facebook: Flag Hill Winery & Distillery
Twitter: @flaghillwinery

Type: Winery / Micro-distillery. Opened in 2004.

Hours of operation:
Wednesday through Sunday, 11:00am to 5:00pm

Tours:
Available weekends from June to September

Types of spirits produced:
Absinthe, brandy, grappa, gin, liqueurs, vodka, rum

Names of spirits:
- General John Stark Vodka
- Josiah Bartlett Barrel Aged Apple Brandy
- Karner Blue Gin
- Moonshine
- Graham's Grappa
- Sugar Maple Liqueur
- Blueberry Liqueur
- Raspberry Liqueur
- Cranberry Liqueur
- Flag Hill White Rum

Best known for / most popular: Karner Blue Gin

Average bottle price: $15.00 to $26.00

Distribution: MA, NH, NY, PA

Interesting facts:
In 2004, Flag Hill became the first distillery in NH

Sea Hagg Distillery

135 Lafayette Road, Unit 9
North Hampton, NH 03862
603-379-2274

Owners / Operators:
Heather Hughes, Managing Member

Email: info@seahaggdistillery.com
Website: www.seahaggdistillery.com
Facebook: The Sea Hagg Distillery LLC

Type: Micro-distillery. Opened in 2012.

Hours of operation: Vary

Tours: Available

Types of spirits produced: Rum, eau de vie, brandy

Names of spirits:
- Sea Hagg Rum (Amber)
- Sea Hagg Silver Rum
- Sea Hagg Peach Rum
- Sea Hagg Blueberry Rum
- Sea Hagg Eau de Vie Pear
- Sea Hagg Eau de Vie Apple

Best known for / most popular: Sea Hagg Rum

Average bottle price: $28.00 to $30.00

Distribution: NH

Interesting facts: Not provided

Big Still Liquors LLC

23 Sebago Street
Clifton, NJ 07013
304-690-2012

Owners / Operators:
Ron Haberman, President / Founder

Email: ron@300joules.com
Website: www.300joules.com
Facebook: 300 Joules
Twitter: @300Joules

Type: Mixing / bottling. Opened in 2011.

Hours of operation:
Monday through Friday, 9:00am to 4:00pm

Tours: Not available

Types of spirits produced: Liqueur

Names of spirits:
• 300 Joules Lemon Infusion
• 300 Joules Ginger Infusion

Best known for / most popular: TBA

Average bottle price: $24.95

Distribution: TBA

Interesting facts:
Joules is a nod to the former profession of the founder, a cardiology specialist.

Don Quixote Distillery & Winery

236 Rio Bravo
Los Alamos, NM 87544
505-695-0864

Owners / Operators:
Ron and Olha Dolin, Owners

Email: ron@dqdistillery.com
Website: www.dqdistillery.com
Facebook: Don Quixote Winery and Distillery

Type: Winery / Micro-distillery. Opened in 2003.

Hours of operation: Tuesday through Sunday, 12:00pm to 6:00pm

Tours: Available

Types of spirits produced:
Eau de vie, vodka, bourbon, gin, whiskey, brandy, grappa

Names of spirits:
- Don Quixote Angelica
- Don Quixote Blue Corn Vodka
- Don Quixote Blue Corn Bourbon
- Don Quixote Gin
- Don Quixote Pisco
- Don Quixote Qalvados – Apple Brandy
- Don Quixote Grappa
- Don Quixote Malvasia Bianca Grappa
- Don Quixote Mon Cherie Cherry Eau de Vie
- Spirit of Santa Fe Gin
- Spirit of Santa Fe Brandy
- Spirit of Santa Fe Vodka

Best known for / most popular: Blue Corn Vodka, Pisco, Angelica, Gin

Average bottle price: $25.00 to $50.00

Distribution: NM

Interesting facts:
Don Quixote Distillery is New Mexico's first and only distillery specializing in premium spirits made from New Mexico agricultural products.

189

Rancho de Los Luceros Destilaría

183 County Road 41
Alcalde, NM 87511
505-404-6101

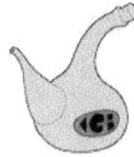

KGB Spirits
Los Luceros Destilaría

Owners / Operators:
John Bernasconi, President / Owner
George Shurman, Owner
Karen Lubliner, Owner
Caitlin Richards, Operation Manager
Steven Jarrett, Distiller
John Cox, Sales Manager

Email: info@kgbspirits.com
Website: www.KGBspirits.com

Type: Micro-distillery. Opened in 2012.

Hours of operation: Vary

Tours: Not available

Types of spirits produced:
Gin, vodka, liqueur, absinthe, bourbon, rye

Names of spirits:
- Los Luceros Hacienda Gin
- Vodka Viracocha
- Brimstone Absinthe
- Naranjo Orange Liqueur
- John David Albert's Taos Lightning
  Single barrel straight Rye Whiskey, 5 year
- Ceran St. Vrain's Taos Lightning
  Single barrel straight Rye Whiskey, 15 year
- Thomas Tate Tobin's Taos Lightning
  Single barrel straight Bourbon
- Simeon Turley's Taos Lightning
  Single barrel straight Bourbon, 6 year

Best known for / most popular: Taos Lightning Rye

Average bottle price: $35.00 to $90.00

Distribution: NM

Interesting facts: Rancho de Los Luceros Destilaría is located on the property of the historic ranch of the same name in Alcalde, NM, in the straw bale building that was once home to the Los Luceros Winery – the second straw bale built winery in the United States.

Santa Fe Spirits

7505 Mallard Way, Unit I
Santa Fe, NM 87507
505-467-8892

Owners / Operators:
Colin Keegan, Owner
Nick Jones, Master Distiller

Email: info@santafespirits.com
Website: www.santafespirits.com
Facebook: Santa Fe Spirits
Twitter: @SantaFeSpirits

Type: Micro-distillery. Opened in 2011 .

Hours of operation:
Wednesday and Friday, 3:00pm to 7:00pm
Saturday, 3:00pm to 5:00pm

Tours: Available

Types of spirits produced: Whiskey, brandy

Names of spirits:
- Santa Fe Silver Coyote Pure Malt Whiskey
- Santa Fe Apple Brandy

Best known for: The Whiskeyrita
A margarita that substitutes tequila with Silver Coyote

Average bottle price: $29.99 to $45.99

Distribution: NM

Interesting facts: Not provided

191

Adirondack Distilling Company

601 Varick Street
Utica, NY 13502
315-316-0387

Owners / Operators:
Steve Cox, Co-owner
Bruce Elsell, Co-owner
Jordan Karp, Co-owner

Email: info@adirondackdistilling.com
Website: www.adirondackdistilling.com
Facebook: Adirondack Distilling Company
Twitter: @ADKDistillingCo
YouTube: Adirondack Distilling
Pinterest: AdirondackDistilling

Type: Micro-distillery. Opened in 2012.

Hours of operation: Friday, 5:00pm to 8:00pm
Saturday, 1:00pm to 4:00pm

Tours: Available

Types of spirits produced: Vodka

Names of spirits:
• Adirondack ADK Vodka

Best known for / most popular: Adirondack ADK Vodka

Average bottle price: $32.95

Distribution: NY

Interesting facts: Not provided

Albany Distilling Company

78 Montgomery Street
Albany, NY 12207
518-621-7191

Owners / Operators:
John Curtin, Co-owner
Matthew Jager, Co-owner

Email: info@albanydistilling.com
Website: www.albanydistilling.com
Facebook: The Albany Distilling Company, Inc.
Twitter: @AlbDistCo

Type: Micro-distillery. Opened in 2012.

Hours of operation: Vary

Tours: Available Tuesdays, 4:00pm to 8:00pm;
Saturdays, 12:00pm to 8:00pm or by appointment.

Types of spirits produced: Whiskey, rum

Names of spirits:
- Coal Yard New Make Whiskey
- Ironweed
- Quackenbush Still House Rum

Best known for / most popular: Ironweed

Average bottle price: $30.00 to $44.00

Distribution: Albany, NY area

Interesting facts:
The distillery occupies a renovated, century old building.

Beak & Skiff Distillery

4472 Cherry Valley Turnpike
LaFayette NY 13084
316-677-5105

Owners / Operators:
Steve Morse, Co-owner
Candy Morse, Co-owner
David Pittard, Co-owner
Tim Beak, Co-owner
Jackie Beak, Co-owner
Ed Brennan, Co-owner
Steve Brennan, Co-owner

Email: beakandskiff@gmail.com
Website: www.1911spirits.com
Facebook: 1911 Spirits
Twitter: @1911spirits

Type: Micro-distillery. Opened in 2009.

Hours of operation: Daily, 10:00m to 5:00pm (May 15th to December 31st)

Tours: Available

Types of spirits produced: Vodka, gin, hard cider

Names of spirits:
- 1911 Vodka
- 1911 Gin
- 1911 Hard Cider
- 1911 Wine

Best known for / most popular: 1911 Vodka

Average bottle price: $9.99 to $34.99

Distribution: NY

Interesting facts: Not provided

Black Dirt Distillery

385 Glenwood Road
Pine Island, NY 10969
845-258-6020

Owners / Operators:
Jeremy Kidde, Co-owner
Jason Grizzanti, Co-owner

Email: info@blackdirtdistillery.com
Website: www.blackdirtdistillery.com
Facebook: Black Dirt Distillery
Twitter: @BDDistillery

Type: Craft-distillery. Opened in 2012.

Hours of operation: Not provided

Tours: Not available

Types of spirits produced: AppleJack, bourbon

Names of spirits:
• Black Dirt Bourbon

Best known for / most popular: Black Dirt Bourbon

Average bottle price: $44.00

Distribution: NJ, NY

Interesting facts: Not provided

Breuckelen Distilling Company Inc.

77 19th Street
Brooklyn, NY 11232
347-725-4985

Owners / Operators:
Brad Estabrooke, Founder

Email: info@brkdistilling.com
Website: www.brkdistilling.com
Facebook: Breuckelen Distilling
Twitter: @BrkDistilling

Type: Micro-distillery. Opened in 2010.

Hours of operation:
Tasting room Saturday, 12:00pm to 6:00pm or by appointment

Tours: Available

Types of spirits produced: Gin, whiskey

Names of spirits:
• Glorious Gin
• 77 Whiskey

Best known for / most popular: 77 Whiskey

Average bottle price: $35.00

Distribution: IL, NJ, NV, NYC

Interesting facts: Not provided

Cacao Prieto LLC

CACAO PRIETO

218 Conover Street
Brooklyn, NY 11231
347-225-0130

Owners / Operators:
Daniel Preston, CEO / Engineer
Alex Clark, Sales Director
Layton Cutler and Celina Perez, Distillers
Michele Clark, Art Director

Email: info@cacaoprieto.com
Website: www.cacaoprieto.com, www.widowjanespirits.com
Facebook: Cacao Prieto
Twitter: @CacaoPrieto
YouTube: CacaoPrieto
Vimeo: CacaoPrieto
Instagram: cacao_prieto

Type: Micro-distillery. Opened in 2008.

Hours of operation: Daily

Tours: Available by appointment

Types of spirits produced: Whiskey, rum, vodka, rye, gin
rum liqueur, bourbon whiskey, bourbon whiskey, white dog

Names of spirits:
- Mamajuana
- Chamomile Rum
- Cacao Prieto White Rum
- Cacao Prieto Don Rafael Cacao Rum
- Cacao Prieto Don Daniel Cacao Rum Liqueur
- Cacao Prieto Don Esteban Cacao Rum Liqueur
- Brooklyn Roasting Company Coffee Liqueur
- Widow Jane Rye
- Widow Jane Bourbon Whiskey
- Widow Jane Wapsie Valley Bourbon Whiskey
- Bloody Butcher Bourbon Whiskey

Best known for / most popular: Widow Jane Bourbon Whiskey

Average bottle price: $29.00 to $53.00

Distribution: NY

Interesting facts: Not provided

Catskill Distilling Company Ltd.

2037 Route 17B
Bethel, NY 12720
845-583-3141

Owners / Operators:
Monte Sachs, President
Stacy Cohen, Vice President

Email: msachs@hvc.rr.com
Website: www.catskilldistillingco.com
Facebook: Catskill Distilling Company, Dancing Cat Distillery and Saloon
Twitter: @catskillDistill

Type: Micro-distillery. Opened in 2011.

Hours of operation: Friday through Sunday, 2:00pm to 8:00pm

Tours: Available

Types of spirits produced: Vodka

Names of spirits:
• Peace Vodka

Best known for / most popular: Peace Vodka

Average bottle price: $34.99

Distribution: Not provided

Interesting facts: Not provided

Celk Distilling
Apple Country Spirits

3274 Eddy Road
Williamson, NY 14589
315-589-8733

Owners / Operators:
David DeFisher, Founder

Email: info@applecountryspirits.com
Website: www.applecountryspirits.com
Facebook: Tree Vodka

Type: Micro-distillery. Opened in 2012.

Hours of operation: Monday through Friday, by appointment
                      Saturday, 11:00am to 5:00pm; Sunday, 12:00pm to 5:00pm

Tours: Available

Types of spirits produced: Vodka

Names of spirits:
• Tree Vodka

Best known for / most popular: Tree Vodka

Average bottle price: Not provided

Distribution: NY

Interesting facts: Tree Vodka is gluten free

Delaware Phoenix Distillery

144 Delaware Street
Walton, NY 13856
610-865-5056

Owners / Operators:
Cherl Lins, Owner / Distiller

Email: cheryllins@frontiernet.net
Website: www.delawarephoenix.com
Facebook: Delaware Phoenix Distillery Absinthes

Type: Micro-distillery. Opened in 2011.

Hours of operation: Not provided

Tours: Not provided

Types of spirits produced: Whiskey, absinthe

Names of spirits:
- Delaware Phoenix Walton Waters Absinthe
- Delaware Phoenix Meadow of Love Absinthe
- Delaware Phoenix Corn Whiskey
- Delaware Phoenix Rye Whiskey
- Delaware Phoenix Rye Dog

Best known for / most popular: Not provided

Average bottle price: Not provided

Distribution: Not provided

Interesting facts: Not provided

200

Demarest Hill Winery

81 Pine Island Turnpike
Warwick, NY 10990
845-986-4723

Owners / Operators:
Francesco Ciummo, Owner

Email: info@demaresthillwinery.com
Website: www.demaresthillwinery.com
Facebook: Demarest Hill Winery

Type: Winery / Micro-distillery. Opened in 2010.

Hours of operation: Daily, 11:00am to 6:00pm

Tours: Available

Types of spirits produced: Grappa, brandy, liqueur, limoncella, orancella

Names of spirits:
- Demarest Hill Winery Grappa
- Demarest Hill Winery Special Reserve Brandy
- Demarest Hill Winery Tropical Liqueur
- Demarest Hill Winery Amarena Aperitivo
- Demarest Hill Winery Limoncella
- Demarest Hill Winery Orancella

Best known for / most popular: Not provided

Average bottle price: Not provided

Distribution: Not provided

Interesting facts: Not provided

Eight Buffalo Spirits LLC

255 Great Arrow Avenue, Ste. 31
Buffalo, NY 14207
716-983-4025

Owners / Operators:
Niko Georgiadis, Partner / President
Chad Vosseller, Partner / Vice President of Operations
Jon Mirro, Partner / Vice President of Marketing
Thomas Jablonski, Business Manager

Email: info@eightbuffalospirits.com
Website: www.eightbuffalospirits.com
Facebook: Eight Buffalo Spirits
Twitter: @8BuffaloSpirits

Type: Micro-distillery. Under construction.

Hours of operation: Not provided

Tours: Not available

Types of spirits produced: TBA

Names of spirits:
- TBA

Best known for / most popular: TBA

Average bottle price: TBA

Distribution: Not provided

Interesting facts: Buffalo's first operating distillery since Prohibition.

Finger Lakes Distilling

4676 NYS Route 414
Burdett, NY 14818
607-546-5510

Owners / Operators:
Brian McKenzie, President / Owner
Thomas McKenzie, Distiller

Email: brian@fingerlakesdistilling.com
Website: www.fingerlakesdistilling.com
Facebook: Finger Lakes Distilling

Type: Craft-distillery. Opened in 2008.

Hours of operation: Daily, 11:00am to 5:00pm

Tours: Special event tours available by appointment

Types of spirits produced: Vodka, gin, whiskey, liqueurs, grappa, brandy

Names of spirits:
- Vintner's Vodka
- Vintner's Wild Berry Vodka
- Seneca Drums Gin
- McKenzie Distiller's Reserve Gin
- McKenzie Pure Potstill Whiskey
- McKenzie Bourbon Whiskey
- McKenzie Rye Whiskey
- Glen Thunder Corn Whiskey
- Pear Brandy
- Riesling Grappa
- Gewurztraminer Grappa
- White Pike Whiskey
- Maplejack Liqueur
- Cassis Liqueur
- Raspberry Liqueur
- Cherry Liqueur
- Grape Brandy

Best known for:
Seneca Drums Gin and McKenzie Bourbon and McKenzie Rye Whiskey

Average bottle price: $19.00 to $48.00

Distribution: CT, DC, IL, MA, MD, NY, NJ, PA

Interesting facts: The first standalone distillery in the Finger Lakes region.

Greenhook Ginsmiths

208 Dupont Street
Brooklyn, NY 11222
646-339-3719

Owners / Operators:
Steven DeAngelo, Ginsmith

Email: steven@greenhookgin.com
Website: www.greenhookgin.com
Facebook: Greenhook Ginsmiths
Twitter: @GreenhookGin

Type: Micro-distillery. Open in 2012.

Hours of operation: Not open to the public

Tours: Not available

Types of spirits produced: Gin, liqueur

Names of spirits:
- Greenhook Ginsmiths American Dry Gin
- Greenhook Ginsmiths Beach Plum Gin Liqueur

Best known for / most popular: Greenhook Ginsmiths American Dry Gin

Average bottle price: Not provided

Distribution: Not provided

Interesting facts: Not provided

Harvest Spirits LLC

3074 US Route 9
Valatie, NY 12184
518-261-1625

Owners / Operators:
Derek Grout, Owner

Email: info@harvestspirits.com
Website: www.harvestspirits.com
Facebook: Harvest Spirits Farm Distillery
Twitter: @HarvestSpirits

Type: Micro-distillery. Opened in 2008 .

Hours of operation: Saturday and Sunday, 12:00pm to 5:00pm

Tours: Available

Types of spirits produced: Vodka, brandy, grappa and applejack. In development: Himbeer Geist, frozen applejack, bacon-washed applejack, fruit-in-bottle and various fruit and herbal infused spirits

Names of spirits:
- Core Vodka
- Cornelius Applejack
- Apple Eau de Vie
- Pear Eau de Vie
- Grappa
- Rare Pear Brandy

Best known for / most popular: Applejack, vodka

Average bottle price: $25.00 to $40.00

Distribution: NY

Interesting facts: Not provided

Hidden Marsh Distillery

2981 Auburn Road (U.S. Route 20)
Seneca Falls, NY 13148
315-568-8190

Owners / Operators:
George, Ginny, Bill & Ed Martin, Owners

Email: info@beevodka.com
Website: www.beevodka.com
Facebook: Montezuma Winery & Hidden Marsh Distillery
Twitter: @MontezumaWinery

Type: Winery / Micro-distillery. Opened in 2008.

Hours of operation: Daily, 9:00am to 6:00pm

Tours: Not available

Types of spirits produced: Vodka, brandy, whiskey, liqueurs

Names of spirits:
- BEE Vodka
- Queen's Flight
- Apple Brandy
- Raspberry Liqueur
- Maple Liqueur

Best known for / most popular: BEE Vodka

Average bottle price: $24.99 to $48.99

Distribution: NY

Interesting facts: Not provided

Hillrock Estate Distillery

408 Pooles Hill Road
Ancram, NY 12502
518-329-1023

Owners / Operators:
Jeffrey Baker, Owner
Dave Pickerell, Master Distiller
Tim Welly, Head of Operations / Distiller
Danielle Eddy, Director of PR Marketing & Sales

Email: info@hillrockdistillery.com
Website: www.hillrockdistillery.com
Facebook: Hillrock Estate Distillery

Type: Micro-distillery. Opened in 2011.

Hours of operation: Available by appointment

Tours: Available by appointment

Types of spirits produced: Whiskey

Names of spirits:
- Hillrock Soera Aged Bourbon Whiskey
- Estate Single Malt
- Estate Rye

Best known for / most popular:
Hillrock Soera Aged Bourbon Whiskey

Average bottle price: Not provided

Distribution: NY

Interesting facts: Field-to-glass operation with on-site floor malthouse.

1806

HILLROCK

207

Industry City Distillery Inc.

33 35th Street, Unit 6A
Brooklyn, NY 11232
917-727-5309

Owners / Operators:
Dave Kyrejko - Co-founder / Chief Engineer
Peter Simon - Co-founder / Director of Sales and Operations
Rich Watts - Co-founder / Design Director
Zachary Bruner - Co-founder / Fabricator & Machinist, CEO
Max Hames - Co-founder / Production Manager

Email: tours@drinkicd.com
Website: www.drinkicd.com
Facebook: Industry City Distillery
Twitter: @drinkicd
Yelp: Industry City Distillery
FourSquare: Industry City Distillery
Flickr: The City Foundry's photostream

Type: Micro-distillery. Opened in 2011.

Hours of operation:
Monday through Friday, 9:30am to 6:00pm
Saturday and Sunday, 10:00pm to 5:00pm

Tours: Available on Sunday at 4:00pm

Types of spirits produced: Vodka

Names of spirits:
- Industry City Distillery Batch No. 3 (no longer produced)
- Industry City Distillery Batch No. 4 (currently on shelves)

Best known for / most popular:
Industry City Distillery Batch No. 3

Average bottle price: $20.00 to $22.00

Distribution: NYC area

Interesting facts:
ICD uses a custom-built immobilized cell bioreactor system for continuous fermentation. This, along with their steam stripping still and their batch fractional column still, was designed and built in-house by the team.

Jack From Brooklyn Inc.

177 Dwight Street
Red Hook, NY 11231

Owners / Operators:
Alan Camlet, Co-founder
Timothy Kealey, Co-founder

Email: info@jackfrombrooklyn.com
Website: www.jackfrombrooklyn.com
Facebook: The Liquortarian
Twitter: @TheLiquortarian

Type: Micro-distillery. Opened in 2011.

Hours of operation: Not provided

Tours: Not provided

Types of spirits produced: Liqueur

Names of spirits:
• Sorel

Best known for / most popular: Sorel

Average bottle price: Not provided

Distribution: Not provided

Interesting facts: Sorel is a hibiscus-based liqueur

Kings County Distillery

Brooklyn Navy Yard, Building 121
Brooklyn, NY 11205

Owners / Operators:
Colin Spoelman, Co-Founder / Master Distiller
David Haskell, Co-Founder
Nicole Austin, Master Blender
Matthew Million, Distillery Manager

Email: info@kingscountydistillery.com
Website: www.kingscountydistillery.com
Facebook: Kings County Distillery
Twitter: @KingsCoWhiskey

Type: Micro-distillery. Opened in 2010.

Hours of operation: Daily, 9:00am to midnight

Tours: Available on Saturdays from 2:30pm to 5:30pm

Types of spirits produced: Whiskey, bourbon

Names of spirits:
* Kings County Moonshine
* Kings County Bourbon
* Kings County Chocolate Whiskey

Best known for / most popular: Kings County Moonshine, neat

Average bottle price: $20.00 to $40.00

Distribution: NY, NJ

Interesting facts:
Kings County Distillery operates out of
the century old Paymaster Building in
the Brooklyn Navy Yard.

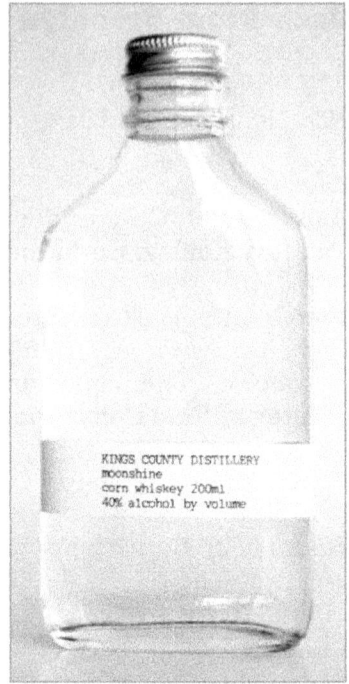

KyMar Farm Distillery

P.O. Box 72
Charlotteville, NY 12036
518-290-0051

Owners / Operators:
Kenneth Wortz, Founder / Managing Member / Distiller
Lori Wortz, Managing Member / Operations
Bill Martz, Member/ Operations

Email: info@ky-mar.com
Website: www.ky-mar.com
Facebook: KyMar Farm Distillery

Type: Micro-distillery. Opened in 2011.

Hours of operation: Weekends by appointment only

Tours: Available Fall 2013

Types of spirits produced: Eau de Vie, shine, liqueur

Names of spirits:
* Schoharie Mapple Jack
* Schoharie Shine
* Schoharie Eau de Vie de Pomme

Best known for / most popular: Schoharie Mapple Jack

Average bottle price: $30.00 to $35.00

Distribution: CT, MA, NY, RI

Interesting facts:
* Schoharie Mapple Jack is the perfect liqueur served neat, on the rocks or in cocktails.
* Schoharie Shine is made from Sweet Sorghum instead of traditional grains and cane sugar

211

Lake Placid Spirits LLC

Lake Placid, NY 12946

Owners / Operators:
Ann Stillman O'Leary, Owner
Twig McGlynn, Manager

Email: info@lakeplacidspirits.com
Website: www.lakeplacidspirits.com
Facebook: P3 Placid Vodka, Lake Placid Spirits, LLC
YouTube: Lake Placid Spirits--Cool Runnings

Type: Craft-distillery. Opened in 2007.

Hours of operation: Daily

Tours: Not available

Types of spirits produced: Vodka

Names of spirits:
• 46 Peaks Potato Vodka
• P3 Placid Vodka
• Alpen Glow

Best known for / most popular: P3 Placid Vodka

Average bottle price: $28.00 to $32.00

Distribution: NY

Interesting facts: Not provided

Long Island Spirits

2182 Sound Avenue
Baiting Hollow, NY 11933
631-630-9322

Owners / Operators:
Richard Stabile, Owner / Founder / Master Distiller

Email: info@lispirits.com
Website: www.lispirits.com
Facebook: LiV® Vodka
Twitter: @LiVGUY

Type: Micro-distillery. Opened in 2007.

Tasting room hours: Monday through Thursday, 10:00am to 5:00pm
Friday and Saturday, 10:00am to 6:00pm; Sunday, 11:00am to 6:00pm

Tours: Not available

Types of spirits produced:
Potato Vodka, liqueurs, single malt whisky, bourbon, rye

Names of spirits:
- LiV Vodka
  Original LiV, Ristretto Espresso Flavored Vodka
- Sorbetta Liqueurs
  Lemon, Lime, Orange, Strawberry, Raspberry
- Pine Barrens Single Malt Whisky
- Rough Rider Rye
- Rough Rider Straight Bourbon Whisky

Best known for / most popular: LiV Vodka

Average bottle price: $27.00

Distribution: CO, CT, DC, GA, IL, MA, NJ, NY, PA, RI

Interesting facts:
- Long Island Spirits is the first craft distillery on Long Island Since the 1800s.
- LiV Vodka is crafted from 100% locally and sustainably marcy russet Long Island Potatoes, creating a gluten-free product.
- The Sorbetta Liqueurs are the first known ever potato based liqueurs to be available in the U.S. They are crafted using all natural macerated fruits, including Long Island strawberries and raspberries.

213

Magnanini Farm Winery Inc.

172 Strawridge Road
Wallkill, NY 12589
845-895-2767

Owners / Operators:
Richard Magnanini, Owner
Robert Magnanini, Operator / Manager
David Magnanini, Operator
Rachel Magnanini, Owner / Operator

Email: info@magwine.com
Website: www.magwine.com

Type: Winery / Micro-distillery. Opened in 2008.

Hours of operation: Saturday and Sunday

Tours: Available by appointment

Types of spirits produced: Grappa, liqueur

Names of spirits:
- Grappa Del Nonno
- Grappa & Miele
- Grappa & Limone
- Pear Liqueur

Best known for / most popular: Grappa Del Nonno

Average bottle price: $19.00 to $32.50

Distribution: On-site

Interesting facts:
- Magnanini Farm Winery Grappa del Nonno is one of the only grappas in the world that is made in small batches from Dechaunac grape marc.
- Grappa Del Nonno won a Bronze Medal at the 7th Annual Judging of Artisan American Spirits.

214

Mazza Chautauqua Cellars

4717 Chautauqua Stedman Road
Mayville, NY 14575
716-269-3000

Owners / Operators:
Mazza Family

Email: info@mazzawines.com
Website: www.mcc.mazzawines.com
Facebook: Mazza Wines
Twitter: @MazzaWines

Type: Winery / Micro-distillery. Opened in 2006.

Hours of operation:
Monday through Saturday, 9:00am to 5:30pm
Sunday, 12:00am to 4:40pm

Tours: Available

Types of spirits produced: Eau de Vie, grappa

Names of spirits:
- Pear in the Bottle Pear Eau de Vie
- Apple Eau de Vie
- Plum Eau de Vie
- Cherry Eau de Vie
- Pear Eau de Vie
- Grappa of Steuben

Best known for / most popular: Not provided

Average bottle price: $24.95 to $79.95

Distribution: Not provided

Interesting facts: Not provided

Myer Farm Distillers

7350 State Route 89
Ovid, NY 14521
607-532-4800

Owners / Operators:
Joseph Myer, President / Master Distiller
John Myer, Vice President

Email: joe@myerfarmdistillers.com
Website: www.myerfarmdistillers.com
Facebook: Myer Farm Distillers
Twitter: @MFDistillers

Type: Micro-distillery. Opened in 2012.

Hours of operation:
Tasting Room, Thursday through Sunday 10:30am to 5:00pm

Tours: Available by appointment

Types of spirits produced:
Vodka, gin, whiskey, wheat spirit, bourbon

Names of spirits:
- Myer Farm Gin
- Myer Farm Vodka
- Myer Farm Ginger Vodka
- Myer Farm Blueberry Orange Vodka
- Myer Farm White Dog Wheat Spirit
- Myer Farm White Dog Corn Whiskey
- Myer Farm Strawberry-Mint Wheat Spirit
- Myer Farm Wheat Whiskey
- Myer Farm Rye Whiskey
- Myer Farm Bourbon

Best known for / most popular: Myer Farm Gin

Average bottle price: $15.00 to $38.00

Distribution: NY

Interesting facts: Not provided

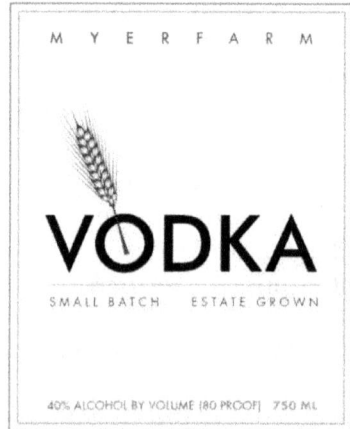

Nahmias et Fils

201 Saw Mill River Road, Bldg. C
Yonkers, NY   10701
914-294-0055

Owners / Operators:
Dorit Nahmias, President
David Nahmias, Master Distiller

Email: Dorit Nahmias: dorit@baronnahmias.com
David Nahmias: david@baronnahmias.com
Website: www.nahmiasetfils.com
Facebook: Nahmias et Fils distillery
Twitter: @nahmiasetfils

Type: Micro-distillery. Opened in 2012.

Hours of operation:
Monday through Friday, 8:00am to 6:00pm

Tours: Not available

Types of spirits produced:
Mahia and un-aged rye whiskey

Names of spirits:
- Mahia
- Legs Diamond Whiskey

Best known for / most popular: Mahia

Average bottle price: $34.99 to $44.99

Distribution: NY

Interesting facts:
Not provided

New York Distilling

79 Richardson Street
Brooklyn, NY 11211
718-412-0874

Owners / Operators:
Tom Potter, Co-founder / President
Allen Katz, Co-founder / Vice-president
Bill Potter, Co-founder / Production Manager

Email: info@nydistilling.com
Website: www.nydistilling.com
Facebook: New York Distilling Company
Twitter: @nydistilling

Type: Micro-distillery. Opened in 2011.

Hours of operation:
Monday, 6:00pm to 12:00am; Tuesday through Friday, 6:00pm to 2:00am
Saturday, 3:00pm to 2:00am; Sunday, 3:00pm to 12:00am

Tours: Available

Types of spirits produced: American rye whiskey, gin

Names of spirits:
- Perry's Tot - Navy Strength Gin
- Dorothy Parker - American Gin
- Chief Gowanus - New-Netherland Gin
- Mister Katz's Rock & Rye

Best known for / most popular:
Dorothy Parker – American Gin

Average bottle price: $31.00

Distribution: NY

Interesting facts:
Chief Gowanus - New-Netherland Gin is based on an early 19th century recipe for 'Resemblance of Holland Gin that was made in the U.S. to mimic Genever

Port Morris Distillery

PORT MORRIS DISTILLERY

780 E 133rd Street
Port Morris
Bronx, NY 10454
718-585-3192

Owners / Operators:
Rafael Barbosa, Co-owner
William Valentin, Co-owner

Email: rbarbosa@portmorrisdistillery.com
wvalentin@portmorrisdistillery.com
Website: www.portmorrisdistillery.com
Facebook: Port Morris Distillery

Type: Micro-distillery. Opened in 2012.

Hours of operation:
Monday through Friday, 9:00am to 6:00pm
Saturday, 9:00am to 8:00pm

Tours: Available by appointment

Types of spirits produced: Rum

Names of spirits:
- Pitorro Rum
- Alpunto Platinum Rum

Best known for / most popular:
Pitorro Rum

Average bottle price: $35.00

Distribution: NY

Interesting facts:
The legacy of Pitorro began in the lush mountains of Guayama, Puerto Rico.

Prohibition Distillery LLC

10 Union Street
Roscoe, NY 12776
917-685-8989

Owners / Operators:
Brian Facquet, Co-founder
John Walsh, Co-founder

Email: brian@prohibitiondistillery.com
Website: www.prohibitiondistillery.com
Facebook: Bootlegger 21 New York Vodka
Twitter: @Bootlegger21

Type: Micro-distillery. Opening in 2013.

Hours of operation: Daily

Tours: Available

Types of spirits produced: Vodka

Names of spirits:
• Bootlegger 21 Vodka

Best known for / most popular: Bootlegger 21 Vodka

Average bottle price: $25.00 to $29.00

Distribution: AZ, CA, CT, GA, MA, MD, NJ, NY, RI, TN

Interesting facts:
• The distillery is located in an old, restored, firehouse.
• Starting to make bourbon, rye, moonshine and gin

Saratoga Distilleries Inc.

2474 Old Mill Road
Galway, NY 12074
518-879-1793

Owners / Operators:
Richard F. DeVall, President / Head Distiller
David F. DeVall, Vice-president / Plant Manager

Email: richdevall@saratogadistilleries.com
Website: www.saragogadistilleries.com
Facebook: Saratoga Distilleries, Inc.

Type: Micro-distillery. Opened in 2011.

Hours of operation: Vary

Tours: Available by appointment

Types of spirits produced: Bourbon

Names of spirits:
• Saratoga Single Barrel Bourbon

Best known for / most popular:
Saratoga Single Barrel Bourbon

Average bottle price: Not provided

Distribution: NY

Interesting facts: Not provided

Shinn Estate Vineyards and Farmhouse

2000 Oregon Road
Mattituck, NY 11952
631-804-0367

Owners / Operators:
David Page, Owner / Distiller

Email: info@shinnestatevineyards.com
Website: www.shinnestatevineyards.com
Facebook: Shinn Estate Vineyards
Twitter: @shinnvineyard

Type: Winery / Micro-distillery. Opened in 2010.

Hours of operation:
Monday through Thursday, 10:30am to 5:00pm
Friday and Saturday, 10:30am to 8:00pm; Sunday, 10:30am to 5:00pm

Tours: Available

Types of spirits produced: Brandy, grappa

Names of spirits:
- Shinn Estate Vineyards Eau de Vie
- Shinn Estate Vineyards Shine

Best known for / most popular: Shinn Estate Vineyards Shine

Average bottle price: $25.00 to $48.00

Distribution: NY

Interesting facts: Not provided

Six Mile Creek Winery & Distillery

1551 Slaterville Road
Ithaca, NY 14850
607-272-9463

Owners / Operators:
Nancy and Roger Battistella, Owners
Paul King, Production Supervisor
Peter Masse, General Manager
Will Adams, Tasting Room Manager
Melissa Croes, Asst. Tasting Room Manager

Email: info@sixmilecreek.com
Website: www.sixmilecreek.com
Facebook: Six Mile Creek
Twitter: @SixMileCreek
Yelp: Six Mile Creek Vineyard

Type: Winery / Micro-distillery. Opened in 1987.

Hours of operation:
Monday through Thursday, 11:00am to 6:00pm
Friday and Saturday, 10:00am to 6:00pm; Sunday, 11:00am to 5:00pm

Tours: Available

Types of spirits produced: Vodka, gin, limoncella, grappa

Names of spirits:
- Six Mile Creek Vodka
- Six Mile Creek Gin
- Six Mile Creek Grappa
- Six Mile Creek Limoncella

Best known for / most popular: Six Mile Creek Vodka

Average bottle price: Not provided

Distribution: Not provided

Interesting facts: Not provided

StilltheOne Distillery LLC

1 Martin Place
Port Chester, NY 10573
914-217-0347

Owners / Operators:
Ed and Laura Tiedge, Owners

Email: ed@stilltheonedistillery.com
Website: www.combvodka.com
Facebook: COMB Vodka, StilltheOne Distillery
Twitter: @Comb_CTO

Type: Micro-distillery. Opened in 2007.

Hours of operation: Daily, 7:00am to 5:00pm

Tours: Available by appointment

Types of spirits produced: Vodka, whiskey, gin, brandy

Names of spirits:
- COMB Vodka
- COMB 9 Gin
- COMB Blossom Brandy
- Westchester Whiskey

Best known for / most popular: COMB Vodka

Average bottle price: $34.00

Distribution: CA, CT, IL, ND, NY

Interesting facts: This is the first legal distillery in Westchester since Prohibition.

COMB
SPIRITS
Distilled From Honey

COMB VODKA • COMB 9 GIN

224

Stoutridge Distillery

10 Ann Kaley Lane
Marlboro, NY 12542
845-236-7620

Owners / Operators:
Stephen Osborn, Owner / Operator
Kimberly Wagner, Owner / Operator

Email: steve@stoutridge.com
Website: www.stoutridge.com

Type: Winery / Micro-distillery. Opened in 2009.

Hours of operation: Friday through Sunday, 11:00am to 6:00pm year-round

Tours: Available.

Types of spirits produced:
Brandy, grappa, vodka, gin, corn, rye whiskey

Names of spirits:
- Northern Threat Yankee Bourbon
- Wagner's White Lightning
- Stoutridge Vodka
- Stoutridge Gin

Best known for / most popular: Stoutridge Gin

Average bottle price: Not provided

Distribution: Sold exclusively at the winery / distillery

Interesting facts: The distillery is built on the site of a Prohibition era distillery.

The Noble Experiment NYC

23A Meadow Street
Brooklyn, NY 11206
718-381-3693

Owners / Operators:
Bridget C. Firtle, Founder / President

Email: info@tnenyc.com
Website: www.tnenyc.com
Facebook: The Noble Experiment NYC
Twitter: @tneNYC, @owneysNYC
Instagram: tnenyc

Type: Micro-distillery. Opened in 2012.

Hours of operation: Monday through Saturday, 10:00am to 6:00pm

Tours: Available Saturdays at 2:00pm, 4:00pm

Types of spirits produced: Rum

Names of spirits:
• Owney's NYC Rum

Best known for / most popular: Owney's NYC Rum

Average bottle price: $34.00 to $36.00

Distribution: NY

Interesting facts: The distillery is housed in a, turn of the century, warehouse.

Tirado Distillery

888 E. 163rd Street
Bronx, NY   10459

Owners / Operators:
Dr. Renee Hernandez Tirado, Owner

Email: madhern@yahoo.com
Website: www.tiradowhiskey.com
Facebook: Tirado Whiskey

Type: Micro-distillery. Opened in 2011.

Hours of operation: Monday through Friday, 9:00am to 5:00pm

Tours: Available

Types of spirits produced: Whiskey, rum, liqueur

Names of spirits:
- Tirado Gold
- Tirado NY Corn Whiskey
- Tirado El Caribe Whiskey
- Tirado Maple Delight
- Tirado El Pitito Rum

Best known for / most popular: Not provided

Average bottle price: Not provided

Distribution: NY

Interesting facts:
First legal distillery in the Bronx since prohibition

Tuthilltown Spirits Distillery

14 Grist Mill Lane
Gardiner, NY 12525
Tuthilltown office: 845-255-1527
Retail store / Tour reservations: 845-633-8734

Owners / Operators:
Ralph Erenzo, Founder / Distiller
Brian Lee, Founder / Distiller
Gable Erenzo, Distiller / Ambassador / Manager
Joel Elder, Chief R & D Distiller
Cathy Erenzo, Executive Manager
Michael Chichetti, Whiskey Production Manager
Brendan O'Rourke, Rick House and Packaging Manager

Email: info@tuthilltown.com
Website: www.tuthilltown.com
Facebook: Tuthilltown Spirits, Hudson Whiskey
Twitter: @Tuthilltown, @HudsonWhiskey

Type: Micro-distillery. Opened in 2005.

Hours of operation:
Thursday through Monday, 11:00am to 6:00pm
Sunday, 12:00pm to 6:00pm

Tours: Available

Types of spirits produced:
Bourbon, rum, whiskey, vodka, seasonal liqueurs, eau de vie

Names of spirits:
Hudson Whiskeys
- Single Malt
- Baby Bourbon
- Four Grain Bourbon
- Manhattan Rye
- Indigenous Vodka: Fresh Pressed Apple
- New York Corn Whiskey
- Half Moon Gin
- Tuthilltown Barrel Aged Cassis
- Basement Bitters

Best known for: Hudson Baby Bourbon

Average bottle price: $28.00 to $45.00

Distribution: International

Interesting facts:
- Tuthilltown Spirits is New York's first whiskey distillery since Prohibition.
- Hudson Baby Bourbon was the first bourbon whiskey to be distilled in NY.

228

Van Brunt Stillhouse

6 Bay Street
Brooklyn, NY 11231
718-852-6405

Owners / Operators:
Daric Schlesselman, Owner / Distiller

Email: info@VanBruntStillhouse.com
Website: www.vanbruntstillhouse.com
Facebook: Van Brunt Stillhouse
Twitter: @VBStillhouse

Type: Micro-distillery. Opened in 2012.

Hours of operation: Not provided

Tours: Available by appointment

Types of spirits produced: Rum, whiskey, grappa

Names of spirits:
- Due North Rum
- Red Hook Grappa
- Van Brunt Stillhouse Whiskey

Best known for / most popular: Due North Rum

Average bottle price: $25.00 to $50.00

Distribution: NYC metro area

Interesting facts: Not provided

Warwick Valley Distillery

114 Little York Road
Warwick, NY 10990
845-258-6020

Owners / Operators:
Jason Grizzanti, Owner
Jeremy Kidde, Owner
Joseph Grizzanti, Owner

Email: wvwinery@warwick.net
Website: www.wvwinery.com
Facebook: Warwick Valley Winery and Distillery

Type: Winery / Micro-distillery. Opened in 2002.

Hours of operation: Daily, 11:00am to 6:00pm

Tours: Available by appointment only

Types of spirits produced: Bourbon, gin, brandy, liqueurs

Names of spirits:
- American Fruits™ Apple Brandy
- American Fruits™ Pear Brandy
- American Fruits™ Black Currant Cordial
- American Fruits™ Bartlett Pear Liqueur
- American Fruits™ Sour Cherry Cordial
- American Fruits™ Burbon Barrel Aged Apple Liqueur
- Warwick Rustic American Gin

Best known for / most popular: Warwick Rustic American Gin

Average bottle price: Not provided

Distribution: U.S.

Interesting facts:
In 2002, Warwick Valley Winery & Distillery became the first licensed distillery in the Hudson Valley since Prohibition.

Adam Dalton Distillery

251 Biltmore Avenue
Asheville, NC 28801
336-413-1657

Owners / Operators:
Adam Dalton, Owner / Manager / Distiller
Joan Dalton, Owner / Manager / CFO

Email: adamdaltondistillery@gmail.com
Website: www.addistillery.com
Facebook: Adam Dalton Distillery
Twitter: @ADDistillery

Type: Micro-distillery. Opened in 2011.

Hours of operation:
Monday through Friday, 5:00pm until close
Saturday and Sunday, 3:00pm until close

Tours: Available by appointment

Types of spirits produced: Rum, blue agave, vodka, moonshine, whiskey

Names of spirits:
• White Widow

Best known for / most popular: White Widow

Average bottle price: $19.99

Distribution: North Carolina

Interesting facts: First legal distillery in Asheville NC since prohibition.

Asheville Distilling Company

12 Old Charlotte Highway
Asheville, NC 28803
828-575-2000

Owners / Operators:
Troy Ball, Owner / Founder
Charlie Ball, Master Distiller

Email: info@troyandsons.com
Website: www.troyandsons.com
Facebook: Troy and Sons
Twitter: @troyandsons
Youtube: Asheville Distilling

Type: Micro-distillery. Opened in 2010.

Hours of operation: Thursday through Saturday, 5:00pm to 7:00pm

Tours: Available

Types of spirits produced: Moonshine

Names of spirits:
- Troy & Sons Blonde Whiskey
- Troy & Sons Oak Reserve Whiskey
- Troy & Sons Platinum Heirloom Moonshine Whiskey

Best known for / most popular: Troy & Sons Platinum Moonshine

Average bottle price: $29.95 to $49.95

Distribution: FL, NC, SC, TN, TX

Interesting facts: Troy is the first woman to start a whiskey distillery in modern times.

Blue Ridge Distilling Company

228 Redbud Lane
Bostic, NC 28018
828-245-2041

Owners / Operators:
Tim Ferris, Owner

Email: info@blueridgedistilling.com
Website: www.blueridgedistilling.com
Facebook: Blue Ridge Distilling Co., Inc.
Twitter: @blueridgedistil
Instagram: BlueRidgeDistilling

Type: Micro-distillery. Opened in 2010.

Hours of operation: Daily

Tours: Available by appointment

Types of spirits produced: Whisky

Names of spirits:
- Defiant Whisky, An American Single Malt

Best known for / most popular: Defiant American Single Malt Whisky

Average bottle price: $54.95

Distribution: NC. Expanded distribution in 2013.

Interesting facts: "Defiantly Redefining Whisky" - Tim Ferris

The History

NESTLED IN THE GOLDEN VALLEY REGION OF BOSTIC, NORTH CAROLINA, BLUE RIDGE DISTILLING CO. BEGAN IN A BARN ON A FORGOTTEN CORNER OF THE FAMILY FARM. REMNANTS OF OLD MOONSHINE STILLS ARE A COMMON SIGHT UP THE SURROUNDING CREEKS. FOUNDER, TIM FERRIS, TRAVELS THE WORLD AS A DEEP-SEA DIVER, VISITING MANY DISTILLERIES ON HIS JOURNEY AND FINDING INSPIRATION ALONG THE WAY. AT BLUE RIDGE DISTILLING CO., OUR PASSIONS ARE THE CREATION OF THE FINEST SPIRITS KNOWN TO MAN AND THE DISCOVERY OF HOW TO MAKE THEM EVEN BETTER. VISIT OUR WEBSITE blueridgedistilling.com TO LEARN MORE ABOUT US AND WHAT MAKES US DEFIANT.

TIM FERRIS
FOUNDER

DEFIANT.

AMERICAN SINGLE MALT

WHISKY

Distilled from 100% Malted Barley & Pure Mountain Spring Water

BY
BLUE RIDGE DISTILLING CO.
GOLDEN VALLEY, NC

(82 PROOF) 750ML 41% ALC./VOL. CASK#

The Whisky

DEFIANT SINGLE MALT WHISKY STARTS WITH WATER DRAWN FROM DEEP UNDER THE DISTILLERY AND IS OF SUCH NATURAL PURITY, IT IS NOT ALTERED IN ANY WAY. WE USE 100% MALTED BARLEY, COLD-GROUND ON OUR GRANITE STONE MILL. THE FRESHLY MILLED GRIST BEGINS THE MASHING PROCESS JUST MOMENTS LATER. SPECIALLY CULTURED YEAST, EXPERTLY PITCHED, GIVES IT LIFE. A HANDBUILT COPPER POTSTILL CAPTURES THE ELUSIVE SPIRIT. TOASTED AMERICAN WHITE OAK SOFTENS THE WHISKY, DEVELOPING A RICH AMBER COLOR AND DELICATE NOTES OF HONEY, VANILLA, CARAMEL AND TANNINS.

Blue Ridge
DISTILLING CO.
GOLDEN VALLEY, NORTH CAROLINA

Broadslab Distillery LLC

4870 NC Highway 50 South
Benson, NC 27504
919-291-0691

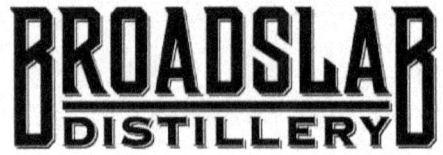

Owners / Operators:
Jeremy Norris, Owner / Distiller

Email: broadslabdistillery@gmail.com
Website: www.broadslabdistillery.com
Facebook: Broadslab Distillery
Twitter: @BroadslabStill

Type: Micro-distillery. Opened in 2011.

Hours of operation: Not open to the public

Tours: Available by appointment

Types of spirits produced: Moonshine, rum

Names of spirits:
* Broadslab Legacy Shine
* Broadslab Legacy Reserve
* Carolina Coast Rum

Best known for / most popular: Broadslab Legacy Shine

Average bottle price: $22.95 to $25.95

Distribution: GA, NC, SC

Interesting facts: Broadslab Distillery is located in "Broadslab," which is the infamous moonshine capital of Johnston County, NC.

Howling Moon Distillery

Asheville, NC 28814

Owners / Operators:
Cody Bradford, Owner / CEO
Chivous Downey, President
Austin Bradford, Bottling and Packaging / Operations Manager

Email: info@howlingmoonshine.com
Website: www.howlingmoonshine.com
Facebook: Howling Moon Distillery

Type: Micro-distillery. Opened in 2010.

Hours of operation: Not open to the public

Tours: Not available

Types of spirits produced: Moonshine

Names of spirits:
• Raymond Fairchilds Mountain Moonshine
• Apple Pie Moonshine

Best known for / most popular: Raymond Fairchilds Mountain Monshine

Average bottle price: $24.95

Distribution: NC

Interesting facts:
• Cody is a fifth generation moonshiner
• Some of his equipment was his great-great-grandfathers.
• The moonshine recipe is 150 years old.

Muddy River Distillery

1500 River Drive, #250
Belmont, NC 28012
336-516-4190

Owners / Operators:
Robbie Delaney, Owner

Email: muddyriverdistillery@gmail.com
Website: www.carolinarum.com
          www.muddyriverdistillery.com
Facebook: Muddy River Distillery LLC
Twitter: @1stCarolinaRum

Type: Micro-distillery. Opened in 2012.

Hours of operation: Friday and Saturday

Tours: Available

Types of spirits produced: Rum

Names of spirits:
• Carolina Rum

Best known for: Carolina Rum

Distribution: NC

Interesting facts:
• First legal rum distillery in NC
• American made equipment designed and built by the distiller
• Winner of the 2012 Big Sip Cup Best in Show for Spirituous Liquor

236

Piedmont Distillers

3690 US Hwy 220
Madison, NC 27025
336-445-0055

Owners / Operators:
Joe Michalek, Founder
Junior Johnson, Co-Owner

Email: info@piedmontdistillers.com
Website: www.piedmontdistillers.com
Facebook: Junior Johnson's Midnight Moon, Catdaddy
Carolina Moonshine
Twitter: @JJMidnightMoon, @CatdaddyShine

Type: Micro-distillery. Opened in 2005.

Hours of operation: N/A

Tours: Not available

Types of spirits produced: Moonshine

Names of spirits:
- Junior Johnson's Midnight Moon
- Catdaddy Spiced Moonshine

Best known for:
Junior Johnson's Midnight Moon and
Catdaddy Spiced Moonshine

Average bottle price: $20.00 to $30.00

Distribution: Available in all 50 states

Interesting facts:
Midnight Moon is one of the only legal moonshine made with real fruit.

Southern Artisan Spirits

Kings Mountain, NC 28086
704-297-0191

Owners / Operators:
Charlie Mauney, Co-owner
Alex Mauney, Co-owner

Email: info@southernartisanspirits.com
Website: www.southernartisanspirits.com
Facebook: Southern Artisan Spirits
Twitter: @CardinalGin

Type: Micro-distillery. Opened in 2010.

Hours of operation: Not provided

Tours: Not provided

Types of spirits produced: Gin

Names of spirits:
• Cardinal Gin

Best known for / most popular: Not provided

Average bottle price: Not provided

Distribution: DC, GA, MD, NC, NJ, SC, VA

Interesting facts: Not provided

The Brothers Vilgalys Spirits Company

803 D Ramseur Street
Durham, NC 27701

Owners / Operators:
Rimas Vilgalys, Founder / CEO

Email: vilgalys@gmail.com
Website: www.brothersvilgalys.com
Facebook: Brothers Vilgalys Spirits
Twitter: @BrosVilgalys

Type: Micro-distillery. Opened in 2012.

Hours of operation: Vary

Tours: Not available

Types of spirits produced: Spiced Honey Liqueur (presently from GNS)

Names of spirits:
• Krupnikas

Best known for: Krupnikas

Average bottle price: $29.95

Distribution: NC

Interesting facts:
Krupnikas is a spiced honey liqueur traditional to Lithuanian and Polish communities

239

Top of the Hill Distillery

505 West Franklin Street, Suite C
Chapel Hill, NC 27516
919-699-8703

Owners / Operators:
Scott Maitland, Proprietor
Esteban McMahan, Spirit Guide
George Dusek, Head Distiller
Keith Crissman, Distiller

Email: info@topodistillery.com
Website: www.topodistillery.com
Facebook: TOPO Distillery
Twitter: @TOPOdistillery

Type: Micro-distillery. Opened in 2012.

Hours of operation: Monday through Friday, 8:00am to 5:00pm

Tours: Online scheduling via website

Types of spirits produced: Vodka, gin, whiskey

Names of spirits:
- TOPO Vodka
- TOPO Carolina Whiskey
- TOPO Piedmont Gin
- TOPO Age Your Own Whiskey Kits

Best known for / most popular: TOPO Vodka

Average bottle price: $21.95 to $28.95

Distribution: NC

Interesting facts: TOPO is NC's only local and organic distillery and is grain to glass

240

Windsor Run Cellars

6531 Windsor Road
Hamptonville, NC 27020
336-468-8400

VINEYARD · WINERY · DISTILLERY

Owners / Operators:
Chuck Johnson, Co-owner
Jamey Johnson, Co-owner

Email: info@windsorrun.com
Website: www.windsorrun.com
Facebook: Windsor Run Cellars

Type: Micro-distillery. Opened in 2012.

Hours of operation: Wednesday through Saturday, 10:00am to 5:00pm
                                     Sunday, 1:00pm to 5:00pm

Tours: Available

Types of spirits produced: TBA

Names of spirits:
• TBA

Best known for / most popular: TBA

Average bottle price: TBA

Distribution: TBA

Interesting facts: Not provided

Maple River Distillery

4 Langer Avenue
North Casselton, ND 58012
701-347-5900

Owners / Operators:
Greg Kempel, Co-owner
Susan Kempel, Co-owner

Email: greg@mapleriverwinery.com
Website: www.mapleriverdistillery.com
Facebook: Maple River Distillery
Twitter: @MapleRiverWine
YouTube: Maple River Winery

Type: Winery / Micro-distillery. Opened in 2009.

Hours of operation: Monday through Saturday, 9:00am to 5:00pm

Tours: Not available

Types of spirits produced: Vodkas, cordials, brandies

Names of spirits:
- Maple River Distillery Flavored Vodka
  Rhubarb, Chokecherry, Apple, Apricot, Grape, Pear, Wild Plum
- Maple River Distillery Cordial
  Chokecherry, Apple, Pear, Red Currant, Aronia Black Currant, Wild Plum
- Maple River Distillery Brandy
  Rhubarb, Chokecherry, Apricot, Apple, Grape, Pear, Wild Plum, Aronia

Best known for / most popular:
Chokecherry Brandy

Average bottle price: $9.99 to $29.99

Distribution: ND

Interesting facts: Not provided

25th Street Spirits

1947 West 25th Street
Cleveland, OH 44113
216-621-4000

Owners / Operators:
Sam McNulty, Partner
Mark Priemer, Partner
Mike Foran, Partner
Andy Tveekrem, Partner

Email: marketgardenbrewery@gmail.com
Website: www.25thstreetspirits.com
Facebook: 25th Street Spirits
Twitter: @25thSpirits

Type: Micro-distillery. Opened in 2012.

Hours of operation: Monday through Friday, 8:00am to 8:00pm

Tours: Available by appointment

Types of spirits produced: Whiskey, gin

Names of spirits:
- McNulty Whiskey
- Starling Gin

Best known for / most popular: McNulty Whiskey

Average bottle price: Not provided

Distribution: Not provided

Interesting facts: Not provided

Buckeye Distillery Inc.

130 W. Plum Street
Tipp City, OH 45371
937-877-1901

Owners / Operators:
Aaron Lee, Owner

Email: info@buckeyedistillery.com
Website: www.buckeyedistillery.com
Facebook: Buckeye Distillery

Type: Micro-distillery. Opened in 2009.

Hours of operation: Monday through Friday, 9:00am to 5:00pm

Tours: Not available

Types of spirits produced: Liqueurs

Names of spirits:
• Buckeye Distillery Cherry Liqueur
• Buckeye Distillery Blackberry Liqueur
• Buckeye Distillery Raspberry Liqueur

Best known for / most popular: Buckeye Distillery Cherry Liqueur

Average bottle price: $16.95 to $19.00

Distribution: IL, MI, OH, TN

Interesting facts: Not provided

Cleveland Whiskey LLC

1768 E 25th Street
Cleveland, OH 44114
216-881-8481

Owners / Operators:
Tom Lix, CEO

Email: tlix@clevelandwhiskey.com
Website: www.clevelandwhiskey.com
LinkedIn: www.linkedin.com/in/tomlix
Facebook: Cleveland Whiskey
Twitter: @CleveWhiskey
Pinterest: Cleveland Whiskey

Type: Micro-distillery. Opened in 2009.

Hours of operation: Daily

Tours: Appointment

Types of spirits produced: Bourbon whiskey

Names of spirits:
• Black Reserve Bourbon Whiskey

Best known for / most popular: Black Reserve

Average bottle price: $34.95

Distribution: Limited

Interesting facts: Pressure-Aged™

Crystal Spirits LLC

Dayton, OH

Owners / Operators:
Jim Finke, CEO
Tom Rambasek, President
Chris Finke, Co-founder

Email: info@crystalspiritsllc.com
Website: www.buckeyevodka.com
Facebook: Buckeye Vodka
Twitter: @BuckeyeVodka

Type: Micro-distillery. Opened in 2011.

Hours of operation: Not provided

Tours: Not provided

Types of spirits produced: Vodka

Names of spirits:
- Buckeye Vodka

Best known for / most popular: Buckeye Vodka

Average bottle price: $20.00

Distribution: Available through The Party Source

Interesting facts: Not provided

Dancing Tree Distillery

41625 Bearwallow Ridge Road
Shade, OH 45776
740-696-1159

Owners / Operators:
Kelly Sauber, Owner / Distiller
Deanna Schwartz, Project Coordinator

Email: Kelly@dancingtreedistillery.com
Website: www.dancingtreedistillery.com
Facebook: Dancing Tree Distillery
Twitter: @dtdistillery

Type: Micro-distillery. Opened in 2011.

Hours of operation: Available by appointment

Tours: Available by appointment

Types of spirits produced: Vodka, gin

Names of spirits:
- Dancing Tree Spicebush Gin
- Dancing Tree Vodka from grapes
- Dancing Tree Vodka from grains
- Dancing Tree Coffee Liqueur
- Seasonal Spirits:
  - Elderberry Brandy
  - Sorghum Rum
  - Whiskey Is In The Wood

Best known for / most popular: Dancing Tree Gin

Average bottle price: $35.00

Distribution: OH

Interesting facts:
100% distilled on premises; locally sourced, organic and non-GMO ingredients

Ernest Scarano Distillery

4487 Hayes Avenue
Freemont, OH 43420
419-205-8734

Owners / Operators:
Ernest Scarano, Owner

Email: ernie@esdistillery.com
Website: www.esdistillery.com
Facebook: Ernest Scarano Distillery

Type: Micro-distillery. Opened in 2010.

Hours of operation: Monday through Saturday, 7:30am to 8:00pm

Tours: Available by appointment. One week notice required.

Types of spirits produced: Whiskey

Names of spirits:
• Old Homicide
• Whiskey Dick

Best known for: Old Homicide

Average bottle price: $45.00 to $95.00

Distribution: Not provided

Interesting facts: Not provided

Flat Rock Spirits

5380 Intrastate Drive
Fairborn, OH 45324
937-879-4447

Owners / Operators:
James Bagford, Co-founder
Brad Measel, Co-founder
Shawn Measel, Co-founder

Email: james@flatrockspirits.com
Website: www.flatrockspirits.com
Facebook: Flat Rock Spirits
Twitter: @FlatRockSpirits

Type: Micro-distillery. Opened in 2010.

Hours of operation: Not provided

Tours: Not provided

Types of spirits produced: Bourbon

Names of spirits:
• Stillwrights Bourbon

Best known for / most popular: TBA

Average bottle price: TBA

Distribution: OH

Interesting facts: Bourbon is currently aging.

Indian Creek Distillery

7095 Staley Road
New Carlisle, OH 45344
937-846-1443

Owners / Operators:
Joe and Melissa Duer, Owners

Email: jmduer76@gmail.com
Website: www.staleymillfarmanddistillery.com
Facebook: Indian Creek Distillery

Early Stillhouse Spirits

Type: Early American Stillhouse. Opened in December 2012.

Hours of operation:
Thursday 10:00am to 5:00pm
Friday 10:00am to 7:00pm
Saturday 10:00am to 5:00pm

Tours:
Available Saturday 12:00pm, 2:00pm, 4:00pm

Types of spirits produced:
Rye whiskey, un-aged whiskey

Names of spirits:
- Staley Rye Whiskey
- Elias Staley Un-aged Rye Whiskey

Best known for / most popular:
Double Copper Distilled Rye Whiskey

Average bottle price: $50.00 to $60.00

Distribution: On-site, OH

Interesting facts:
"Created and crafted in the hearts and hands of the 6th generation, this rare and unique early American distillery brings the flavor of our storied American Rye Whiskey out of the 1800's and dares to create a hand-made authentic spirit, distinct and relevant for today."

– Indian Creek Distillery

Middle West Spirits LLC

1230 Courtland Avenue
Columbus, OH 43201
614-299-2460

Owners / Operators:
Brady Konya, General Manager / Owner
Ryan Lang, Head Distiller / Owner
Eric Boettcher, Production Manager
Josh Daily. Director of Sales
Cris Dehlavi, Brand Mixologist

Email: info@middlewestspirits.com
Website: www.middlewestspirits.com
Facebook: Middle West Spirits
Twitter: @MiddleWestSpts
LinkedIn: Middle West Spirits, LLC

Type: Craft-distillery. Opened in 2010.

Hours of operation:
Office Hours: Monday through Friday, 9:00am to 6:00pm
Gift Shop: Monday through Friday, Noon to 6pm
Gift Shop Holiday Hours: Monday through Saturday, 10:00am to 7:00pm

Tours: Available Friday and the first Saturday of each month starting at 6:00pm. There is a $15.00 fee per person effective May 1, 2013.

Types of spirits produced:
Vodka, infused seasonal vodkas, whiskey, bourbon

Names of spirits:
- OYO Vodka
- OYO Honey Vanilla Bean Vodka
- OYO Stone Fruit Vodka
- OYO Whiskey (100% Wheat)
- OYO Bourbon, Michelone Reserve (4-Grain)
- OYO Rye Whiskey (100% Dark Pumpernickel)

Best known for / most popular: OYO Whiskey

Average bottle price: $30.00 to $45.00

Distribution: DC, FL, GA, KY, LA, MD, NJ, NY, OH, PA

Interesting facts:
Middle West Spirits is the first modern craft distillery to operate in Columbus, OH, the birthplace of Prohibition.

Portside Distillery

983 Front Street
Cleveland, OH 44113
216-568-6633

Owners / Operators:
Dan Malz, Co-owner
Keith Sutton, Co-owner
John Marek, Co-owner
Matt Zappernick, Co-owner

Email: dan@portsidedistillery.com
Website: www.portsidedistillery.com
Facebook: Portside Distillery
Twitter: @_Portside_

Type: Micro-distillery. Opened in 2011.

Hours of operation:
Monday through Friday, 5:00pm to 8:00pm
Saturday, 12:00pm to 4:00pm

Tours: Not provided

Types of spirits produced: Rum

Names of spirits:
Portside Distillery Silver Rum

Best known for / most popular:
Portside Distillery Silver Rum

Average bottle price: Not provided

Distribution: Not provided

Interesting facts: Portside Distillery is the first craft-distillery in Cleveland, OH since prohibition.

252

Red Eagle Spirits

6202 South River Road
Geneva, OH 44041
440-466-6604

Owners / Operators:
Gene and Heather Sigel, Owners

Email: info@redeaglespirits.com
Website: www.redeaglespirits.com
Facebook: Red Eagle Distillery

Type: Micro-distillery. Opened in 2012.

Hours of operation:
Saturday, 1:00pm to 9:00pm
Sunday, 1:00pm to 6:00pm

Tours: Available

Types of spirits produced: Bourbon

Names of spirits:
• TBA

Best known for / most popular: TBA

Average bottle price: $23.00

Distribution: OH

Interesting facts: Bourbon is currently aging

Seven Brothers Distilling Company

7755 Brakeman Road
Painesville, OH 44077
440-897-9311

Owners / Operators:
Kevin Suttman, President

Email: promo@seven-brothers.com
Website: www.seven-brothers.com
Facebook: Seven Brothers Distilling Co

Type: Micro-distillery. Opened in 2010.

Hours of operation: Vary

Tours: Available by appointment

Types of spirits produced: Vodka, White
Rum, aged rum, spice rum, aged whiskey,
flavored vodkas, flavored rums, flavored
whiskey

Names of spirits:
- Seven Brothers Vodka
- Seven Brothers Silver Rum
- Seven Brothers 100-Proof Spiced Rum

Best known for / most popular: Seven Brothers Vodka

Average bottle price: $24.50 to $32.00

Distribution: OH

Interesting facts:
- Seven Brothers Distilling Company is one of the smallest and most unique distilleries in America.
- Seven Brothers Distilling Company has pioneered a unique "Low-Temperature" distillation technique. This process significantly lowers the distillation temperature, creating unique flavor profiles. They plan to use this technology to create many more unique and flavorful products.

Tom's Foolery
Tomsfoolery LLC

Chagrin Falls, OH 44022

Owners / Operators:
Tom Herbruck, President / Master Distiller
Lianne Herbruck, Plant Manager
Erik Rothschiller, Brewer / Distiller

Email: tom@tomsfoolery.com
            lianne@tomsfoolery.com
Website: www.tomsfoolery.com
            www.applejackohio.com
Facebook: Tom's Foolery—A Spirited Venture

Type: Micro-distillery. Opened in 2008.

Hours of operation: Daily, hours vary

Tours: Not available

Types of spirits produced: Applejack, bourbon, rye

Names of spirits:
• Tom's Foolery Applejack

Best known for / most popular: Tom's Foolery Applejack

Average bottle price: $38.00

Distribution: OH

Interesting facts: Tomsfoolery is certified organic.

Watershed Distillery

1145 Chesapeake Avenue
Columbus, OH 43221
614-357-1936

Owners / Operators:
Greg Lehman, Co-owner
Dave Rigo, Co-owner

Email: info@watersheddistillery.com
Website: www.watersheddistillery.com
Facebook: Watershed Distillery
Twitter: @Watershed_Ohio
Pinterest: Watershed Distillery
YouTube: watersheddistillery1

Type: Micro-distillery. Opened in 2010.

Hours of operation: Daily

Tours: Available

Types of spirits produced: Vodka, gin, bourbon

Names of spirits:
• Watershed Distillery Bourbon
• Watershed Distillery Bourbon Barrel Gin
• Watershed Distillery Four Peel Gin
• Watershed Distillery Vodka

Best known for / most popular: Bourbon

Average bottle price: $22.99 to $34.99

Distribution: OH

Interesting facts:
• The first bourbon distilled in Columbus since prohibition.
• Watershed's use of "spent grains'" reduces the cost of farming and provides for a more sustainable Ohio.

256

Woodstone Creek

4934 Provident Drive
Cincinnati, OH 45246

Owners / Operators:
Donald Outterson, Owner / Distiller

Email: woodstonecreek@yahoo.com
Website: www.woodstonecreek.com
Facebook: Woodstone Creek

Type: Micro-distillery. Opened in 1999.

Hours of operation: Saturday, 1:00pm to 5:00pm

Tours: Not available

Types of spirits produced: Bourbon, single malt (peated and unpeated), white dogs, varietal whisky (barley, rye, wheat, corn), vodka, rum, gin, grape brandy, honey brandy, bierschnaps

Names of spirits:
- Woodstone Creek 5 Grain Straight Bourbon Whisky
- Woodstone Creek Vodka
- Woodstone Creek Single Barrel Peated Single Malt Whisky

Best known for / most popular:
Woodstone Creek 5-Grain Straight Bourbon Whiskey

Average bottle price: $20.00 to $185.00

Distribution: CO, IL, IN, KY, OH

Interesting facts:
Woodstone Creek is Ohio's first licensed micro-distillery.

Donald originated the micro-distillery license in Ohio in 1998. Additionally, he worked to change the liquor law in 2008 when he introduced legislation to allow self-sales for micros in the state. Legislation to allow spirits tastings was finally passed in 2012.

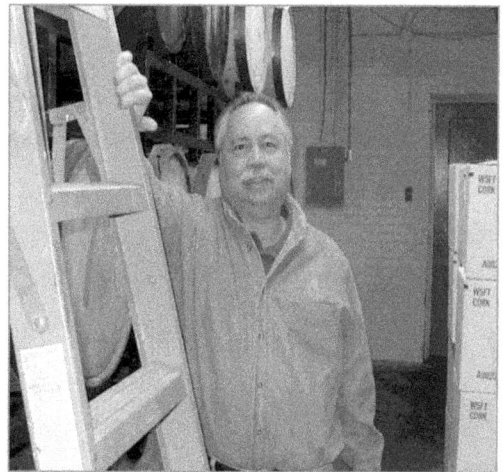

Prairie Wolf Spirits

124 East Oklahoma Avenue
Guthrie, OK 73044
405-590-7619

Owners / Operators:
David Merritt, President
Hunter Merritt, Manager
Blake Merritt, Head Distiller

Email: info@prairiewolfspirits.com
Website: www.prairiewolfspirits.com
Facebook: Prairie Wolf Spirits
Twitter: @PWSpirits

Type: Micro-distillery. Opened in 2013.

Hours of operation: Not open to the public

Tours: Not available

Types of spirits produced: Vodka

Names of spirits:
• Prairie Wolf Vodka

Best known for / most popular:
Prairie Wolf Vodka

Average bottle price: $20.00

Distribution: OK

Interesting facts:
• Prairie Wolf Spirits is fully wind powered.
• The first licensed active distiller in Oklahoma.

4 Spirits Distillery

6040 NE Marcus Harris Avenue
Adair Village, OR 97330
541-760-0696

Owners / Operators:
Dawson Officer, Owner / Distiller
Sarah Wayt, Marketing and Sales Director

Email: dawson@4spiritsdistillery.com, sarah@4spiritsdistillery.com
Website: www.4spiritsdistillery.com
Facebook: 4 Spirits Distillery

Type: Micro-distillery. Opened in 2011.

Hours of operation: Vary

Tours: Available

Types of spirits produced: Vodka, whiskey

Names of spirits:
- WebFoot Vodka
- SlapTail Vodka
- 4 Spirits Whiskey

Best known for / most popular: All

Average bottle price: $11.95 to $26.50

Distribution: OR

Interesting facts: 4 Spirits Distillery pays homage to all U.S. war veterans and active service members so that we should never forget their service and sacrifice to our country. Specifically and on a very personal level of the owner, the distillery is dedicated to four combat soldiers who he served with in the Oregon National Guard 2 Battalion, 162 Infantry Brigade. They are Lt. Erik McCrae, Sgt. Justin Linden, Sgt. Justin Eyerly and Sgt. David Roustum. These four men lost their lives in 2004 serving in Baghdad, Iraq. They were combat soldiers and fought side by side in Delta Co. 2-162 Infantry.

259

Bendistillery

19330 Pinehurst Road
Bend, OR 97701
541-318-0200

Owners / Operators:
Jim Bendis, Founder & Chairman
Alan Dietrich, Chief Executive Officer
Jennah Padilla, Vice President/Operations
James Padilla, National Sales Manager
Francoise Labbe, Private Label Director

Email: info@bendistillery.com
Website: www.bendistillery.com
Facebook: Crater Lake Vodka & Gin, Bend Distillery
Twitter: @bendistillery

Type: Micro-distillery. Opened in 1995.

Hours of operation:
Monday through Thursday, 9:00am to 5:00pm
Friday, 9:00am to 6:00pm; Saturday, noon to 6:00pm

Tours: Available

Types of spirits produced: Gin, vodka, rum

Names of spirits:
• Crater Lake Gin
• Crater Lake Vodka
• Crater Lake Reserve Vodka
• Crater Lake Hazelnut Espresso Vodka
• Crater Lake Pepper Vodka
• Crater Lake Sweet Ginger Vodka

Best known for / most popular: Crater Lake Gin

Average bottle price: $22.95 to $29.95

Distribution: AZ, CA, DC, GA, HI, ID, IL, MA, MD, MN, MT, NM, OR, PA, RI, TN, TX, WA, WI, WY

Interesting facts: Will be launching an Estate line of spirits that are crafted from products grown entirely at the distillery. The first in the series will be a gin.

Big Bottom Whiskey

21420 NW Nicholas Court, Ste. D-9
Hillsboro, OR 97124
503-608-7816

Owners / Operators:
Ted Pappas, Founder / Owner

Email: info@bigbottomwhiskey.com
Website: www.bigbottomwhiskey.com
Facebook: Big Bottom Whiskey
Twitter: @bbwhiskey

Type: Craft-distillery/ Independent Bottler. Opened in 2010.

Hours of operation:
Tasting Room: Saturdays, 12:00pm to 4:00pm or by appointment

Tours: Available by appointment

Types of spirits produced: Straight bourbon whiskey

Names of spirits:
- Big Bottom Whiskey American Straight Bourbon Whiskey
- Big Bottom Whiskey Straight Bourbon Whiskey Finished in Port Casks
- Big Bottom Whiskey Straight Bourbon Whiskey Finished in Zinfandel Casks

Best known for / most popular: Pear's Big Bottom

Average bottle price: $29.95 to $34.95

Distribution: CA, GA, IL, NV, OR, SC, TN, WA

Black Rock Distillery LLC

32405 Highway 19-207
Spray, OR 97874
541-420-4748

Owners / Operators:
Galen B. Fischer, Co-owner
Isaiah Fischer, Co-owner
Wes Whelchel, Co-owner

Email: 9rocksvodka@gmail.com
Website: www.blackrockdistillery.com, www.ninerocksvodka.com
        www.9rocksvodka.com
Facebook: 9 Rocks Vodka Southern Oregon, Nine Rocks Vodka
Twitter: @9rocksvodka

Type: Micro-distillery. Opened in 2010.

Hours of operation: N/A

Tours: Available by appointment

Types of spirits produced: Vodka

Names of spirits:
• 9 Rocks Vodka

Best known for / most popular:
9 Rocks Vodka

Average bottle price: $23.95

Distribution: OR

Interesting facts: 9 Rocks Vodka is gluten free. Made in Spray, Oregon; a small rural outpost located on the unabated John Day River 2.5 hrs NE of Bend, OR.

Brandy Peak Distillery

18526 Tetley Road
Brookings, OR 97415
541-469-0194

Owners / Operators:
David and Georgia Nowlin, Owners

Email: distiller@brandypeak.com
Website: www.brandypeak.com
Facebook: Brandy Peak Distillery

Type: Micro-distillery. Opened in 1994.

Hours of operation:
Open March through the first weekend of January
Tuesday through Saturday, 1:00pm to 5:00pm

Tours: Available

Types of spirits produced:
Brandy, grappa, liqueur

Names of spirits:
- Brandy Peak Natural Pear Brandy
- Brandy Peak Aged Pear Brandy
- Brandy Peak Aged Pinot Noir Brandy
- Brandy Peak Spirit of Muscat Brandy
- Brandy Peak Aged Muscat Brandy
- Brandy Peak Grappa
- Brandy Peak Aged Grape Brandy
- Brandy Peak Blackberry Liqueur

Best known for / most popular:
Brandy Peak Aged Pear Brandy

Average bottle price: $20.00 to $32.00

Distribution: CA, OR

Interesting facts
- Spirits are distilled in wood-fired pot stills that are unique in the industry.
- It takes fourteen pounds of pears to make a 375ml bottle of the pear brandy.
- No artificial additives, colorings or flavorings are used.
- Brandy Peak is named after the highest mountain in Curry County.

Bull Run Distilling Company

2259 NW Quimby Street
Portland, OR 97210
503-224-3483

Owners / Operators:
Lee Medoff, Co-founder / Head Distiller
Patrick Bernards, Co-founder / Chief Enthusiast
John Rudi, President

Email: patrick@bullrundistillery.com
Website: www.bullrundistillery.com
Facebook: Bull Run Distilling Company
Twitter: @BullRunSpirits
YouTube: BullRunDistillingCo. Channel

Type: Micro-distillery. Opened in 2011.

Hours of operation:
Monday through Friday, 9:00am to 5:00pm
Tasting Room and Retail Store Hours, Vary. See website.

Tours:
Available Thursday through Sunday by reservation only

Types of spirits produced: Rum, gin, whiskey, vodka, limited release line of sweet and bitter liqueurs, schnapps, aquavit

Names of spirits:
- Pacific Rum
- Oregon Whiskey
- Medoyeff Vodka
- Aria Portland Dry Gin
- Temperance Trader Bourbon Barrel Strength
- Temperance Trader Straight Bourbon Whiskey
- Temperance – A limited release line of spirits sold exclusively at Bull Run Distillery that may include, but may not be limited to: Aquavit, Sweet & Bitter Liqueurs, Flavored Vodka, Absinthe, Flavored Rums, and Schnapps

Best known for / most popular:
The Medoyeff Mule, Bull Run Distillings take on the famous Moscow Mule, the cocktail that put vodka on the map in the U.S. back in the 1950's

Average bottle price: $27.95 to $32.95

Distribution: CA, DC, IL, KS, NY, OR, TX, WA

Interesting facts: Not provided

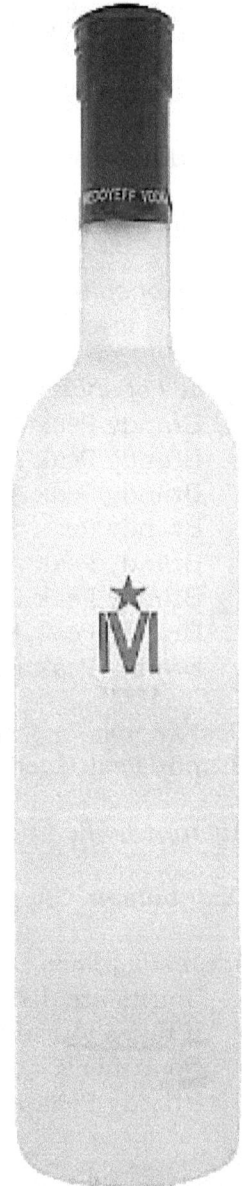

Cascade Peak Spirits Distillery
Home of Organic Nation

280 E. Hersey Street
Ashland, OR   97520
541-482-3160

Owners / Operators:
Diane Paulson, Co-founder / Owner
David Eliasen, Co-founder / Owner / Distiller

Email: spirits@organicnationspirits.com
Website: www.organicnationspirits.com
Facebook: Organic Nation Spirits
Twitter: @OGNationSpirits
LinkedIn: Diane Paulson
YouTube: Certified Organic Spirits

Type: Micro-distillery. Opened in 2007.

Hours of operation: Open year-round on a short schedule and by appointment

Tours: Available by appointment only

Types of spirits produced:
Certified organic vodka, gin, rye whiskey

Names of spirits:
• Organic Nation Vodka
• Organic Nation Gin
• Oldfield Rye Whiskey

Best known for / most popular:
Organic Nation Gin and Vodka, and a Bees Knees cocktail

Average bottle price: $30.00 to $55.00

Distribution: CA, OR

Interesting facts
Cascade Peak Spirits is the first certified organic artisan distiller in the Pacific Northwest creating uniquely crafted organic spirits.

Clear Creek Distillery

2389 NW Wilson
Portland, OR 97210
503-248-9470

Owners / Operators:
Steve McCarthy, Owner

Email: steve@clearcreekdistillery.com

Website: www.clearcreekdistillery.com

Facebook: Clear Creek Distillery

Type: Micro-distillery. Opened in 1985.

Hours of operation: Vary by season
Tasting Room and Store hours: Monday through Saturday, 9:00am to 5:00pm

Tours: Available

Types of spirits produced: Whiskey, brandy, grappa, liqueur

Names of spirits
- Williams Pear Brandy
- Pear in the Bottle
- Eau de Vie de Pomme
- Apple Brandy
- Apple in the Bottle
- Kirschwasser (Cherry Brandy)
- Blue Plum Brandy (Slivovitz)
- Framboise (Raspberry)
- Eau de Vie of Douglas Fir
- Grappa Moscato
- Marc de Gewürztraminer
- Grappa of Oregon Pinot Noir
- McCarthy's Oregon Single Malt Whiskey
- Grappa of Pinot Grigio
- Cavatappi Nebbiolo Grappa
- Cavatappi Sangiovese Grappa
- Oregon Pot Distilled Brandy
- Cranberry Liqueur
- Blackberry Liqueur
- Loganberry Liqueur
- Cassis Liqueur
- Cherry Liqueur
- Raspberry Liqueur
- Pear Liqueur
- Mirabelle Plum

Best known for / most popular:
McCarthy's Oregon Single Malt Whiskey

Average bottle price: $25.00 to $80.00

Distribution: 35 states

Interesting facts: Not provided

266

Dogwood Distilling

1835 19th Avenue
Forest Grove, OR 97116
503-359-7705

Owners / Operators:
Matt Hottenroth, Owner

Email: info@dogwooddistilling.com
Website: www.dogwooddistilling.com
Facebook: Dogwood Distilling
Twitter: @UnionGin

Type: Craft-distillery. Opened in 2010.

Hours of operation: Not provided

Tours: Not provided

Types of spirits produced: Gin, vodka

Names of spirits:
- Union Gin
- DL Franklin Vodka

Best known for / most popular: DL Franklin Vodka

Average bottle price: $15.95 to $21.95

Distribution: OR

Interesting facts: Not provided

Eastside Distilling
Formerly Deco Distilling

1512 SE 7th Avenue
Portland, OR 97214
503-926-7060

Owners / Operators:
Lenny Gotter, Owner
Bill Adams, Owner

Email: info@eastsidedistilling.com
events@eastsidedistilling.com
Website: www.eastsidedistilling.com
Facebook: Eastside Distilling
Twitter: @eastsidedistill
Yelp: Eastside Distilling
YouTube: Eastside Distilling Channel

Type: Micro-distillery. Opened in 2008.

Tasting room hours:
Monday through Thursday, 12:00pm to 5:00pm
Friday, 12:00pm to 7:30pm
Saturday, 11:00am to 6:00pm
Sunday, 12:00pm to 5:00pm

Tours: Available with Groupon, Living Social, Mercperk, and Fox12 Daily Deals

Types of spirits produced:
Rum, bourbon, vodka, seasonal liqueurs

Names of spirits:
- Below Deck Silver Rum
- Below Deck Coffee Rum
- Below Deck Ginger Rum
- Burnside Bourbon
- Double Barrel Burnside Bourbon
- Portland Potato Vodka
- Cherry Bomb Whiskey
- Peppermint Bark Liqueur
- Egg Nog Advocaat Liqueur
- Holiday Spiced Liqueur

Best known for / most popular: Burnside Bourbon

Average bottle price: $15.95 to $43.95

Distribution: OR, WA

Interesting facts: Not provided

Elixir Inc.

1050 Bethel Drive
Eugene, OR 97405
541-345-2257

Owners / Operators:
Andrea Loreto, President / CEO

Email: contact@elixir-us.com
Website: www.calisaya.net, www.irisliqueur.com
Twitter: @CalisayaLiqueur, @IrisLiqueur

Type: Micro-distillery. Opened in 2011.

Hours of operation:
Monday through Friday, 9:00am to 5:00pm

Tours: Available by appointment

Types of spirits produced: Liqueurs

Names of spirits:
- Calisaya
- Iris

Best known for / most popular: Calisaya

Average bottle price: $47.00

Distribution: CA, DC, OR, WA

Interesting facts:
- Elixir® craft distillery, founded by Italian brothers Andrea and Mario Loreto in Eugene, Oregon, is dedicated to revivifying traditional spirits in the Italian tradition using the finest all-natural ingredients. All of Elixirs spirits are composed of pure McKenzie River water and grain neutral spirit.
- Elixir® is producing two botanical liqueurs Calisaya® and Iris™. Iris™ is a floral liqueur derived from pure iris root and Calisaya® is an "amaro" based on cinchona bark.

269

Glaser Estate Winery and Distillery

213 Independence Lane
Roseburg, OR 97471
541-580-4867

Owners / Operators:
David and Sandra Glaser, Owners
Leon Glaser, Master Distiller

Email: info@glaserestatewinery.com
Website: www.glaserestatewinery.com
Facebook: Glaser Estate Winery

Type: Winery / Micro-distillery. Opened in 2011.

Hours of operation: Friday through Sunday, 11:00am to 5:00pm

Tours: Not available

Types of spirits produced: Rum, vodka, whisky, liqueur, limoncello

Names of spirits:
• TBA

Best known for / most popular: Not provided

Average bottle price: Not provided

Distribution: Not provided

Interesting facts: Not provided

Hard Times Distillery LLC

175 S. 5th
Monroe, OR 97456
541-207-8354

Owners / Operators:
Dudley Clark, Owner / Distiller

Email: info@hardtimesdistillery.com
         dudley@hardtimesdistillery.com
Website: www.hardtimesdistillery.com
Facebook: Hard Times Distillery LLC
Twitter: @hardtimesdstlry
YouTube: Hardtimesdistillery's Channel

Type: Micro-distillery. Opened in 2009.

Hours of operation:
Saturday and Sunday, 12:00pm to 5:00pm

Tours: Available

Types of spirits produced: Vodka, whiskey

Names of spirits:
• Apple Shine
• Green Geisha
• Sweet Baby Moonshine

Best known for / most popular: Green Geisha Wasabi Bloody Mary

Average bottle price: $18.00 to $27.00

Distribution: OR

Interesting facts: Not provided

HillCrest Winery and Distillery

240 Vineyard Lane
Roseburg, OR 97471
541-673-3709

Owners / Operators:
Dyson and Susan DeMara, Owners

Email: info@hillcrestvineyard.com
Website: www.hillcrestvineyard.com
Facebook: HillCrest Winery and Distillery
Yelp: Hillcrest Winery & Distillery
Tripadvisor: HillCrest Winery and Distillery

Type: Winery / Micro-distillery. Opened in 2003.

Hours of operation: Not provided

Tours: Not provided

Types of spirits produced: Eaux de Vie, vodka

Names of spirits:
• Not provided

Best known for / most popular: Not provided

Average bottle price: Not provided

Distribution: Not provided

Interesting facts: Oregon's oldest estate winery

House Spirits Distillery

2025 SE 7th Avenue
Portland, OR 97214
503-235-3174

Owners / Operators:
Christian Krogstad, Co-owner
Thomas Mooney, Co-owner

Email: info@housespirits.com
Website: www.housespirits.com, www.avaiationgin.com
   www.westwardwhiskey.com
Facebook: Westward Whiskey, Aviation Gin, House Spirits Distillery
Twitter: @AviationGin
Pinterest: House Spirits

Type: Micro-distillery. Opened in 2004.

Hours of operation:
Wednesday through Saturday, 12:00pm to 6:00pm
Sunday, 12:00pm to 5:00pm

Tours: Available on Saturday

Types of spirits produced:
Gin, whiskey, liqueur, rum, white dog

Names of spirits:
- Aviation Gin
- House Spirits Rum
- House Spirits White Dog
- House Spirits Coffee Liqueur
- Krogstad Festlig Aquavit
- Krogstad Gamel Aquavit
- Westward Oregon Straight Malt Whiskey

Best known for / most popular: Aviation Gin

Average bottle price: Not provided

Distribution: AZ, CA, GA, ID, KS, LA,
MT, NJ, NY, OR, PA, TN, TX, WA, WY

Interesting facts: Not provided

Immortal Spirits & Distilling Company

3582 S Pacific Highway, Unit D.
Medford, OR 97501
541-646-8144

Owners / Operators:
Jesse Gallagher, Co-owner / Operator
Enrico Carini, Co-owner / Operator

Email: info@immortalspirits.com
Website: www.immortalspirits.com
Facebook: Immortal Spirits and Distilling Company
Twitter: @immortalspirits

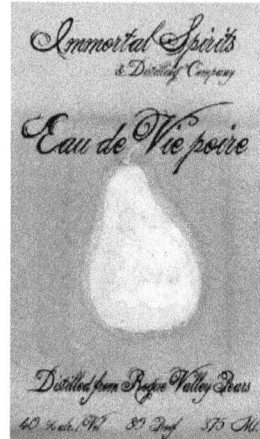

Type: Micro-distillery. Opened in 2010.

Hours of operation: Not provided

Tours: Available by appointment

Types of spirits produced: Whiskey, rum, brandy, absinthe

Names of spirits:
- Eau de Vie Poire
- Knarr- Absinthe Verte
- State of Jefferson Rum (currently aging)

Best known for / most popular: Knarr- Absinthe Verte

Average bottle price: $44.00

Distribution: OR

Interesting facts: The stills were made in house by the owners, a 2,000 gallon mash tun and 1,200 gallon still is possibly the largest micro-distillery capacity in Oregon. Additionally the are currently producing custom smoked Oregon Single Malt Whiskey.

McMenamins Cornelius Pass Roadhouse Distillery

4045 N.W. Cornelius Pass Road
Hillsboro, OR 97124
503-640-6174

Owners / Operators:
Clark McCool, Distillery Manager
Bart Hance, Head Distiller
Arthur Price, Distiller

Email: cpr@mcmenamins.com
Website: www.mcmenamins.com
Facebook: McMenamins Cornelius Pass Roadhouse

Type: Micro-distillery. Opened in 2011.

Hours of operation: Daily, 9:00am to 5:00pm

Tours: Available

Types of spirits produced: Whiskey, brandy

Names of spirits:
- White Owl Whiskey
- Morning Dew
- Gables Gin

Best known for / most popular: White Owl Whiskey

Average bottle price:
$12.75 to 37.50

Distribution: OR, WA

Interesting facts:
Set in an old granary barn constructed by the pioneer Imbrie family in the mid-1850s, the Cornelius Pass Roadhouse Distillery boasts a century-year-old, 160-gallon Alambic Charentais pot still.

McMenamins Edgefield Distillery

2126 SW Halsey Street
Troutdale, OR 97060
503-669-8610

Owners / Operators:
Clark McCool, Manager
James Whelan, Head Distiller
Jarod Davis, Distiller

Email: distillery@mcmenamins.com
Website: www.mcmenamins.com
Facebook: McMenamins Edgefield Distillery
YouTube: McMenaminsVIDEO's channel
Pinterest: McMenamins
Flickr: McMenamins Photos' photostream

Type: Micro-distillery. Opened in 1998.

Hours of operation: Daily, 9:00am to 5:00pm

Tours: Available

Types of spirits produced:
Whiskey, brandy, gin, liqueur, rum

Names of spirits:
- Hogshead Whiskey
- White Dog Whiskey
- Monkey Puzzle Whiskey
- Devils Bit Whiskey
- Alambic 13 Brandy
- Edgefield Potstill Brandy
- Pear Brandy
- Longshot Brandy
- Penny's Gin
- Professors Gin
- Coffee Liqueur
- Herbal Liqueur
- Edgefield Rum

Best known for / most popular: Hogshead Whiskey

Average bottle price: $12.75 to 37.50

Distribution: OR, WA

Interesting facts: Edgefield also has a brewery and a winery.

276

New Deal Distillery

900 SE Salmon Street
Portland, OR 97214
503-234-2513

Owners / Operators:
Tom Burkleaux, Owner
Matthew VanWinkle, Owner

Email: info@newdealdistillery.com, tom@newdealdistillery.com
Website: www.NewDealDistillery.com
Facebook: New Deal Distillery
Twitter: @NewDealPDX

Type: Micro-distillery. Opened in 2004.

Hours of operation:
Wednesday through Friday, 1:00pm to 4:00pm
Saturday and Sunday, 12:00pm to 5:00pm

Tours: Available

Types of spirits produced: Vodka, infused vodka, rum, liqueurs, gin

Names of spirits:
- New Deal Vodka
- Portland 88 Vodka
- Hot Monkey Pepper Vodka
- Mud Puddle Chocolate Vodka
- Coffee Liqueur
- Ginger Liqueur
- Gin No.1
- Gin No. 33
- Clawfoot Gin
- Distiller's Workshop Rum

Photo by: Jeremy Dunham, Polara Studios, 2009

Best known for / most popular: New Deal Vodka

Average bottle price: $20.00 to $50.00

Distribution: OR, VT, WA; Canada

Interesting facts:
New Deal uses water from the Bull Run Reservoir, one of North America's largest gravity-fed water supplies. This water, which comes from the melted snow pack from Mt. Hood's annual accumulation of 500-600 inches of snow each season, is considered by many to be among the most pure water in the nation.

Oregon Spirit Distillers

490 NE Butler Market Road, Ste. 110
Bend, OR 97701
541-382-0002

Owners / Operators:
Brad and Kathy Irwin, Owners / Operators

Email: info@oregonspiritdistillers.com
Website: www.oregonspiritdistillers.com
Facebook: Oregon Spirit Distillers
Twitter: @oregonspirit

Type: Micro-distillery. Opened in 2009.

Hours of operation:
Wednesday, Thursday, 1:00pm to 5:00pm
Friday, 1:00pm to 7:00pm; Saturday, 12:00pm to 5:00pm

Tours: Available during open hours

Types of spirits produced: Vodka, cordial, bourbon, gin, absinthe

Names of spirits:
- Merrylegs Genever
- Wild Card Absinthe
- Oregon Spirit Vodka
- C.W. Irwin Straight Bourbon
- Black Mariah (Marionberry Cordial)

Best known for / most popular: Not provided

Average bottle price: $30.00 to $50.00

Distribution: OR

Interesting facts: Not provided

278

Ransom Spirits

23101 Houser Road
Sheridan, OR 97378
503-876-5022

Owners / Operators:
Tad Seestedt, Sole Proprietor

Email: info@ransomspirits.com
Website: www.ransomspirits.com
Facebook: Ransom Spirits

Type: Winery / Micro-distillery. Opened in 1997.

Hours of operation: Not open to the public

Tours: Not available

Types of spirits produced:
Gin, whiskey, brandy, grappa, vodka

Names of spirits:
- WhipperSnapper Oregon Spirit Whiskey
- Old Tom Gin
- Small's Gin
- Gewürztraminer Grappa
- The Vodka

Best known for / most popular: Old Tom Gin

Average bottle price: $25.00 to $37.00

Distribution:
CA, CO, DC, IL, MA, MO, NJ, NV, NY, OR, TN, TX, WA, WI

Interesting facts:
The name Ransom was initially chosen to represent the investment necessary to become self-employed. It has since come to represent the amount of debt owed to banks and other loaning institutions.

Photos courtesy of Ransom Spirits. Photos by: "Eye of the Lady Photography Studio"

Rogue Spirits

Rum Distillery:
Rogue Ales Public House and Distillery
1339 Northwest Flanders Street
Portland, OR 97209
503-222-5910

Main Distillery:
Rogue House of Spirits
2122 Marine Science Drive
Newport, OR 97365
541-867-3673

Owners / Operators:
Mike Higgins, President Rogue Spirits
Jeff Alexander, Master Distiller

Email: m.higgins@rogue.com
Website: www.rogue.com
          www.roguespirits.com
Facebook: Rogue Ales

Twitter: @RogueAles
YouTube: Rogue Ales HQ
Instagram: rogueales

Type: Brewery / Micro-distillery. Opened Portland in 2003, Newport in 2006.

Hours of operation:

Portland	Newport
Sun. through Thur., 11am to 12am	Friday, 4:00pm to 8:00pm
Fri. & Sat., 11am to 1am	Saturday, 12:00pm to 8:00pm
	Sunday, 12:00pm to 6:0pm

Tours: Available at both facilities. Days and times vary.

Types of spirits produced: Artisan, varietal whiskey, gin, rum, vodka

Names of spirits:
- Rogue Spruce Gin
- Rogue Pink Gin
- Rogue Dead Guy Whiskey
- Rogue Oregon Single Malt Whiskey
- Rogue Chipotle Whiskey
- Rogue Hazelnut Spice Rum
- Rogue Dark Rum
- Rogue Vintage Vodka

Best known for / most popular: Rogue Spirits are best known for creating unique, varietal, hand-crafted, small-batch spirits that are grown, harvested, malted, smoked, roasted, milled, mashed, brewed, distilled and barrel-aged using ingredients fresh from Rogue Farms.

Average bottle price: $34.00 to $44.00

Distribution: 45 states and 5 countries

Interesting facts: The Rogue distillery in Portland was Oregon's first rum distillery.

Stein Distillery

604 N. Main Street
Joseph, OR 97846
503-642-2659

Owners / Operators:
Austin Stein, Co-owner
Heather Stein, Co-owner

Email: whiskey@steindistillery.com
Website: www.steindistillery.com

Type: Micro-distillery. Opened in 2012.

Hours of operation: Not provided

Tours: Not provided

Types of spirits produced: Whiskey

Names of spirits:
• TBA

Best known for / most popular: Not provided

Average bottle price: Not provided

Distribution: OR

Interesting facts: Not provided

Stone Barn Brandyworks

3315 SE 19th, Ste. B
Portland, OR 97202
503-775-6747

Owners / Operators:
Sebastian and Erika Degens, Founders

Email: degens@stonebarnbrandyworks.com
Website: www.stonebarnbrandyworks.com
Facebook: Stone Barn Brandyworks

Type: Micro-distillery. Opened in 2009.

Hours of operation:
Saturday and Sunday, 12:00pm to 6:00pm
Monday, 12:00pm to 7:00pm

Tours: Available during open hours

Types of spirits produced:
Brandy, liqueur, grappa, whiskey

Names of spirits:
- Oregon Apple Brandy (oaked)
- Bartlett Pear Brandy
- Comice Pear Brandy
- Pacific Northwest Cherry Brandy
- Pacific Northwest Plum Brandy
- Biggs Junction Apricot Liqueur
- Golden Quince Liqueur
- Cranberry Liqueur
- Oregon Blush Rhubarb Liqueur
- Strawberry Liqueur
- Red Wing Roast Coffee Liqueur
- Nocino Green Walnut Liqueur
- Easy Eight Unoaked Oat Whiskey
- Hard Eight Rye Whiskey
- Hoppin' Eights Whiskey
- Pinot Noir Grappa
- Eastside Ouzo

Best known for / most popular: Fruit liqueurs, brandies; rye and oat whiskey

Average bottle price: $25.00 to $32.00

Distribution: OR

Interesting facts: Stone Barn's whiskeys are made from Bob's Red Mill Flour.

Stringer's Orchard Winery and Distillery

New Pine Creek, OR 97635
530-946-4112

Owners / Operators:
Joanne and John Stringer, Owners

Email: winemaker@stringersorchard.com
Website: www.stringersorchard.com

Type: Winery / Micro-distillery. Opened in 2005.

Hours of operation:
Closed January through March
April to December, Monday through Saturday, 10:00am to 5:00pm

Tours: Tours are available.

Types of spirits produced: Brandy, liqueur

Names of spirits:
- Wild Plum Wine
- Plum Brandy (Slivovitz)
- Pacific Plum Liqueur
- Pacific Plum Gin
- Plum Jam and Syrup

Best known for / most popular: Pacific Plum Liqueur

Average bottle price: $19.95 to $28.00

Distribution: Sold locally

Interesting facts:
Only known distillery making alcohol from wild Pacific plum

Sub Rosa Spirits

876 SW Alder Drive
Dundee, OR 97115
503-476-2808

Owners / Operators:
Michael Sherwood, Owner

Email: sub-rosa@comcast.net
Website: www.subrosaspirits.com
Facebook: Sub Rosa Spirits

Type: Craft-distillery. Opened in 2007.

Hours of operation: Not provided

Tours: Not provided

Types of spirits produced: Vodka

Names of spirits:
- Sub Rosa Tarragon Vodka
- Sub Rosa Saffron Vodka

Best known for / most popular:
Sub Rosa Tarragon Vodka and Sub Rosa Saffron Vodka

Average bottle price: $29.95

Distribution: CA, DC, IL, OR, WA

Interesting facts:
Sub Rosa Saffron Vodka is the first commercial savory spiced vodka that captures the flavors of India and Asia.

The words "sub rosa" come from the Latin "under the rose," from the association of the rose with confidentiality. Use of a rose at secret meetings was a symbol of the sworn confidence of the participants. The ceilings of ancient banquet rooms were often decorated with roses to remind guests that what was spoken within was private.

Lovers of Sub Rosa distillates carry on the tradition of elixirs consumed in private, a shared secret with a select few. Anyone who is familiar with secret societies such as the Illuminati, Freemasons, Priory of Scion, or Knights Templar will be familiar with the concept of "sub rosa." By sampling Sub Rosa elixirs, you become part of the cadre. Membership is open to a select few who quest after the true spirit.

Superfly Distilling Company

16399 Ste. B Lower Harbor Road
Brookings, OR 97415
530-520-8005

Owners / Operators:
Ryan Webster, Owner

Email: ryanwebster@msn.com
Website: www.superflybooze.com
Facebook: Superfly Distilling Company

Type: Micro-distillery. Opened in 2008.

Hours of operation: Not provided

Tours: Available occasionally

Types of spirits produced: Vodka, rum, whiskey

Names of spirits:
• Superfly Vodka

Best known for / most popular: Superfly Vodka

Average bottle price: $20.00

Distribution: Not provided

Interesting facts: Not provided

Vinn Distillery

7990 SW Boeckman Road
Wilsonville, OR 97070
503-957-9210

Owners / Operators:
Michelle Ly, Co-owner
Quyen Ly, Co-owner
Vicki Ly, Co-owner
Lien Ly, Co-owner

Email: Michelle Ly, michelle@vinndistillery.com
  Quyen Ly, quyen@vinndistillery.com
  Vicki Ly, vicki@vinndistillery.com
  Lien Ly, lien@vinndistillery.com
Website: www.vinndistillery.com
Facebook: Vinn Distillery
Twitter: @vinndistillery

Type: Micro-distillery. Opened in 2009.

Tasting room location / hours:
833 SE Main Street Ste. 125, Portland, OR 97214
Saturday and Sunday, 12:00pm to 5:00pm

Tours: Not available

Types of spirits produced: Rice vodka, baijiu, rice wine

Names of spirits:
• Vinn Mijiu (pronounced "Mee-Je-oh") Ice
• Vinn Mijiu (pronounced "Mee-Je-oh") Fire
• Vinn Baijiu (pronounced "By-Je-oh")
• Vin Vodka

Best known for / most popular: Vinn Baijiu

Average bottle price: $18.95 to $35.95

Distribution: OR

Interesting facts:
• The recipe used to make all three of Vinn Distillery spirits is over 7 generations old.
• Baijiu - considered the national drink of China - is a Chinese distilled alcoholic beverage. The name baijiu literally means "white liquor."
• Vinn Distillery products are gluten free.
• First known rice vodka produced and bottled in the U.S.

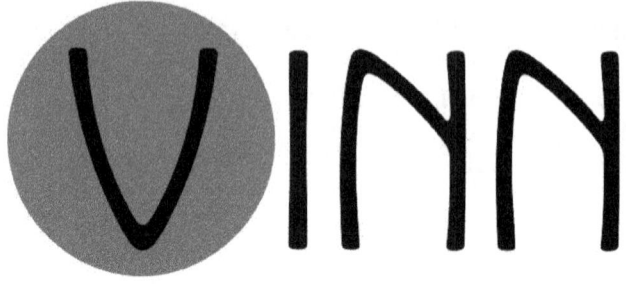

Vivacity Spirits

720 NE Granger Ave #C
Corvallis, OR 97330
541-286-4285

Owners / Operators:
Caitlin Prueitt, Owner / Distiller
Chris Neumann, Owner / Distiller

Email: vivacityspirits@gmail.com
Website: www.vivacityspirits.com
Facebook: Vivacity Spirits
Twitter: @VivacitySpirits

Type: Micro-distillery. Opened in 2011.

Hours of operation: Tasting room open first and third Saturday of the month

Tours: Available by appointment

Types of spirits produced: Vodka, gin, rum

Names of spirits:
• Vivacity Fine Vodka
• Vivacity Bankers' Gin
• Vivacity Native Gin

Best known for / most popular:
Vivacity Native Gin

Average bottle price: $23.95 to $28.95

Distribution: OR

Interesting facts: The base for the vodka and gin are made with American grown organic corn.

287

Ye Ol' Grog Distillery

35855 Industrial Way, Unit C
Saint Helens, OR 97051
503-366-4001

Owners / Operators:
Lloyd Williams, Owner
Ken McFarland, Owner
Greg Scott, Owner
Marcus Alden, Owner

Email: info@yeolgrogdistillery.com
Website: www.yeolgrogdistillery.com, www.grogme.com
Facebook: Ye Ol Grog Distillery, Grog Wench Libations
Twitter: @GrogMe

Type: Micro-distillery. Opened in 2009.

Hours of operation: Monday through Saturday, 1:00pm to 4:00pm

Tours: Available by appointment

Types of spirits produced:
Specialty distilled spirits, vodka

Names of spirits:
- Dog Watch Vodka
- Dutch Harbor Breeze (Grog)
- Good Morning Glory (Grog)

Best known for / most popular: Grog

Average bottle price: Mid-range

Distribution: AK, CA, CO, DC, DE, FL, GA, HI, IL, LA, MO, OR, PA, WA and online at www.cellar.com

Interesting facts:
You'll notice that most of Ye Ol' Grog products have an "FPC" brand that is their corporate take on political correctness. PC is for politically correct, the "F," well, you can figure that out for yourself.

Mountain Laurel Spirits LLC

925 Canal Street
Bristol, PA 19007
215-781-8300

Owners / Operators:
Herman C. Mihalich, Co-owner
John S. Cooper, Co-owner

Email: info@dadshatrye.com
Website: www.dadshatrye.com
Facebook: Dad's Hat Rye
Twitter: @dadshatrye

Type: Craft-distillery. Opened in 2011.

Hours of operation: Not provided

Tours:
Available Saturday afternoons by appointment

Types of spirits produced: Rye whiskey, white rye

Names of spirits:
* Dad's Hat™ Pennsylvania Rye Whiskey
* Dad's Hat™ Pennsylvania White Rye
* Dad's Hat™ Pennsylvania Rye Whiskey Finished in Vermouth Barrels
* Dad's Hat™ Pennsylvania Rye Whiskey Finished in Sweet Wine Barrels

Best known for / most popular:
Dad's Hat™ Pennsylvania Rye Whiskey

Average bottle price: $30.00 to $40.00

Distribution:
CA, DC, ID, MA, NJ, NY, OR, PA, RI

Interesting facts: Not provided

Naoj and Mot Inc.

2519 Moore Street
Philadelphia, PA 19145
215-271-1161

Owners / Operators:
Joan Verratti, CEO / President
Tom Cavaliere, Plant Manager

Email: joan@naojandmotinc.com
Website: www.pollyodd.com
Facebook: Pollyodd

Type: Micro-distillery. Opened in 2012.

Hours of operation:
Monday through Friday, 8:00am to 12:00pm

Tours: Not available

Types of spirits produced: Liqueurs

Names of spirits:
- Pollyodd Lemoncello
- Pollyodd Limecello
- Pollyodd Orangecello
- Pollyodd Chocolatecello
- Pollyodd Mangocello
- Pollyodd Lemoncreamcello
- Pollyodd Orangecreamcello
- Pollyodd Bananacreamcello
- Pollyodd Chocolatecreamcello
- Pollyodd Strawberrycreamcello

Best known for / most popular: Pollyodd Lemoncello

Average bottle price: $23.00 to $26.00

Distribution: PA

Interesting facts:
One of only a few woman owned and
operated distilleries in the U.S.

pollyodd

...and as always, "Dalle Mia Mani Al Tuo Cuore"

LIQUEUR
A HANDCRAFTED LEMONCELLO CREAM
MADE FOR THE AMERICAN PALATE
ALC. BY VOL 20%.. (40 PROOF) 750 ML

pollyodd

...and as always, "Dalle Mia Mani Al Tuo Cuore"

LIQUEUR
A HANDCRAFTED BANANACELLO CREAM
MADE FOR THE AMERICAN PALATE
ALC. BY VOL 14%.. (28 PROOF) 750 ML

pollyodd

...and as always, "Dalle Mia Mani Al Tuo Cuore"

LIQUEUR
A HANDCRAFTED CHOCOLATECELLO CREAM
MADE FOR THE AMERICAN PALATE
ALC. BY VOL 21%.. (42 PROOF) 750 ML

Pennsylvania Pure Distilleries LLC

1101 William Flinn Highway
Glenshaw, PA 15116
412-486-8666

Owners / Operators:
Barry L. Young, Owner
C. Prentiss Orr, Owner

Email: info@boydandblair.com
Website: www.boydandblair.com
Facebook: Boyd and Blair Potato Vodka
Twitter: @BoydBlairVodka
LinkedIn: Pennsylvania Pure Distilleries LLC

Type: Micro-distillery. Opened in 2008.

Hours of operation:
Monday through Friday 9:30am to 6:00pm

Tours: By appointment for industry professionals

Types of spirits produced: Potato vodka

Names of spirits:
- Boyd & Blair Potato Vodka (80 proof)
- Boyd & Blair Professional Proof 151 Potato Vodka

Best known for / most popular:
Boyd & Blair Potato Vodka

Average bottle price: $29.00 to $49.00

Distribution: CA, CT, DC, DE, FL, GA, ID, IL, IN, MA, MD, MO, NC, NJ, NV, NY, OR, PA, RI, TN, TX, WA, WI, WV; Canada ON; Singapore

Interesting facts: Pennsylvania Pure Distilleries LLC was founded as Pennsylvania's first vodka distillery.

Philadelphia Distilling

12285 McNulty Road #105
Philadelphia, PA 19154
215-671-0346

Owners / Operators:
Andrew Auwerda, President
Tim Yarnall, Vice President
Robert Cassell, Master Distiller

Email: info@philadelphiadistilling.com
Website: www.philadelphiadistilling.com, www.bluecoatgin.com
         www.penn1681vodka.com, www.vieuxcarreabsinthe.com
         www.shinewhiskey.com, www.thebayvodka.com
Facebook: Bluecoat American Dry Gin, Penn 1681 Rye Vodka
          Vieux Carré Absinthe Supérieure, Shine Whiskey
          Philadelphia Distilling, THE BAY Seasoned Vodka
Twitter: @bluecoatgin, @vcabsinthe, @TheBayVodka
         @Penn1681Vodka, @shinewhiskey

Type: Micro-distillery. Opened in 2005.

Hours of operation: Regular

Tours: Available

Products produced: Absinthe, gin, vodka, whiskey

Names of spirits:
• Bluecoat American Dry Gin
• Penn 1681 Rye Vodka
• Vieux Carré Absinthe Supérieure
• XXX Shine Whiskey (range)
• The Bay Seasoned Vodka

Best known for / most popular:
Bluecoat American Dry Gin

Average bottle price: $28.00

Distribution:
40 U.S. States, Bermuda, France, Spain, Italy, East Africa

Interesting facts:
• The first craft distillery in Pennsylvania since Prohibition
• The first spirit released was Bluecoat American Dry Gin
• The first East Coast distillery to distill authentic absinthe in over 100 years

Pittsburgh Distilling Co.

2401 Smallman Street
Pittsburgh, PA 15222
412-728-0053

Owners / Operators:
Alex Grelli, Meredith Grelli,
Eric Meyer, Mark Meyer, Mary Ellen Meyer

Email: meredith@wiglewhiskey.com
Website: www.wiglewhiskey.com
Facebook: Wigle Whiskey
Twitter: @WigleWhiskey

Type: Micro-distillery. Opened in 2012.

Hours of operation:
Tuesday through Sunday, 10:00am to 6:00pm

Tours:
Available Saturdays and by appointment
Register at website

Types of spirits produced:
Whiskey, Genever-style gin, rum, bitters

Names of spirits:
- Wigle Organic White Rye Whiskey
- Wigle Organic White Wheat Whiskey
- Wigle Organic Ginever
- Organic Aged Wheat Whiskey – Small Cask Series
- Organic Aged Rye Whiskey-Small Cask Series

Best known for / most popular:
Small batch, from scratch organic whiskey

Average bottle price: $25.00 to $35.00

Distribution: On-site

Interesting facts:
Pittsburgh Distilling makes Monongahela Rye, the original form of American Whiskey and offers historical tours about the Whiskey Rebellion.

293

Newport Distilling Company

293 JT Connell Road
Newport, RI 02840
401-849-5232

Owners / Operators:
Brent Ryan, President / Head Distiller
Derek Luke, Founder / Brewmaster

Email: information@thomastewrums.com
Website: www.thomastewrums.com
Facebook: Thomas Tew Rum
Twitter: @ThomasTewRum

Type: Brewery / Micro-distillery. Opened in 2006.

Hours of operation: Wednesday through Monday, 12:00pm to 5:00pm

Tours: Available

Types of spirits produced: Rum

Names of spirits:
• Thomas Tew Single Barrel Rum

Best known for / most popular:
Thomas Tew Single Barrel Rum

Average bottle price: $30.00 to $35.00

Distribution: RI

Interesting facts: Newport Distilling Company received the first license to distill in the state since the close of the John Dyer distillery in Providence in 1872.

Sons of Liberty Spirits Co.

1425 Kingstown Road
South Kingstown, RI 02879
401-284-4006

Owners / Operators:
Mike Reppucci, Owner / Founder
Chris Guillette, The Fashionista
Danny Murphy, The Mayor
Bryan Ricard, The Gopher

Email: info@solspirits.com
Website: www.solspirits.com
Facebook: Sons of Liberty Spirits Co.

Type: Micro-distillery. Opened in 2011.

Hours of operation: Vary

Tours: Wednesdays and Saturdays, 12:00pm to 4:00pm

Types of spirits produced: Whiskey, vodka

Names of spirits:
- UPRISING American Whiskey
- Sons of Liberty Seasonals
- The 1765 Collection
  (Limited release, single malt whiskies)
- Loyal 9 Vodka
- Loyal 9 Seasonal Vodkas

Best known for / most popular:
UPRISING American Whiskey

Average bottle price: $27.00 to $42.00

Distribution: MA, RI

Interesting facts:
- UPRISING American Whiskey is distilled from a flavorful stout beer.
- Sons of Liberty Seasonals is the first seasonal line of whiskies ever.
- Loyal 9 Vodka is chill filtered through charcoal 99 times for an incredibly smooth taste.
- Loyal 9 Seasonal Vodkas use fresh and locally grown ingredients.

Dark Corner Distillery

241-B North Main Street
Greenville, SC 29601
864-631-1144

Owners / Operators:
Joe Fenten, Founder

Email: joe@darkcornerdistillery.com
Website: www.darkcornerdistillery.com
Facebook: Dark Corner Distillery
Twitter: @DCDistillery

Type: Micro-distillery. Opened in 2011.

Hours of operation: Monday through Saturday, 12:00pm to 6:00pm

Tours: Available by appointment

Types of spirits produced: Whiskey, bourbon, gin, absinthe

Names of spirits:
- Moonshine
- Hot Mama
- White Tiger
- The Green Villain
- Apple-achian Shine
- Butterscotch Shine
- Carolina Peach Shine
- Wildberry Shine
- Honeysuckle Shine
- Lewis Redmond Carolina Bourbon Whiskey

Best known for / most popular: Apple-achian Margarita

Average bottle price: $32.00

Distribution: DC, SC

Interesting facts: Makers of mighty fine shine!

Firefly Distillery

6775 Bears Bluff Road
Wadmalaw Island, SC 29487
843-557-1405

Owners / Operators:
Jim Irvin and Scott Newitt, Owners

Email: info@fireflyvodka.com
info@fireflymoonshine.com
Website: www.fireflyvodka.com, www.fireflymoonshine.com
Facebook: The Official Firefly Sweet Tea Vodka Page, Firefly Moonshine
Twitter: @FireflyVodka, @TheFireflyShine

Type: Micro-distillery. Opened in 2007.

Hours of operation: Closed January
Production: Monday through Friday, 8:30am to 4:30pm (closed to public)
Retail: Tuesday through Saturday, 11:00am to 5:00pm

Tours: Video tour is available

Types of spirits produced:
Vodka, moonshine, rum, liqueur, ready-to-drink cocktails

Names of spirits:
- Firefly Sweet Tea Flavored Vodka
- Firefly Skinny Tea
- Firefly Sweet Tea Flavored Bourbon
- Firefly Peach Tea Vodka
- Firefly Handcrafted Vodka
- Firefly Moonshines:
  - White Lightning Moonshine
  - Strawberry
  - Cherry
  - Peach
  - Caramel
  - Apple Pie
- Sea Island Gold, Java and Spiced Rums
- Southern Accents Liqueurs

Best known for / most popular: Firefly Sweet Tea Vodka

Average bottle price: Under $20.00

Distribution: Nationwide

Interesting facts:
Firefly was the first distillery to make a sweet tea flavored vodka.

Palmetto Moonshine

200 W. Benson Street
Anderson, SC 29624
864-226-9917

Owners / Operators:
Trey Boggs, Owner / Operator
Bryan Boggs, Owner / Operator

Email: Trey Boggs: ahboggsiii@gmail.com
        Bryan Boggs: bboggs@hotmail.com
Website: www.palmettomoonshine.com
Facebook: Palmetto Moonshine
Twitter: @palmettomoonshn
YouTube: PalmettoMoonshine

Type: Micro-distillery. Opened in 2011.

Hours of operation:
Monday through Friday, 10:00am to 7:00pm; Saturday 9:00 to 7:00pm

Tours: Available

Types of spirits produced: Moonshine

Names of spirits:
- Palmetto Moonshine
- Palmetto Blackberry Moonshine
- Palmetto Apple Pie Moonshine
- Palmetto Peach Moonshine

Best known for / most popular:
Moonshine Margarita and Redneck Tea

Average bottle price: $24.95 to $34.90

Distribution: SC

Interesting facts:
Palmetto Moonshine is South Carolinas first legal moonshine distillery.

298

Six & Twenty Distillery

3109 Highway 153
Piedmont, SC 29673
864-263-8312

Owners / Operators:
David Raad, Head Distiller
Robert Redmond, Marketing and Sales

Email: info@sixandtwentydistillery.com
Website: www.sixandtwentydistillery.com
Facebook: Six & Twenty Distillery

Type: Micro-distillery. Opened in 2012.

Hours of operation:
Monday through Saturday, 9:00am to 6:30pm

Tours: Available by appointment

Types of spirits produced: Whiskey

Names of spirits:
- Six & Twenty Whiskey "Blue"
- Carolina Virgin Wheat Whiskey

Best known for / most popular: Six & Twenty Whiskey "Blue"

Average bottle price: $49.95

Distribution: Not provided

Interesting facts: "BLUE" was named after the old adage, "something old, something new, something borrowed, something blue".

The five year old bourbon (something old), the virgin wheat whiskey (something new), re-barrel age those together (something borrowed--time in a barrel) to get perfect harmony (something "Blue").

What's on the label? "At first sight, you see its youthfulness. Your nose alerts you to the sweetness of South Carolina's soft red winter wheat. The pride of the Carolinas comes out when you taste this hand-crafted spirit made from the pure Blue Ridge Mountain water. This is why we call it Virgin Wheat Whiskey."

Striped Pig Distillery

2225 Old School Road
Charleston, SC 29405
504-957-2147

Owners / Operators:
Todd Weiss, Proprietor
Casey Lillie, Proprietor
Johnny Pieper, Proprietor

Email: todd@stripedpigdistillery.com
Website: www.stripedpigdistillery.com
Facebook: Striped Pig Distillery
Twitter: @DstillD

Type: Micro-distillery. Opened in 2013.

Hours of operation: Monday through Saturday, 10:00am to 6:00pm

Tours: Available

Types of spirits produced: Vodka, rum, whiskey

Names of spirits:
• TBA

Best known for / most popular: TBA

Average bottle price: $25.00 to $36.00

Distribution: SC

Interesting facts: What's in a name?
The earliest temperance laws sought to eliminate the rum seller's trade by prohibiting the sale of liquor in quantities smaller than fifteen gallons. The failure of such measures is gleefully recounted in "The Dedham Muster."

Citizen soldiers would parade and stage mock maneuvers while townsfolk cheered them on. Traditionally after the muster were games, food, and much drinking. The fifteen gallon law was aimed at eliminating this last feature.

One clever fellow got a license, not to sell liquor, but to exhibit a striped pig. The price of admission coincided with the usual price of a drink and, one was included, as well. He gave away the liquor and only charged for admission to see the pig.

Striped Pig,
As Sung with unbounded applause.
Tune—King and Countryman.

300

Tiger Juice Distillery

1438 Cedar Creek Road
Hartsville, SC 29550
843-498-7202

Owners / Operators:
Michael Joseph Flynn

Email: tiger6@shtc.net
Website: www.tigerjuicedistillery.com
Facebook: Tiger Juice Distillery
Twitter: @TJ_Distillery

Type: Micro-distillery. Opened in 2011.

Hours of operation: Not provided

Tours: Not provided

Types of spirits produced: Whiskey

Names of spirits:
• New Age Spirit Whiskey

Best known for / most popular: New Age Spirit Whiskey

Average bottle price: Not provided

Distribution: SC

Interesting facts: Not provided

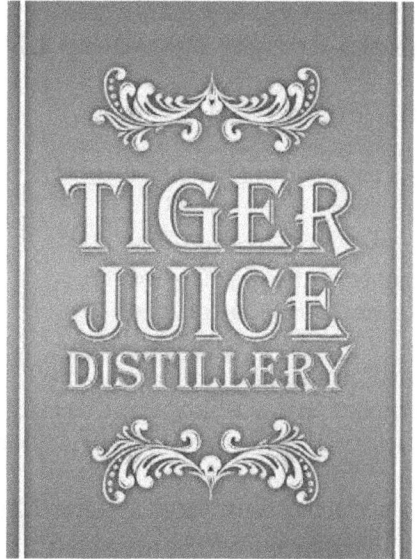

Sometimes the best ideas are in your own backyard. Whether your roots are Native American or Scotch/Irish like mine, some traditions are time-honored for great and delicious reasons. With a combination of family tradition, adventurous spirit and an innovative, patented technology, we're proud to share our New Age Spirit Whiskey. Virtually free of impurities, it's still full of nuanced flavor and an ultimately smooth taste you'll want to sip and savor.

To all of you, thanks – and enjoy our libations responsibly. And please, do your part to support the farmers who nurture the land and harvest our favorite grains. Be kind to your fellow man and animals that share this earth we've been chosen to explore. Welcome to the New Age of Spirits.

Michael Joseph Flynn

Michael Joseph Flynn

301

Dakota Spirits Distillery LLC

3601 Airport Road
Pierre, SD 57501
605-494-1009

DAKOTA SPIRITS DISTILLERY

Owners / Operators:
Jamison Rounds, Co-founder
Tom Rounds, Co-founder

Email: info@dakotaspirits.com
Website: www.dakotaspirits.com
Facebook: Dakota Spirits Distillery LLC

Type: Micro-distillery. Opened in 2010.

Hours of operation: Not provided

Tours: Not provided

Types of spirits produced: Vodka, whiskey, brandy

Names of spirits:
- Ringneck Vodka
- Blended Whiskey
- Coyote 100 Light Whiskey
- Bickering Brothers Brandy

Best known for / most popular: Not provided

Average bottle price: Not provided

Distribution: SD

Interesting facts: Dakota Spirits Distillery is South Dakota's first legal distillery.

Chattanooga Whiskey Company

Chattanooga, TN

Owners / Operators:
Joe Ledbetter, Co-founder
Tim Piersant, Co-founder

Email: info@chattanoogawhiskey.com
Website: www.chattanoogawhiskey.com
Facebook: Chattanooga Whiskey
Twitter: @ChattWhiskey
Pinterest: Chattanooga Whiskey

Type: Planning and business development stage

Hours of operation: Not provided

Tours: Not provided

Types of spirits produced: Whiskey

Names of spirits:
• 1816 Reserve
• 1816 Cask

Best known for / most popular: TBA

Average bottle price: Not provided

Distribution: Not provided

Interesting facts: Not provided

Collier and McKeel

1200 Clinton Street
Nashville, TN 37212

Owners / Operators:
Mike Williams, Owner

Email: info@collierandmckeel.com
Website: www.collierandmckeel.com
Facebook: Collier and McKeel Handcrafted Tennessee Whiskey
Twitter: @TNsourmash

Type: Micro-distillery. Opened in 2011.

Hours of operation: Not provided

Tours: Not provided

Types of spirits produced: Vodka, whiskey

Names of spirits:
- Snow Creek Vodka
- Collier and McKeel White Dog
- Collier and McKeel Tennessee Whiskey
- Collier and McKeel Sour Mash Whiskey
- Collier and McKeel Fiery Gizzard Cinnamon Whiskey

Best known for / most popular: Not provided

Average bottle price: Not provided

Distribution: TN

Interesting facts: As a sign of their commitment to quality and attention to detail the master distiller personally puts his thumbprint on every single bottle of Collier and McKeel Handcrafted Tennessee Whiskey they make.

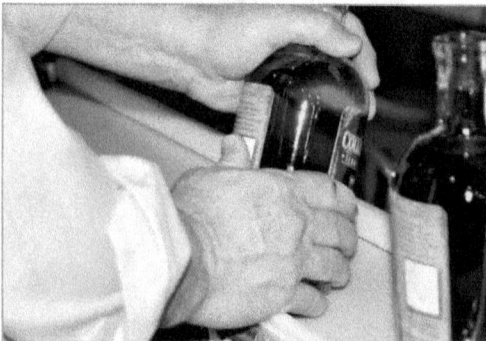

Corsair Artisan Distillery

1200 Clinton Street, #110
Nashville, TN 37203
615-200-0320

400 East Main Street, #110
Bowling Green, KY 42101
270-904-2021

Owners / Operators:
Darek Bell and Andrew Webber, Owners

Email: info@corsairartisan.com
Website: www.corsairartisan.com
Facebook: Corsair Artisan Distillery
Twitter: @corsairartisan
YouTube: Corsair Artisan

Type: Micro-distillery. Opened TN in 2010. Open KY in 2008.

Hours of operation:

Nashville, TN
Mon. through Sat., 9:00am to 8:00pm

Bowling Green, KY
Mon. through Sat. 8:00am to 6:00pm

Tours: Available
Nashville, TN; Tuesday through Saturday from 3:00pm to 8:00pm
Bowling Green, KY; Friday and Saturday from 10:00am to 6:00pm

Types of spirits produced: Gin, rum, absinthe, vodka, whiskeys

Names of spirits:
- Corsair Gin
- Corsair Spiced Rum
- Corsair Red Absinthe
- Corsair Vanilla Vodka
- Corsair Barrel Aged Gin
- Corsair Wry Moon Un-aged Rye Whiskey
- Corsair Triple Smoke Single Malt Whiskey
- Corsair Pumpkin Spice Moonshine
- Corsair Quinoa Whiskey
- Corsair Ryemageddon Whiskey
- Corsair Genever
- Corsair Rasputin Hopped Whiskey

Best known for / most popular: Corsair Triple Smoke Whiskey

Average bottle price: $25.00 to $55.00

Distribution: AK, CA, CO, CT, DC ,DE, FL, IL, IL, GA, KY, MD, MI, MO, NC, NJ, NV, NY, OR, TN, TX, WA, WV

Interesting facts:
- 2013 Craft Whiskey of the Year, Whisky Advocate
- 2013 Craft Distillery of the Year, Whisky Magazine
- 2013 Innovator of the Year, Whisky Magazine

East Tennessee Distillery

220 Piney Flats Road
Piney Flats, TN 37686

Owners / Operators:
Neil "Tiny" Roberson, President / Master Distiller
Byron Reece, VP Sales & Marketing
Gary Melvin, VP Finance
Darrell Hunt, Chairman of the Board

Email: tennesseemellomoon@gmail.com
Website: www.mellomoon.com
Facebook: East Tennessee Distillery

Type: Micro-distillery. Opened in 2011.

Hours of operation: Not available

Tours: Not available

Types of spirits produced: Moonshine

Names of spirits:
• Roberson's Tennessee Mellomoon

Best known for / most popular: Roberson's Tennessee Mellomoon

Average bottle price: $25.00

Distribution: TN

Interesting facts:
• ETD was the 9th federally licensed distiller in TN since prohibition.
• ETD was the 1st legal distillery in Sullivan County, TN

306

Nelson's Green Brier Distillery

1412 Clinton Street
Nashville, TN 37203
615-207-7467

Owners / Operators:
Charles (Charlie) Nelson, President
William (Andy) Nelson, Vice President

Email: Charlie, charlie@greenbrierdistillery.com
       Andy, andy@greenbrierdistillery.com
Website: www.greenbrierdistillery.com
Facebook: Nelson's Green Brier Distillery
Twitter: @TNWhiskeyCo

Type: Micro-distillery. Opened in 2009.

Hours of operation: Not provided

Tours: Not available

Types of spirits produced: Whiskey

Names of spirits:
- Belle Meade™ Bourbon

Best known for / most popular:
- Belle Meade Manhattan
- Fortified Belle
- Belle Meade Mint Julep

Average bottle price: $35.00 to $44.00

Distribution: AL, AR, DC, FL, GA, IL, MD, SC, TN, TX

Interesting facts: Nelson's Green Brier Distillery was one of the largest distilleries in the country before Prohibition. It was known as "Old No. 5". The founder Charles Nelson produced the original Tennessee Whiskey, before Jack Daniel's, and was one of the first to bottle and sell whiskey rather than selling it by the barrel or jug.

Ole Smoky Distillery LLC

903 Parkway
Gatlinburg, TN 37738
865-436-6995

Owners / Operators:
Justin King, Master Distiller

Email: General info: shine@osdistillery
          Justin King: justin@osdistillery.com
Website: www.olesmokymoonshine.com
Facebook: Ole Smoky Moonshine Distillery
Twitter: @OleSmoky

Type: Micro-distillery. Opened in 2010.

Hours of operation:
Daily, 10:00am to 10:00pm
No alcohol sold on Sundays

Tours: Self-guided tours are available. Guests can read the storyboards, see the working still, and speak with the distillers.

Types of spirits produced: Moonshine

Names of spirits:
• Ole Smoky® Original Moonshine (Corn Whiskey)
• Ole Smoky® White Lightnin'™ (Neutral Spirits)
• Ole Smoky® Moonshine Cherries™
• Ole Smoky® Apple Pie Moonshine™
• Ole Smoky® Grape Moonshine™ (seasonal)
• Ole Smoky® Hunch Punch Moonshine™ (seasonal)
• Ole Smoky® Peach Moonshine™ (seasonal)

Best known for / most popular: Moonshine

Average bottle price: $24.95 to $34.95

Distribution: 30 states. Visit website for complete list.

Interesting facts:
• Tennessee's first legal moonshine distillery
• The original, unaged corn whiskey is made from a 100-year-old family recipe

Popcorn Sutton's Distillery

Nashville, TN 37209

Owners / Operators:
Jamey Grosser, Master Distiller

Email: info@popcornsuttonswhiskey.com
Website: www.popcornsuttonswhiskey.com
Facebook: Popcorn Sutton's Tennessee White Whiskey

Type: Micro-distillery. Opened in 2011.

Hours of operation: Not provided

Tours: Not provided

Types of spirits produced: Whiskey

Names of spirits:
- Popcorn Sutton's Tennessee White Whiskey

Best known for / most popular: Popcorn Sutton's Tennessee White Whiskey

Average bottle price: Not provided

Distribution: TN

Interesting facts: Not provided

Prichard's Distillery Inc.

11 Kelso Smithland Road
Kelso, TN 37348
931-433-5454

Owners / Operators:
Phil Prichard, President / Master Distiller

Email: phil@pdspirits.com
Website: www.pdspirits.com
Facebook: Prichard's Distillery
Twitter: @prichardspirits
Pinterest: Pricard's Distillery

Type: Micro-distillery. Opened in 1999.

Hours of operation: 8:00am to 4:00pm

Tours: Available

Types of spirits produced: Rum, whiskey, liqueurs

Names of spirits:

Rums
- Prichard's Fine Rum
- Prichard's Cranberry Rum
- Prichard's Crystal Rum
- Prichard's Key Lime Rum
- Prichard's Private Stock Rum
- Prichard's Sweet Georgia Bell

Whiskey
- Benjamin Prichard's Double Barreled Bourbon
- Benjamin Prichard's Double Chocolate Bourbon Whiskey
- Benjamin Prichard's Lincoln County Lightning
- Benjamin Prichard's Rye Whiskey
- Benjamin Prichard's Single Malt Whiskey
- Benjamin Prichard's Tennessee Whiskey

Liqueurs
- Benjamin Prichard's Cranberry Liqueur
- Benjamin Prichard's Sweet Lucy Bourbon Liqueur
- Benjamin Prichard's Sweet Lucy Bourbon Cream Liqueur

Best known for / most popular: Sweet Lucy

Average bottle price: $19.95 to $72.00

Distribution: 44 U.S. states; 8 European countries

Interesting facts: The first legal distillery in Tennessee in almost fifty years

SPEAKeasy Spirits

900 44th Avenue North, Ste. 100
Nashville, TN 37209
615-347-9543

Owners / Operators:
Jeff Pennington, Co-owner
Jenny Pennington, Co-owner

Email: info@tennesseesippingcream.com
Website: www.tennesseesippingcream.com
Facebook: Speakeasy Spirits
Twitter: @SpeakeasySpirit, @TNSippingCream

Type: Micro-distillery. Opened in 2012.

Hours of operation: Not provided

Tours: Available

Types of spirits produced: Liqueur

Names of spirits:
• Whisper Creek Tennessee Sipping Cream

Best known for / most popular:
Whisper Creek Tennessee Sipping Cream

Average bottle price: Not provided

Distribution: TN

Interesting facts: Not provided

Azar Distillery

8501 Cover Road
San Antonio, TX 78263
210-648-1500

Owners / Operators:
Richard N. Azar III (Trey), Founder / Master Distiller
Kimberly R. Azar, Founder

Email: trey@cincovodka.com
Website: www.cincovodka.com
Facebook: Cinco Vodka
Twitter: @CincoVodka
YouTube: Azar Distilling
Flickr: Cinco Vodka

Type: Micro-distillery. Opened in 2011.

Hours of operation: Monday through Friday, 9:00am to 5:00pm

Tours: Available by appointment

Types of spirits produced: Vodka

Names of spirits:
• Cinco ~ The Five Star Vodka

Best known for / most popular: Cinco Martini (Cincotini)

Average bottle price: $24.99 to $39.99

Distribution: CA, GA, TX

Interesting facts: Not provided

312

Balcones Distillery

212 S. 17th Street
Waco, TX 76701
254-755-6003

Owners / Operators:
Chip Tate, President and Head Distiller

BALCONES
DISTILLING

Email: info@balconesdistilling.com
Website: www.balconesdistilling.com
Facebook: Balcones Distillery
Twitter: @BalconesWhisky

Type: Micro-distillery. Opened in 2008.

Hours of operation:
Monday through Friday, 9:00am to 5:00pm

Tours: Available by appointment only

Types of spirits produced:
Whisky, rumble (sugar, honey and fig spirit), rum

Names of spirits:
• Rumble
• Rumble Cask Reserve
• Baby Blue Whisky
• True Blue Whisky
• Brimstone Whisky
• '1' Texas Single Malt Whisky

Best known for / most popular:
Baby Blue Corn Whisky and '1' Texas Single Malt Whisky

Average bottle price: $35.00 to $65.00

Distribution: CA, CT, DC, DE, FL, IL, KY, LA, MD, MN, NJ, NM, NY, TX

Interesting facts
Balcones Distilling are the producers of the first legal Texas whiskey since Prohibition, the only 100% Blue Corn whisky, and Texas' first single malt.

Bone Spirits

802 Northeast 1st Street
Smithville, TX 78957
512-237-5000

Owners / Operators:
Jeff Peace, Founder

Email: info@bonespirits.com
Website: www.bonespirits.com
Facebook: Bone Spirits LLC
Twitter: @BoneSpiritsLLC
LinkedIn: Jeff Peace

Type: Micro-distillery. Opened in 2010.

Hours of operation: Not provided

Tours: Not provided

Types of spirits produced:
Vodka, moonshine, whiskey, gin

Names of spirits:
- Smiths Premium Vodka
- Fitch's Goat Moonshine
- Fitch's Goat 100% Corn Whiskey
- Moody June American Dry Gin

Best known for / most popular: Not provided

Average bottle price: Not provided

Distribution: FL, GA, LA, OK, TN, TX

Interesting facts: Not provided

D.E.W. Distillation LLC

1400 Jacob's Well Road
Wimberley, TX 78676
512-847-6874

Owners / Operators:
David Watson, Owner/President
Laura Watson, Vice President
Walter Smith, General Manager

Email: David Watson, david@cypresscreekreserve.com
Laura Watson, laura@cypresscreekreserve.com
Walter Smith , walterlsmithjr@yahoo.com
Website: www.cypresscreekreserve.com
Facebook: Cypress Creek Reserve Rum

Type: Micro-distillery. Opened in 2010.

Hours of operation: Monday through Friday, 7:00am to 5:00pm

Tours: Available by appointment

Types of spirits produced: Rum

Names of spirits:
• Cypress Creek Reserve Crystal Rum
• Cypress Creek Reserve Vanilla Flavored Rum

Best known for / most popular: Cypress Creek Reserve Vanilla Citrus Martini

Average bottle price: $17.00 to $25.00

Distribution: TX

Interesting facts: Owner David Watson designed and built the distillery.

Firestone & Robertson Distilling Co.

901 W. Vickery
Fort Worth, TX 76104
817-840-9140

Owners / Operators:
Leonard Firestone, Co-founder / Distiller
Troy Robertson, Co-Founder / Distiller

Email: info@frdistilling.com
Website: www.frdistilling.com
Facebook: Firestone & Robertson Distilling Co.
Twitter: @FRDistilling

Type: Micro-distillery. Opened in 2012.

Hours of operation: Not provided

Tours: Available

Types of spirits produced: Bourbon, whiskey

Names of spirits:
• TX Blended Whiskey
• Straight Bourbon

Best known for / most popular: TX Blended Whiskey

Average bottle price: Not provided

Distribution: TX

Interesting facts: Not provided

316

Garrison Brothers Distillery

1827 Hye Albert Road
Hye, TX 78635
830-392-0246

Owners / Operators:
Dan Garrison, Proprietor

Email: dan@garrisonbros.com
Website: www.garrisonbros.com
Facebook: Garrison Brothers Distillery
Twitter: @garrisonbros

Type: Craft-distillery. Opened in 2005.

Hours of operation: Daily, 10:00am to 6:00pm

Tours: Available
Wednesday through Sunday, 10:00am, 12:00pm, 2:00pm, 4:00pm

Types of spirits produced: Straight Bourbon Whiskey

Names of spirits:
• Garrison Brothers Texas Straight Bourbon Whiskey

Best known for / most popular:
Garrison Brothers Texas Straight Bourbon Whiskey

Average bottle price: Not provided

Distribution: TX

Hideous LC

5276 Barth Road
Lockhart, TX 78644
512-443-3687

Owners / Operators:
Michael E. Klein, Owner

Email: hideousinfo@hideous.com
Website: www.hideous.com
Facebook: Hideous Liqueur
Twitter: @hideousliqueur

Type: Micro-distillery. Opened in 2012.

Hours of operation: Not open to the public

Tours: Not available

Types of spirits produced: Liqueur

Names of spirits:
- Hideous Liqueur

Best known for / most popular: Hideous Liqueur

Average bottle price: $27.00

Distribution: TX

Interesting facts:
- Hideous Liqueur is an all-natural 70 proof berry citrus liqueur that was created at a fraternity house in 1999 while Michael Klein was an undergraduate at The University of Texas at Austin.
- Hideous is one of the top selling on-premise spirits in Texas
- The H-Bomb (Hideous and energy drink is the most popular drink with the brand, however it is great in margaritas, martinis, or as a mixer with almost any other spirit or flavor.

HIDEOUS

LIQUEUR

JEM Beverage Company

2525 Tarpley Road #104
Carrollton, TX 75006

Owners / Operators:
Evan Batt, Co-Owner
John Straits, Co-Owner
Mike Pfeiffer, Co-Owner / Master Distiller

Email: info@jembevco.com
Website: www.westernsonvodka.com, www.redriverwhiskey.com
　　　　www.stingrayspicedrum.com, www.southernsonvodka.com
Facebook: Western Son Vodka, Southern Son Vodka
　　　　Red River Whiskey, Stingray Spiced Rum
Twitter: @westernsonvodka, @StingrayRum, @SouthrnSonVodka

Type: Micro-distillery. Opened in 2011.

Hours of operation: Vary

Tours: Available by appointment

Types of spirits produced:
Rum, whiskey, vodka

Names of spirits:
* Stingray Spiced Rum
* Southern Son Vodka
* Western Son Texas Vodka
* Red River Texas Bourbon Whiskey

Best known for / most popular:
Western Son Texas Vodka

Average bottle price: $17.99 to $27.99

Distribution:
AK, GA, LA, MA, MS, OK, RI, TN, TX

Interesting facts: JEM donates to two charities for their brands. The Peter Burks Unsung Hero Fund for both vodkas and Native Texas Wildlife Conservation for the Whiskey.

319

Quentin D. Witherspoon Distillery LLC

Lewisville, TX

Owners / Operators:
Quentin D. Witherspoon, CEO / Master Distiller
M. Ryan Dehart, CFO
Laurent Spamer, COO

Email: info@witherspoondistillery.com
Website: www.witherspoondistillery.com
Facebook: Quentin D. Witherspoon Distillery
Twitter: @River_Rum
Pinterest: Quentin Witherspoon

Type: Micro-distillery. Opened in 2011.

Hours of operation: Monday through Friday, 9:00 to 5:00pm

Tours: Private by appointment

Types of spirits produced: Rum, whiskey

Names of spirits:
- Witherspoon's River Rum
- Witherspoon's Texas Whiskey

Best known for / most popular:
Witherspoon's River Rum
Witherspoon's Texas Whiskey

Average bottle price: $20.00 to $40.00

Distribution: TX

Interesting facts:
Quentin Witherspoon began distilling water from the Congo River in Africa over 20 years ago, he also learned that water wasn't the only necessity one could provide with a still; and began making his own spirits. He spent 15 years in the Carolina's, Georgia, & Tennessee transforming legendary river waters into fine sipping whiskey.

Railean Distillers
Eagle Point Distillery

341 5th Street
San Leon, TX 77539
713-545-2742

Owners / Operators:
Kelly Railean, Owner / Master Distiller
Erik Bauer, EVP Sales

Email: Kelly Railean: krailean@railean.com
　　　　Erik Bauer: ebauer@railean.com
Website: www.railean.com
Facebook: Railean Handmade Texas Rum
Twitter: @RaileanRum
Flickr: Railean Rum

Type: Micro-distillery. Opened in 2007.

Hours of operation: Open to the public by appointment only

Tours: Available by appointment only

Types of spirits produced:
Rum (white and aged), 100% Blue Agave Spirit

Names of spirits:
- Railean Texas White Rum
- Railean Reserve XO Dark Rum
- Railean Small Cask Single Barrel Dark Rum
- Railean "El Perico" 100% Blue Agave Spirit
- Railean Spiced Rum
- Railean "El Perico" Blue Agave Reposado

Best known for / most popular:
Reserve XO Dark Rum

Average bottle price: $16.99 to $29.99

Distribution: AK, CA, TX

Interesting facts:
- First and only distillery in the Houston / Galveston area
- First and only certified American made rum in the USA
- Blue Agave Spirits is certified "Made in America"

Ranger Creek Brewing & Distilling

4834 Whirlwind Drive
San Antonio, TX 78217
210-775-2099

Owners / Operators:
Mark McDavid, Co-Founder, Sales / Marketing
TJ Miller, Co-founder / Operations / Head Distiller
Dennis Rylander, Co-founder / Finance / Accounting

Email: General Info, info@drinkrangercreek.com
       Mark McDavid, mark@drinkrangercreek.com
Website: www.drinkrangercreek.com
Facebook: Ranger Creek Brewing & Distilling
Twitter: @rangercreek
YouTube: DrinkRangerCreek

Type: Brewery / Micro-distillery. Opened in 2010.

Hours of operation: Open for tours only

Tours: Saturdays, 3:00pm to 5:00pm.
       Check the website for availability and to RSVP

Types of spirits produced: Whiskey

Names of spirits:
• Ranger Creek .36 Texas Bourbon Whiskey
• Ranger Creek Rimfire Mesquite Smoked Texas Single Malt Whiskey

Best known for / most popular:
Ranger Creek .36 Texas Bourbon Whiskey

Average bottle price: $35.00

Distribution: TX

Interesting facts: Ranger Creek is a combined brewery/distillery located in San Antonio, TX. They make beer and whiskey in their "brewstillery" and make it by hand one batch at a time. They primarily focus on the relationship between beer and whiskey. As a combined operation, they can do things to highlight this relationship that no one else can. For example, they age their own beer in bourbon barrels and distill their beers into whiskeys. They also use much of the same equipment to make both beer and whiskey because there are a lot of similarities between the two processes.

Rebecca Creek Distillery LLC

REBECCA CREEK™

A SPIRITED TEXAS DISTILLERY

Texas Hill Country

★

26605 Bulverde Road, Ste. B
San Antonio, TX 78260
830-714-4581

Owners / Operators:
Mike Cameron, Co-Founder / Owner
Steve Ison, Co-Founder / Owner

Email: info@rebeccacreekdistillery.com
Website: www.rebeccacreekdistillery.com, www.texasvodka.com
     www.rebeccacreekwhiskey.com
Facebook: Enchanted Rock Vodka,
     Rebecca Creek Fine Texas Spirit Whiskey
Twitter: @TXvodka

Type: Micro-distillery. Opened in 2010.

Hours of operation: Monday through Friday, 8:00am to 5:00pm

Tours: Available Saturdays, 12:00pm to 5:00pm

Types of spirits produced: Vodka, whiskey

Names of spirits:
- Enchanted Rock Vodka
- Rebecca Creek Fine Texas Whiskey

Best known for / most popular:
Enchanted Rock Ultra-Premium Texas Vodka

Average bottle price: $18.00 to $35.00

Distribution: TX

Interesting facts:
Rebecca Creek Distillery was the first legal
distillery in south Texas since Prohibition.

San Luis Spirits

PURE TEXAS VODKA

Dripping Springs, TX 78620
512-858-1199

Owners / Operators:
Kevin Kelleher, Owner

Email: info@sanluisspirits.com
Website: www.drippingspringsvodka.com
Facebook: Dripping Springs Vodka
Twitter: @DSVodka

Type: Micro-distillery. Opened in 2012.

Hours of operation: Not provided

Tours: Not provided

Types of spirits produced: Vodka

Names of spirits:
• Dripping Springs Texas Vodka

Best known for / most popular:
Dripping Springs Texas Vodka

Average bottle price: Not provided

Distribution: AZ, CO, LA, NM, OK, TX

Interesting facts: Not provided

SAVVY Distillers LP

13805 Quitman Pass
Austin, TX 78728
512-476-4477

Owners / Operators:
Chad Auler, Founder / President
Clayton Christopher, CEO
John Potts, VP of Sales
Brandon Cason, VP of Marketing
John Scarborough, CFO
Gary Crowell, Special Operations
Kevin Coles, Production Manager

Email: info@savvyvodka.com
Website: www.savvyvodka.com
Facebook: SAVVY Vodka
Twitter: @SavvyMartini

Type: Micro-distillery. Opened in 2007.

Hours of operation: Monday through Friday, 8:00 am to 5:00pm

Tours: Not available

Types of spirits produced: Vodka

Names of spirits:
• SAVVY Vodka

Best known for / most popular: SAVVY Vodka

Average bottle price: $20.00 to $25.00

Distribution: TX

Interesting facts: Not provided

South Congress Distillery

16525 Decker Creek Drive
Manor, TX 78563
512-589-3939

Owners / Operators:
Mike Jakle, Owner
Miles Ponder, Owner

Email: mike@whitehatrum.com
Website: www.whitehatrum.com
Facebook: White Hat Rum
Twitter: @WhiteHatRum

Type: Micro-distillery. Opened in 2009.

Hours of operation: Monday through Friday, 8:00am to 5:00pm

Tours: Available by request

Types of spirits produced: Rum

Names of spirits:
• White Hat Rum

Best known for / most popular:
White Hat Rum

Average bottle price: $19.99

Distribution: TX

Interesting facts:
Gold Medal - The Fifty Best White Rum Tasting 2013 NYC

Silver Medal - Ministry of Rum Tasting Competition 2012 Chicago

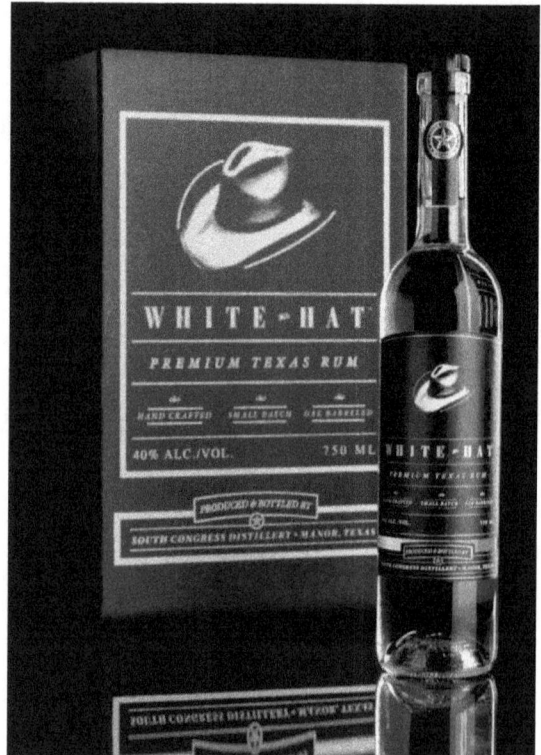

326

Spink Distillery

12732 Cimarron Path, Ste. 102
San Antonio, TX 78249
210-787-9020

Owners / Operators:
Nick Spink, Owner / Founder
Rachel Price, Master Distiller

Email: info@spikevodka.com
Website: www.spikevodka.com
Facebook: Spike Vodka

Type: Micro-distillery. Opened in 2012.

Hours of operation: Monday through Friday, 9:00am to 5:00pm

Tours: Not available

Types of spirits produced: Vodka

Names of spirits:
• Spike Vodka

Best known for / most popular: Spiked Lemon and Spikerita

Average bottle price: $22.00 to $26.00

Distribution: TX

Interesting facts:
Spike Vodka is made from fermenting cactus.

Spirit of Texas LLC

1715 Dalshank Street, Ste. A
Pflugerville, TX 78660
512-789-1600

Owners / Operators:
Shaun Siems, Co-founder
Jason Malik, Co-founder
Michael Rajski, Partner

Email: General info: info@spiritoftx.com
          Shaun Siems: shaun.siems@spiritoftx.com
          Jason Malik: jason.malik@spiritoftx.com
          Michael Rajski: michael.rajski@spiritoftx.com
Website: www.spiritoftx.com www.pecanstreetrum.com
Facebook: Spirit of Texas Distillery Pecan Street Rum
Twitter: @spiritoftx1

Type: Micro-distillery. Opened in 2010.

Hours of operation:
Monday through Friday, 8:00am to 5:00pm

Tours: Not available

Types of spirits produced: Rum

Names of spirits:
• Pecan Street Rum
• Spirit of Texas Rum

Best known for / most popular: Pecan Street Rum

Average bottle price: $20.00

Distribution: TX

Interesting facts:
Pecan Street Rum is the first known rum to be
aged in American oak barrels with Texas pecans.

Texacello LLC

5214 Burleson Road
Austin, TX 78744
512-636-6389

Owners / Operators:
Paula Angerstein, Founder / Owner
Dee Kelleher, Managing Partner

Email: info@paulastexasspirits.com
Website: www.paulastexasspirits.com
Facebook: Paula's Texas Spirits
Twitter: @PaulasTXSpirits

Type: Small batch macerate. Opened in 2004.

Hours of operation: Vary

Tours: Not available

Types of spirits produced: Liqueur

Names of spirits:
- Paula's Texas Orange
- Paula's Texas Lemon

Best known for / most popular:
Margarita, Lemon Drop

Average bottle price: $22.00

Distribution: TX

Interesting facts:
- Paula is the organizer and charter board member of Texas Distilled Spirits Association.
- Paula's Texas Lemon is one of only a handful of limoncellos made in the USA.
- Paula's Texas Orange is one of only a few orange liqueurs made in the USA.

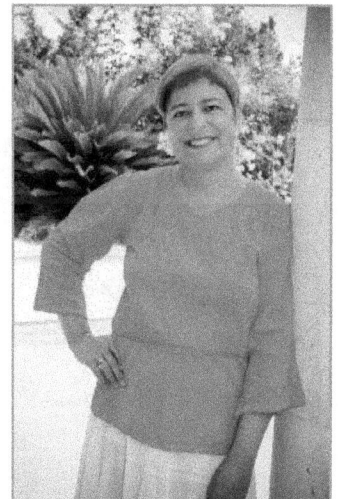

The Original Texas Legend Distillery

1501 Simmons
Orange, TX 77630

Owners / Operators:
Thomas Germann, CEO
William Manning, Operations Manager
Benjamin Higgs, Director of Leisure

Email: tger68@yahoo.com
Website: www.theoriginaltexaslegenddistillery.com
Facebook: Friends of The Original Texas Legend Distillery

Type: Micro-distillery. Opened in 2012.

Hours of operation: Vary

Tours: Not available

Types of spirits produced: Vodka, bourbon, blended whiskey

Names of spirits:
- Troubador Vodka
- Troubadour Texas Bourbon
- Troubadour Blended Whiskey

Best known for / most popular: Troubador Vodka

Average bottle price: $18.00

Distribution: United Wine & Spirits, Houston TX

Interesting facts: True handcrafted batch blended vodka. Each and every bottle of Troubadour Vodka is hand signed by the distiller that made that vodka.

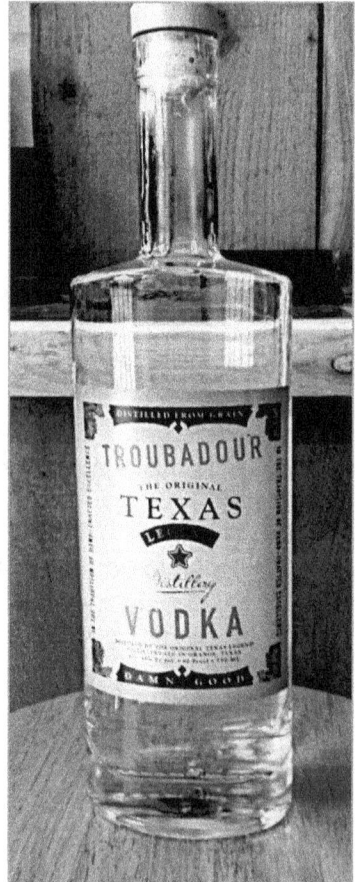

Tito's Handmade Vodka

Fifth Generation, Inc.
Mockingbird Distillery

1406 Smith Road
Austin, TX 78721
512-389-9011

Owners / Operators:
Tito Beveridge, Owner

Email: info@titosvodka.com
Website: www.titosvodka.com
Facebook: Titos Handmade Vodka
Twitter: @TitosVodka
Flicker: Titos Vodka
Pinterest: TitosVodka

Type: Micro-distillery. Opened in 1995.

Hours of operation:
Monday through Friday, 8:00am to 5:00pm

Tours: Not available

Types of spirits produced: Vodka

Names of spirits:
• Tito's Handmade Vodka

Best known for / most popular: Tito's Handmade Vodka

Average bottle price: $20.00

Distribution: Throughout the U.S. and Canada

Interesting facts:
• Tito's Handmade Vodka is Texas' first and oldest legal distillery.
• Tito's Handmade Vodka is gluten free.

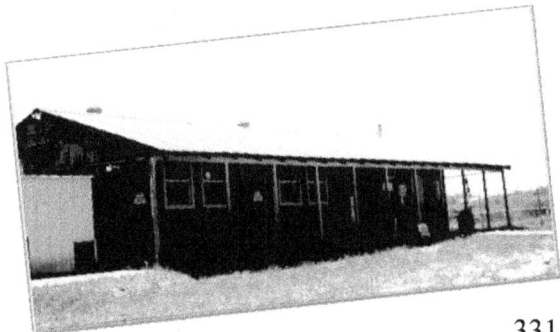

Treaty Oak Distilling Co.

13011 DeBarr Drive
Austin, TX 78729
512-699-5041

Owners / Operators:
Daniel R. Barnes, Owner

Email: info@treatyoakrum.com
Website: www.treatyoakdistilling.blogspot.com
Facebook: Treaty Oak Distilling Co.
Twitter: @TreatyOakTX

Type: Micro-distillery. Opened in 2005.

Hours of operation: Not provided

Tours: Not provided

Types of spirits produced: Rum, gin, vodka

Names of spirits:
- Treaty Oak Platinum Rum
- Treaty Oak Aged Rum
- Waterloo Gin
- Starlite Vodka
- Graham's Texas Tea

Best known for / most popular: Not provided

Average bottle price: Not provided

Distribution: Not provided

Interesting facts: Not provided

Whitmeyer's Distilling Co. LLC

12821 Duncan Road, Bldg. 5 Ste. G
Houston, TX 77067
713-623-1637

Owners / Operators:
Travis Whitmeyer, Founder / Owner
Chris Whitmeyer, Founder / Owner
Wesley Whitmeyer, Founder / Owner
Sam Freeman, Director of Operations

Email: info@whitmeyers.com
Website: www.whitmeyers.com
Facebook: Whitmeyer's Distilling
Twitter: @HOU_Distillery

Type: Micro-distillery. Opened in 2012.

Hours of operation: Open for tours only

Tours: Available

Types of spirits produced: Vodka, bourbon whiskey, moonshine whiskey, flavored whiskey

Names of spirits:
- Space City Vodka
- Whitmeyer's Texas Moonshine Whiskey
- Whitmeyer's Texas Peach Whiskey
- Whitmeyer's Texas Single Barrel
- Cask Strength Straight Bourbon Whiskey

Best known for / most popular: Not provided

Average bottle price: $18.00 to $70.00

Distribution: TX

Interesting facts: Not provided

Yellow Rose Distilling LLC

34444 Wright Road
Pinehurst, TX 77362
281-305-8106

Owners / Operators:
Troy Smith, Founding Partner / Master Distiller
Ryan Baird, Founding Partner
Randy Whitaker, Managing Partner

Email: info@yellowrosedistilling.com
Website: www.yellowrosedistilling.com
Facebook: Yellow Rose Distilling
Twitter: @YR_Distilling

Type: Micro-distillery. Opened in 2012.

Hours of operation: Not provided

Tours: Not available

Types of spirits produced: Whiskey

Names of spirits:
- Outlaw Bourbon Whiskey
- Straight Rye Whiskey

Best known for / most popular:
Outlaw Bourbon Whiskey

Average bottle price: $30.00 to $65.00

Distribution: TX

Interesting facts: Not provided

334

High West Distillery

703 Park Avenue
Park City, UT 84060
435-649-8300

Owners / Operators:
David Perkins, Owner

Email: info@highwest.com
Website: www.highwest.com
Facebook: High West Distillery
Twitter: @HighWest
Yelp: High West Distillery & Saloon

Type: Micro-distillery. Opened in 2009.

Hours of operation: Daily, 10:00am to 10:00pm

Tours: Available

Types of spirits produced: Whiskey, vodka

Names of spirits:
- High West Whiskey Rendezvous Rye
- High West Whiskey Double Rye
- High West Silver Whiskey Western Oat
- High West Vodka 7000
- High West Vodka 7000 Peach
- High West Distillery Barreled Manhattan
- High West Double Rye
- High West Son Of Bourye
- High West OMG Pure Rye
- High West Valley Tan

Best known for / most popular:
High West Whiskey Rendezvous Rye

Average bottle price: $30.00 to $130.00

Distribution: AZ, CA, CO, DC, FL, GA, IL, KY, LA, NM, MA, MD, MN, MO, NV, NY, OR, PA, SC, TN, TX, UT, VA, WA, WI, WY; UK; Quebec, Alberta

Interesting facts:
- High West Distillery became the first legal distillery in Utah since 1870.
- High West Distillery and Saloon is the only ski-in gastro-distillery in the world.

Ogden's Own Distillery

2679 Midland Drive #4
Ogden, UT 84401
801-458-1995

Owners / Operators:
Tim Smith, Founder / Distiller
Steve Conlin, Partner / Marketing
Mike Glasmann, Partner / Executive
Stu Smith, Partner / Executive

Email: info@ogdensown.com
Website: www.ogdensown.com
Facebook: Five Wives Vodka
              Underground Herbal Spirit
Twitter: @OgdensOwn

Type: Micro-distillery. Opened in 2009.

Hours of operation: Monday through Friday, 9:00am to 5:00pm

Tours: Not available

Types of spirits produced: Liqueur, vodka

Names of spirits:
- Underground Herbal Spirit
- Five Wives Vodka
- Five Wives Sinful Vodka

Best known for / most popular:
Underground Herbal Spirit and Five Wives Vodka

Average bottle price: $19.95

Distribution: AK, AL, CA, CO, ID, MI, MO, MT, NV, OR, PA, TX, UT, WA, WY

Interesting facts:
- "Distillery of the Year" 2012 New York International Spirits Competition
- Awards - Underground Herbal Spirit
  - 2013 Best of Category "Liqueurs" in Spirits of the Americas Competition
  - 2013 Gold, Denver Int. Spirits Competition
- Awards - Five Wives Vodka
  - 2012 Bronze in New York International Spirits Competition
  - 2013 Silver in Spirits of the Americas Competition
  - 2013 Silver Medal, Denver International Spirits Competition
  - 2013 Silver Medal, San Francisco World Spirits Competition

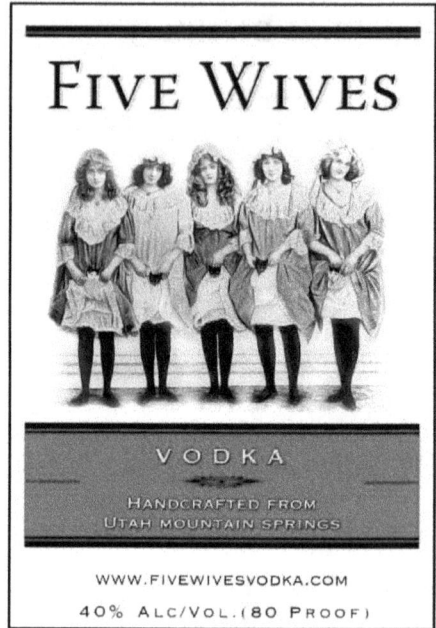

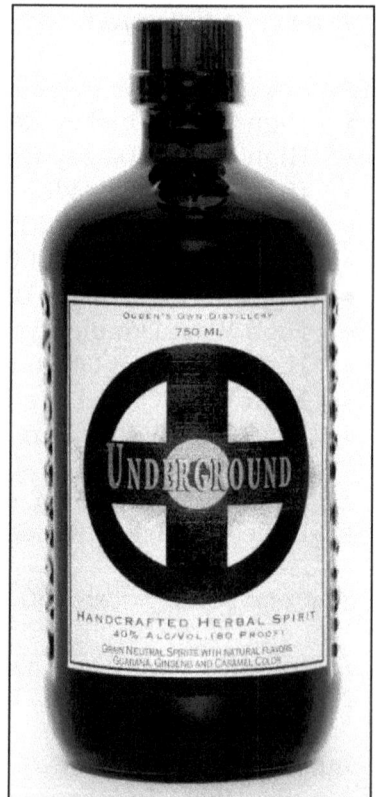

336

Boyden Valley Winery & Spirits

64 Vermont Route 104
Cambridge, VT 05444
802-644-8151

Owners / Operators:
David Boyden, Co-owner
Linda Boyden, Co-owner

Email: info@boydenvalley.com
Website: www.boydenvalley.com
Facebook: Boyden Valley Winery
Twitter: @Bwinery

Type: Micro-distillery. Opened in 2010.

Hours of operation: Daily, 10:00am to 5:00pm

Tours: Available

Types of spirits produced: Liqueurs

Names of spirits:
• Vermont Ice Apple Crème
• Vermont Ice Maple Crème

Best known for / most popular: Not provided

Average bottle price: Not provided

Distribution: Not provided

Interesting facts: Not provided

Caledonia Spirits Inc.
Caledonia Winery Inc.

46 Buffalo Mountain Commons Drive
Hardwick, VT 05843
802-472-8000

Owners / Operators:
Todd Hardie, Owner

Email: info@caledoniaspirits.com
Website: www.caledoniaspirits.com
Facebook: Caledonia Spirits & Winery
Twitter: @CaledoniaSpirit

Type: Winery / Micro-distillery. Opened in 2011.

Hours of operation: Monday through Saturday, 10:00am to 6:00pm

Tours: Not provided

Types of spirits produced: Vodka, cordial

Names of spirits:
- Barr Hill Vodka
- Barr Hill Honey Vodka
- Caledonia Spirits Elderberry Cordial

Best known for / most popular: Not provided

Average bottle price: Not provided

Distribution: DC, MA, MD, NJ, NY, VT

Interesting facts: Not provided

Dunc's Mill

622 Keyser Hill Road
St. Johnsbury, VT 05819
802-745-9486

Aged and flavored rums made from Fair Trade, organic cane and Vermont flavors

Owners / Operators:
Duncan Holaday, Owner

Email: duncan@duncsmill.com
Website: www.duncsmill.com

Type: Micro-distillery. Opened in 1998.

Hours of operation: Not provided

Tours: Available by appointment

Types of spirits produced: Rum

Names of spirits:
- Dunc's Mill Maple Flavored Rum
- Dunc's Mill Elderflower Flavored Rum
- Backwoods Reserve Straight Rum

Best known for / most popular: Dunc's Mill Elderflower Flavored Rum

Average bottle price: Not provided

Distribution: Not provided

Interesting facts: The oldest continuously operating distillery in VT.

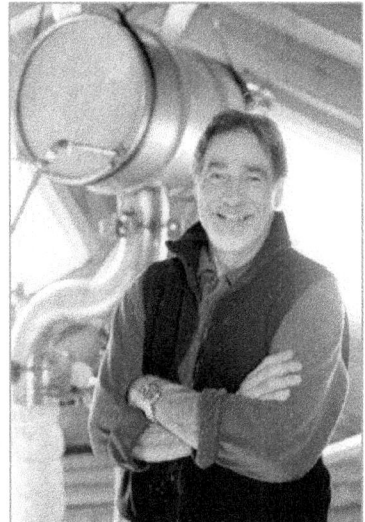

Elm Brook Farm

250 Elm Brook Road
East Fairfield, VT 05448
802-782-5999

Owners / Operators:
David Howe, Owner

Email: ebf@elmbrookfarm.com
Website: www.elmbrookfarm.com
Twitter: @ElmBrookFarm

Type: Micro-distillery. Opened in 2012.

Hours of operation: Available by appointment

Tours: Available by appointment

Types of spirits produced:
Vodka, barrel aged specialty spirit

Names of spirits:
• Literary Dog Premium Sipping Vodka
• Rail Dog Barrel Aged Eau de Vie
• Aged Maple Specialty Spirit
• Literary Dog Maple Based Premium Sipping Vodka

Best known for / most popular: Not provided

Average bottle price: $53.99

Distribution:
Elm Brook Farm, Burlington VT Farmers' Market and most VT Liquor Outlets

Interesting facts:
• Literary Dog Vodka is distilled more than 20 times
• Elm Brook Farm does not use charcoal filtering

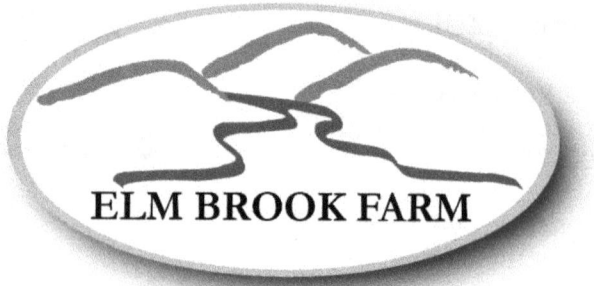

340

Flag Hill Farm

135 Ewing Road
Vershire, VT 05079
802-685-7724

Owners / Operators:
Sebastian Lousada and Sabra Ewing, Owners

Email: flaghillfarm@wildblue.net
Website: www.flaghillfarm.com
Facebook: Flag Hill Farm Vermont Hard Cyder

Type: Micro-distillery. Winery in 1986. Distillery in 2002

Hours of operation: Appointment only

Tours: Appointment only

Types of spirits produced: Brandy

Names of spirits:
- Pomme de Vie - Vermont Apple Brandy
- Stair's Pear - Vermont Pear Brandy

Best known for / most popular: Apple Brandy

Average bottle price: $17.50 to $20.00

Distribution: VT

Interesting facts:
- Produced the first legal Vermont brandies since Prohibition
- Flag Hill Farm Winery and Distillery is certified organic

Green Mountain Distillers

192 Thomas Lane, Ste. 1
Stowe, VT 05672
802-253-0064

Owners / Operators:
Timothy Danahy, Founder / Distiller
Harold Faircloth III, Founder / Distiller

Email: info@greendistillers.com
Website: www.greendistillers.com
Facebook: Green Mountain Distillers

Type: Micro-Distillery. Opened in 2002.

Hours of operation: Not provided

Tours: Not provided

Types of spirits produced: Vodka, gin

Names of spirits:
* Green Mountain Organic Gin
* Green Mountain Organic Sunshine Vodka
* Green Mountain Organic Lemon Vodka
* Green Mountain Organic Orange Vodka
* Green Mountain Organic Maple Liqueur

Best known for / most popular: Not provided

Average bottle price: Not provided

Distribution: Not provided

Interesting facts: Not provided

Saxtons River Distillery LLC

485 West River Road
Brattleboro, VT 05301
802-246-1128

Owners / Operators:
Christian Stromberg, Owner

Email: sapling@saplingliqueur.com
Website: www.saplingliqueur.com
Facebook: Sapling Vermont Maple Liqueur

Type: Micro-distillery. Opened in 2007.

Hours of operation:
Tuesday through Friday, 9:00am to 5:00pm
Saturday, 10:00am to 5:00pm; Sunday and Monday, Closed

Tours: Not provided

Types of spirits produced: Liqueur

Names of spirits:
• Sapling Vermont Maple Liqueur

Best known for / most popular: Sapling Vermont Maple Liqueur

Average bottle price: Not provided

Distribution: CA, MA, PA, VT

Interesting facts: Not provided

Shelburne Orchards Distillery

216 Orchard Road
Shelburne, VT 05482
802-985-2753

Owners / Operators:
Nick Cowles, Owner

Email: apple100@together.net
Website: www.shelburneorchards.com
Facebook: Shelburne Orchards

Type: Micro-distillery. Opened in 2009.

Hours of operation:
Monday through Saturday, 9:00am to 6:00pm
Sunday, 9:00am to 5:00pm

Tours: Available

Types of spirits produced: Brandy

Names of spirits:
• Dead Bird Apple Brandy

Best known for / most popular:
Dead Bird Apple Brandy

Average bottle price: Not provided

Distribution: Not provided

Interesting facts: Not provided

344

Smugglers' Notch Distillery

276 Main Street
Jeffersonville, VT 05363
802-309-3077

Owners / Operators:
Ron Elliott, Co-owner
Jeremy Elliott, Co-owner / President

Email: jeremy@smugglersnotchdistillery.com
Website: www.smugglersnotchdistillery.com
Facebook: Smugglers Notch Distillery

Type: Micro-distillery. Opened in 2010.

Hours of operation: Monday through Sunday, 1:00pm to 5:00pm

Tours: Not available

Types of spirits produced: Vodka, rum, gin

Names of spirits:
- Smugglers' Notch Vodka
- Smugglers' Notch Gin
- Smugglers' Notch Rum

Best known for / most popular: Smugglers' Notch Vodka

Average bottle price: $26.99 to $29.99

Distribution: NH, VT

Interesting facts: The name, Smugglers' Notch, captures the legacy of the smugglers who used this thickly forested, rugged mountain pass with its surrounding caves to move goods and liquor from Canada into the United States. This route was first explored as a secret passageway during the Embargo Act of 1807 and then again in the 1920s to transport liquor during prohibition.

Vermont Distillers

7755 Route 9 East
West Marlboro, VT 05363
802-464-2003

Owners / Operators:
Edward C. Metcalfe, Jr., CEO
Augustus (Gus) Metcalfe, Production and Marketing
Dominic Metcalfe, Marketing and Sales

Email: info@vermontdistillers.com
Website: www.vermontdistillers.com
Facebook: Vermont Distillers

Type: Micro-distillery. Opened in 2012.

Hours of operation: Daily, 10:00am to 5:00pm

Tours: Not available

Types of spirits produced: Cordials, vodka

Names of spirits:
• Metcalfe's Vermont Maple Cream Liqueur
• Metcalfe's Raspberry Liqueur
• Ciriaco's Limoncello
• Mount Snow Vodka

Best known for / most popular:
Metcalfe's Vermont Maple Cream Liqueur

Average bottle price: $24.95 to $29.95

Distribution: AZ, CT, FL, MA, MN, ND, NH, NJ, NV, NY, OR, TX, VT, WA, WI

Interesting facts: Not provided

Vermont Spirits Distilling Co.

Quechee Gorge Village
5573 Woodstock Road
Quechee, VT 05059
866-998-6352

Owners / Operators:
Steve Johnson, President / CEO
Harry Gorman, Vice President / Distiller
Mimi Buttenheim, General Manager

Email: info@vermontspirits.com
Website: www.vermontspirits.com
Facebook: Vermont Spirits Distilling Co.
Twitter: @VermontSpirits

Type: Micro-distillery. Opened in 2012.

Hours of operation:
Monday through Sunday, 10:00am to 5:00pm
Call for seasonal hours

Tours: Not available

Types of spirits produced: Vodka

Names of spirits:
- Vermont Gold Vodka
- Vermont White Vodka
- Vermont Spirits Limited Release Vodka

Best known for / most popular: Vermont Vodka

Average bottle price: $20.00 to $50.00

Distribution: CT, DC, MA, ME, NH, NJ, NY, OR, RI, TN, VA, VT, WA

Interesting facts:
- Vermont White Vodka is lactose free
- Both vodkas are gluten free

347

A. Smith Bowman Distillery

One Bowman Drive
At Deep Run
Fredericksburg, VA 22408
540-373-4555

Owners / Operators:

Email: pioneer@asmithbowman.com
Website: www.asmithbowman.com
Facebook: A. Smith Bowman Distillery

Type: Micro-distillery. Opened in 1935, moved in 1988.

Hours of operation:
Distillery is open from 9:00am to 4:00pm
Gift shop is open from 9:00am to 3:00pm leaving every hour

Tours: Available at 10:00am, 2:00pm and by appointment

Types of spirits produced:
Bourbon, limited edition whiskeys, gin, vodka, rum

Names of spirits:
- Bowman Brothers Small Batch Virginia Straight Bourbon Whiskey
- John J. Bowman Single Barrel Virginia Straight Bourbon Whiskey
- Abraham Bowman Limited Edition Whiskey
- George Bowman Colonial Era Dark Caribbean Rum
- Deep Run Virginia Vodka
- Sunset Hills Virginia Gin
- Virginia Gentleman

Best known for / most popular:
Hand crafted small batch VA bourbons

Average bottle price: Not provided

Distribution: CO, DC, FL, IL, KY, LA, MA, MD,
MI, MO, NJ, NY, OR, PA, SC, TN, TX, VA

Interesting facts:
Gold Medal, John J. Bowman Single Barrel Bourbon & Bowman Brothers
Small Batch Bourbon, San Francisco World Spirits Competition.

348

Appalachian Mountain Spirits LLC
Virginia Sweetwater Distillery

760 Walkers Creek Road
Marion, VA 24365
276-782-0932

Owners / Operators:
Scott Schumaker, Owner

Email: appmtnspirits@yahoo.com
Website: www.virginiasweetwaterdistillery.com
Facebook: Appalachian Mountain Spirits LLC

Type: Micro-distillery. Opened in 2013.

Hours of operation: Not provided

Tours: Not provided

Types of spirits produced: Moonshine, whiskey

Names of spirits:
• Virginia Sweetwater Moonshine
• War Horn Whiskey

Best known for / most popular:
Virginia Sweetwater Moonshine

Average bottle price: Not provided

Distribution: Not provided

Interesting facts: Not provided

Belmont Farms Distillery

13490 Cedar Run Road
Culpeper, VA 22701
540-825-3207

Owners / Operators:
Chuck and Jeanette Miller, Owners

Email: jtmiller46@aol.com
Website: www.virginiawhiskey.com

Type: Micro-distillery. Opened in 1987.

Hours of operation: Tuesday through Saturday, 10:00am to 5:00pm

Tours:
Available from April 1st through December 15th
Tuesday through Saturday, from 10:00am to 5:00pm

Types of spirits produced: Virginia whiskey, corn whiskey

Names of spirits:
- Kopper Kettle Virginian Whiskey
- Virginia Lightning Whiskey

Best known for / most popular: Virginia Lightning Whiskey

Average bottle price: $17.95 to $29.95

Distribution: VA

Interesting facts:
Belmont Farms Distillery has appeared on "How It's Made" on the Science Channel and has been featured on "The History Channel" and "The National Geographic Channel." Additionally, Author Patricia Cornwell visited the still and did her own filming.

Catoctin Creek Distilling Co. LLC

37251C East Richardson Lane
Purcellville, VA 20132
540-751-8404

Owners / Operators:
Scott and Becky Harris, Owners

Email: info@catoctincreek.com
Website: www.catoctincreek.com
Facebook: Catoctin Creek Distilling Company
Twitter: @catoctincreek
YouTube: Catoctin Creek Distilling Company
LinkedIn: Catoctin Creek Distilling Company

Type: Micro-distillery. Opened in 2009.

Hours of operation:
Monday through Friday, 8:00am to 3:00pm
Saturday, 11:00am to 4:00pm

Tours: Available

Types of spirits produced:
Rye whiskey, gin, fruit spirits

Names of spirits:
- Catoctin Creek Organic Roundstone Rye™
- Catoctin Creek Organic Mosby's Spirit™
- Catoctin Creek Organic Watershed Gin®
- Catoctin Creek Pearousia®
- Catoctin Creek 1757 Virginia Brandy™

Best known for / most popular:
Catoctin Creek Organic Roundstone Rye™

Average bottle price: $38.90

Distribution: CA, DC, GA, KY, MD, TN, VA, WA

Interesting facts:
- First legal distillery in Loudoun County, VA since Prohibition
- Certified organic and kosher

Photo by: Ed Felker, Mayfly Design

Chesapeake Bay Distillery LLC

2669 Production Road #106
Virginia Beach, VA 23454
757-692-4083

Owners / Operators:
Chris Richeson, Managing member

Email: info@chesapeakebaydistillery.com
Website: www.chesapeakebaydistillery.com
Facebook: Spirits of the Blue Ridge Vodka
Twitter: @blueridgevodka

Type: Micro-distillery. Opened in 2006.

Hours of operation: Not open to the public

Tours: Not available

Types of spirits produced: Vodka, rum

Names of spirits:
- Spirits of the Blue Ridge Vodka
- Chick's Beach Rum

Best known for / most popular:
Spirits of the Blue Ridge Vodka

Average bottle price: $19.95 to $22.45

Distribution: VA

Interesting facts: Not provided

Copper Fox Distillery

9 River Lane
Sperryville, VA 22740
540-987-8554

Owners / Operators:
Richard Wasmund, Owner / Master Distiller

Email: rwasm@aol.com
Website: www.copperfox.biz
Facebook: Copper Fox Distillery
Twitter: @cufoxdistillery
YouTube: Copper Fox Distillery

Type: Micro-distillery. Opened in 2005.

Hours of operation:
Monday through Saturday, 10:00am to 6:00pm

Tours: Available

Types of spirits produced: Single malt whisky, rye whisky

Names of spirits:
- Wasmund's Single Malt Whisky
- Wasmund's Single Malt Spirit
- Copper Fox Rye Whisky
- Wasmund's Rye Spirit

Best known for / most popular:
Wasmund's Single Malt Whisky

Average bottle price: Not provided

Distribution: 24 U.S. states

353

Parched Group LLC

2700 Hardy Street
Richmond, VA 23220
804-231-3000

Owners / Operators:
Paul McCann, Owner

Email: info@cirrusvodka.com
Website: www.cirrusvodka.com
Facebook: Cirrus Vodka
Twitter: @CirrusVodka

Type: Micro-distillery. Opened in 2009.

Hours of operation: Not provided

Tours: Not provided

Types of spirits produced: Vodka

Names of spirits:
• Cirrus Vodka

Best known for / most popular: Cirrus Vodka

Average bottle price: Not provided

Distribution: DC, GA, IN, MD, MI, TN, VA

Interesting facts: Not provided

Reservoir Distillery

1800 A Summit Avenue
Richmond, VA 23230
804-912-2621

Owners / Operators:
David Cuttino, General Manager / Co-owner
James H. Carpenter, Master Distiller / Co-owner

Email: info@reservoirdistillery.com
Website: www.reservoirdistillery.com
Facebook: Reservoir Distillery
Twitter: @ReservoirDist

Type: Micro-distillery. Opened in 2009.

Hours of operation: Daily

Tours: Not available

Types of spirits produced: Bourbon, whiskey

Names of spirits:
- Reservoir Bourbon
- Reservoir Rye Whiskey
- Reservoir Wheat Whiskey

Best known for / most popular: Not provided

Average bottle price: $40.00 to $80.00

Distribution: DC, DE, FL, MD, VA

355

Virginia Distillery Company

299 Eades Lane
Lovingston, VA 22949
434-325-1299

Owners / Operators:
George Moore, Chairman
John McCray, President

Email: info@vadistillery.com
Website: www.vadistillery.com
Facebook: Virginia Distillery
Twitter: @VADistillery

Type: Craft-distillery. Opened in 2010.

Hours of operation: Not provided

Tours: Not provided

Types of spirits produced: Whisky

Names of spirits:
• Virginia Highland Malt Whisky

Best known for / most popular: Not provided

Average bottle price: $55.00

Distribution: DC, DE, IL, MA, MD, NYC, VA

Interesting facts: Not provided

2bar® Spirits

2960 4th Avenue S, #106
Seattle, WA 98134
206-801-1113

Owners / Operators:
Nathan Kaiser, Owner

Email: info@2barspirits.com
Website: www.2barspirits.com
Facebook: 2bar Spirits
Twitter: @2bar
Pinterest: 2bar Spirits
Flicker: 2bar Spirits' Photostream
Vimeo: 2bar Spirits

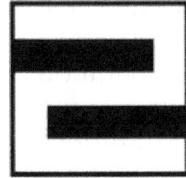

Type: Micro-distillery. Opened in 2012.

Hours of operation: Monday through Friday, 9:00am to 5:00pm

Tours: Available

Types of spirits produced: Vodka, moonshine

Names of spirits:
- 2bar Vodka
- 2bar Moonshine

Best known for / most popular:
Moonshine over Manhattan

Average bottle price: $30.00

Distribution: Seattle, WA

Interesting facts:
2bar Spirits is descended from five generations who ranched their land under the 2bar brand. For more than a century they have stood for quality, independence and hard work. Now those characteristics transcend to 2bar Spirits, handcrafted in Seattle, Washington.

357

Bainbridge Organic Distillers

9727 Coppertop Loop NE, Unit 101
Bainbridge Island, WA   98110
206-842-3184

Owners / Operators:
Keith Barnes, Owner / Distiller

Email: info@bainbridgedistillers.com
Website: www.bainbridgedistillers.com
Facebook: Bainbridge Organic Distillers
Yelp: Bainbridge Organic Distillers

Type: Craft-distillery. Opened in 2009.

Hours of operation:
May to Oct.: Monday through Sunday, 12:00pm to 5:00pm
Nov. to April: Monday through Saturday, 12:00pm to 5:00pm

Tours: Available

Types of spirits produced: Vodka, whiskey, gin

Names of spirits:
- Bainbridge Legacy Organic Vodka
- Bainbridge Battle Point Organic Whiskey
- Bainbridge Heritage Organic Gin
- Bainbridge Rolling Bay Organic Rye
- Bainbridge 'The Whiskey Forty Saloon' Organic Whiskey

Best known for / most popular: Bainbridge Battle Point Whiskey

Average bottle price: $34.95 to $48.95

Distribution: WA (CA in 2013)

Interesting facts: Not provided

Batch 206 Distillery

1417 Elliott Avenue West
Seattle, WA 98119

Owners / Operators:
Jeff and Daleen Steichen, Owners
Rusty Figgins, Master Distiller

Email: info@batch206.com
Website: www.batch206.com
Facebook: Batch 206
Twitter: @batch206

Type: Micro-distillery. Opened in March 2012.

Hours of operation:
Wednesday through Friday, 2:00pm to 7:00pm
Saturday and Sunday, 12:00pm to 6:00pm

Tours: Available

Types of spirits produced: Vodka, gin, moonshine

Names of spirits:
- Batch 206 Vodka
- Batch 206 Mad Mint Vodka
- Counter Gin
- See 7 Stars Moonshine

Best known for / most popular:
Batch 206 Vodka and Counter Gin

Average bottle price: $24.95

Distribution: AZ, CA, CT, DE, FL, GA, MD, NJ, NM, NV, OR, SC, TX, WA

Interesting facts: Not provided

BelleWood Distilling

6140 Guide Meridian
Lynden, WA 98264
360-318-7720

Owners / Operators:
John & Dorie Belisle, Owners
Jake Fowler, Manager
Jessie Parker, Distiller

Email: info@bellewoodfarms.com
Website: www.bellewoodfarms.com, www.bellewooddistilling.com
Facebook: BelleWood Acres - Apples and Apple Cider
YouTube: BelleWood Acres TV Commerical
Flickr: Bellewood Acres

Type: Micro-distillery. Opened in 2012.

Hours of operation:
Daily, 9:00am to 5:00pm, Sept. through Dec.
Mondays, Closed, January through August

Tours: Available

Types of spirits produced:
Vodka, eau de vie brandy, gin

Names of spirits:
• BelleWood Vodka
• BelleWood Apple Eau de Vie
• BelleWood Gin

Best known for / most popular:
BelleWood Vodka

Average bottle price: $23.00 to $49.00

Distribution:
On farm sales at BelleWood Acres, Haggen and Top Food, a 28 store local grocery chain, plus local restaurants and bars. A complete list can be found on our web site.

Interesting facts: They are growers as well as distillers. They raise 25,000 trees in the most Northwest corner of our nation and results in over 1.7 million pounds of fruit. Their farm provides a true farm to glass experience.

Black Heron Spirits Distillery

8011 Keene Road
West Richland, WA 99353
509-967-0781

Owners / Operators:
Joel Tefft, Owner

Email: info@blackheronspirits.com
Website: www.blackheronspirits.com
Facebook: Black Heron Spirits

Type: Micro-distillery. Opened in 2010.

Hours of operation: Friday and Saturday, 12:00pm to 5:00pm

Tours: Available

Types of spirits produced: Vodka, gin, whisky, lemoncello

Names of spirits:
- Ink Vodka
- Rayn Anjel Gin
- Desert Lightning Corn Whisky
- Lemoncello
- Black Heron Brandy
- Coyote Howl Whisky
- Finn Huckleberry Vodka
- Brushfire Pepper Vodka
- Huckleberry Cordial

Best known for / most popular:
Desert Lightning and Lemoncello

Average bottle price: $30.00

Distribution: WA

Interesting facts: Not provided

Black Rock Spirits LLC

1952 1st Avenue South #5
Seattle, WA 98134

Owners / Operators:
Sven Liden, Co-founder / Owner
Stefan Schachtell, Co-founder / Owner
Chris Marshall, Co-founder / Owner

Email: info@blackrockspirits.com
Website: www.blackrockspirits.com, www.bakonvodka.com
         www.sparkledonkey.com
Facebook: Black Rock Spirits, Bacon Vodka
Twitter: @baconvodka, @BlackRockSp
LinkedIn: Black Rock Spirits LLC

Type:
Contract distilled at Koenig Distillery, ID. Opened in 2008.

Hours of operation:
Monday through Friday, 9:00am to 6:00pm

Tours: Not available

Types of spirits produced: Vodka

Names of spirits:
- Bakon Vodka

Best known for / most popular: Bakon Bloody Mary

Average bottle price: $28.00

Distribution: 46 U.S. states and 5 countries

Interesting facts:
Passed $1M in sales of Bakon Vodka in 2012

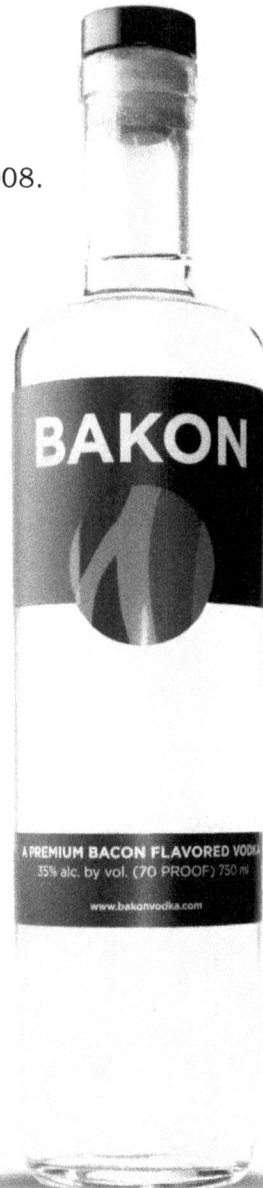

Black Sam Distillery Co.

430 South First Street
Montesano, WA 98563
360-580-0304

Owners / Operators:
Bob & Myrna Bellamy, Owners

Email: blacksaminc@comcast.net
Website: www.blacksamdistillery.com

Type: Micro-distillery. Opened in 2012.

Hours of operation: Daily, 10:00am to 5:00pm

Tours: Available by appointment

Types of spirits produced: Whiskey, vodka, gin

Names of spirits:
- Black Sam
- Down & Dirty

Best known for / most popular: Not provided

Average bottle price: Not provided

Distribution: On-site, local liquor stores

Interesting facts:
- The distillery was named after Pirate Black Sam Bellamy, a family ancestor.
- The still was hand fabricated on site from copper and stainless.
- The mash cooker and still are heated with a glycol hot water system instead of steam.

Blue Flame Spirits

2880 Lee Road, Ste. B
Prosser, WA 99350
509-778-4036

Owners / Operators:
Brian Morton, Co-owner
Charles Isley, Co-owner

Email: info@blueflamespirits.com
Website: www.blueflamespirits.com
Facebook: Blue Flame Spirits
Twitter: @BlueFlamespirit
Yelp: Blue Flame Spirits

Type: Craft-distillery. Opened in 2010.

Hours of operation: Monday through Saturday, 11:00am to 5:00pm

Tours: Available

Types of spirits produced: Whiskey, vodka, gin, brandy

Names of spirits:
- Blue Flame Grappa
- Blue Flame Brandy
- Blue Flame Gin
- Blue Flame Ultra Premium Gin
- Blue Flame Vodka
- Blue Flame Peppered Vodka
- Blue Flame Ultra Premium Vodka
- Blue Flame Rye
- Blue Flame Wheat Whiskey

Best known for / most popular: All products

Average bottle price: $35.00

Distribution: OR, WA

Interesting facts:
- 100% percent handcrafted farm to bottle
- All ingredients are sourced within 45 miles of the distillery
- Gold Medal winner, San Francisco World Spirits Competition

Bluewater Distilling

1205 Craftsman Way, Ste. 116
Everett, WA 98201
206-369-0739

Owners / Operators:
John Lundin, President / Distiller

Email: info@bluewaterdistilling.com
Website: www.bluewaterdistilling.com
Facebook: Bluewater Distilling
Twitter: @BWDistilling
Instagram: bluewaterdistilling

Type: Micro-distillery. Opened in 2012.

Hours of operation: Tuesday through Sunday, 12:00pm to 7:00pm

Tours: Available

Types of spirits produced: Vodka, gin, specialty spirits

Names of spirits:
- Bluewater Organic Vodka
- Halcyon Organic Distilled Gin
- Bluewater Organic Liqueur - Limited Release

Best known for / most popular:
Bluewater Organic Vodka

Average bottle price: $24.00 to 32.00

Distribution: CA, KS, MT, NJ, NY, OR, WA

Interesting facts:
- Certified organic
- American-Made bottles
- Member of 1% for the Planet

365

broVo Spirits

Seattle, WA 98117
206-496-2613

Owners / Operators:
Erin Brophy, Co-founder / COO
Mhairi Voelsgen, Co-founder / CEO
Kat Uzzelle, Co-founder

Email: info@brovospirits.com
Website: www.brovospirits.com
Facebook: BroVo Spirits
Twitter: @broVoSpirits

Type: Micro-distillery. Opened in 2011.

Hours of operation: Not provided

Tours: Not provided

Types of spirits produced: Liqueur, amaro

Names of spirits:
- broVo+RG Rose Geranium Liqueur
- broVo+L Lavender Liqueur
- broVo+LB Lemon Balm Liqueur
- broVo+G Ginger Liqueur
- broVo+DF Douglas Fir Liqueur
- broVo Amaro No 1
- broVo Amaro No 2
- broVo Amaro No 3
- broVo Amaro No 4
- broVo Amaro No 5
- broVo Amaro No 6

Best known for / most popular:
broVo+RG Rose Geranium Liqueur

Average bottle price: Not provided

Distribution: WA; Canada: BC

Interesting facts: Not provided

Captive Spirits

1518 NW 52nd Street
Seattle, WA 98107
206- 852-4794

Owners / Operators:
Ben Capdevielle, Owner / Founder / Head Distiller
Todd Leabman, Owner / Founder / CFO
Holly Robinson, Owner / Head of Marketing and PR

Email: ben@captivespiritsdistilling.com
todd@captivespiritsdistilling.com
holly@captivespiritsdistilling.com
Website: www.captivespiritsdistilling.com
Facebook: Captive Spirits
Twitter: @captivespirits

Type: Micro-distillery. Opened in 2012.

Hours of operation: Vary

Tours: Available by appointment

Types of spirits produced: Gin

Names of spirits:
• Big Gin

Best known for / most popular: Big Gin

Average bottle price: $30.00 to $50.00

Distribution: WA

Interesting facts:
• Ben is a 3rd Generation distiller.
• Captive Spirits is the only known, strictly gin distillery, in Washington.
• Captive Spirits uses a custom built Vendome Pot still, specifically designed to make gin.

367

Carbon Glacier Distillery

533 Church Street
Wilkeson, WA 98396
360-989-9700

Owners / Operators:
Christopher W. Lyons, Owner
Keith Quimby, Owner

Email: admin@carbonglacierdistillery.com
Website: www.carbonglacierdistillery.com
Facebook: Carbon Glacier Distillery
Twitter: @CGDistillery
Pinterest: Carbon Glacier Distillery

Type: Micro-distillery. Opened in 2012.

Hours of operation:
Monday, Thursday, Friday: 2:00 pm to 6:00 pm
Saturday and Sunday 12:00 pm to 6:00 pm

Tours: Available upon request

Types of spirits produced: Vodka, gin, whiskey
(Apple Brandy and absinthe coming soon)

Names of spirits:
• Stocking Stuffer Whiskey
  (Seasonal Avail. Dec. 1st)
• Pump Trolley Whiskey
  (Seasonal – Avail. 3rd weekend in July)
• B4 Premium Handcrafted Vodka
• Quimby and Jack's Distilled Dry Gin
• Moose Shine Pacific Northwest Un-aged Whiskey

Best known for / most popular:
Moose Shine Pacific Northwest Un-aged Whiskey
B4 Premium Handcrafted Vodka

Average bottle price: $25.00 to $35.00

Distribution: WA

Interesting facts: Founded by Keith Quimby (a Washington native) and Christopher Lyons (a transplant from Kentucky), Carbon Glacier Distillery is nestled in the foothills of the Cascade Mountains, just a few miles from the entrance to Mount Rainier National Park, on WA State Route 165, in the historic town of Wilkeson.

Chuckanut Bay Distillery

1115 Railroad Avenue
Bellingham, WA 98225
360-739-0361

Owners / Operators:
Kelly Andrews, Co-owner
Rob Andrews, Co-owner
Ethan Lynette, Co-owner
Matt Howell, Co-owner

Email: chuckanutbaydistillery@yahoo.com
Website: www.chuckanutbaydistillery.com
Facebook: Chuckanut Bay Distillery
Twitter: @ChuckanutBay

Type: Micro-distillery. Opened in 2011.

Hours of operation: Friday through Sunday, 12:00pm to 4:00pm

Tours: Not provided

Types of spirits produced: Vodka, gin

Names of spirits:
- Chuckanut Bay Gin
- Chuckanut Bay Vodka

Best known for / most popular: Not provided

Average bottle price: Not provided

Distribution: Not provided

Interesting facts: Not provided

Copperworks Distilling Co.

51 University Street
Seattle, WA 98101
206-504-7604

Owners / Operators:
Jason Parker, Owner / Distiller
Micah Nutt, Owner / Distiller

Email: info@copperworksdistilling.com
Website: www.copperworksdistilling.com
Facebook: Copperworks Distilling & Tasting Room

Type: Micro-distillery. Opening in 2013.

Hours of operation: TBA

Tours: Available after opening

Types of spirits produced: Whiskey, gin

Names of spirits:
• TBA

Best known for / most popular: TBA

Average bottle price: TBA

Distribution: TBA

Interesting facts:
• Copperworks spirits will be distilled in four traditional copper stills which were handcrafted by expert coppersmiths in the highlands of Scotland.
• Copperworks' largest still—the wash still—weighs nearly three tons and stands more than 15 feet tall.

Dark Moon Artisan Distillery

1830 Bickford Avenue, Ste. 108
Snohomish, WA 98290

Owners / Operators:
Kathy Alley, Owner
John Dawson, Master Distiller

Email: info@darkmoondistillery.com
Facebook: Dark Moon Artisan Distillery

Type: Micro-distillery. Opened in 2012.

Hours of operation:
Monday through Friday, 7:30am to 5:00pm
Saturday, 11:00am to 5:00pm

Tours: Available

Types of spirits produced:
Apple-based vodka, rum, mixed cider and vodka

Names of spirits:
• Singing Whale Vodka
• Turtle Island Rum-style Spirits
• Apple Knocker

Best known for / most popular: Apple Knocker
A 40 proof mixed cider and vodka with cinnamon,
vanilla and other natural flavors.

Average bottle price: $20.00

Distribution: OR, WA

Interesting facts:
All spirits are distilled from Washington apples.

Double V Distillery

1315 SE Grace Avenue, Unit 118
Battle Ground, WA 98604
360-606-9423

Owners / Operators:
John Vissotzky, Co-owner
Steve Vissotzky, Co-owner
Nicholas Vissotzky, Operations

Email: vvspirits@gmail.com
Website: Not provided
Facebook: Double V Distillery
Twitter: Not provided

Type: Craft-distillery. Opened in 2009.

Hours of operation:
Monday through Friday, 9:00am to 6:00pm

Tours: Available by appointment

Types of spirits produced: Vodka, gin, whiskey

Names of spirits:
- Viscova (vodka)
- Brodie (gin)
- Washington Select (whiskey)

Best known for / most popular: Viscova Craft Vodka

Average bottle price: $25.00 to $30.00

Distribution: Self

Interesting facts:
- Mashes are hand made using an open vat style fermentation process.
- Uses only organically grown corn and barley from the state of Washington.
- Their copper still was manufactured in Germany and it features a 21 plate vodka tower.
- They distill their vodka and gin three times for the best overall character.
- They age their whiskey in charred oak barrels made in Kentucky for a minimum of 4 years.

372

Dry County Distillery LLC

1326 6th Street
Marysville, WA 98270
425-343-8021

Owners / Operators:
Howard V.O. Johnston, Owner
Jennifer Johnston, Manager

Email: info@drycountydistillery.com
Website: www.drycountydistillery.com
Facebook: Dry County Distillery

Type: Micro-distillery. Opened in June 2012.

Hours of operation:
Monday through Friday, 11:00am to 6:00pm; Sunday by appointment

Tours: Available by appointment

Types of spirits produced: Gin, vodka, whisky, liqueur

Names of spirits:
- Dry County Gin
- Dry County Vodka
- Black Rope Anis
- Dry County Rum

Best known for / most popular: Black Rope Anis

Average bottle price: $25.00 to $30.00

Distribution: Pilchuck Distributors Inc.

Interesting facts: Not provided

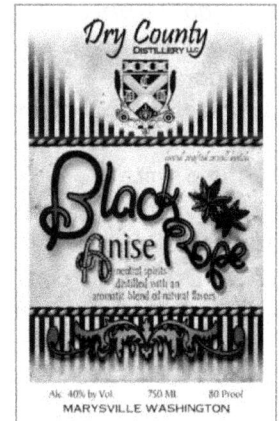

Dry Fly Distilling

1003 E. Trent, Ste. 200
Spokane, WA 99202
509-489-2112

Owners / Operators:
Don Poffenroth, Owner
Kent Fleischmann, Owner

Email: don@dryflydistilling.com, kent@dryflydistilling.com
Website: www.dryflydistilling.com
Facebook: Dry Fly Distilling
Twitter: @dryflydistiller

Type: Micro-distillery. Opened in 2007.

Hours of operation:
Monday through Friday, 8:00am to 5:00pm
Saturday, 10:00am to 3:00pm

Tours: Available

Types of spirits produced: Vodka, gin, whisky

Names of spirits:
- Dry Fly Washington Wheat Vodka
- Dry Fly Washington Wheat Gin
- Dry Fly Washington Wheat Whiskey
- Dry Fly Washington Bourbon Whiskey
- Dry Fly Washington Triticale Whiskey

Best known for / most popular:
A "PMD" - Dry Fly Vodka from the freezer and a splash of cranberry juice

Average bottle price: $29.95 to $49.95

Distribution:
30 U.S. states, Europe and the Caribbean.

Interesting facts
- Dry Fly Distillery is Washington's first craft-distillery producing vodka, gin, and whiskey.
- The "Dry Fly" company name stemmed from Kent and Don's mutually shared passion for fly fishing.

Ezra Cox Distillery

719 N. Tower Avenue
Centralia, WA 98531
360-736-1033

Owners / Operators:
Ezra Cox III, Distiller / Manager

Email: ezracoxiii@gmail.com
Website: www.ezracox.com
Facebook: Ezra Cox Distillery

Type: Micro-distillery. Opened in 2011.

Hours of operation: Advanced notice requested

Tours: Available

Types of spirits produced: Moonshine, whiskey, vodka, flavored moonshine

Names of spirits:
- Ezra Cox Moonshine
- Ezra Cox Single Malt Whiskey
- Ezra Cox Single Malt Vodka

Best known for / most popular: Ezra Cox Moonshine, Flavored Moonshine

Average bottle price: $20.00 to $30.00

Distribution: WA

Interesting facts:
Specializing in spirits made from single malt mash and a variety of real fruit flavored moonshines.

Four Lakes

223 Howard Flats Road
Chelan, WA 98816
509-542-7927

Owners / Operators:
Don Koester, Owner
Karl Koester, Manager / Winemaker / Grower

Email: info@fourlakeswinery.com
Website: www.fourlakeswinery.com
Facebook: Four Lakes Winery
Twitter: @FourLakesWinery

Type: Winery / Micro-distillery. Opened in 2004.

Hours of operation: Not provided

Tours: Not provided

Types of spirits produced: Grappa, brandy

Names of spirits:
• Not provided

Best known for / most popular: Not provided

Average bottle price: Not provided

Distribution: Not provided

Interesting facts: Not provided

Fremont Mischief

132 N. Canal Street
Seattle, WA 98103
206-547-0838

Owners / Operators:
Mike Sherlock, Founder

Email: info@fremontmischief.com
Website: www.fremontmischief.com
Facebook: Freemont Mischief
Twitter: @FreemontMischief

Type: Micro-distillery. Opened in 2011

Hours of operation:
Wednesday through Saturday, 11:00am to 6:00pm
Sunday, 11:00am to 4:00pm

Tours: Not available

Types of spirits produced: Whiskey, gin, vodka

Names of spirits:
- Rex Velvet Sinister Spirit
- John Jacob Whiskey
- Freemont Mischief Gin

Best known for / most popular: Rex Velvet

Average bottle price: Not provided

Distribution: Not provided

Interesting facts: Not provided

Glass Distillery

1712 1ˢᵗ Avenue S
Seattle, WA 98134
206-686-7210

Owners / Operators:
Ian MacNeil, Founder / Distiller

Email: tastings@glassdistillery.com
Website: www.glassdistillery.com
Facebook: Glass Distillery
Twitter: @GlassDistillery

Type: Micro-distillery. Opened in 2012.

Hours of operation: Available by appointment

Tours: Available by appointment
(call or email tastings@glassdistillery.com)

Types of spirits produced: Vodka

Names of spirits:
- Glass Vodka
- Gridiron Vodka
- Glass Kona Coffee Vodka

Best known for / most popular: Glass Vodka

Average bottle price: $20.00 to $50.00

Distribution: CA, HI, MI, TX, WA; Canada BC

Interesting facts:
- Glass Vodka is distilled from grapes harvested from the Pacific Northwest and distilled using a state-of-the-art, 17.5 foot tall copper German still.
- Glass Vodka won a Bronze in the Vodka category and Best in Class Platinum for bottle/package design at the 2012 International SIP Awards.
- Gridiron Vodka was recently introduced as a premium vodka selection at Century Link Field home of the Seattle Seahawks and Seattle Sounders.
- Glass Kona Coffee Vodka is an infusion of Keala's Hapuna Blend Kona Coffee.

Gnostalgic Spirits Distillery

1518 NW 52nd Street
Seattle, WA 98107
206-257-2306

Owners / Operators:
Gwydion Stone, Owner

Email: contact@gnostalgicspirits.com
Website: www.gnostalgicspirits.com
Facebook: Gnostalgic Spirits Distillery

Type: Micro-distillery. Opened in 2012.

Hours of operation: Not provided

Tours: Not provided

Types of spirits produced: Absinthe

Names of spirits:
• Marteau Absinthe de la Belle Époque

Best known for / most popular: Not provided

Average bottle price: Not provided

Distribution: Not provided

Interesting facts: Not provided

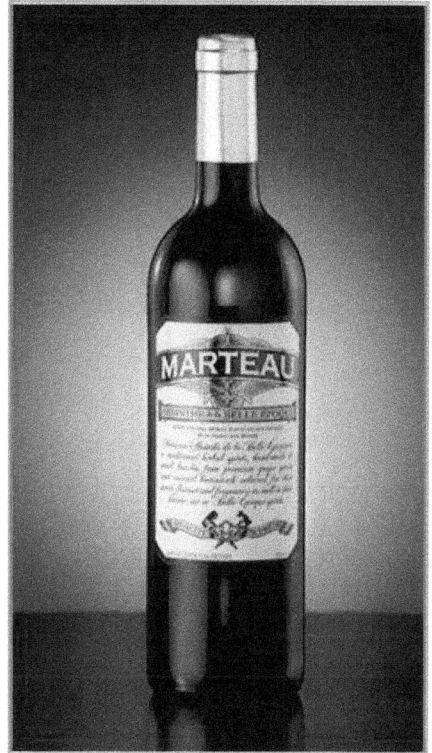

Golden Distillery

9746 Samish Island Road
Bow, WA 98232
360-542-8332

Owners / Operators:
Bob Stilnovich and Jim Caudill, Owners

Email: goldendistillery@gmail.com
Website: www.goldendistillery.com
Facebook: Golden Distillery

Type: Micro-distillery. Opened in 2010.

Hours of operation:
Thursday through Sunday, 11:00am to 5:00pm

Tours: Available

Types of spirits produced: Whiskey, brandy

Names of spirits:
- Golden Samish Bay Single Malt Whiskey
- Golden Samish Bay Whiskey Reserve
- Golden White Gold Whiskey
- Golden Apple Brandy

Best known for / most popular: Golden Samish Bay Single Malt Whiskey

Average bottle price: $40.00 to $50.00

Distribution: WA

Interesting facts:
- Golden Distillery is the first distillery to open in Skagit County.
- Samish Bay Single Malt Whiskey won Gold at the ADI convention in KY.
- Samish Bay Single Malt Whiskey received 88.5 points in the Whiskey Bible.
- Golden Apple Brandy is being aged in used whiskey barrels.

380

Heritage Distilling Company Inc.

3207 57th Street Court NW
Gig Harbor, WA 98335
253-509-0008

SMALL-BATCH SPIRITS
HERITAGE
DISTILLING CO. INC.
Every spirit has a story.

Owners / Operators:
Jennifer Stiefel, Co-Founder / President
Justin Stiefel, Co-Founder / CEO / Head Distiller

Email: info@heritagedistilling.com
Website: www.heritagedistilling.com
Facebook: Heritage Distilling Company, Inc.
Twitter: @heritagedistill
Pinterest: Heritage Distilling Company
LinkedIn: Heritage Distilling Co.
Flickr: Heritage Distilling Company's Photostream
Blog: Official HDC™ Blog: On the Rocks
Tripadvisor: Heritage Distilling Company

Type: Micro-distillery. Opened in 2012.

Hours of operation: Vary. Refer to website.

Tours: Available daily at 4:00pm or by appointment

Types of spirits produced: Whiskey, gin, vodka

Names of spirits:
- HDC Vodka
- HDC Gin
- HDC Light Whiskey
- Commander's Rye Whiskey
- Elk Rider Vodka
- Elk Rider Gin
- Elk Rider Whiskey

Best known for / most popular:
HDC Vodka, Triple distilled

Average bottle price: $29.00 to $47.00

Distribution: WA

Interesting facts:
- Wherskey Gin and Wherskey Vodka are gluten free.
- Commander's Rye Whiskey won a Bronze Medal from the Beverage Testing Institute International Review of Spirits.

It's 5 Artisan Distillery

207 Mission Avenue
Cashmere, WA 98801
509-679-9771

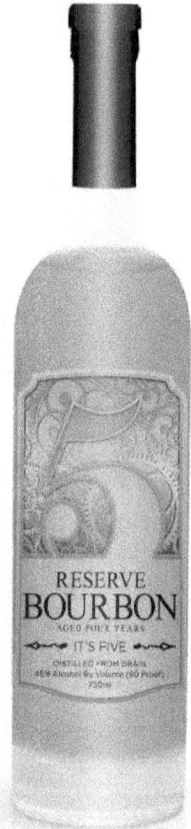

Owners / Operators:
Colin Levi, Owner

Email: 5@its5distillery.com
Website: www.its5distillery.com
Facebook: It's 5

Type: Micro-distillery. Opened in 2009.

Hours of operation:
Monday, Tuesday and Sunday by appointment
Wednesday through Friday, 10:00am to 5:00pm
Saturday, 1:00pm to 5:00pm

Tours: Available by appointment

Types of spirits produced:
Eau de vie, brandy, grappa, whiskey, gin, liqueurs

Names of spirits:
- Block and Tackle Moonshine 100% Corn Whiskey Un-aged
- Block and Tackle Sunshine 100% Corn Whiskey Aged
- Reserve Bourbon (aged 4 years)
- Vodka
- Northwest Dry Gin
- Grappa
- Eaux de Vie: Voignier, Apple, Pear, Apricot, Cherry, Plum
- Liqueur: Raspberry, Blueberry, Elderberry, Blackberry, Pear, Apricot, Cherry

Best known for / most popular: Reserve Bourbon

Average bottle price: $30.00

Distribution: WA

Interesting facts:
Seventh craft distillery since Prohibition in North Central WA

J.P. Trodden Small Batch Bourbon

18646 142nd Avenue NE
Woodinville, WA 98072
206-399-6291

Owners / Operators:
Mark Nesheim, Owner / Distiller
Jennifer Seversen, Owner

Email: Mark Nesheim: mark@jptroddendistilling.com
        Jennifer Seversen: jennifer@jptroddendistilling.com
Website: www.jptroddendistilling.com
Facebook: JP Trodden, JP Trodden Distilling

Type: Micro-distillery. Opened in 2011.

Hours of operation:
Monday through Friday, 7:00am to 5:00pm
Saturday, 8:00am to 1:00pm

Tours: Available by appointment

Names of spirits: Bourbon

Names of spirits:
• JP Trodden Small Batch Bourbon

Best known for / most popular:
JP Trodden Small Batch Bourbon

Average bottle price: $62.00

Distribution: WA

Interesting facts: Not provided

Kayak Spirits Distillery LLC

5490 Cameron Road
Freeland, WA 98249
360-672-4920

Owners / Operators:
Eric R. Stallman, Co-owner
Kathy Stallman, Co-owner

Email: lwa@whidbey.com
Website: www.sites.google.com/site/kayakspiritsdistillery
Facebook: Kayak Spirits Distillery LLC

Type: Craft-distillery. Opening in 2013.

Hours of operation: Not provided

Tours: Not provided

Types of spirits produced: Whiskey, vodka

Names of spirits:
* TBA

Best known for / most popular: TBA

Average bottle price: TBA

Distribution: TBA

Interesting facts: TBA

Letterpress Distilling

85 South Atlantic Street, #110
Seattle, WA 98134
206-227-4522

Owners / Operators:
Eric "Skip" Tognetti, Owner / Distiller

Email: skip@letterpressdistilling.com
Website: www.letterpressdistilling.com
Facebook: Letterpress Distilling
Twitter: @lp_distilling

Type: Micro-distillery. Opened in 2010.

Hours of operation: Saturday and Sunday, 12:00pm to 6:00pm

Tours: Not provided

Types of spirits produced: Gin, vodka, limoncello

Names of spirits:
- Letterpress Gin
- Letterpress Vodka
- Letterpress Limoncello

Best known for / most popular: Not provided

Average bottle price: Not provided

Distribution: Not provided

Interesting facts: Not provided

Mac Donald Distillery

104 Avenue C
Snohomish, WA 98290
425-275-1328

Owners / Operators:
Glen Mac Donald, Owner

Email: info@macdonalddistillery.com
Website: www.macdonalddistillery.com
Facebook: Mac Donald Distillery

Type: Micro-Distillery. Opened in 2010.

Hours of operation:
Monday through Friday, 8:00am to 5:00pm
Saturday, 12:00pm to 5:00pm

Tours: Available

Types of spirits produced: Gin, vodka, whiskey

Names of spirits:
• Isis Vodka
• Isis Premium Gin
• Ty Wolfe Whiskey

Best known for / most popular: Isis Vodka

Average bottle price: Not provided

Distribution: Not provided

Interesting facts: Not provided

386

Meriwether Distilling Co.

5840 Airport Way S., Ste. 200
Seattle, WA 98108

Owners / Operators:
Whitney D. Meriwether, Owner / Distiller

Email: info@meriwetherdistilleries.com
Website: www.meriwetherdistilleries.com
Facebook: Meriwether Distilling Company
Twitter: @Daily_Drinker

Type: Craft-distillery. Opened in 2011.

Hours of operation: Not provided

Tours: Not provided

Types of spirits produced: Vodka

Names of spirits:
• Speakeasy Vodka

Best known for / most popular: Speakeasy Vodka

Average bottle price: Not provided

Distribution: Not provided

Interesting facts: Not provided

Mount Baker Distillery

1305 Fraser Street, Ste. D2
Bellingham, WA 98229
360-734-3301

Owners / Operators:
Troy Smith, Owner

Email: info@mountbakerdistillery.com
Website: www.mountbakerdistillery.com
Facebook: Mount Baker Distillery
Twitter: @MtBDistillery

Type: Craft-distillery. Opened in 2011.

Hours of operation:
Friday and Saturday, 11:00am to 6:00pm

Tours: Available by appointment

Types of spirits produced: Vodka, moonshine

Names of spirits:
- Mount Baker Vodka
- Mount Baker Moonshine

Best known for / most popular: Mount Baker Moonshine

Average bottle price: Not provided

Distribution: WA

Interesting facts: The recipe for the Moonshine comes from an old family recipe perfected by Grandpa Abe Smith. The story of Abe Smith is told on the label of MBD's Moonshine.

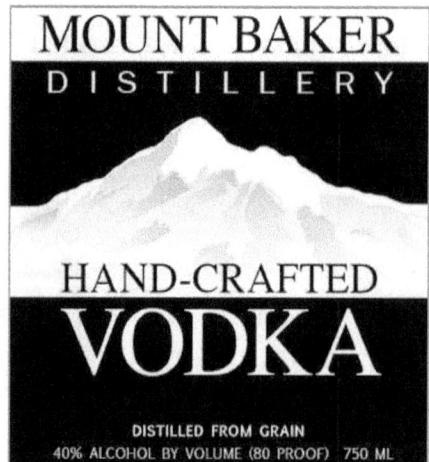

Oola Distillery

1314 East Union Street
Seattle, WA 98122
206-709-7909

Owners / Operators:
Kirby Kallas-Lewis, Founder / Distillery
Jeana Harrington, Managing Director

Email: info@ooladistillery.com
Website: www.ooladistillery.com
Facebook: Oola Distillery
Twitter: @OolaDistillery

Type: Micro-distillery. Opened in 2011.

Hours of operation:
Tuesday through Thursday, 2:00pm to 8:00pm
Friday and Saturday, 2:00 to 10:00pm

Tours: Available Saturday, 3:00pm by reservation

Types of spirits produced: Gin, vodka, whiskey

Names of spirits:
- Oola Gin
- Oola Vodka
- Oola Citrus Vodka
- Oola Chili Pepper Vodka
- Oola Rosemary Vodka
- Oola Waitsburg Bourbon Whiskey

Best known for / most popular: Oola Waitsburg Bourbon Whiskey

Average bottle price: $20.00 to $50.00

Distribution: IL, OR, WA

Interesting facts:
- Oola is also the name of Kirby's German Shepherd.
- Oola Distillery is located in Seattle's dense, urban Capitol Hill neighborhood.

Photos by: David Clugston

389

Pacific Distillery LLC

18808-142nd Avenue NE #4B
Woodinville, WA 98072
425-350-9061

Owners / Operators:
Marc Bernhard, Owner / Master Distiller

Email: mbernhard@pacificdistillery.com
Website: www.pacificdistillery.com
Facebook: Pacific Distillery
Twitter: @PacificDistill

Type: Micro-distillery. Opened in 2008.

Hours of operation: Not provided

Tours: Available

Types of spirits produced: Absinthe, gin

Names of spirits:
- Voyager Single Batch Distilled Gin
- Pacifique Absinthe Verte

Best known for / most popular: Pacifiqua Absinthe

Average bottle price: $30.00 to $63.00

Distribution: CA, IL, LA, MT, NY, OR, VT, WA

Interesting facts: Pacific Distillery products are distilled in a genuine direct-fired 500 liter copper alambic-pot still using all-organic botanicals.

Parliament Distillery

13708 24th Street, Ste. 103
Sumner, WA 98390
253-447-8044

Owners / Operators:
Jarrett Tomal, Owner / Distiller
Flynn Huntington, Owner
Matt McCartney, Operations Manager / Distiller

Email: ghostowlsales@gmail.com
Website: www.ghostowlwhisky.com
Facebook: Parliament Distillery
Twitter: @ghostowlwhisky

Type: Micro-distillery. Opened in 2012.

Hours of operation: Monday through Saturday, 12:00pm to 6:00pm

Tours: Available by appointment

Types of spirits produced: Whisky

Names of spirits:
• Ghost Owl Pacific Northwest Whisky

Best known for / most popular: Whisky

Average bottle price: $39.99

Distribution: WA

Interesting facts: Not provided

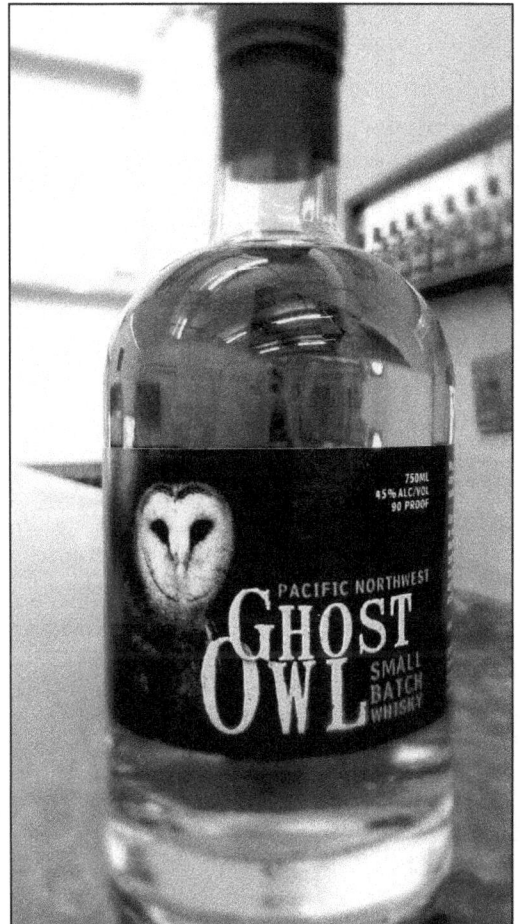

Port Steilacoom Distillery

1601 Lafayette Street
Steilacoom, WA 98388
253-212-0090

Owners / Operators:
Kevin Laughlin Stewart, Co-owner
Jennifer Laughlin Stewart, Co-owner

Email: portsteilacoomdistillery@yahoo.com
Website: www.portsteilacoomdistillery.com
Facebook: Port Steilacoom Distillery

Type: Micro-distillery. Opened in 2012.

Hours of operation:
Wednesday through Sunday, 3:30pm to 6:30pm

Tours: Available

Types of spirits produced: Gin, vodka

Names of spirits:
- Homeport Craft Distilled Gin
- Chambers Bay Craft Distilled Vodka

Best known for / most popular: Not provided

Average bottle price: $22.55

Distribution: Not provided

Interesting facts:
All products are made from local blackberry honey. Kevin learned to distill as a teenager spending summers with his moonshining grandfather who is now 100 years old.

Chambers Bay Craft Distilled Vodka
Port Steilacoom Distillery
750 ml — 48% Alc./Vol. (96 proof)

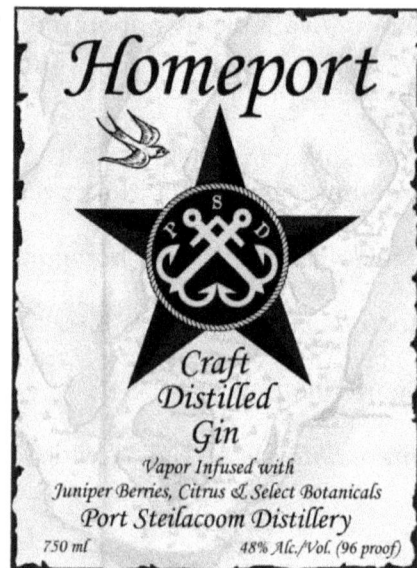

Homeport Craft Distilled Gin
Vapor Infused with Juniper Berries, Citrus & Select Botanicals
Port Steilacoom Distillery
750 ml — 48% Alc./Vol. (96 proof)

392

Project V Distillery and Sausage Company

19495 144th Avenue NE
Woodinville, WA 98072
425-398-1738

Owners / Operators:
Mo Heck, President / Founder / Distiller

Email: projectvdistillery@gmail.com
Website: www.projectvdistillery.com
Facebook: Project V Distillery & Sausage Co.
Twitter: @ProjectVDistill
Yelp: Project V Distillery & Sausage Company
Flickr: ProjectVDistillery's protostream

Type: Micro-distillery. Opened in 2010.

Hours of operation: Not provided

Tours: Available Saturday and Sunday, 12:00pm to 5:00pm or by appointment

Types of spirits produced: Vodka

Names of spirits:
- Single Silo Vodka
- Single Silo Distiller's Cut Vodka
- Single Silo Ultra Filtered Vodka
- Single Silo Chai Infused Vodka
- Double Silo (160 Proof)

Best known for / most popular:
Chai Vodka Moscow Mule

Average bottle price: $30.00

Distribution: WA

Interesting facts: Not provided

Image by: Amy Louise Herndon

Rain City Spirits

4660 East Marginal Way
South Seattle, WA 98134
206-464-7246

Owners / Operators:
Cory Duffy, Distiller / Managing Partner
Joe Matthys, VP Marketing / Sales / Partner

Email: cory@raincityvodka.com, joe@raincityvodka.com
Website: www.raincityvodka.com, www.raincitydistillery.com
Facebook: Rain City Spirits
Twitter: @RainCitySpirits

Type: Micro-distillery. Opened in 2011.

Hours of operation: Not open to the public

Tours: Available by appointment

Types of spirits produced: Vodka

Names of spirits:
• Rain Ciy Vodka
• Drip Coffee Liqueur

Best known for / most popular: Rain City Vodka

Average bottle price: $22.95

Distribution: WA

Interesting facts: Not provided

San Juan Island Distillery

12 Anderson Lane
Friday Harbor, WA 98250
360-378-2606

Owners / Operators:
Suzy Pingree, President
Hawk Pingree, Vice President
Rich Anderson, Treasurer

Email: suzy@sanjuanislanddistillery.com
Website: www.sanjuanislanddistillery.com
Facebook: San Juan Island Distillery
Twitter: @sjidistillery
Foursquare: San Juan Island Distillery

Type: Micro-distillery. Opened in 2011.

Hours of operation: Thursday through Sunday afternoons

Tours: Available

Types of spirits produced: Gin, brandy, liqueur

Names of spirits:
- Spy Hop Gin
- Apple Eau de vie
- Lavender and Wild Rose Liqueur
- Blackberry Brandy
- Thimbleberry Brandy
- Winterberry Brandy
- Madrone Brandy
- Red Sky at Night Cocktail
- Pommeau

Best known for / most popular: Spy Hop Gin

Average bottle price: $25.00 to $80.00

Distribution: WA

Interesting facts: Not provided

395

Seattle Distilling Company

19429 Vashon Highway SW
Vashon, WA 98070
206-463-0830

Owners / Operators:
Ishan D. Dillon, President
John P. (Paco) Joyce III, VP Head Distiller
David E. Waterworth, VP Marketing

Email: info@seattledistillingcompany.com
Website: www.seattledistillingcompany.com
Facebook: Seattle Distilling Company
Twitter: @RocketVodka

Type: Micro-distillery. Opened in 2011.

Hours of operation: Monday; Thursday
through Saturday, 12:00pm to 5:00pm

Tours: Available by appointment

Types of spirits produced:
Vodka, gin, whiskey

Names of spirits:
• the Alpinist Gin
• the Rocket Vodka
• the Vashon Idle Hour Whiskey

Best known for / most popular: Rocket Vodka

Average bottle price: $25.00 to $30.00

Distribution: WA, Total Wine & More

Interesting facts: Custom built in-house still and columns.

Sidetrack Distillery

27010 78th Avenue S.
Kent, WA 98032
206-963-5079

Owners / Operators:
Larry Person, Partner
Linda Person, Partner
David O'Neal, Partner

Email: info@sidetrackdistillery.com
Website: www.sidetrackdistillery.com
Facebook: Sidetrack Distillery
Pinterest: Sidetrack Distillery

Type: Micro-distillery. Opened in 2011.

Hours of operation:
Saturdays 11:00am to 5:00pm
All other days by appointment

Tours: Available by appointment

Types of spirits produced: Liqueurs, specialty spirits, eaux de vie

Names of spirits:
- Sidetrack Distillery Strawberry Liqueur
- Sidetrack Distillery Blueberry Liqueur
- Sidetrack Distillery Blackberry Liqueur
- Sidetrack Distillery Raspberry Liqueur
- Sidetrack Distillery Cassis
- Sidetrack Distillery Nocino
- Sidetrack Distillery BETE (a beet spirit)

Best known for / most popular: Raspberry Liqueur

Average bottle price: $24.95 to $49.95

Distribution: WA

Interesting facts:
Raspberry Liqueur was awarded
"Best of Category" Gold Medal at the
2012 annual American Distilling
Institutes tasting competition.

Skip Rock Distillers

104 Avenue C
Snohomish, WA 98290
360-862-0272

Owners / Operators:
Ryan Hembree, Co-owner
Julie Hembree, Co-owner

Email: info@skiprockdistllers.com
Website: www.skiprockdistillers.com
Facebook: Skip Rock Distillers
Twitter: @SkipRockDistill

Type: Micro-distillery. Opened in 2009.

Hours of operation:
Monday through Friday, 12:00pm to 5:00pm
Saturday: 11:00am to 5:00pm

Tours: Available

Types of spirits produced:
Vodka, whiskey, liqueurs, gin

Names of spirits:
- Skip Rock Potato Vodka
- Headwaters White Whiskey
- Spiced Apple Liqueur
- Blackberry Liqueur
- Raspberry Liqueur
- Nocino, Walnut Liqueur
- Rye Whiskey

Best known for / most popular:
Skip Rock Potato Vodka, Spiced Apple Liqueur

Average bottle price: Vary

Distribution: CA, ID, LA, OR, WA

Interesting facts:
Ryan made beer, wine and cider at home before being interested in spirits. He has two year certificate in winemaking from Washington State University.

Sodo Spirits Distillery

2228 Occidental Ave. S.
Seattle, WA 98134
206-399-2645

Owners / Operators:
Not provided

Email: info@sodospirits.com
Website: www.sodospirits.com
Facebook: Sodo Spirits Distillery

Type: Micro-distillery. Opened in 2009.

Hours of operation: Not provided

Tours: Not provided

Types of spirits produced: Hankaku Shochu

Names of spirits:
- Evenstar
- Evenstar Mint
- Evenstar Ginger
- Evenstar Chiles

Best known for / most popular: Evenstar

Average bottle price: Not provided

Distribution: WA

Interesting facts: America's only craft Shochu distillery.

Soft Tail Spirits

12280 NE Woodinville Drive, Suite C
Woodinville, WA 98072

Second location:
14356 Woodinville Redmond Road
Redmond, WA 98052

425-770-1154, 425-770-1158

Owners / Operators:
Dennis Robertson, Owner
Tammy Robertson, Owner
Cameron Robertson, Distiller
Matthew Farmer, Distiller

Email: Dennis Robertson: dennis@softtailspirits.com
            Tammy Robertson: tammy@softtailspirits.com
            Matthew Farmer: matthew@softtailspirits.com
Website: www.softtailspirits.com
Facebook: Soft Tail Spirits
Twitter: @softtailspirits

Type: Micro-distillery.
Woodinville Distillery Opened 2008.
Redmond Distillery Opened 2011.

Hours of operation:
Woodinville, Monday through Saturday, 12:00pm to 5:00pm
Redmond, Friday through Sunday, 12:00pm to 5:00pm

Tours: Available

Types of spirits produced: Grappa, vodka

Names of spirits:
* Soft Tail Vodka
* Soft Tail Blanco Grappa
* Giallo Grappa
* Sangiovese Grappa
* Woodstock Reserve
  A 24- month aged Grappa blend of Merlot, Cab & Syrah

Best known for: Soft Tail Martini

Average bottle price: $32.00 to $38.00

Distribution: OR, WA

Interesting facts: Soft Tail Vodka is gluten free.

Sound Spirits

1630 15th Avenue West
Seattle, WA 98119
206-651-5166

Owners / Operators:
Steven Stone, Founder / Head Distiller

Email: info@drinksoundspirits.com
Website: www.drinksoundspirits.com
Facebook: Sound Spirits
Twitter: @Sound_Spirits

Type: Micro-distillery. Opened in 2010.

Hours of operation: Daily

Tours: Available

Types of spirits produced: Vodka, gin, old tom gin, aquavit

Names of spirits:
- Ebb+Flow Vodka
- Ebb+Flow Gin
- Sound Spirits – Old Tom Gin
- Sound Spirits – Aquavit

Best known for / most popular: Ebb+Flow Gin

Average bottle price: $33.00

Distribution: WA

Interesting facts:
Sound Spirits is Seattle's first
craft distillery since Prohibition.

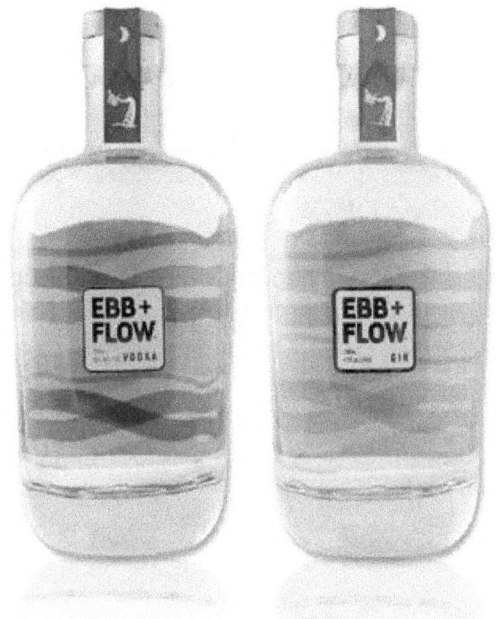

Sun Liquor Distillery

514 E. Pike Street
Seattle, WA 98122
206-720-1600

Owners / Operators:
Michael Klebeck, Founder / President
Erik Chapman, Manager / Head Distiller

Email: sunliquorseattle@gmail.com
        michael@sunliquor.com
Website: www.sunliquor.com
Facebook: Sun Liquor
Twitter: @SunLiquor
Tumblr: Sun Liquor

Type: Micro-distillery. Opened in 2011.

Hours of operation: Daily, 11:00am to 2:00am

Tours: Available by appointment

Types of spirits produced:
Gin, vodka, bitters, seasonal specialty products

Names of spirits:
• Gun Club Gin
• Hedge Trimmer Gin
• Sun Liquor Unxld Vodka
• Orange Bitters

Best known for / most popular: Gun Club 100 Proof Gin

Average bottle price: Not provided

Distribution: OR, WA

Interesting facts: The distillery is also a cocktail lounge

Tatoosh Craft Distillery

Seattle, WA
206-412-1000

Owners / Operators:
Mark Simon, Co-Founder / CEO
Troy Turner, Co-Founder / COO
Michael Carrosino, Co-Founder / CFO
Joe Eliasen, Co-Founder / Head Distiller

Email: info@tatooshdistillery.com
Website: www.tatooshdistillery.com
Facebook: Tatoosh Distillery & Spirits
Twitter: @TatooshSpirits

Type: Micro-distillery. Opened in 2012.

Hours of operation: Not provided

Tours: Not provided

Types of spirits produced: Whiskey, bourbon

Names of spirits:
• Tatoosh Single Malt Whiskey
• Tatoosh Bourbon

Best known for / most popular: Tatoosh Bourbon

Average bottle price: Not provided

Distribution: Not provided

Interesting facts: Not provided

The Ellensburg Distillery

1000 N. Prospect Street
Ellensburg, WA 98926
509-925-1295

Owners / Operators:
Ralph Bullock, Owner

Email: info@theellensburgdistillery.com
Website: www.wildcatwhite.com
Facebook: The Ellensburg Distillery
Twitter: @GoldBuckleClub

Type: Micro-distillery. Opened in 2008.

Hours of operation: By appointment

Tours: Available by appointment

Types of spirits produced: Whisky, brandy

Names of spirits:
- Gold Buckle Club Malt Whisky
- El Chalán Pisco-style Brandy
- Wildcat White Whisky

Best known for / most popular: Wildcat White Whiskey

Average bottle price: $28.00 to $110.00

Distribution: WA

Interesting facts:
- The Ellensburg Distillery is Washington's second licensed distillery.
- It's known for making brandy and whisky.

404

The Hardware Distillery Co.

24210 N. Highway 101
Hoodsport, WA 98548
206-300-0877

Owners / Operators:
Chuck and Jan Morris, Owners

Email: jan@hardwaredistillery.com
      chuck@hardwaredistillery.com
Website: www.thehardwaredistillery.com
Facebook: Hardware Distillery Co.
Twitter: @HDistillery

Hoodsport, Washington

Type: Craft-distillery. Opened in 2013.

Hours of operation:
Summer hours: Thursday through Sunday, 11:00am to 5:00pm
Winter hours: By appointment

Tours: Available

Types of spirits produced: Whiskey, gin, brandy, aquavit, absinthe

Names of spirits:
- Aquavit
- R Gin
- Crabby Ginny
- Green Cat Absinthe
- Hardware Distillery Whiskey

Best known for / most popular: Not provided

Average bottle price: Not provided

Distribution: WA

Interesting facts:
The Hardware Distillery and tasting room are located in an old hardware store

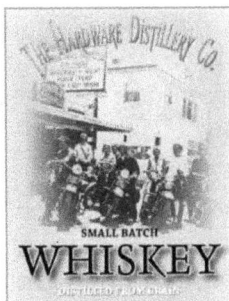

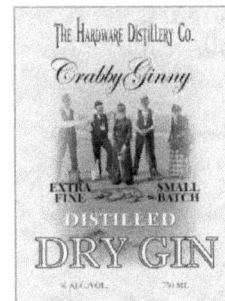

Walla Walla Distilling Company
Walla Walla Wine & Spirits Inc.

1105 "C" Street (at the Regional Airport)
Walla Walla, WA 99362
509-301-8834

Owners / Operators:
Jeremy W. Barker, Co-founder
Katrina Roberts Barker, Co-founder

Email: info@wallawalladistillingcompany.com
Website: www.wallawalladistillingcompany.com
Facebook: Walla Walla Distilling Company

Type: Craft-distillery. Opened in 2008.

Hours of operation: Open only by appointment

Tours: Not available

Types of spirits produced:
Vodka, gin, whisky, grappa, eau de vie, brandy

Names of spirits:
• Walla Walla Gin
• Walla Walla Vodka
• Walla Walla Whisky
• Walla Walla Light Whisky
• Tytonidae Grappa
• Tytonidae Brandy
• Tytonidae Eau-de-Vie
• Tytonidae Gin

Best known for / most popular: Walla Walla Gin

Average bottle price: Not provided

Distribution: WA

Interesting facts:
Walla Walla valley's first craft distillery

Photos by: Greg Lehman Photography

Whidbey Island Distillery

3466 Craw Road
Langley, WA 98260
360-321-4715

Owners / Operators:
Steve Heising, Owner / Operator
Beverly Heising, Owner / Operator
James Heising, Owner / Operator
Kris Heising, Owner / Operator

Email: info@whidbeydistillery.com
Website: www.whidbeydistillery.com
Facebook: Whidbey Island Distillery
Twitter: @whidbeyspirits

Type: Micro-distillery. Opened in 2010.

Hours of operation:
Saturday and Sunday, 11:00am to 5:00pm or by appointment

Tours: Available

Types of spirits produced: Neutral grapes spirits, whiskey, liqueur

Names of spirits:
- Whidbey Island Distillery Loganberry Liqueur
- Whidbey Island Distillery Raspberry Liqueur
- Whidbey Island Distillery Whidskey

Best known for / most popular:
Whidbey Island Distillery Loganberry

Average bottle price: $32.80

Distribution: WA

Interesting facts: Not provided

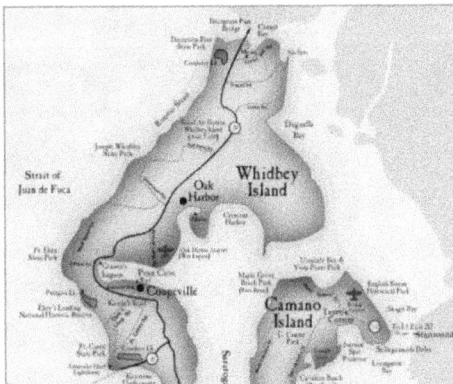

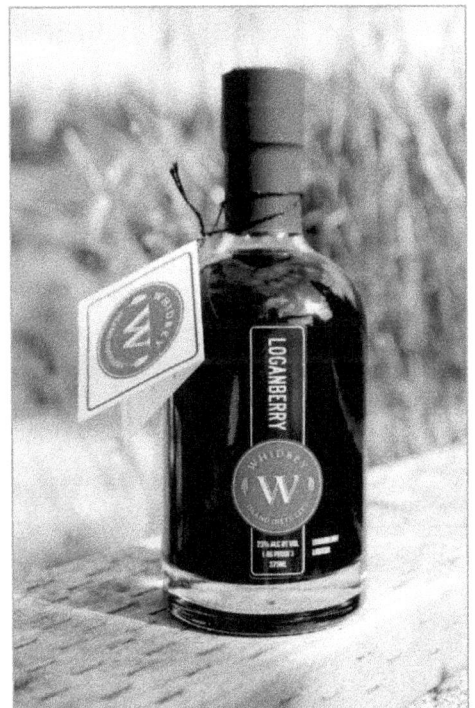

407

Wishkah River Distillery

2210 Port Industrial Road, Ste. A
Aberdeen, WA 98520
360-612-4756

Owners / Operators:
Josh Mayr, Co-owner / Lead Distiller
Patrick O'Donnell, Co-owner
Chris Olsen, Co-owner
Paul Stutzenburg, Co-owner

Email: josh@wishkahriver.com
        tours@wishkahriver.com
Website: www.wishkahriver.com
Facebook: Wishkah River Distillery
Twitter: @WRDistillery

Type: Micro-distillery. Opened in 2011.

Hours of operation:
Tuesday through Saturday, 12:30pm to 5:30pm

Tours: Available

Types of spirits produced:
Vodka, un-aged whiskey, aged whiskey, gin

Names of spirits:
• Wishkah River Distillery Vodka Distilled from Grains
• Wishkah River Distillery Vodka Distilled from Honey
• Thirteen Corners Virgin Cask American Malt Whiskey
• Bulfinch 83 Redistilled Gin

Best known for / most popular:
Wishkah River Distillery Vodka Distilled from Honey

Average bottle price: $20.00 to $50.00

Distribution: OR, WA

Interesting facts: Not provided

Woodinville Whiskey Co.

WOODINVILLE
• handcrafted small-batch spirits •
WHISKEY CO.

16110 Woodinville Redmond Rd. NE, Ste. 3
Woodinville, WA 98072
425-486-1199

Owners / Operators:
Orlin Sorensen, Owner / Operator
Brett Carlile, Owner / Operator

Email: Orlin Sorensen: orlin@woodinvillewhiskeyco.com
        Brett Carlile: brett@woodinvillewhiskeyco.com
Website: www.woodinvillewhiskeyco.com
Facebook: Woodinville Whiskey Co.

Type: Micro-distillery. Opened in 2010.

Hours of operation:
Monday through Sunday, 5:00am to 6:00pm
Tasting room: Wed. through Sun., 12:00pm to 5:00pm

Tours:
Available Wednesday through Sunday at 4:00pm

Types of spirits produced:
Bourbon, rye whiskey, American whiskey, vodka

Names of spirits:
- The Microbarreled™ Collection - Bourbon and Rye Whiskey
- Peabody Jones™ Vodka
- Age Your Own™ Whiskey Kit

Best known for / most popular:
The Microbarreled™ Collection

Average bottle price: $29.95 to $39.95

Distribution: WA

Interesting facts:
- Produced the first rye whiskey in WA State since Prohibition.
- Mentored by David Pickerell, former Master Distiller at Maker's Mark.

Bloomery Plantation Distillery

16357 Charles Town Road
Charles Town, WV 25414
304-725-3036

Owners / Operators:
Tom Kiefer, CEO / CFO / Owner
Linda Losey, COO / CCO / Owner
Rob Losey, Sales and Distribution

Email: LLosey@aol.com
Website: www.bloomeryplantation.com
Facebook: Bloomery Plantation Distillery

Type: Micro-distillery. Opened in 2011.

Hours of operation: Fridays and Saturday, 11:00am to 8:00pm

Tours: Available Fridays and Saturdays

Types of spirits produced:
Farm-fresh cocktail liqueurs

Names of spirits:
- Limoncello
- Raspberry Limoncello
- Cremma Lemma
- Lemon Ice
- Chocolate Raspberry
- Peaches and Cream
- Ginger SweetShine

Best known for / most popular:
Raspberry Limoncello

Average bottle price: $20.00 to $30.00

Distribution: DC, WV

Interesting facts:
- The iron ore from the original Bloomery was used to make the ship carrying the Lewis and Clark Expedition in the early 1800s.
- The current distillery is housed in an original 1840s log cabin slave quarters that was on the plantation.
- In the mid-1800's, the historic site housed six stills.
- The tiny hamlet of Bloomery held the honor of being the largest bootlegging operation in WV. More illegal 'shine came through this area than in any other place in the state.

410

Pinchgut Hollow Distillery

1602 Tulip Lane
Fairmont, WV 26554
304-366-9463

Owners / Operators:
Mikey Heston, Owner

Email: info@hestonfarm.com
Website: www.hestonfarm.com
Facebook: Heston Farm
Twitter: @hestonfarm

Type: Craft-distillery. Opened in 2011.

Hours of operation:
Monday through Saturday, 9:00am to 9:00pm
Sunday, 11:00am to 5:00pm

Tours: Available

Types of spirits produced: Moonshine

Names of spirits:
- Pinchgut Hollow Distillery Buckwheat Moon
- Pinchgut Hollow Distillery Corn Shine
- Pinchgut Hollow Distillery Honey Peach Moon
- Pinchgut Hollow Distillery Apple Pie Shine

Best known for / most popular: Pinchgut Hollow Corn Shine

Average bottle price: Not provided

Distribution: Not provided

Interesting facts: Not provided

411

Smooth Ambler Spirits Company

745 Industrial Park Road
Maxwelton, WV 24957
304-497-3123

Owners / Operators:
John Little, John Foster, Owners
TAG Galyean, Greg Parseghian, Owners

Email: sales@smoothambler.com
Websites: www.smoothambler.com
Facebook: Smooth Ambler Spirits
Twitter: @SmoothAmbler

Type: Micro-distillery. Opened in 2010.

Hours of operation:
Monday through Friday, 10:00am to 6:00pm; Saturday, 11:00am to 3:00pm

Tours: Friday, 2:00pm and 4:00pm; Saturday, 12:00pm and 2:00pm

Types of spirits produced: Vodka, gin, bourbon, rye

Names of spirits:
- Smooth Ambler Old Scout
- Smooth Ambler Greenbrier Gin
- Smooth Ambler Whitewater Vodka
- Smooth Ambler Yearling Bourbon
- Smooth Ambler Barrel Aged Gin
- Smooth Ambler Old Scout Straight Rye
- Smooth Ambler Old Scout Straight Bourbon Whiskey

Best known for / most popular: Smooth Ambler Old Scout

Average bottle price: $28.00 to $34.00

Distribution: AZ, CA, CO, CT, DC, DE, FL, IL, IN, KY, LA, MD, NC, NJ, NV, NY, OH, PA, RI, TN, VA, WA, WI, WV

412

WV Distilling Co. LLC

1380 Fenwick Avenue
Morgantown, WV 26505
304-599-0960

Owners / Operators:
Payton Fireman, Owner

Email: pfireman@frontier.com
Website: www.mountainmoonshine.com
Twitter: @wvdistilling

Type: Micro-distillery. Opened in 1999.

Hours of operation: Not provided

Tours: Not available

Types of spirits produced: Corn whiskey

Names of spirits:
• Mountain Moonshine Spirit Whiskey
• Mountain Moonshine Old Oak Recipe

Best known for / most popular: Mountain Moonshine Spirit Whiskey

Average bottle price: $15.00

Distribution: Not provided

Interesting facts: First legal distilled spirits company in WV since Prohibition.

45th Parallel Spirits LLC

1570 Madison Avenue
New Richmond, WI 54017
715-246-0565

Owners / Operators:
Paul Werni Jr., Owner / Distiller
Scott Davis, Distiller
Tom Gunn, Distiller
Ryan Brown, Sales Manager

Email: Paul Werni Jr.: paul@45thparallelspirits.com
            Ryan Brown: ryan@45thparallelspirits.com
Website: www.45thparallelspirits.com
Facebook: 45th Parallel Vodka
Twitter: @45th_Distillery

Type: Micro-distillery. Opened in 2007.

Hours of operation:
Tuesday through Friday, 9:00am to 7:00pm
Saturday, 12:00pm to 6:00pm

Tours:
Available by appointment Fridays and Saturdays
Exceptions for other days are made by request

Types of spirits produced:
Grain based whiskies, vodka, gin, aquavit, cellos

Names of spirits:
- 45th Parallel Vodka
- Border Bourbon
- New Richmond Rye
- Midwest Vodka
- Midwest Gin
- Madison Avenue Limoncello
- Madison Avenue Orancello

Contract Labels
- Referent Horseradish vodka
- Gamle Ode Dill Aquavit
- Gamle Ode Holiday Aquavit

Best known for / most popular:
45th Parallel Vodka, Border Bourbon, New Richmond Rye

Average bottle price: $14.00 to $45.00

Distribution: GA, IL, MN, OR, UT, WI

Interesting facts: 45th Parallel Spirits is also the location

AEppelTreow Winery & Distillery

1072 288th Avenue
Burlington, WI 53105
262-878-5345

Owners / Operators:
Charles and Milissa McGonegal, Owners

Email: cider@appletrue.com
cpm@appletrue.com
Website: www.appletrue.com
Facebook: AEppelTreow Winery Artisan Ciders

Type: Winery / Micro-distillery. Opened in 2009.

Hours of operation:
Open seasonally, May through December. Visit website for details.

Tours: Available

Types of spirits produced: Apple brandy, hard cider

Names of spirits:
* AEppelTreow WI Apple Brandy
* Brown Dog Whiskey

Best known for / most popular:
Sparkling cider

Average bottle price: $20.00 to $30.00

Distribution: WI

Interesting facts:
AEppelTreow (pronounced Apple True) Winery & Distillery specializes in Wisconsin grown and produced artisan hard cider, brandy and specialty spirits to make craft beverages from heirloom apples.

415

Death's Door Spirits

2220 Eagle Drive
Middleton, WI 53562
608-831-1083

Owners / Operators:
Brian Ellison, President / Founder
John Jeffery, Distiller
John Kinder, National Brand Manager / Contract Sales

Email: Brian Ellison: brian@deathsdoorspirits.com
          John Jeffery: johnny@deathsdoorspirits.com
          John Kinder: john@deathsdoorspirits.com
Website: www.deathsdoorspirits.com
Facebook: Death's Door Spirits
Twitter: @deathsdoor

Type: Micro-distillery. Opened in 2007.

Hours of operation: Daily, 9:00am to 5:00pm

Tours: Friday 6:00pm; Saturday 12:00pm , 2:00pm

Types of spirits produced: Gin, vodka, white whisky

Names of spirits:
- Death's Door Gin
- Death's Door Vodka
- Death's Door White Whisky

Best known for / most popular: Death's Door Gin

Average bottle price: $29.99 to $34.99

Distribution: 40 U.S. states, 9 countries

Interesting facts:
Death's Door takes its name from the body of water between Door County peninsula and Washington Island. Potowatami and Winnebego tribesmen originally named the waterway, while the French called it *Port de Morts* when trading in the area to ward off other traders.

Door County Distillery

5806 Highway 42
Carlsville, WI 54235
920-746-8463

Owners / Operators:
Door County Distillery

Email: info@doorcountydistillery.com
Website: www.doorcountydistillery.com
Facebook: Door County Distillery
Twitter: @DoorDistillery

Type: Micro-distillery. Opened in 2011.

Hours of operation:
April to October, Daily 10:00am to 6:00pm
Off-Season, Friday through Saturday vary

Tours: Not available

Types of spirits produced:
Brandy, bitters, gin, vodka, whiskey

Names of spirits:
- Door County Cherry Infused Vodka
- Door County Gin
- Door County Vodka
- Luminous Vodka
- Apple Brandy
- Cherry Brandy
- Cherry Infused Bitters
- Brandy – Aged in Oak Casks
- Whiskey

Best known for / most popular:
Luminous Vodka and Door County Gin

Average bottle price: $19.99 to $29.99

Distribution: WI, IL

Interesting facts: Not provided

Great Lakes Distillery LLC

616 W. Virginia Street
Milwaukee, WI 53204
414-431-8683

Owners / Operators:
Guy Rehorst, Owner

Email: info@greatlakesdistillery.com
Website: www.GreatLakesDistillery.com
Facebook: Great Lakes Distillery
Twitter: @GLDistillery
Foursquare: Great Lakes Distillery
Yelp: Great Lakes Distillery

Type: Micro-distillery. Opened in 2004.

Hours of operation: Monday through Saturday, 12:00pm to 6:00pm

Tours: Available

Types of spirits produced:
Vodka, flavored vodka, gin, rum, brandy, absinthe, whiskey

Names of spirits:
- Rehorst Premium Milwaukee Vodka
- Rehorst Citrus Honey Flavored Vodka
- Rehorst Premium Milwaukee Gin
- Roaring Dan's Rum
- Kinnickinnic Whiskey
- Great Lakes Seasonal Pumpkin Spirit
- Amerique 1912 Absinthe Verte
- Amerique 1912 Absinthe Rouge
- Great Lakes Artisan Series Grappa
- Great Lakes Artisan Series Pear Eau-de-Vie
- Great Lakes Artisan Series Kirschwasser
- Various extremely small batch whiskeys

Best known for / most popular:
Rehorst Premium Milwaukee Vodka

Average bottle price: $29.00

Distribution: AZ, CA, CO, IL, MN, WI

Interesting facts:
Great Lakes Distillery was the first
legal distillery in WI since Prohibition.

Lo Artisan Distillery LLC

1607 South Stevenson Pier Road
Sturgeon Bay, WI 54235
337-660-1600

Owners / Operators:
Po Lo, Owner
Chong Va Lo, Operations Supervisor

Email: poclo@lo-artisandistillery.com
Website: www.lo-artisandistillery.com
Facebook: Lo Artisan Distillery, Yerlo Rice Spirits

Type: Micro-distillery. Opened in 2011.

Hours of operation: Not provided

Tours: Available by appointment

Types of spirits produced: Hmong Rice Spirits

Names of spirits:
- Yerlo (120 Proof)
- Yerlo Reserve (130 Proof)
- Yerlo X Whisky (90 Proof)

Best known for / most popular: Hmong Rice Spirits

Average bottle price: $33.00 to $145.00

Distribution:
CA, CT, IL, LA, MA, MN, MT, RI, SC, TX, WI

Interesting facts:
- Lo Artisan Distillery uses all-natural rice grains, no additives or neutral spirits are added.
- Gluten Free

Minhas Micro Distillery

1404 13th Street
Monroe, WI 53566
608-328-5550

Owners / Operators:
Gary Olson, Manager
Michael Connolly, Production Supervisor
Carol Tallman, Staff Accountant
Lance Ray, Tour / Tasting Room Guide

Email: tours@minhasdistillery.com
Website: www.minhasdistillery.com
Facebook: Minhas Micro Distillery
Twitter: @MinhasDistiller

Type: Micro-distillery. Opened in 2011.

Hours of operation: Monday through Friday, 8:00am to 5:00pm
Saturday and Sunday, 11:00am to 5:00pm

Tours: Monday, 1:00pm; Tuesday through Thursday, 12:00pm and 3:00pm
Friday through Sunday, 12:00pm, 2:00pm, 4:00pm

Types of spirits produced: Vodka, whisky, rum, irish cream, horchata

Names of spirits:
- Chinook Canadian Whisky USA
- Chinook Canadian Whisky
- XO Gold Coast Rum USA
- XO Gold Coast Rum
- Rum of the Gods
- Blackstone Vodka USA
- Stars Vodka
- Stars Rye Whisky
- Stars White Rum
- Stars Spiced Rum
- Blarney's Irish Cream
- St. Patrick's Irish Cream
- Uptown Girl Chocolate Wine
- Aristo Gold Rum
- Aristo White Rum
- Aristo Spiced Rum
- Aristo Gold Rum
- Aristo Rye Whisky
- Aristo Vodka
- Sailboat Gold Rum
- Sailboat White Rum
- Sailboat Spiced Rum
- Sailboat Gold Rum
- Sailboat Spiced Rum
- Sailboat Rye Whisky
- Royal Crest Rye Whisky
- Maya Horchata (USA)
- Maya Rum Horchata

Best known for / most popular: Maya Horchata

Average bottle price: $5.99 TO $19.99

Distribution: CA, MA, OR, WA; Canada, AB, SK

Interesting facts: Home to "GODSTILLA". A 1,000 gallon tank still, located right in the tasting room.

Old Sugar Distillery

931 East Main Street, Ste. 8
Madison, WI 53703
608-260-0812

Owners / Operators:
Nathan Greenawalt, Owner / Distiller

Email: madisondistillery@gmail.com
Website: www.madisondistillery.com
Facebook: Old Sugar Distillery

Type: Micro-distillery. Opened in 2010.

Hours of operation:
Thursday and Friday, 4:00pm to 10:00pm
Saturdays, noon to 10:00pm

Tours: Available

Types of spirits produced:
Sorghum whiskey, rum, honey liqueur, ouzo,
and seasonal grappa and brandy

Names of spirits:
- Cane and Abe Small-Barrel Rum
- Old Sugar Factory Honey Liqueur
- Americanaki Ouzo
- Queen Jennie Sorghum Whiskey
- Brandy Station
  (brandy distilled from Wisconsin grapes)

Best known for / most popular: Rum

Average bottle price: $30.00 to $35.00

Distribution: CT, DC, DE, FL, IL, MD, NJ, NY WI

Interesting facts:
One of the only American Ouzo producers

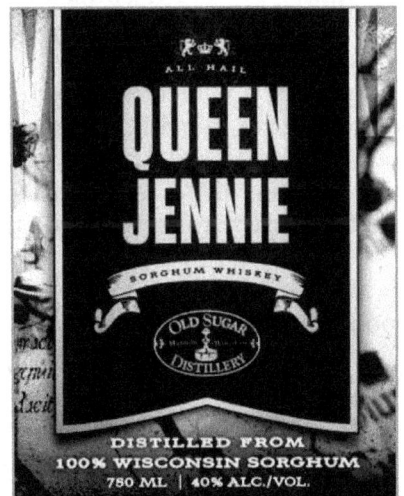

The North Woods Distillery LLC

135 W. Main Street
Coleman, WI 54112
920-819-6083

North Woods
DISTILLERY

Owners / Operators:
Curt A. Naegeli, Owner

Email: curt@northwoodsdistillery.com
Website: www.northwoodsdistillery.com
Facebook: The North Woods Distillery LLC

Type: Micro-distillery. Opened in 2011.

Hours of operation: Available by appointment

Tours: Available by appointment

Types of spirits produced: Rum

Names of spirits:
• Heath Rum
• Chocolat Mint Rum

Best known for / most popular: Heath Rum

Average bottle price: $21.00

Distribution: WI

Interesting facts:
"We operate under the assumption that today's consumer is health conscious and wants clean tasting spirits with little in the way of off flavors or burn.

Congeners in alcohol produce character and a sad feeling in the morning. Ethanol is what makes us happy and by refining their rum through two careful distillations, little is left in the way of congeners. We take great strides to produce our rums' character through flavoring.

Heath Rum tastes like candy; it's sweet, smooth, and has a toffee flavor. It's good straight up or on the rocks, but also mixes well. The North Woods Distillery grows Chocolat Mint, a variety of peppermint, naturally which is then distilled to make the flavoring. Mint is highlighted with a subtle chocolate flavor. Chocolat Mint Rum is great on the rocks and mixes well." - Curt Naegeli

Rum made by The North Woods Distillery is gluten free.

White Wolf Distillery

23396 Thompson Road
Shell Lake, WI 54871
715-468-4224

Owners / Operators:
Laura and Patrick Walters, Alexia and Jason Gannon, Owners
Ryan and Armani Walters and James Walters, Owners

Email: info@whitewolfdistillery.com
Website: www.whitewolfdistillery.com
Facebook: White Wolf Distillery

Type: Winery / Micro-distillery. Opened in 2011.

Hours of operation:
May 1 to October 31
Thursday through Saturday 12:00 to 9:00pm; Sunday, 12:00pm 6:00pm

November 1 to April 30
Saturday and Sunday, 12:00pm to 4:00pm

Tours: Not available

Types of spirits produced: Brandy, neutral spirit, whisky

Names of spirits:
- White Wolf Plum Brandy
- White Wolf Apple Brandy
- White Wolf Grape Brandy
- White Wolf Raspberry Brandy
- White Wolf Blackberry Brandy
- White Wolf Apple Neutral Spirit
- White Wolf Grape Neutral Spirit
- White Wolf Rye Whisky

Best known for / most popular: White Wolf Blackberry Brandy

Average bottle price: $35.00 to $70.00

Distribution: WI

Interesting facts:
- White Wolf Distillery is 100% certified organic and a travel green Wisconsin business.
- White Wolf Distillery generates 100% of their electricity needs using solar and wind energy

Yahara Bay Distillers

3118 Kingsley Way
Madison, WI 53713
608-275-1050

Owners / Operators:
Nick Quint and Catherine Forde Quint, Owners
Lars Forde, Head Distiller
Jill Skowronski, VP of Sales and Marketing

Email: jill@yaharabay.com
Website: www.yaharabay.com
Facebook: Yahara Bay Distillery
Twitter: @SeraphineVodka
YouTube: Yahara Bay Distillery

Type: Micro-distillery. Opened in 2007.

Hours of operation:
Monday through Friday, 9:00am to 5:00pm

Tours: Public house (tours/sampling) every Thursday, 5:00pm to 10:00pm.
All others by appointment.

Types of spirits produced:
Gin, rum, vodka, whiskey, brandy, liqueur

Names of spirits:
- Yahara Bay Premium Rum
- Mad Bird Rum (aged)
- Yahara Bay Extra Dry Gin
- Yahara Bay Premium Vodka
- Seraphine Chai Tea Vodka
- Yahara Bay Whiskey
- V Bourbon Whiskey
- Lightning Whiskey
- Charred Oak Bourbon Whiskey
- Charred Oak Rye Whiskey
- Yahara Bay Apple Brandy
- Kirschwasser Cherry Brandy
- Yahara Bay Pear Brandy
- Cocoa Liqueur
- Coffee Liqueur
- Lemoncella

Average bottle price: $13.99 to $34.99

Distribution: CA, FL, GA, IA, IL, MD, MI, MN, OK, TX WI, WY

Interesting facts: First legal distillery in Dane County WI.

Kolts Fine Spirits

Sheridan, WY 82801
307-673-5410

Owners / Operators:
Robert Koltiska, CEO
Jason Koltiska, Head of Distribution and Production
Justin Koltiska, Head of Marketing

Email: info@koltsfinespirits.com
Website: www.koltsfinespirits.com
Facebook: Koltiska Original & KO 90

Type: Micro-Distillery. Opened in 2006.

Hours of operation: Not provided

Tours: Not provided

Types of spirits produced: Liqueur

Names of spirits:
- Koltiska 90 Proof Liqueur
- Koltiska Original Liqueur

Best known for / most popular: Not provided

Average bottle price: Not provided

Distribution: ID, MT, NE, WA, WY

Interesting facts: Not provided

Wyoming Whiskey Distillery

100 South Nelson
Kirby, WY 82430
307-864-2116

Owners / Operators:
Brad Mead, Owner
Kate Mead, Owner
David DeFazio, Owner / COO

Email: info@wyomingwhiskey.com
Website: www.wyomingwhiskey.com
Facebook: Wyoming Whiskey
Twitter: @WyoWhiskey

Type: Micro-distillery. Opened in 2009.

Hours of operation:
Monday, Tuesday, Thursday, Friday 10:00am to 4:00pm

Tours: Available Monday through Saturday, 10:00 to 4:00pm

Types of spirits produced: Bourbon

Names of spirits:
* Wyoming Whiskey

Best known for / most popular: Wyoming Whiskey

Average bottle price: $43.00

Distribution: Currently WY only. Additional select markets in 2014.

Interesting facts: The Meads are fourth generation Wyoming ranchers who run cattle in Kirby and in Jackson. Brad's grandfather, Cliff Hansen, was a US senator and governor. Brad's brother, Matt, is the current governor.

426

Island Spirits Distillery

4605 Roburn Road
Hornby Island, BC V0R 1Z0
250-335-0630

Owners / Operators:
Peter Kimmerly, Co-owner
Naz Abudurahman, Co-owner

Email: pckimmer@telus.net
Website: www.islandspirits.ca

Type: Micro-distillery. Opened in 2009.

Hours of operation: Not provided

Tours: Not provided

Types of spirits produced: Gin, vodka

Names of spirits:
- Phrog Premium Gin
- Phrog Premium Vodka

Best known for / most popular: Phrog Premium Gin

Average bottle price: Not provided

Distribution: Vancouver Island, Vancouver, Alberta

Interesting facts: Not provided

427

Long Table Distillery Ltd.

1451 Hornby Street
Vancouver, BC V6Z 1W8
604-266-0177

Owners / Operators:
Charles Tremewen, Founder / Distiller
Rita Tremewen, Distillery General Manager

Email: info@longtabledistillery.com
Website: www.longtabledistillery.com
Facebook: Long Table Distillery
Twitter: @LT_Distillery

Type: Craft-distillery. Opened in 2012.

Hours of operation:
Friday and Saturday, 11:00am to 6:00pm
Sunday through Thursday by appointment only

Tours: Check distillery website for seasonally adjusted public tasting/sales room hours.

Types of spirits produced: Gin, vodka, whisky (2016)

Names of spirits:
- Long Table Distillery London Dry Gin
- Long Table Distillery Texada Vodka

Best known for / most popular: LTD Gin

Average bottle price: $45.00 to $50.00

Distribution: British Columbia

Interesting facts:
- Vancouver's first micro-distillery.
- Long Table Distillery focuses on handcrafted, small batch spirits incorporating locally produced and hand harvested botanicals and base ingredients.
- Spirits made on premises are available for purchase on site along with mixers, locally produced bitters and cocktail paraphernalia.
- Expect to release a wider range of spirits including a line of small batch apothecary spirits and liquors.

428

Maple Leaf Spirit Inc.

1386 Carmi Avenue
Penticton, BC V2A 3H2
250-493-0180

Owners / Operators:
Jorg and Anette Engel, Owners

Email: info@engel.ca
Website: www.mapleleafspirits.ca
Facebook: Maple Leaf Spirits Inc
Twitter: @mapleleafspirit

Type: Micro-distillery. Opened in 2006.

Hours of operation: Open by appointment

Tours: Available by appointment

Types of spirits produced: Eau de vie, brandy, liqueur

Names of spirits:
- Canadian Kirsch
- Maple Liqueur
- Cherry Liqueur
- Pear Williams
- Pear Liqueur
- Skinny

Best known for / most popular: Canadian Kirsch

Average bottle price: $30.00 to $50.00

Distribution: British Columbia

Interesting facts:
First licensed distillery in the South Okanagan

429

Merridale Ciderworks Corp.

1230 Merridale Road
Cobble Hill, BC V0R 1L0
800-998-9908

Owners / Operators:
Not provided

Email: info@merridalecider.com
Website: www.merridalecider.com
Facebook: Merridale Ciderworks
Twitter: @merridalecider
Pinterest: Merridale Ciderworks

Type: Micro-distillery. Opened in 2008.

Hours of operation:
Monday through Thursday, 11:00am to 7:30pm
Friday and Saturday, 11:00am to 6:00pm
Sunday, 11:00am to 7:30pm

Tours: Available by appointment

Types of spirits produced: Eau de vie, vodka

Names of spirits:
• Frizz Vodka

Best known for / most popular: Frizz Vodka

Average bottle price: Not provided

Distribution: British Columbia

Interesting facts: Not provided

Okanagan Spirits

267 Bernard Avenue
Kelowna, BC V1Y 6N2
250-549-3120

Owners / Operators:
Tyler Dyck, CEO
Tony Dyck, Owner
Peter von Hahn, Distiller
Rodney Goodchild, Sales & Marketing

Email: info@okanaganspirits.com
Website: www.okanaganspirits.com
Facebook: Okanagan Spirits
Twitter: @okspirits

Type: Craft-distillery. Opened in 2003.

Hours of operation: Daily

Tours: Available

Types of spirits produced:
Fruit spirits, fruit liqueurs, gin, rye whisky, vodka, absinthe, grappa, aquavit

Names of spirits:

- Okanagan Spirits Liqueur
  Raspberry, Cherry, Blueberry,
  Blackcurrant, Cranberry,
  Blackberry, Sea Buckthorn

- Okanagan Spirits Eau de Vie
  Poire Williams, Canados, Old
  Italian Prune, Italian Prune,
  Raspberry Framboise, Kirsch
  Danbue, Kirsch Virginiana,
  Apricot

- Okanagan Spirits Grappa
  Gewurztraminer, Pinot Noir,
  Riesling

- Okanagan Spirits Gin
- Okanagan Spirits Whisky
- Okanagan Spirits Vodka
- Okanagan Spirits Single Malt Whisky
- Okanagan Spirits Aquavit – Aquavitus

- Absinthe
  Okanagan Spirits Taboo Gold
  Okanagan Spirits Taboo Genuine

Average bottle price: $40.00

Distribution: Throughout Canada

Interesting facts:
- Distillery of the Year - 2013 World Spirits Awards
- Spirit of the Year 2013 - 2013 World Spirits Awards
- Received "World Class Distillery" - 2013 World Spirits Awards

Pemberton Distillery Inc.

1954 Venture Place
Pemberton, BC V0N2L0
604-894-0222

Owners / Operators:
Tyler Schramm, Owner

Email: info@pembertondistillery.ca
Website: www.pembertondistillery.ca
Facebook: Pemberton Distillery Inc.
Twitter: @pembydistillery
YouTube: Pemberton Distillery
Tripadvisor: Pemberton Distillery
Tumblr: Pemberton Distillery
Instagram: pembydistillery
Pinterest: Pemberton Distillery

Type: Micro-distillery. Opened in 2009.

Hours of operation:
Winter (October 15 - May 15): Friday & Saturday
Summer (May 15 - October 15): Wednesday - Saturday

Tours: Yes, tours run on Saturdays at 4pm

Types of spirits produced:
Vodka, gin, whisky, absinthe, brandy, liqueur

Names of spirits:
*   Schramm Organic Gin
*   Schramm Organic Potato Vodka
*   Pemberton Distillery Organic Single Malt Whisky
*   The Devil's Club Organic Absinthe

Best known for / most popular: Schramm Vodka

Average bottle price: $40.00 to $50.00

Distribution: Alberta, British Columbia

Interesting facts: The distillery uses a geothermal ground loop system to heat and cool water used in the distilling process reducing their energy usage by 35-70%, depending on the function that it is providing.

Shelter Point Distillery

4650 Regent Road
Campbell River, BC V9H 1E3
778-420-2200

Owners / Operators:
Patrick Evans, Co-owner
James Marinus, Co-owner

Email: info@shelterpointdistillery.com
Website: www.shelterpointdistillery.com
Facebook: Shelter Point Distillery
Twitter: @ShelterPoint

Type: Micro-distillery. Opened in 2011.

Hours of operation: Not provided

Tours: Available

Types of spirits produced: Whisky

Names of spirits:
- Shelter Point Distillery Single Malt Whisky

Best known for / most popular: Shelter Point Distillery Single Malt Whisky

Average bottle price: Not provided

Distribution: Not provided

Interesting facts: Not provided

Urban Distilleries

6-325 Bay Avenue
Kelowna, BC V1Y 7S3
778-478-0939

Owners / Operators:
Mike Urban, Owner / Master Distiller

Email: info@urbandistilleries.ca
Website: www.urbandistilleries.ca
Facebook: Urban Distilleries
Twitter: @SpiritBearVodka
YouTube: Urban Distilleries

Type: Micro-distillery. Opened in 2011.

Hours of operation:
May to October – Daily, 11:00am to 6:00pm
November to April – Monday through Saturday, 11:00am to 5:00pm

Tours: Available

Types of spirits produced: Gin, vodka, rum, whisky, brandy

Names of spirits:
- Spirit Bear Gin
- Spirit Bear Vodka
- Spirit Bear Espresso Vodka
- Urban White Rum
- Urban Amber Rum
- Urban Single Malt Whisky

Best known for / most popular: Spirit Bear Gin

Average bottle price: $48.00

Distribution: Alberta, British Columbia

Interesting facts:
- Urban Distilleries is a hand craft micro producing top-shelf Okanagan Gin, Vodkas, Rums and Whisky including the signature "Spirit Bear" line in Kelowna, BC.
- Each batch is crafted in Artesian copper stills from premium 100% British Columbia grains and agricultural inputs along with pure spring water from the Kootneys.
- All products are gluten free.

434

Victoria Spirits

6170 Old West Saanich Road
Victoria, BC V9E 2G8
250-544-8217

Owners / Operators:
Valerie and Bryan Murray, Owners
Peter Hunt, Distiller

Email: info@victoriaspirits.com
Website: www.victoriaspirits.com
Facebook: Victoria Spirits
Twitter: @victoriaspirits

Type: Micro-distillery. Opened in 2008.

Hours of operation:
Weekends and holidays, April through September, 10:00am to 5:00pm

Tours: Available

Types of spirits produced:
Gin, vodka, oak barrel aged gin, whisky, bitters

Names of spirits:
- Victoria Gin
- Left Coast Hemp Vodka
- Oaken Gin
- Craigdarroch Whisky
- Twisted and Bitter Bitters

Best known for / most popular: Victoria Gin

Average bottle price: $50.00

Distribution:
Provincial Government Liquor Stores, independent retail outlets in Alberta, British Columbia, Manitoba, Ontario, Saskatchewan, Quebec.

Interesting facts:
First artisan producer of premium gin in Canada

Winegarden Estate Ltd.

851 Route 970
Baie Verte, NB E4M 1Z7
506-538-7405

Owners / Operators:
The Rosswog Family, Owners / Operators
Steffen Rosswog, Distiller / Winemaker

Email: srosswog@nbnet.nb.ca
Website: www.winegardenestate.com

Type: Winery / Micro-distillery. Opened in 1991.

Hours of operation: Vary

Tours: Available

Types of spirits produced: Eau de vie, brandy, liqueur

Names of spirits:
- Johnny Ziegler Grappa
- Johnny Ziegler Sibowitz
- Johnny Ziegler Myrtille
- Johnny Ziegler Elderberry
- Johnny Ziegler Cassis
- Johnny Ziegler Kirsch
- Johnny Ziegler Obstler
- Johnny Ziegler Brandy
- Plaisir Apple Liqueur
- Blue Hill Blueberry Liqueur
- Wild Cherry Liqueur
- Maple Dream liqueur
- Elderberry Liqueur
- Pear Liqueur
- Cranberry Liqueur
- Cassis Liqueur
- Honey Liqueur
- Blackberry Liqueur
- Raspberry Liqueur
- Mocca Gino Coffee Liqueur

Best known for / most popular: Johnny Ziegler Apple Schnaps

Average bottle price: $16.00 to $45.00

Distribution: On-site, NB, Co-op cottage wineries

Interesting facts:
- First fruit wine distillery in Atlantic Canada, established in 1991
- Pioneered New Brunswick's cottage distillery and winery industry

Glenora Distillery

13727 Route 19, Glenville
Cape Breton, NS B0E 1X0
902-258-2662, 1-800-839-0491

Owners / Operators:
Lauchie MacLean, President / CEO

Email: info@glenora1.ca
Website: www.glenoradistillery.com
Facebook: Glenora Inn & Distillery
Twitter: @GlenBreton

Type: Micro-distillery. Opened in 1990.

Hours of operation: Open May through October

Tours: Available on the hour, 9:00am to 5:00pm.

Types of spirits produced: Single malt whisky

Names of spirits:
• Glen Breton Canadian Single Malt Whisky
• Glen Breton Ice
• Battle of the Glen

Best known for / most popular: Glen Breton Ice

Average bottle price: $50.00 to $300.00

Distribution: Canada, U.S., Europe

Interesting facts:
• Glen Breton Rare Aged 10 years won a gold medal in international competition 2006
• Glen Breton Ice won a International Silver Award in 2008.
• Battle of the Glen Aged 15 years, 95 Points out of 100.
• In the early 1800's, Scottish immigrants chose Cape Breton Island for their new home as its beauty resembled the Highlands and Islands of Scotland. Many traditions and secrets came with these pioneers. The making of a spirited whisky was one of them. Scottish descendants passionately keep the dearest aspects of their colourful culture alive. This is especially evident in Inverness County, Nova Scotia, which is home to Glenora Distillery, the First Single Malt Whisky Distillery in North America.

Ironworks Distillery

2 Kempt Street
Lunenburg, NS B0J 2C0
902-640-2424

Owners / Operators:
Lynne MacKay, Co-owner
Pierre Guevremont, Co-owner

Email: spirits@ironworksdistillery.com
Website: www.ironworksdistillery.com
Facebook: Ironworks Distillery
Twitter: @Ironworks_NS

Type: Micro-distillery. Opened in 2009.

Hours of operation: 2013 Schedule
January to May 18, Thursday, Friday & Saturday, 12:00pm to 5:00pm
May 19 to June 25, Wednesday through Monday, 12:00pm to 5:00pm
June 26 to September 2, Daily 11:00am to 7:00pm
September 3 to December 31, Daily 12:00pm to 5:00pm

Tours: Available

Types of spirits produced:
Vodka, rum, eaux de vie, brandy, liqueur

Names of spirits:
- Amber Rum
- Bluenose Black Rum
- Ironworks Vodka
- Ironworks Eaux de Vie
- Ironworks Apple Brandy
- Ironworks Blueberry Liqueur
- Ironworks Cranberry Liqueur

Best known for / most popular:
Ironworks Vodka

Average bottle price: $25.00 to $38.00

Distribution: Lunenburg, Halifax NS

Interesting facts: Ironworks Distillery is housed in a heritage blacksmith shop built in the 1890s in the UNESCO designated town of Lunenburg Nova Scotia.

438

Six Owls Spirits

4614 Main Street
Weymouth, NS B0W 3T0

Owners / Operators:
Craig Melanson, Owner / Distiller
Nicole Leblanc, Owner / Marketing / Sales

Email: sixowls@hotmail.ca
Facebook: SIX OWLS Spirits
Twitter: @sixowls

Type: Micro-distillery. Opening in 2013.

Hours of operation: Not provided

Tours: Not available

Types of spirits produced: Vodka, rum

Names of spirits:
- White Owl Vodka
- Six Owls Rum

Best known for / most popular: TBA

Average bottle price: $25.00

Distribution: Not provided

Interesting facts: First distillery in southwestern Nova Scotia

66 Gilead Distillery

66 Gilead Road
Bloomfield, ON K0K 1G0
613-393-1890

Owners / Operators:
Sophia Pantazi, Co-owner
Peter Stroz, Co-owner

Email: info@66gileaddistillery.com
Website: www.66gileaddistillery.com
Facebook: 66 Gilead Distillery
Twitter: @66Gilead

Type: Craft-distillery. Opened in 2011.

Hours of operation:
Daily from Victoria Day to Labour Day. Check website for exact hours.
Weekends year-round. Check website for exact hours.

Tours: Available on weekends from Victoria Day to Labour Day

Types of spirits produced:
Vodkas, gin, shochu, rum, Canadian rye whisky

Names of spirits:
• Loyalist Gin
• Duck Island Rum
• Whole Wheat Vodka
• Canadian Rye Vodka
• Canadian Pine Vodka
• White Dragon Shochu

Best known for / most popular: Canadian Pine Vodka

Average bottle price: $36.95 to $45.95

Distribution: Alberta, Ontario

Interesting facts: Not provided

440

Forty Creek Distillery

297 South Service Road West
Grimsby, ON L3M 1Y6
905-945-9225

Owners / Operators:
John K. Hall, Owner

Email: Admin@FortyCreekDistillery.com
Website: www.fortycreekwhisky.com
   www.princeigorvodka.com, www.canadagoldwhisky.com
Facebook: Forty Creek Whisky
Twitter: @FortyCreek_John

Type: Micro-distillery. Opened in 1992.

Hours of operation:
Monday through Saturday, 10:00am to 6:00pm
Sunday and Holidays, 11:00am to 5:00pm

Tours: Available

Types of spirits produced: Whisky, vodka, liqueur

Names of spirits:
- Forty Creek Carrel Select Whisky
- Forty Creek Copper Pot Whisky
- Forty Creek Port Wood Reserve
- Forty Creek Small Batch Reserve
- Forty Creek Double Barrel Reserve
- Forty Creek Confederation Oak Reserve
- Forty Creek John's Private Cask No. 1
- Forty Creek Whisky Cream Liquor
- Canada Gold Premium Barrel Aged Canadian Whisky
- Prince Igor Vodka

Best known for / most popular: Not provided

Average bottle price: Not provided

Distribution: Throughout U.S. and Canada

Interesting facts: Not provided

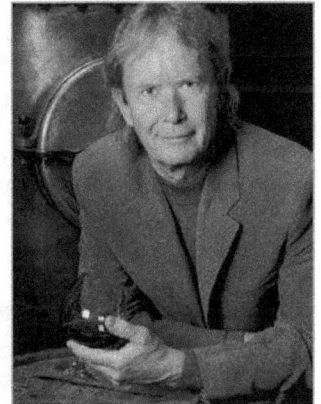

Mary Jane's

Niagara Falls, ON
289-257-0420

Owners / Operators:
Scott Collier, Owner

Email: drinkmaryjanes@live.com
Website: www.drinkmaryjanes.com
Facebook: Drink Mary Jane's

Type: Micro-distillery. Opened in 2012.

Hours of operation: Not provided

Tours: Not provided

Types of spirits produced: Vodka, gin

Names of spirits:
- Mary Jane's Primo Hemp Vodka
- Mary Jane's Premium Hemp Gin

Best known for / most popular: Mary Jane's Primo Hemp Vodka

Average bottle price: Not provided

Distribution: Not provided

Interesting facts: Handcrafted and multi-distilled in alembic copper using select grains and fastidiously filtered BC spring water.

442

Still Waters Distillery

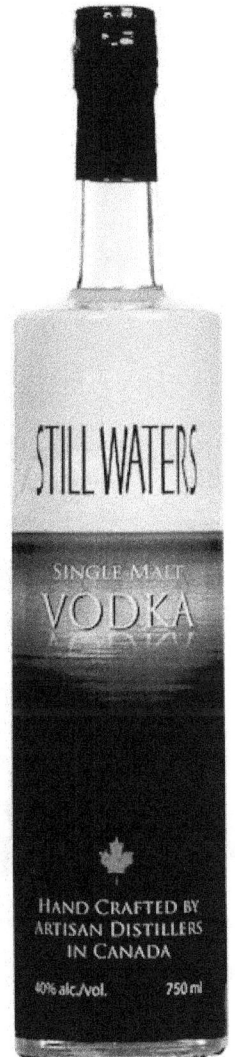

150 Bradwick Drive, Unit # 26
Concord, ON L4K 4M7
905-482-2080

Owners / Operators:
Barry Bernstein and Barry Stein, Owners

Email: info@stillwatersdistillery.com
Website: www.stillwatersdistillery.com
Facebook: Still Waters Distillery
Twitter: @StillWatersD
Flickr: Still Water Distillery's photostream

Type: Micro-distillery. Opened in 2009

Hours of operation: Monday through Friday, 10:00am to 5:00pm
                      Weekends by appointment

Tours: Available by appointment

Types of spirits produced: Single malt whisky, rye whisky,
Canadian whisky, vodka, brandy

Names of spirits:
- Stalk & Barrel Single Malt Whisky
- Special 1+11 Blend Canadian Whisky
- Still Waters Single Malt Vodka

Best known for / most popular:
Stalk & Barrel Single Malt Whisky

Average bottle price: $30.00 to $40.00

Distribution: Liquor Control Board of Ontario and across
Canada as well as through Purple Valley Imports for the U.S.

Interesting facts: The first micro-distillery in Ontario

443

Waverley Spirits

34 Herriott Street
Perth, ON K7H 1T2
613-601-8810

Owners / Operators:
James Snasdell-Taylor, Co-founder
Barbara Snasdell-Taylor, Co-founder

Email: info@waverleyspirits.com
Website: www.waverleyspirits.com
Facebook: Waverley Spirits Limited
Twitter: @waverleyspirits

Type: Micro-distillery under construction. Opening in 2013.

Hours of operation: TBA

Tours: TBA

Types of spirits produced: Vodka

Names of spirits:
• TBA

Best known for: TBA

Average bottle price: TBA

Distribution: TBA

Interesting facts: The first craft-distillery in Perth, Ontario since 1916

where tradition begins

Myriad View Artisan Distillery Inc.

Prince Edward Island 2
Rollo Bay, PE C0A 2B0
902-687-1281

Owners / Operators:
Dr. Paul and Angie Berrow, Owners
Ken and Danielle Mill, Owners

Email: info@straitshine.com
Website: www.straitshine.com
Facebook: Strait Shine

Type: Micro-distillery. Opened in 2007.

Hours of operation: Vary

Tours: Available

Types of spirits produced: Moonshine, rum, gin, whisky, vodka

Names of spirits:
- Strait Shine
- Strait Lightning
- Strait Rum (historic 100 proof 57.1%)
- Strait Rum (40%)
- Strait Vodka
- Strait Gin
- Strait Pastis
- Strait Whisky

Best known for / most popular: Strait Shine

Average bottle price: $26.00 to $42.00

Distribution: PEI, Calgary Alberta

Interesting facts: Prince Edward Island's first distillery

445

Prince Edward Distillery

9985 Route 16
Hermanville, PE C0A 2B0
902-687-2586

Owners / Operators:
Julie Shore, Co-owner
Arla Johnson, Co-owner

Email: info@princeedwarddistillery.com
Website: www.princeedwarddistillery.com
Facebook: Prince Edward Distillery

Type: Micro-distillery. Opened in 2008.

Hours of operation: Daily, 10:00am to 6:00pm

Tours: Available

Types of spirits produced: Vodka, gin, rum, whiskey

Names of spirits:
- Prince Edward Potato Vodka
- Prince Edward Wild Blueberry Vodka
- Prince Edward Wild Blueberry Gin
- Prince Edward Merchantman Rum
- Prince Edward I.C. Shore Whiskey
- Prince Edward Canadian Rye

Best known for / most popular:
Prince Edward Potato Vodka

Average bottle price: Not provided

Distribution: PEI, Nova Scotia

Interesting facts: Not provided

Cidrerie Michel Jodoin

1130 Petite Caroline
Rougemont, QC JOL 1M0
450-469-2676

Owners / Operators:
Michel Jodoin, Owner

Email: info@micheljodoin.ca
Website: www.micheljodoin.ca
Facebook: Cidrerie Michel Jodoin
Twitter: @cidrerie

Type: Micro-distillery. Opened in 1999.

Hours of operation:
Monday through Friday, 9:00am to 5:00pm
Saturday and Sunday, 10:00am to 4:00pm

Tours: Available

Types of spirits produced:
Apple liquor, brandy, eau de vie, fortified cider

Names of spirits:
- Calijo
- Calijo XO
- Fine Caroline
- Pom de vie
- Ambre de pomme (fortified cider)

Best known for / most popular: Calijo

Average bottle price: $33.00

Distribution: Alberta

Interesting facts:
In 1999, the cidrerie became the first micro-distillery of apples in Canada.

The Subersives Distillers

449 Gardenville
Longueuil, QC J4H 2H5
514-316-6692

Owners / Operators:
Fernando Balthazard, Co-owner
Pascal Gervais, Co-owner
Stéphan Ruffo, Co-owner
Robert Paradis, Co-owner

Email: info@lat45.ca
Website: www.distillateurssubversifs.com, www.pigerhenricus.com
Facebook: Piger Henricus Gin
Twitter: @PigerHenricus

Type: Micro-distillery. Opened in 2012.

Hours of operation: Not provided

Tours: No provided

Types of spirits produced: Gin

Names of spirits:
• Piger Henricus Gin

Best known for / most popular: Piger Henricus Gin

Average bottle price: Not provided

Distribution: Not provided

Interesting facts: Not provided

Last Mountain Distillery Ltd.

70 Highway 20
Lumsden, SK S0G 3C0
306-731-3930

Owners / Operators:
Colin Schmidt, President / Distiller
Meredith Schmidt, Retail Manager / Secretary
Darryl Babey, Co-owner / Manager of Fixed Operations
Shannon Babey, Co-owner

Email: colin@lastmountaindistillery.com
Website: www.lastmountaindistillery.com
Facebook: Last Mountain Distillery
Twitter: @skdistillery

Type: Micro-distillery. Opened in 2011.

Hours of operation:
Tuesday through Saturday, 12:00pm to 6:00pm

Tours: Available by appointment

Types of spirits produced: Vodka, whisky, liqueur

Names of spirits:
- Last Mountain Vodka
- Last Mountain Canadian Rye Whisky

Best known for / most popular: Last Mountain Vodka

Average bottle price: $35.00

Distribution: Saskatchewan

Interesting facts: Saskatchewan's first micro distillery

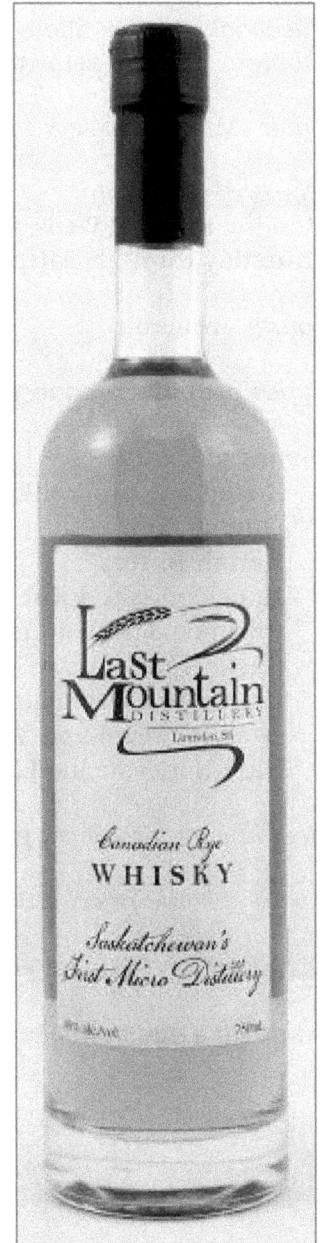

LB Distillers

1925 Avenue B North
Saskatoon, SK S7L 4K9
306-979-7280

Owners / Operators:
Cary Bowman, President of Good Times
Lacey Crocker, Chief Operating Officer Lady
Michael Goldney, President of Vice

Email: lucky@luckybastard.ca
Website: www.luckybastard.ca
Facebook: LB Distillers
Twitter: @luckybastardSK

Type: Micro-distillery. Opened in 2012.

Hours of operation:
Monday through Wednesday, 11:00am to 5:00pm
Thursday through Saturday, 11:00am to 6:00pm

Tours: Available

Types of spirits produced: Vodka, gin, whisky

Names of spirits:
- Lucky Bastard Vodka
- Gambit Gin
- Bettah Bitters
- Knock on Wood Rum
- Carmine Jewel Liqueur
- Saskatoon Liqueur
- Crème de Cassis Liqueur
- Seabuckthorn and Wildflower Honey Liqueur
- Blue Honeysuckle Liqueur

Best known for / most popular: Lucky Bastard Vodka

Average bottle price: $35.00 to $37.77

Distribution: Saskatchewan

Interesting facts: Not provided

Klondike River Distillery

Across the river from Dawson City, YT Y0B1G0
867-993-3487

Owners / Operators:
Dorian and Bridget Amos, Owners

Email: info@klondikeriverdistillery.com
Website: www.klondikeriverdistillery.com
Facebook: Klondike River Distillery

Type: Micro-distillery. Opened in 2007.

Hours of operation: Vary

Tours: Not available

Types of spirits produced: Vodka

Names of spirits:
• Klondike Vodka -The Spirit of the Yukon

Best known for / most popular: Klondike Vodka

Average bottle price: $39.99

Distribution: Yukon

Interesting facts:
Klondike Vodka is the first spirit to be legally produced in the Yukon Territory

Yukon Spirits

102A Copper Road
Whitehorse, YT Y1A 2Z6
867-668-4183

Owners / Operators:
Alan Hansen and Bob Baxter, Owners

Email: bob@yukonbeer.com
Website: www.yukonbeer.com, www.yukonspirits.ca
Facebook: Yukon Spirits
Twitter: @YukonSpirits

Type: Brewery / Micro-distillery. Opened in 2010.

Hours of operation: Monday through Sunday, 8:00am to 6:00pm

Tours: Available

Types of spirits produced: Vodka, whisky (still aging)

Names of spirits:
• Solstice Infused Vodka

Best known for / most popular: Solstice Infused Vodka

Average bottle price: $44.95

Distribution: Yukon

Interesting facts: Not provided

Distilling Associations and Guilds

American Distilling Institute
Email: bill@distilling.com
Website: www.distilling.com
Facebook: American Distilling Institute
Twitter: @Distilling

Artisan Distillers Guild of British Columbia
Facebook: Artisan Distillers Guild of British Columbia
Twitter: @ADG_BC

California Artisanal Distillers Guild
Email: info@cadsp.org
Website: www.cadsp.org
Facebook: California Artisanal Distillers Guild

Colorado Distillers Guild
Email: coloradodistillers@gmail.com
Website: www.coloradodistillersguild.com
Facebook: Colorado Distillers Guild

Distilled Spirits Council of Vermont
Website: www.distilledvermont.org
Facebook: Distilled Spirits Council of Vermont

Distillery Row Association
Website: www.distilleryrowpdx.com
Facebook: Distillery Row
Twitter: @DistilleryRow

Distilled Spirits Council of the United States (DISCUS)
Website: www.discus.org
Facebook: Distilled Spirits Council of the United States

Florida Craft Distillers Guild
Website: www.floridadistillers.org
Facebook: Florida Craft Distillers Guild

Illinois Craft Distillers Association
Facebook: Illinois Craft Distillers Association

Kentucky Distillers' Association (Kentucky Bourbon Trail)
Email: enjoy@kybourbon.com
Website: www.kybourbon.com, www.kybourbontrail.com
Facebook: Kentucky Bourbon Trail
Twitter: KentuckyBourbonTrail

National Alcohol Beverage Control Association (NABCA)
Website: www.nabca.org

New York Craft Distillers Guild
Email: site_distiller@burningstill.com
Website: www.burningstill.com

Ohio Distillers Guild
Website: www.distillersguild.org

Oregon Distillers Guild
Email: director@oregondistillersguild.org
Website: www.oregondistillersguild.org
Facebook: Oregon Distillers Guild
Twitter: @OregonDistilled

Texas Distilled Spirits Association
Email: info@texasdistilledspirits.org
Website: www.texasdistilledspirits.org

United Craft Distillers
Email: info@unitedcraftdistillers.com
Website: www.unitedcraftdistillers.com

Washington Distillers Guild
Website: www.washingtondistillersguild.org

Wine & Spirits Wholesales of America
Email: info@wswa.org
Website: www.wswa.org

Wisconsin Distillers Association
Website: www.widistillers.org

Resources and Information

Alcohol and Tobacco Tax and Trade Bureau – Distilled Spirits
Website: www.ttb.gov/spirits

American Craft Spirits – Reviews & Interviews
Email: info@americancraftspirits.com
Website: www.americancraftspirits.com
Facebook: American Craft Spirits

Beverage World Magazine
Website: www.beverageworld.com
Facebook: Beverage World Magazine
Twitter: @Beverage_World

BevX – A Beverage & Lifestyle Magazine
Email: sean@bevx.com
Website: www.bevx.com
Facebook: BevX.com

Beverage Information Group – Info Source for the Beverage Alcohol Industry
Website: www.beveragenet.net

Cheers Magazine
Website: www.alturl.com/6v27z
Facebook: Cheers Magazine

Chilled Magazine
Website: www.chilledmagazine.com
Facebook: Chilled Magazine
Twitter: @chilledmagazine

Cigars & Spirits Magazine
Email: customerservice@cigarandspirits.com
Website: www.cigarandspirits.com

Drink Me – Lifestyle Beyond The Glass
Email: info@drinkmemag.com
Website: www.drinkmemag.com
Facebook: Drink Me Magazine
Twitter: Drink Me Magazine

Imbibe Magazine – Liquid Culture
Email: info@imbibemagazine.com
Website: www.imbibemagazine.com
Facebook: Imbibe Magazine
Twitter: Imbibe Magazine
Pinterest: Imbibe Magazine

Micro Liquor – Liquor Entrepreneurship + Innovation
Email: contact@MicroLiquor.com
Website: www.microliquor.com
Facebook: MicroLiquor
Twitter: MicroLiquor

MicroShiner Magazine
Email: microshiner@gmail.com
Website: www.microshiner.com
Facebook: MicroShiner
Twitter: @MicroShiner
Pinterest: MicroShiner

Modern Distillery Age – Spirits Business e-newsletter
Email: gregg@distilleryage.com
Website: www.distilleryage.com
Facebook: Modern Distillery Age

F. Paul Pacult's Spirit Journal
Email: mail@spiritjournal.com
Website: www.spiritjournal.com

The Tasting Panel – Connection for Beverage Trends
Website: www.tastingpanelmag.com
Facebook: The Tasting Panel Magazine
Twitter: @TastingPanel

Whisky Advocate
Email: info@whiskyadvocate.com
Website: www.whiskyadvocate.com
Facebook: The Whisky Advocate Magazine
Twitter: @JohnHansell

Whisky Magazine
Website: www.whiskymag.com
Facebook: Whisky Magazine
Twitter: @Whisky_Magazine

Wine & Spirits Magazine
Email: info@wineandspiritsmagazine.com
Website: www.wineandspiritsmagazine.com
Facebook: Wine & Spirits Magazine
Twitter: Wine & Spirits Mag

Spirit Events and Festivals

Art of the Cocktail – Victoria BC, Canada
Email: sip@artofthecocktail.ca
Website: www.artofthecocktail.ca

Breckenridge Craft Spirits Festival – Breckenridge, CO
Website: www.breckenridgecraftspiritsfestival.com

Chicago Craft Spirit Week – Chicago, IL
Email: chicagocraftspirits@gmail.com
Website: www.craftspiritweekchicago.com
Facebook: Chicago Craft Spirit Week

Chicago Independent Spirits Expo – Chicago, IL

Cocktail Camp – Portland, OR
Website: www.cocktailcamp.net
Twitter: @CocktailCamp

Colorado Distillers Festival – Denver, CO
Website: www.coloradodistillersfestival.com
Twitter: CODistFest

Distill America – Madison, WI
Website: www.distillamerica.com

Great American Distillers Festival – Portland, OR
Website: www.distillersfestival.com
Facebook: Great American Distillers Festival

Independent Spirits Expo - U.S. cities change
Email: indiespirits@gmail.com
Website: www.indiespiritsexpo.com

Kentucky Bourbon Festival – Bardstown, KY
Website: www.kybourbonfestival.com

Los Angeles International Spirits Expo
Website: www.laspiritsexpo.com
Facebook: Los Angeles International Spirits Expo
Twitter: @LASPIRITSEXPO

Manhattan Cocktail Classic – New York, NY
Website: www.manhattancocktailclassic.com
Facebook: Manhattan Cocktail Classic
Twitter: @cocktailclassic

Midtown Cocktail Week – Sacramento, CA
Website: www.midtowncocktailweek.org
Facebook: Midtown Cocktail Week
Twitter: @SacMCW

Nashville Whiskey Festival – Nashville, TN
Website: www.nashvillewhiskeyfestival.com
Facebook: Nashville Whiskey Festival
Twitter: @NashWhiskeyFest

Northwest Food and Wine Festival – Portland, OR
Website: www.nwwinefestival.com
Facebook: Northwest Food & Wine Festival

Philadelphia Whiskey & Fine Spirits – Philadelphia, PA
Website: www.phillymag.com/whiskeyfest

Pittsburgh Whiskey & Fine Spirits Festival – Pittsburgh, PA
Website: www.pittsburghwhiskeyfestival.com

Portland Cocktail Week – Portland, OR
Website: www.portlandcocktailweek.com
Facebook: Portland Cocktail Week
Twitter: @PDXCocktailWeek

San Diego Spirits Festival – San Diego, CA
Website: www.sandiegospiritsfestival.com
Facebook: San Diego Spirits Festival
Twitter: @spiritsfestival

San Francisco Cocktail Week – San Francisco Bay Area, CA
Website: www.sfcocktailweek.com
Facebook: SF Cocktail Week
Twitter: @CocktailWeek

Speakeasy Cocktail Festival – Atlanta, GA
Website: www.speakeasycocktailfestival.com
Facebook: Speakeasy Cocktail Festival
Twitter: @speakeasyfest

St. Louis Classic Cocktail Party – St. Louis MO
Facebook: St. Louis Classic Cocktail Party

Tails of the Cocktail – New Orleans, LA
Website: www.talesofthecocktail.com
Facebook: Tales of the Cocktail
Twitter: @totc

The Liquid Projects – Mia, FL
Website: www.theliquidprojects.com

Ultimate Beverage Challenge – New York, NY
Website: www.ultimate-beverage.com
Facebook: Ultimate Beverage Challenge

Whisky Live – U.S. / Canadian cities change
Website: www.whiskylive.com

Miscellaneous

Museum of the American Cocktail – New Orleans, LA
Website: www.museumoftheamericancocktail.org
Facebook: Museum of the American Cocktail

National Absinthe Day – March 5
Facebook: National Absinthe Day

National Bourbon Day – June 14
Website: www.nationalbourbonday.com
Twitter: @BourbonDay

National Bourbon Heritage Month - September

National Repeal Day – December 5
Website: www.repealday.org

National Rum Day – August 16

National Vodka Day – October 4
Website: www.nationalvodkaday.com
Twitter: @NtlVodkaDay

Small Business Saturday – November
Facebook: Small Business Saturday

World Whisky Day – May 18
Facebook: World Whisky Day
Twitter: @WorldWhiskyDay

Absinthe	Absinthe Brun (Barrel-Aged)	Letherbee Distillers, IL
Absinthe	Brimstone Absinthe	Rancho de Los Luceros Destilaría, NM
Absinthe	Delaware Phoenix Meadow of Love Absinthe	Delaware Phoenix Distillery, NY
Absinthe	Delaware Phoenix Walton Waters Absinthe	Delaware Phoenix Distillery, NY
Absinthe	Green Cat Absinthe	The Hardware Distillery Co., WA
Absinthe	Marteau Absinthe de la Belle Époque	Gnostalgic Spirits Distillery, WA
Absinthe	Okanagan Spirits Taboo Genuine Absinthe	Okanagan Spirits, BC Canada
Absinthe	Okanagan Spirits Taboo Gold Absinthe	Okanagan Spirits, BC Canada
Absinthe	Redux Absinthe	Golden Moon Distillery, CO
Absinthe	Redux Absinthe No.2	Golden Moon Distillery, CO
Absinthe	The Green Villain	Dark Corner Distillery, SC
Absinthe Blanche	Extrait d'Absinthe Blanche	Vilya Spirits LLC, MT
Absinthe Bleue	La Sorciere Absinthe Bleue	Old World Spirits LLC, CA
Absinthe Rogue	Amerique 1912 Absinthe Rouge	Great Lakes Distillery LLC, WI
Absinthe Rubra	Absinthia Rubra	Fish Hawk Spirits LLC, FL
Absinthe Superieure	Germain-Robin Absinthe Superieure	Germain-Robin, CA
Absinthe Superieure	Germain-Robin Absinthe Superieure	Greenway Distillers Inc., CA
Absinthe Superieure	Vieux Carré Absinthe Supérieure	Philadelphia Distilling, PA
Absinthe Verte	Amerique 1912 Absinthe Verte	Great Lakes Distillery LLC, WI
Absinthe Verte	Artemisia Superior Absinthe Verte	Fat Dog Spirits LLC, FL
Absinthe Verte	Extrait d'Absinthe Verte	Vilya Spirits LLC, MT
Absinthe Verte	Knarr- Absinthe Verte	Immortal Spirits & Distilling Company, OR
Absinthe Verte	La Sorciere Absinthe Verte	Old World Spirits LLC, CA
Absinthe Verte	Leopold Bros. Absinthe Verte	Leopold Bros., CO
Absinthe Verte	Pacifique Absinthe Verte	Pacific Distillery LLC, WA
Absinthe Verte	Sirène Absinthe Verte	North Shore Distillery, IL
Absinthe Verte	St. George Absinthe Verte	St. George Spirits, CA
Absinthe, Organic	The Devil's Club Organic Absinthe	Pemberton Distillery Inc., BC Canada
Absinthe, Red	Corsair Red Absinthe	Corsair Artisan Distillery, TN
Absinthe, Red	Toulouse Red Absinthe Rouge	Atelier Vie, LA
Agave Spirit	Agua Azul	St. George Spirits, CA
Agave Spirit	California Gold Agave	Saint James Spirits, CA

Category	Product	Distillery
Agave Spirit	Colorado Gold's Own Agave Spirits	Colorado Gold Distillery, CO
Agave Spirit	Dagave Extra	Peach Street Distillers, CO
Agave Spirit	Dagave Gold	Peach Street Distillers, CO
Agave Spirit	Dagave Silver	Peach Street Distillers, CO
Agave Spirit	Midnight Caye Rested 100% Blue Agave Spirit	Tailwinds Distilling Company, IL
Agave Spirit	Midnight Caye Silver 100% Blue Agave Spirit	Tailwinds Distilling Company, IL
Agave Spirit	Railean "El Perico" Blue Agave Reposado	Railean Distillers, TX
Agave Spirit	Railean "El Perico" 100% Blue Agave Spirit	Railean Distillers, TX
Agave Spirit	Rattlesnake Jalapeño Tequila	Spirits of the USA LLC, FL
Agave Spirit	Rattlesnake Tequila	Spirits of the USA LLC, FL
Agave Spirit	Spirit of St. Louis Agave Blue	Square One Brewery and Distillery, MO
Agave Spirit	Colorado Agave Liquor Desert Water	Trail Town Still, CO
Amaro	broVo Amaro No 1	broVo Spirits, WA
Amaro	broVo Amaro No 2	broVo Spirits, WA
Amaro	broVo Amaro No 3	broVo Spirits, WA
Amaro	broVo Amaro No 4	broVo Spirits, WA
Amaro	broVo Amaro No 5	broVo Spirits, WA
Amaro	broVo Amaro No 6	broVo Spirits, WA
Angelica	Don Quixote Angelica	Don Quixote Distillery & Winery, NM
Anis	Black Rope Anis	Dry County Distillery LLC, WA
Aqua Ardiente	Primo Aqua Ardiente	Fog's End Distillery, CA
Aquavit	Aquavit	The Hardware Distillery Co., WA
Aquavit	Aquavit Private Reserve	North Shore Distillery, IL
Aquavit	Krogstad Festlig Aquavit	House Spirits Distillery, OR
Aquavit	Krogstad Gamel Aquavit	House Spirits Distillery, OR
Aquavit	Okanagan Spirits Aquavit – Aquavitus	Okanagan Spirits, BC Canada
Aquavit	Sound Spirits – Aquavit	Sound Spirits, WA
Bitters	Basement Bitters	Tuthilltown Spirits Distillery, NY
Bitters	Bettah Bitters	LB Distillers, SK Canada
Bitters	Cherry Infused Bitters	Door County Distillery, WI
Bitters	Cocktail Kingdom Bitters	Berkshire Mountain Distillers Inc., MA
Bitters	Golden Moon Amer dit Picon	Golden Moon Distillery, CO

Category	Product	Distillery
Bitters	Orange Bitters	Sun Liquor Distillery, WA
Bitters	Turin-Style Bitters	Breckenridge Distillery, CO
Bitters	Twisted and Bitter Bitters	Victoria Spirits, BC Canada
Bourbon	1512 Spirits Bourbon #1	1512 Spirits, CA
Bourbon	Beer Barrel Bourbon	New Holland Artisan Spirits, MI
Bourbon	Bell Bourbon	StiL 630, MO
Bourbon	Berkshire Bourbon	Berkshire Mountain Distillers Inc., MA
Bourbon	Black Dirt Bourbon	Black Dirt Distillery, NY
Bourbon	Breaking & Entering Bourbon	St. George Spirits, CA
Bourbon	Burnside Bourbon	Eastside Distilling, OR
Bourbon	Colorado Straight Bourbon	Peach Street Distillers, CO
Bourbon	Dancing Pines Bourbon	Dancing Pines Distillery, CO
Bourbon	Devils' Share Bourbon	Ballast Point Spirits, CA
Bourbon	DiVine Bourbon	Entente Spirits LLC, MI
Bourbon	Double Barrel Burnside Bourbon	Eastside Distilling, OR
Bourbon	Featherbone Bourbon	Journeyman Distillery, MI
Bourbon	Few Bourbon	Few Spirits LLC, IL
Bourbon	Fireside Bourbon	Mile High Spirits LLC, CO
Bourbon	Gold Coast Bourbon	Cathead Distillery LLC, MS
Bourbon	Heartland Distiller's Reserve Bourbon	Heartland Distillers, IN
Bourbon	Hooker's House Bourbon	HelloCello, CA
Bourbon	Johnny Drum Private Stock	Willett Distillery, KY
Bourbon	JP Trodden Small Batch Bourbon	J.P. Trodden Small Batch Bourbon, WA
Bourbon	Kings County Bourbon	Kings County Distillery, NY
Bourbon	Moylan's Distilling Bourbon Cask Strength	Stillwater Spirits, CA
Bourbon	Myer Farm Bourbon	Myer Farm Distillers, NY
Bourbon	Northern Threat Yankee Bourbon	Stoutridge Distillery, NY
Bourbon	"Master's Select" Kentucky Straight Bourbon	Old Pogue Distillery, KY
Bourbon	OYO Bourbon, Michelone Reserve (4-Grain)	Middle West Spirits LLC, OH
Bourbon	Prohibition Edition Bourbon	Artesian Distillers, MI
Bourbon	Reserve Bourbon	It's 5 Artisan Distillery, WA
Bourbon	Reservoir Bourbon	Reservoir Distillery, VA

463

Type	Product	Distillery
Bourbon	Rocky Mountain Bourbon	Boathouse Distillery, CO
Bourbon	Saratoga Single Barrel Bourbon	Saratoga Distilleries Inc., NY
Bourbon	Simeon Turley's Taos Lightning Bourbon	Rancho de Los Luceros Destilaria, NM
Bourbon	Smooth Ambler Yearling Bourbon	Smooth Ambler Spirits Company, WV
Bourbon	Stillwrights Bourbon	Flat Rock Spirits, OH
Bourbon	Tatoosh Bourbon	Tatoosh Craft Distillery, WA
Bourbon	Temperance Trader Bourbon Barrel Strength	Bull Run Distilling Company, OR
Bourbon	Thomas Tate Tobin's Taos Lightning Bourbon	Rancho de Los Luceros Destilaría, NM
Bourbon	Thunderbeast Baby Buffalo Bourbon	Mad Buffalo Distillery, MO
Bourbon	Troubadour Texas Bourbon	The Original Texas Legend Distillery, TX
Bourbon	Two James Bourbon	Two James Spirits, MI
Bourbon	Watershed Distillery Bourbon	Watershed Distillery, OH
Bourbon	Watershed Distillery Bourbon Barrel Gin	Watershed Distillery, OH
Bourbon	Willett Family Estate Bottled Bourbon	Willett Distillery, KY
Bourbon	Willett Pot Still Reserve Bourbon	Willett Distillery, KY
Bourbon, Black Walnut	Dancing Pines Black Walnut Bourbon	Dancing Pines Distillery, CO
Bourbon, Blue Corn	Feisty Spirits Blue Corn Bourbon	Feisty Spirits, CO
Bourbon, Corn	Don Quixote Blue Corn Bourbon	Don Quixote Distillery & Winery, NM
Bourbon, Flavored	Firefly Sweet Tea Flavored Bourbon	Firefly Distillery, SC
Bourbon, Spiced	Seasonal Spiced Bourbon	Breckenridge Distillery, CO
Bourbon, Straight	Straight Bourbon	Firestone & Robertson Distilling Co., TX
Brandy	A & G Brandy	St. Julian Winery, MI
Brandy	Alambic 13 Brandy	McMenamins Edgefield Distillery, OR
Brandy	Baerenfang Fruit and Honey Blended Brandy	Nashoba Valley Spirits Ltd., MA
Brandy	Bickering Brothers Brandy	Dakota Spirits Distillery LLC, SC
Brandy	Black Heron Brandy	Black Heron Spirits Distillery, WA
Brandy	Blue Flame Brandy	Blue Flame Spirits, WA
Brandy	Brandy – Aged in Oak Casks	Door County Distillery, WI
Brandy	Brandy Station	Old Sugar Distillery, WI
Brandy	Buena Vista Brandy	Deerhammer Distilling Company, CO
Brandy	Catoctin Creek 1757 Virginia Brandy™	Catoctin Creek Distilling Co. LLC, VA
Brandy	Charbay Brandy No. 83 Folle Blanche	Charbay Winery & Distillery, CA

Brandy	Chateau Chantal Brandy – "Cinq à Sept"	Chateau Chantal, MI
Brandy	Chauvet Brandy	HelloCello, CA
Brandy	COMB Blossom Brandy	StilltheOne Distillery LLC, NY
Brandy	Demarest Hill Winery Special Reserve Brandy	Demarest Hill Winery, NY
Brandy	Edgefield Potstill Brandy	McMenamins Edgefield Distillery, OR
Brandy	El Chalán Pisco-style Brandy	The Ellensburg Distillery, WA
Brandy	Foggy Bog Brandy	Nashoba Valley Spirits Ltd., MA
Brandy	Germain-Robin Brandy	Germain-Robin, CA
Brandy	Johnny Hop Appl and Hop flower-infused Brandy	Nashoba Valley Spirits Ltd., MA
Brandy	Johnny Ziegler Brandy	Winegarden Estate Ltd., NB Canada
Brandy	Johnny Ziegler Obstler	Winegarden Estate Ltd., NB Canada
Brandy	Kuchan Alambic Brandy	Old World Spirits LLC, CA
Brandy	Longshot Brandy	McMenamins Edgefield Distillery, OR
Brandy	Madrone Brandy	San Juan Island Distillery, WA
Brandy	Nevada Brandy	Churchill Vineyards and Distillery, NV
Brandy	Northern Comfort Brandy	Nashoba Valley Spirits Ltd., MA
Brandy	Oregon Pot Distilled Brandy	Clear Creek Distillery, OR
Brandy	RE:FIND Botanical Brandy	RE:FIND Distillery, CA
Brandy	RE:FIND Neutral Brandy	RE:FIND Distillery, CA
Brandy	Spirit of Santa Fe Brandy	Don Quixote Distillery & Winery, NM
Brandy	St. George Brandy	St. George Spirits, CA
Brandy	Starlight Distillery Brandy	Huber's Starlight Distillery, IN
Brandy	Starlight Distillery Private Reserve Brandy	Huber's Starlight Distillery, IN
Brandy	Tytonidae Brandy	Walla Walla Distilling Company, WA
Brandy, Apple	AEppelTreow WI Apple Brandy	AEppelTreow Winery & Distillery, WI
Brandy, Apple	American Fruits™ Apple Brandy	Warwick Valley Distillery, NY
Brandy, Apple	Apple Brandy	Clear Creek Distillery, OR
Brandy, Apple	Apple Brandy	Door County Distillery, WI
Brandy, Apple	Apple Brandy	Hidden Marsh Distillery, NY
Brandy, Apple	Apple Brandy	Nashoba Valley Spirits Ltd., MA
Brandy, Apple	Bitterroot Heritage Apple Brandy	Swanson's Mtn. View Distillery, MT
Brandy, Apple	Cedar Ridge Apple Brandy	Cedar Ridge Distillery, IA

Category	Product	Distillery, Location
Brandy, Apple	Don Quixote Qalvados – Apple Brandy	Don Quixote Distillery & Winery, NM
Brandy, Apple	Fine Apple Brandy	Spirits of Maine Distillery, ME
Brandy, Apple	Germain-Robin Apple Brandy	Germain-Robin, CA
Brandy, Apple	Golden Apple Brandy	Golden Distillery, WA
Brandy, Apple	Hubbard's Apple Brandy	Corey Lake Orchards, MI
Brandy, Apple	Ironworks Apple Brandy	Ironworks Distillery, NS Canada
Brandy, Apple	Ivy Mountain Apple Brandy™	Ivy Mountain Distillery LLC, GA
Brandy, Apple	Josiah Bartlett Barrel Aged Apple Brandy	Flag Hill Winery & Distillery, NH
Brandy, Apple	Koval Apple Brandy	Koval Distillery, IL
Brandy, Apple	Maple River Distillery Apple Brandy	Maple River Distillery, ND
Brandy, Apple	Oregon Apple Brandy (oaked)	Stone Barn Brandyworks, OR
Brandy, Apple	Pomme de Vie - Vermont Apple Brandy	Flag Hill Farm, VT
Brandy, Apple	Santa Fe Apple Brandy	Santa Fe Spirits, NM
Brandy, Apple	Starlight Distillery Apple Brandy	Huber's Starlight Distillery, IN
Brandy, Apple	White Wolf Apple Brandy	White Wolf Distillery, WI
Brandy, Apple	Woody Creek Distillers Apple Brandy	Woody Creek Distillers, CO
Brandy, Apple	Yahara Bay Apple Brandy	Yahara Bay Distillers, WI
Brandy, Apple	Dead Bird Apple Brandy	Shelburne Ochards Distillery, VT
Brandy, Apple Aged	Aged Apple Brandy	Westford Hill Distillers, CT
Brandy, Apricot	Koenig Apricot Brandy	Koenig Distillery, ID
Brandy, Apricot	Maple River Distillery Apricot Brandy	Maple River Distillery, ND
Brandy, Aronia	Maple River Distillery Aronia Brandy	Maple River Distillery, ND
Brandy, Asian Pear	Stillwater Spirits Asian Pear Brandy	Stillwater Spirits, CA
Brandy, Blackberry	Blackberry Brandy	San Juan Island Distillery, WA
Brandy, Blackberry	White Wolf Blackberry Brandy	White Wolf Distillery, WI
Brandy, Cherry	Cherry Brandy	Door County Distillery, WI
Brandy, Cherry	Hubbard's Cherry Brandy	Corey Lake Orchards, MI
Brandy, Cherry	Kirschwasser	Clear Creek Distillery, OR
Brandy, Cherry	Kirschwasser	Yahara Bay Distillers, WI
Brandy, Cherry	Koenig Cherry Brandy	Koenig Distillery, ID
Brandy, Cherry	Pacific Northwest Cherry Brandy	Stone Barn Brandyworks, OR
Brandy, Chockcherry	Maple River Distillery Chokecherry Brandy	Maple River Distillery, ND

Brandy, Elderberry	Elderberry Brandy	Nashoba Valley Spirits Ltd., MA
Brandy, Elderberry	Elderberry Brandy	Dancing Tree Distillery, OH
Brandy, Grape	Brandy Peak Aged Grape Brandy	Brandy Peak Distillery, OR
Brandy, Grape	Cedar Ridge Grape Brandy	Cedar Ridge Distillery, IA
Brandy, Grape	Grape Brandy	Finger Lakes Distilling, NY
Brandy, Grape	Hubbard's Grape Brandy	Corey Lake Orchards, MI
Brandy, Grape	Maple River Distillery Grape Brandy	Maple River Distillery, ND
Brandy, Grape	Morning Dew	McMenamins CPR Distillery, OR
Brandy, Grape	White Wolf Grape Brandy	White Wolf Distillery, WI
Brandy, Honey	Queen's Flight	Hidden Marsh Distillery, NY
Brandy, Kirsch	Johnny Ziegler Kirsch	Winegarden Estate Ltd., NB Canada
Brandy, Kirsch	Canadian Kirsch	Maple Leaf Spirits Inc., BC Canada
Brandy, Kirschwasser	Blarney's Irish Cream	Minhas Micro Distillery, WI
Brandy, Kirschwasser	Great Lakes Artisan Series Kirschwasser	Great Lakes Distillery LLC, WI
Brandy, Muscat	Brandy Peak Aged Muscat Brandy	Brandy Peak Distillery, OR
Brandy, Muscat	Brandy Peak Spirit of Muscat Brandy	Brandy Peak Distillery, OR
Brandy, Peach	Hubbard's Peach Brandy	Corey Lake Orchards, MI
Brandy, Peach	Ivy Mountain Georgia Peach Brandy™	Ivy Mountain Distillery LLC, GA
Brandy, Peach	Jack & Jenny Peach Brandy	Peach Street Distillers, CO
Brandy, Peach	Silk Peach Brandy	Nashoba Valley Spirits Ltd., MA
Brandy, Peach Aged	Aged Peach Brandy	Peach Street Distillers, CO
Brandy, Pear	American Fruits™ Pear Brandy	Warwick Valley Distillery, NY
Brandy, Pear	Bartlett Pear Brandy	Stone Barn Brandyworks, OR
Brandy, Pear	Brandy Peak Aged Pear Brandy	Brandy Peak Distillery, OR
Brandy, Pear	Brandy Peak Natural Pear Brandy	Brandy Peak Distillery, OR
Brandy, Pear	Catoctin Creek Pearousia®	Catoctin Creek Distilling Co. LLC, VA
Brandy, Pear	Comice Pear Brandy	Stone Barn Brandyworks, OR
Brandy, Pear	Hubbard's Pear Brandy	Corey Lake Orchards, MI
Brandy, Pear	Jack & Jenny Pear Brandy	Peach Street Distillers, CO
Brandy, Pear	Koenig Pear Brandy	Koenig Distillery, ID
Brandy, Pear	Koval Williams Pear Brandy	Koval Distillery, IL
Brandy, Pear	Maple River Distillery Pear Brandy	Maple River Distillery, ND

Category	Product	Distillery, Location
Brandy, Pear	Pear Brandy	Finger Lakes Distilling, NY
Brandy, Pear	Pear Brandy	McMenamins Edgefield Distillery, OR
Brandy, Pear	Rare Pear Brandy	Harvest Spirits LLC, NY
Brandy, Pear	Stair's Pear - Vermont Pear Brandy	Flag Hill Farm, VT
Brandy, Pear	Williams Pear Brandy	Clear Creek Distillery, OR
Brandy, Pear	Yahara Bay Pear Brandy	Yahara Bay Distillers, WI
Brandy, Pear Aged	Aged Pear Brandy	Peach Street Distillers, CO
Brandy, Pineapple	Saint James Spirits Pineapple Brandy	Saint James Spirits, CA
Brandy, Pinot Noir	Brandy Peak Aged Pinot Noir Brandy	Brandy Peak Distillery, OR
Brandy, Plum	Blue Plum Brandy (Slivovitz)	Clear Creek Distillery, OR
Brandy, Plum	Elephant Heart Plum-infused Brandy	Nashoba Valley Spirits Ltd., MA
Brandy, Plum	Koenig Plum Brandy	Koenig Distillery, ID
Brandy, Plum	Pacific Northwest Plum Brandy	Stone Barn Brandyworks, OR
Brandy, Plum	Plum Brandy (Slivovitz)	Stringer's Orchard Distillery, OR
Brandy, Plum	White Wolf Plum Brandy	White Wolf Distillery, WI
Brandy, Raspberry	White Wolf Raspberry Brandy	White Wolf Distillery, WI
Brandy, Rhubarb	Maple River Distillery Rhubarb Brandy	Maple River Distillery, ND
Brandy, Thimbleberry	Thimbleberry Brandy	San Juan Island Distillery, WA
Brandy, Wild Plum	Maple River Distillery Wild Plum Brandy	Maple River Distillery, ND
Brandy, Winterberry	Winterberry Brandy	San Juan Island Distillery, WA
Cerise	Chateau Chantal Cerise	Chateau Chantal, MI
Cerise	Chateau Chantal Cerise Noir	Chateau Chantal, MI
Cider, Hard	1911 Hard Cider	Beak & Skiff Distillery, NY
Cider, Hard	Harvest Legacy Dessert Cider	Swanson's Mtn. View Apple Distillery, MT
Cocktail	Barrel-Aged Cocktail - East India	Napa Valley Distillery, CA
Cocktail	Barrel-Aged Cocktail - Manhattan	Napa Valley Distillery, CA
Cocktail	Barrel-Aged Cocktail - Mint Julep	Napa Valley Distillery, CA
Cocktail	Barrel-Aged Cocktail - Negroni	Napa Valley Distillery, CA
Cocktail	Barrel-Aged Cocktail - Old Hollywood	Napa Valley Distillery, CA
Cocktail	Gingeroo – an Old New Orleans Rum Bottled Cocktail	Celebration Distillation, LA
Cocktail	Hula Girl RTD Cocktails	Essential Spirits Alambic Distill., CA
Cocktail	Red Sky at Night Cocktail	San Juan Island Distillery, WA

Cocktail	Uncle Don's Country Cocktail, Black Cherry	Uncle Don's Apple Pie Craft Distillery, MI
Cocktail	Uncle Don's Country Cocktail, Blueberry	Uncle Don's Apple Pie Craft Distillery, MI
Cocktail	Uncle Don's Country Cocktail, Fuzzy Peach	Uncle Don's Apple Pie Craft Distillery, MI
Cocktail	Uncle Don's Country Cocktail, Old Fashion Apple	Uncle Don's Apple Pie Craft Distillery, MI
Cocktail	Uncle Don's Country Cocktail, Raspberry	Uncle Don's Apple Pie Craft Distillery, MI
Cordial, Apple	Maple River Distillery Apple Cordial	Maple River Distillery, ND
Cordial, Black Currant	American Fruits™ Black Currant Cordial	Warwick Valley Distillery, NY
Cordial, Black Currant	Maple River Distillery Aronia Black Currant Cordial	Maple River Distillery, ND
Cordial, Chokecherry	Maple River Distillery Chokecherry Cordial	Maple River Distillery, ND
Cordial, Elderberry	Caledonia Spirits Elderberry Cordial	Caledonia Spirits Inc., VT
Cordial, Huckleberry	Huckleberry Cordial Black Heron	Spirits Distillery, WA
Cordial, Pear	Maple River Distillery Pear Cordial	Maple River Distillery, ND
Cordial, Red Currant	Maple River Distillery Red Currant Cordial	Maple River Distillery, ND
Cordial, Sour Cherry	American Fruits™ Sour Cherry Cordial	Warwick Valley Distillery, NY
Cordial, Wild Plum	Maple River Distillery Wild Plum Cordial	Maple River Distillery, ND
Eau de Vie	Ambre de pomme (fortified cider)	Cidrerie Michel Jodoin, QC Canada
Eau de Vie	Calijo	Cidrerie Michel Jodoin, QC Canada
Eau de Vie	Calijo XO	Cidrerie Michel Jodoin, QC Canada
Eau de Vie	CapRock® Organic Eaux de Vie	Peak Spirits® Farm Distillery, CO
Eau de Vie	Eau de Vie de Pomme	Clear Creek Distillery, OR
Eau de Vie	Eau de Vie of Douglas Fir	Clear Creek Distillery, OR
Eau de Vie	Eau de Vie Poire	Immortal Spirits & Distilling Company, OR
Eau de Vie	Fine Caroline	Cidrerie Michel Jodoin, QC Canada
Eau de Vie	Fraise Eau de vie	Westford Hill Distillers, CT
Eau de Vie	Framboise Eau de vie	Westford Hill Distillers, CT
Eau de Vie	Ironworks Eaux de Vie	Ironworks Distillery, NS Canada
Eau de Vie	Johnny Ziegler Myrtille	Winegarden Estate Ltd., NB Canada
Eau de Vie	Johnny Ziegler Sibowitz	Winegarden Estate Ltd., NB Canada
Eau de Vie	Kirsch Eau de vie	Westford Hill Distillers, CT
Eau de Vie	Kuchan Eaux De Vie Indian Blood Peach	Old World Spirits LLC, CA
Eau de Vie	Kuchan Eaux De Vie O'Henry Oak Aged Peach	Old World Spirits LLC, CA
Eau de Vie	Kuchan Eaux De Vie Poire Williams	Old World Spirits LLC, CA

Category	Product	Distillery
Eau de Vie	Poire Prisonniere	Westford Hill Distillers, CT
Eau de Vie	Pom de vie	Cidrerie Michel Jodoin, QC Canada
Eau de Vie	Rail Dog Barrel Aged Eau de Vie	Elm Brook Farm, VT
Eau de Vie	Saint James Spirits Kirsch (Eau de Vie)	Saint James Spirits, CA
Eau de Vie	Schoharie Eau de Vie de Pomme	KyMar Farm Distillery, NY
Eau de Vie	Shinn Estate Vineyards Eau de Vie	Shinn Estate Vineyards, NY
Eau de Vie	Tytonidae Eau-de-Vie	Walla Walla Distilling Company, WA
Eau de Vie	Voignier Eaux de Vie	It's 5 Artisan Distillery, WA
Eau de Vie, Apple	Apple Eau de vie	San Juan Island Distillery, WA
Eau de Vie, Apple	Apple Eau de Vie	Harvest Spirits LLC, NY
Eau de Vie, Apple	Apple Eau de Vie	Mazza Chautauqua Cellars, NY
Eau de Vie, Apple	Apple Eaux de Vie	It's 5 Artisan Distillery, WA
Eau de Vie, Apple	Apple in the Bottle	Clear Creek Distillery, OR
Eau de Vie, Apple	BelleWood Apple Eau de Vie	Bellewood Distilling, WA
Eau de Vie, Apple	Sea Hagg Eau de Vie Apple	Sea Hagg Distillery, NH
Eau de Vie, Apricot	Apricot Eaux de Vie	It's 5 Artisan Distillery, WA
Eau de Vie, Apricot	Okanagan Spirits Apricot Eau de Vie	Okanagan Spirits, BC Canada
Eau de Vie, Canados	Okanagan Spirits Canados Eau de Vie	Okanagan Spirits, BC Canada
Eau de Vie, Cherry	Chateau Chantal Cherry Eau de Vie	Chateau Chantal, MI
Eau de Vie, Cherry	Cherry Eau de vie	Nashoba Valley Spirits Ltd., MA
Eau de Vie, Cherry	Cherry Eau de Vie	Mazza Chautauqua Cellars, NY
Eau de Vie, Cherry	Don Quixote Mon Cherie Cherry Eau de Vie	Don Quixote Distillery & Winery, NM
Eau de Vie, Cherry	Cherry Eaux de Vie	It's 5 Artisan Distillery, WA
Eau de Vie, Elderberry	Johnny Ziegler Elderberry	Winegarden Estate Ltd., NB Canada
Eau de Vie, Honey	Honey Eau de Vie	Spirits of Maine Distillery, ME
Eau de Vie, Kirsch	Okanagan Spirits Kirsch Danbue Eau de Vie	Okanagan Spirits, BC Canada
Eau de Vie, Kirsch	Okanagan Spirits Kirsch Virginiana Eau de Vie	Okanagan Spirits, BC Canada
Eau de Vie, Peach	Peach Eau de Vie	Spirits of Maine Distillery, ME
Eau de Vie, Pear	Chateau Chantal Pear Eau de Vie	Chateau Chantal, MI
Eau de Vie, Pear	Classick Pure Pear Eau-de-Vie	Essential Spirits Alambic Distillery, CA
Eau de Vie, Pear	Great Lakes Artisan Series Pear Eau-de-Vie	Great Lakes Distillery LLC, WI
Eau de Vie, Pear	Okanagan Spirits Poire Williams Eau de Vie	Okanagan Spirits, BC Canada

Eau de Vie, Pear	Pear Eau de Vie	Harvest Spirits LLC, NY
Eau de Vie, Pear	Pear Eau de Vie	Spirits of Maine Distillery, ME
Eau de Vie, Pear	Pear Eau de Vie	Mazza Chautauqua Cellars, NY
Eau de Vie, Pear	Pear Eaux de Vie	It's 5 Artisan Distillery, WA
Eau de Vie, Pear	Pear in the Bottle	Clear Creek Distillery, OR
Eau de Vie, Pear	Pear in the Bottle Pear Eau de Vie	Mazza Chautauqua Cellars, NY
Eau de Vie, Pear	Pear William Eau de vie	Westford Hill Distillers, CT
Eau de Vie, Pear	Pear Williams	Maple Leaf Spirits Inc., BC Canada
Eau de Vie, Pear	Sea Hagg Eau de Vie Pear	Sea Hagg Distillery, NH
Eau de Vie, Pear	Woody Creek Distillers Pear Eau de Vie	Woody Creek Distillers, CO
Eau de Vie, Plum	Chateau Chantal Plum Eau de Vie	Chateau Chantal, MI
Eau de Vie, Plum	Mirabelle Plum	Clear Creek Distillery, OR
Eau de Vie, Plum	Plum Eau de Vie	Mazza Chautauqua Cellars, NY
Eau de Vie, Plum	Plum Eaux de Vie	It's 5 Artisan Distillery, WA
Eau de Vie, Prune	Okanagan Spirits Italian Prune Eau de Vie	Okanagan Spirits, BC Canada
Eau de Vie, Prune	Okanagan Spirits Old Italian Prune Eau de Vie	Okanagan Spirits, BC Canada
Eau de Vie, Raspberry	Raspberry Eau de vie	Nashoba Valley Spirits Ltd., MA
Eau de Vie, Framboise	Okanagan Spirits Raspberry Framboise Eau de Vie	Okanagan Spirits, BC Canada
Entice Chateau	Chantal Entice	Chateau Chantal, MI
Framboise	Framboise (Raspberry)	Clear Creek Distillery, OR
Geist	Raspberry Geist	Spirits of Maine Distillery, ME
Gin	1911 Gin	Beak & Skiff Distillery, NY
Gin	Alaska Distillery Gin	Alaska Distillery< AK
Gin	Anselmo Gin	Headframe Spirits, MT
Gin	Autumnal Gin	Letherbee Distillers, IL
Gin	Aviation Gin	House Spirits Distillery, OR
Gin	Back River Gin	Sweetgrass Farm Winery & Distillery, ME
Gin	Barrel Aged Ethereal Gin	Berkshire Mountain Distillers Inc., MA
Gin	BelleWood Gin	Bellewood Distilling, WA
Gin	Big Gin	Captive Spirits, WA
Gin	Bilberry Black Heart's Gin	Journeyman Distillery, MI
Gin	Black Window Gin	Spirits of the USA LLC, FL

Gin	Blade California Small Batch Gin	Old World Spirits LLC, CA
Gin	Blue Flame Gin	Blue Flame Spirits, WA
Gin	Blue Flame Ultra Premium Gin	Blue Flame Spirits, WA
Gin	Brandon's Gin	Rock Town Distillery Inc., AR
Gin	Bristow Gin	Cathead Distillery LLC, MS
Gin	Brodie	Double V Distillery, WA
Gin	Bulfinch 83 Redistilled Gin	Wishkah River Distillery, WA
Gin	Bullwheel Gin	Deerhammer Distilling Company, CO
Gin	Cardinal Gin	Southern Artisan Spirits, NC
Gin	Chief Gowanus - New-Netherland Gin	New York Distilling, NY
Gin	Chuckanut Bay Gin	Chuckanut Bay Distillery, WA
Gin	Civilized Gin	North. U. Brew. Co. & Distilling, MI
Gin	Clawfoot Gin	New Deal Distillery, OR
Gin	ClearHeart Gin	Cedar Ridge Distillery, IA
Gin	Cold River Gin	Maine Distilleries LLC, ME
Gin	Colorado Fog Gin	Mystic Mountain Distillery LLC, CO
Gin	Colorado Gold Premium Gin	Colorado Gold Distillery, CO
Gin	COMB 9 Gin	StilltheOne Distillery LLC, NY
Gin	Corsair Genever	Corsair Artisan Distillery, TN
Gin	Corsair Gin	Corsair Artisan Distillery, TN
Gin	Counter Gin	Batch 206, WA
Gin	Crabby Ginny	The Hardware Distillery Co., WA
Gin	Crater Lake Gin	Bendistillery, OR
Gin	Dancing Pines Gin	Dancing Pines Distillery, CO
Gin	Dancing Tree Spicebush Gin	Dancing Tree Distillery, OH
Gin	Death's Door Gin	Death's Door Spirits, WI
Gin	DH Krahn Gin	Essential Spirits Alambic Distillery, CA
Gin	Distiller's Gin No. 11	North Shore Distillery, IL
Gin	Distiller's Gin No. 6	North Shore Distillery, IL
Gin	Don Quixote Gin	Don Quixote Distillery & Winery, NM
Gin	Door County Gin	Door County Distillery, WI
Gin	Dry County Gin	Dry County Distillery LLC, WA

Gin	Ebb+Flow Gin	Sound Spirits, WA
Gin	Elk Rider Gin	Heritage Distilling Company Inc., WA
Gin	Ethereal Gin	Berkshire Mountain Distillers Inc., MA
Gin	Freemont Mischief Gin	Freemont Mischief, WA
Gin	Gables Gin	McMenamins CPR Distillery, OR
Gin	Gale Force Gin	Triple Eight Distillery, MA
Gin	Gambit Gin	LB Distillers, SK Canada
Gin	Gin No. 33	New Deal Distillery, OR
Gin	Gin No.1	New Deal Distillery, OR
Gin	Glorious Gin	Breuckelen Distilling Company Inc., NY
Gin	Golden Moon Gin	Golden Moon Distillery, CO
Gin	Green Hat Gin	New Columbia Distillers, DC
Gin	Green Hat Seasonal Gin	New Columbia Distillers, DC
Gin	Greylock Gin	Berkshire Mountain Distillers Inc., MA
Gin	Gun Club Gin	Sun Liquor Distillery, WA
Gin	Half Moon Gin	Tuthilltown Spirits Distillery, NY
Gin	Hana Gin	Essential Spirits Alambic Distillery, CA
Gin	HDC Gin	Heritage Distilling Company Inc., WA
Gin	Healy's Gin	Trailhead Spirits, MT
Gin	Hedge Trimmer Gin	Sun Liquor Distillery, WA
Gin	Homeport Craft Distilled Gin	Port Steilacoom Distillery, WA
Gin	Ingenium Gin	New England Distilling, ME
Gin	Isis Premium Gin	Mac Donald Distillery, WA
Gin	Jack Pine Gin	Northern Latitudes Distillery, MI
Gin	Jackelope and Jenny Gin	Peach Street Distillers, CO
Gin	Jackelope Gin	Peach Street Distillers, CO
Gin	Jagged Peaks Gin	Tahoe Moonshine Distillery Inc., CA
Gin	Karner Blue Gin	Flag Hill Winery & Distillery, NH
Gin	Knickerbocker Gin	New Holland Artisan Spirits, MI
Gin	Knockabout Gin	Ryan & Wood Inc., MA
Gin	Leopold Bros. American Small Batch Gin	Leopold Bros., CO
Gin	Letherbee Gin	Letherbee Distillers, IL

Gin	Letterpress Gin	Letterpress Distilling, WA
Gin	Los Luceros Hacienda Gin	Rancho de Los Luceros Destilaría, NM
Gin	Loyalist Gin	66 Gilead Distillery, ON Canada
Gin	McKenzie Distiller's Reserve Gin	Finger Lakes Distilling, NY
Gin	Midwest Gin	45th Parallel Spirits LLC, WI
Gin	Myer Farm Gin	Myer Farm Distillers, NY
Gin	Nicholas Gin	Fat Dog Spirits LLC, FL
Gin	No. 209 Gin	Distillery No. 209, CA
Gin	Oaken Gin	Victoria Spirits, BC Canada
Gin	Okanagan Spirits Gin	Okanagan Spirits, BC Canada
Gin	Old Grove Gin	Ballast Point Spirits, CA
Gin	Old Hollywood Gin	Napa Valley Distillery, CA
Gin	Old No. 176™ Gin	Quincy Street Distillery, IL
Gin	Old Tom Gin	Ransom Spirits, OR
Gin	Oola Gin	Oola Distillery, WA
Gin	Penny's Gin	McMenamins Edgefield Distillery, OR
Gin	Permafrost Alaska Gin	Alaska Distillery, AK
Gin	Perry's Tot - Navy Strength Gin	New York Distilling, NY
Gin	Phrog Premium Gin	Island Spirits Distillery, BC Canada
Gin	Piger Henricus Gin	The Subersives Distillers, QC Canada
Gin	Professors Gin	McMenamins Edgefield Distillery, OR
Gin	Prohibition Gin	Heartland Distillers, IN
Gin	R Gin	The Hardware Distillery Co., WA
Gin	Rayn Anjel Gin	Black Heron Spirits Distillery, WA
Gin	RE:FIND Gin	RE:FIND Distillery, CA
Gin	Rehorst Premium Milwaukee Gin	Great Lakes Distillery LLC, WI
Gin	River Rose Gin	Mississippi River Distilling Company, IA
Gin	RMD Gin	Artesian Distillers, MI
Gin	Rob's Mountain Gin	Spring44 Distilling, CO
Gin	Rogue Pink Gin	Rogue Spirits, OR
Gin	Rogue Spruce Gin	Rogue Spirits, OR
Gin	Roundhouse Gin	Roundhouse Spirits, CO

Gin	Seneca Drums Gin	Finger Lakes Distilling, NY
Gin	Six Mile Creek Gin	Six Mile Creek Winery & Distillery, NY
Gin	Small's Gin	Ransom Spirits, OR
Gin	Smooth Ambler Greenbrier Gin	Smooth Ambler Spirits Company, WV
Gin	Smugglers' Notch Gin	Smuggler's Notch Distillery, VT
Gin	Sound Spirits – Old Tom Gin	Sound Spirits, WA
Gin	Southern Gin	Thirteenth Colony Distilleries, GA
Gin	Spirit Bear Gin	Urban Distilleries, BC Canada
Gin	Spirit Hound Gin	Spirit Hound Distillers, CO
Gin	Spirit of Santa Fe Gin	Don Quixote Distillery & Winery, NM
Gin	Spirit of St. Louis Regatta Bay Gin	Square One Brewery and Distillery, MO
Gin	Spirit Works Gin	Spirit Works Distillery, CA
Gin	Spring44 Gin	Spring44 Distilling, CO
Gin	Spy Hop Gin	San Juan Island Distillery, WA
Gin	St. George Botanivore Gin	St. George Spirits, CA
Gin	St. George Terroir Gin	St. George Spirits, CA
Gin	Starling Gin	25th Street Spirits, OH
Gin	Stillwater Spirits Gin	Stillwater Spirits, CA
Gin	Stoutridge Gin	Stoutridge Distillery, NY
Gin	Strait Gin	Myriad View Artisan Distill., PE Canada
Gin	Sunset Hills Virginia Gin	A. Smith Bowman Distillery, VA
Gin	the Alpinist Gin	Seattle Distilling Company, WA
Gin	Thunderbeast Prairie Gin	Mad Buffalo Distillery, MO
Gin	TOPO Piedmont Gin	Top of the Hill Distillery, NC
Gin	Trail Town Still Colorado Gin	Trail Town Still, CO
Gin	Treeline Gin	Wood's High Mountain Distillery, CO
Gin	Two James Gin	Two James Spirits, MI
Gin	Tytonidae Gin	Walla Walla Distilling Company, WA
Gin	Ugly Dog Gin	Ugly Dog Distillery LLC, MI
Gin	Union Gin	Dogwood Distilling, OR
Gin	Valentine Liberator Gin	Valentine Distilling Company, MI
Gin	Vernal Gin	Letherbee Distillers, IL

Category	Product	Distillery
Gin	Victoria Gin	Victoria Spirits, BC Canada
Gin	Vivacity Bankers' Gin	Vivcity Spirits, OR
Gin	Vivacity Native Gin	Vivcity Spirits, OR
Gin	Voyager Single Batch Distilled Gin	Pacific Distillery LLC, WA
Gln	Walla Walla Gin	Walla Walla Distilling Company, WA
Gin	Warwick Rustic American Gin	Warwick Valley Distillery, NY
Gin	Waterloo Gin	Treaty Oak Distilling Co., TX
Gin	Watershed Distillery Four Peel Gin	Watershed Distillery, OH
Gin	Whistling Andy Gin	Whistling Andy Distillery, MT
Gin	Whyte Laydie Gin	Montgomery Distillery, MT
Gin	Wildflower Gin	Honey House Distillery, CO
Gin	Wire Works Special Reserve Gin	GrandTen Distilling, MA
Gin, Aged	Corsair Barrel Aged Gin	Corsair Artisan Distillery, TN
Gin, Aged	Imperial Barrel Aged Gin	Roundhouse Spirits, CO
Gin, Aged	Smooth Ambler Barrel Aged Gin	Smooth Ambler Spirits Company, WV
Gin, American	Few American Gin	Few Spirits LLC, IL
Gin, American	Pinckney Bend American Gin	Pinckney Bend Distillery, MO
Gin, American	Wire Works American Gin	GrandTen Distilling, MA
Gin, American	Dorothy Parker	New York Distilling, NY
Gin, American Dry	Bluecoat American Dry Gin	Philadelphia Distilling, PA
Gin, American Dry	Moody June American Dry Gin	Bone Spirits, TX
Gin, Barrel Aged	Rusty Blade Barrel Aged Gin	Old World Spirits LLC, CA
Gin, Dry	Aria Portland Dry Gin	Bull Run Distilling Company, OR
Gin, Dry	Denver Dry Gin	Mile High Spirits LLC, CO
Gin, Dry	Desert Dry Gin	Arizona High Spirits Distillery, AZ
Gin, Dry	Greenhook Ginsmiths American Dry Gin	Greenhook Ginsmiths, NY
Gin, Dry	Northwest Dry Gin	It's 5 Artisan Distillery, WA
Gin, Dry	Quimby and Jack's Distilled Dry Gin	Carbon Glacier Distillery, WA
Gin, Dry	Silvertip American Dry Gin	Vilya Spirits LLC, MT
Gin, Dry Rye	St. George Dry Rye Gin	St. George Spirits, CA
Gin, Extra Dry	Yahara Bay Extra Dry Gin	Yahara Bay Distillers, WI
Gin, Hemp	Mary Jane's Premium Hemp Gin	Mary Jane's, ON Canada

Category	Product	Distillery
Gin, Kosher	No. 209 Kosher-for-Passover Gin	Distillery No. 209, CA
Gin, London Dry	Bardenay London Dry Gin	Bardenay Inc., ID
Gin, London Dry	Long Table Distillery London Dry Gin	Long Table Distilley Ltd., BC Canada
Gin, Organic	Bainbridge Heritage Organic Gin	Bainbridge Organic Distillers, WA
Gin, Organic	CapRock® Organic Gin	Peak Spirits® Farm Distillery, CO
Gin, Organic	Catoctin Creek Organic Watershed Gin®	Catoctin Creek Distilling Co. LLC, VA
Gin, Organic	Green Mountain Organic Gin	Green Mountain Distillers, VT
Gin, Organic	Halcyon Organic Distilled Gin	Bluewater Distilling, WA
Gin, Organic	Schramm Organic Gin	Pemberton Distillery Inc., BC Canada
Gin, Organic	TRU Organic Gin	GreenBar Collective, CA
Gin, Organic	Organic Nation Gin	Cascade Peak Spirits Distillery, OR
Gin, Organic	Wigle Organic Ginever	Pittsburgh Distilling Co., PA
Gin, Plum	Pacific Plum Gin	Stringer's Orchard Winery Distillery, OR
Gin, Sloe	Spirit Works Sloe Gin	Spirit Works Distillery, CA
Gin, Wheat	Dry Fly Washington Wheat Gin	Dry Fly Distilling, WA
Gin, Wild Blueberry	Prince Edward Wild Blueberry Gin	Prince Edward Distillery, PE Canada
Grappa	1512 Spirits Grappa	1512 Spirits, CA
Grappa	Blue Flame Grappa	Blue Flame Spirits, WA
Grappa	Brandy Peak Grappa	Brandy Peak Distillery, OR
Grappa	CapRock® Biodynamic® Estate Grappa	Peak Spirits® Farm Distillery, CO
Grappa	Cavatappi Nebbiolo Grappa	Clear Creek Distillery, OR
Grappa	Cavatappi Sangiovese Grappa	Clear Creek Distillery, OR
Grappa	Cedar Ridge Grappa	Cedar Ridge Distillery, IA
Grappa	Charbay Grappa di Marko	Charbay Winery & Distillery, CA
Grappa	Classick Grappa di Cabernet - Stags Leap	Essential Spirits Alambic Distillery, CA
Grappa	Del Dotto Estates - Howell Mountain Grappa Cabernet	Essential Spirits Alambic Distill., CA
Grappa	Demarest Hill Winery Grappa	Demarest Hill Winery, NY
Grappa	Don Quixote Grappa	Don Quixote Distillery & Winery, NM
Grappa1	Don Quixote Malvasia Bianca Grappa	Don Quixote Distillery & Winery, NM
Grappa	Fiore Grappa	Fiore Winery & Distillery, MD
Grappa	Germain-Robin Grappa	Germain-Robin, CA
Grappa	Gewürztraminer Grappa	Finger Lakes Distilling, NY

Grappa	Gewürztraminer Grappa	Ransom Spirits, OR
Grappa	Giallo Grappa	Soft Tail Spirits, WA
Grappa	Golden Moon Colorado Grappa	Golden Moon Distillery, CO
Grappa	Graham's Grappa	Flag Hill Winery & Distillery, NH
Grappa	Grappa	Harvest Spirits LLC, NY
Grappa	Grappa	It's 5 Artisan Distillery, WA
Grappa	Grappa & Limone	Magnanini Farm Winery Inc., NY
Grappa	Grappa & Miele	Magnanini Farm Winery Inc., NY
Grappa	Grappa Del Nonno	Magnanini Farm Winery Inc., NY
Grappa	Grappa Moscato	Clear Creek Distillery, OR
Grappa	Grappa Muscat	Peach Street Distillers, CO
Grappa	Grappa of Gewurztraminer	Peach Street Distillers, CO
Grappa	Grappa of Oregon Pinot Noir	Clear Creek Distillery, OR
Grappa	Grappa of Pinot Grigio	Clear Creek Distillery, OR
Grappa	Grappa of Steuben	Mazza Chautauqua Cellars, NY
Grappa	Grappa of Viognier	Peach Street Distillers, CO
Grappa	Great Lakes Artisan Series Grappa	Great Lakes Distillery LLC, WI
Grappa	Johnny Ziegler Grappa	Winegarden Estate Ltd., NB Canada
Grappa	Koenig Grappa	Koenig Distillery, ID
Grappa	Marc de Gewürztraminer	Clear Creek Distillery, OR
Grappa	Okanagan Spirits Gewurtztraminer Grappa	Okanagan Spirits, BC Canada
Grappa	Red Hook Grappa	Van Brunt Stillhouse, NY
Grappa	Saint James Spirits Grappa	Saint James Spirits, CA
Grappa	Sangiovese Grappa	Soft Tail Spirits, WA
Grappa	Six Mile Creek Grappa	Six Mile Creek Winery & Distillery, NY
Grappa	Soft Tail Blanco Grappa	Soft Tail Spirits, WA
Grappa	Starlight Distillery Grappa	Huber's Starlight Distillery, IN
Grappa	Stillwater Spirits Cabernet Sauvignon Grappa	Stillwater Spirits, CA
Grappa	T & W Grappa Di Muscatto	Empire Winery & Distillery, FL
Grappa	Two Jays Grappa	Broadbent Distillery, IA
Grappa	Tytonidae Grappa	Walla Walla Distilling Company, WA
Grappa	Vidal Grappa	Nashoba Valley Spirits Ltd., MA

478

Grappa	Vino Robles Grappa de Petite Syrah	Essential Spirits Alambic Distillery, CA
Grappa	Woodstock Reserve	Soft Tail Spirits, WA
Grappa, Pinot Noir	Pinot Noir Grappa	Stone Barn Brandyworks, OR
Grappa, Riesling	Riesling Grappa	Finger Lakes Distilling, NY
Grog	Dutch Harbor Breeze (Grog)	Ye Ol' Grog Distillery, OR
Grog	Good Morning Glory (Grog)	Ye Ol' Grog Distillery, OR
Hankaku Shochu	Evenstar	Sodo Spirits Distillery, WA
Hankaku Shochu	Evenstar Chiles	Sodo Spirits Distillery, WA
Hankaku Shochu	Evenstar Ginger	Sodo Spirits Distillery, WA
Hankaku Shochu	Evenstar Mint	Sodo Spirits Distillery, WA
Liqueur	Angelica - Botanical Liqueur	GrandTen Distilling, MA
Liqueur	Calisaya	Elixir Inc., OR
Liqueur	Carmine Jewel Liqueur	LB Distillers, SK Canada
Liqueur	Cherry Liqueur	Finger Lakes Distilling, NY
Liqueur	Ciriaco's Limoncello	Vermont Distillers, VT
Liqueur	Cremma Lemma	Bloomery Plantation Distillery, WV
Liqueur	Demarest Hill Winery Amarena Aperitivo	Demarest Hill Winery, NY
Liqueur	Demarest Hill Winery Tropical Liqueur	Demarest Hill Winery, NY
Liqueur	Distroya Liqueur	Mile High Spirits LLC, CO
Liqueur	Egg Nog Advocaat Liqueur	Eastside Distilling, OR
Liqueur	Forty Creek Whisky Cream Liquor	Forty Creek Distillery, ON Canada
Liqueur	Germain-Robin Créme de Poête Liqueur	Germain-Robin, CA
Liqueur	Golden Moon Créme de Violette	Golden Moon Distillery, CO
Liqueur	Golden Moon Dry Curacao	Golden Moon Distillery, CO
Liqueur	Golden Quince Liqueur	Stone Barn Brandyworks, OR
Liqueur	Hideous Liqueur	Hideous LC, TX
Liqueur	Hoodoo Chicory Liqueur	Cathead Distillery LLC, MS
Liqueur	Hum Botanical Spirit	Hum Spirits Company, IL
Liqueur	Iris	Elixir Inc., OR
Liqueur	Koltiska 90 Proof Liqueur	Kolts Fine Spirits, WI
Liqueur	Koltiska Original Liqueur	Kolts Fine Spirits, WI
Liqueur	Krupnikas	The Brothers Vilgalys Spirits Company, NC

Liqueur	Malört Liqueur	Letherbee Distillers, IL
Liqueur	Maple Liqueur	Hidden Marsh Distillery, NY
Liqueur	Maui Okolehao (made from Ti root)	Haleakala Distillers, HI
Liqueur	Nocino	HelloCello, CA
Liqueur	Orphan Girl Bourbon Cream Liqueur	Headframe Spirits, MT
Liqueur	Pommeau	San Juan Island Distillery, WA
Liqueur	Saskatoon Liqueur	LB Distillers, SK Canada
Liqueur	Skinny	Maple Leaf Spirits Inc., BC Canada
Liqueur	Sorel	Jack From Brooklyn Inc., NY
Liqueur	Southern Accents Liqueurs	Firefly Distillery, SC
Liqueur	Spirit of St. Louis Vermont Night Whiskey Liqueur	Square One Brewery and Distillery, MO
Liqueur	Strait Pastis	Myriad View Artisan Dist. Inc., PE Canada
Liqueur	T &W Limonela Liqueur	Empire Winery & Distillery, FL
Liqueur	Whisper Creek Tennessee Sipping Cream	SPEAKeasy Spirits, TN
Liqueur	Wild-Harvested Genepi Liqueur	Breckenridge Distillery, CO
Liqueur, Almond Aged	Amandine – Barrel Aged Almond Liqueur	GrandTen Distilling, MA
Liqueur, Apple	Plaisir Apple Liqueur	Winegarden Estate Ltd., NB Canada
Liqueur, Apple	Spiced Apple Liqueur	Skip Rock Distillers, WA
Liqueur, Apple	Vermont Ice Apple Crème	Boyden Valley Winery & Spirits, VT
Liqueur, Apple Aged	American Fruits™ Burbon Barrel Aged Apple Liqueur	Warwick Valley Distillery, NY
Liqueur, Applejack	Cornelius Applejack	Harvest Spirits LLC, NY
Liqueur, Applejack	Golden Moon Colorado Apple Jack	Golden Moon Distillery, CO
Liqueur, Applejack	Starlight Distillery Applejack Brandy	Huber's Starlight Distillery, IN
Liqueur, Applejack	Tom's Foolery Applejack	Tom's Foolery, OH
Liqueur, Applejack	Tree Spirits Applejack	Tree Spirits, ME
Liqueur, Apricot	Apricot Liqueur	It's 5 Artisan Distillery, WA
Liqueur, Apricot	Biggs Junction Apricot Liqueur	Stone Barn Brandyworks, OR
Liqueur, Banana	Pollyodd Bananacreamcello	Naoj and Mot Inc., PA
Liqueur, Black Walnut	Charbay Black Walnut Liqueur	Charbay Winery & Distillery, CA
Liqueur, Black Walnut	Kuchan Nocino Black Walnut Liqueur	Old World Spirits LLC, CA
Liqueur, Blackberry	Blackberry Liqueur	Clear Creek Distillery, OR
Liqueur, Blackberry	Blackberry Liqueur	It's 5 Artisan Distillery, WA

Liqueur, Blackberry	Blackberry Liqueur	Skip Rock Distillers, WA
Liqueur, Blackberry	Blackberry Liqueur	Winegarden Estate Ltd., NB Canada
Liqueur, Blackberry	Brandy Peak Blackberry Liqueur	Brandy Peak Distillery, OR
Liqueur, Blackberry	Buckeye Distillery Blackberry Liqueur	Buckeye Distillery Inc., OH
Liqueur, Blackberry	Leopold Bros. Rocky Mountain Blackberry Liqueur	Leopold Bros., CO
Liqueur, Blackberry	Okanagan Spirits Blackberry Liqueur	Okanagan Spirits, BC Canada
Liqueur, Blackberry	Sidetrack Distillery Blackberry Liqueur	Sidetrack Distillery, WA
Liqueur, Blackcurrant	Okanagan Spirits Blackcurrant Liqueur	Okanagan Spirits, BC Canada
Liqueur, Blu. Honeysuc.	Blue Honeysuckle Liqueur	LB Distillers, SK Canada
Liqueur, Blueberry	Blue Hill Blueberry Liqueur	Winegarden Estate Ltd., NB Canada
Liqueur, Blueberry	Blueberry Liqueur	Flag Hill Winery & Distillery, NH
Liqueur, Blueberry	Blueberry Liqueur	It's 5 Artisan Distillery, WA
Liqueur, Blueberry	Ironworks Blueberry Liqueur	Ironworks Distillery, NS Canada
Liqueur, Blueberry	Okanagan Spirits Blueberry Liqueur	Okanagan Spirits, BC Canada
Liqueur, Blueberry	Sidetrack Distillery Blueberry Liqueur	Sidetrack Distillery, WA
Liqueur, Bourbon	Benj. Prichard's Sweet Lucy Bourbon Cream Liqueur	Prichard's Distillery Inc., TN
Liqueur, Bourbon	Benj. Prichard's Sweet Lucy Bourbon Liqueur	Prichard's Distillery Inc., TN
Liqueur, Brulee	Dancing Pines Brulee Liqueur	Dancing Pines Distillery, CO
Liqueur, Caraway	Koval Caraway Liqueur	Koval Distillery, IL
Liqueur, Cassis	Cassis Liqueur	Clear Creek Distillery, OR
Liqueur, Cassis	Cassis Liqueur	Finger Lakes Distilling, NY
Liqueur, Cassis	Cassis Liqueur	Winegarden Estate Ltd., NB Canada
Liqueur, Cassis	Crème de Cassis Liqueur	LB Distillers, SK Canada
Liqueur, Cassis	Johnny Ziegler Cassis	Winegarden Estate Ltd., NB Canada
Liqueur, Cassis	Sidetrack Distillery Cassis	Sidetrack Distillery, WA
Liqueur, Cassis	Tuthilltown Barrel Aged Cassis	Tuthilltown Spirits Distillery, NY
Liqueur, Chai	Dancing Pines Chai Liqueur	Dancing Pines Distillery, CO
Liqueur, Cherry	Buckeye Distillery Cherry Liqueur	Buckeye Distillery Inc., OH
Liqueur, Cherry	Cherry Liqueur	Clear Creek Distillery, OR
Liqueur, Cherry	Cherry Liqueur	It's 5 Artisan Distillery, WA
Liqueur, Cherry	Cherry Liqueur	Maple Leaf Spirits Inc., BC Canada
Liqueur, Cherry	Okanagan Spirits Cherry Liqueur	Okanagan Spirits, BC Canada

Liqueur, Cherry Tart	Dancing Pines Cherry Tart Liqueur	Dancing Pines Distillery, CO
Liqueur, Choc. Rasp.	Chocolate Raspberry	Bloomery Plantation Distillery, WV
Liqueur, Chocolatecream	Pollyodd Chocolatecreamcello	Naoj and Mot Inc, PA
Liqueur, Chrysanthemum	Koval Chrysanthemum & Honey Liqueur	Koval Distillery, IL
Liqueur, Cocoa	Cocoa Liqueur	Yahara Bay Distillers, WI
Liqueur, Coffee	Brooklyn Roasting Company Coffee Liqueur	Cacao Prieto LLC, NY
Liqueur, Coffee	Coffee Liqueur	New Deal Distillery, OR
Liqueur, Coffee	Coffee Liqueur	Yahara Bay Distillers, WI
Liqueur, Coffee	Coffee Liqueur	McMenamins Edgefield Distillery, OR
Liqueur, Coffee	Colorado Coffee Liqueur	Mancos Valley Distillery, CO
Liqueur, Coffee	Corretto Coffee Liqueur	Roundhouse Spirits, CO
Liqueur, Coffee	Dancing Tree Coffee Liqueur	Dancing Tree Distillery, OH
Liqueur, Coffee	Dream Bean Coffee Liqueur	Tahoe Moonshine Distillery Inc., CA
Liqueur, Coffee	Drip Coffee Liqueur	Rain City Spirits, WA
Liqueur, Coffee	House Spirits Coffee Liqueur	House Spirits Distillery, OR
Liqueur, Coffee	Koval Coffee Liqueur	Koval Distillery, IL
Liqueur, Coffee	Frenchpress Style American Coffee Liqueur	Leopold Bros., CO
Liqueur, Coffee	Mocca Gino Coffee Liqueur	Winegarden Estate Ltd., NB Canada
Liqueur, Coffee	Red Wing Roast Coffee Liqueur	Stone Barn Brandyworks, OR
Liqueur, Coffee	Richardo's Coffee Liqueur	Spirit Hound Distillers, CO
Liqueur, Cranberry	Benjamin Prichard's Cranberry Liqueur	Prichard's Distillery Inc., TN
Liqueur, Cranberry	Cranberry Liqueur	Clear Creek Distillery, OR
Liqueur, Cranberry	Cranberry Liqueur	Stone Barn Brandyworks, OR
Liqueur, Cranberry	Cranberry Liqueur	Flag Hill Winery & Distillery, NH
Liqueur, Cranberry	Cranberry Liqueur	Winegarden Estate Ltd., NB Canada
Liqueur, Cranberry	Craneberry - Massachusetts Cranberry Liqueur	GrandTen Distilling, MA
Liqueur, Cranberry	Ironworks Cranberry Liqueur	Ironworks Distillery, NS Canada
Liqueur, Cranberry	Leopold Bros. New England Cranberry Liqueur	Leopold Bros., CO
Liqueur, Cranberry	Okanagan Spirits Cranberry Liqueur	Okanagan Spirits, BC Canada
Liqueur, Douglas Fir	broVo+DF Douglas Fir Liqueur	broVo Spirits, WA
Liqueur, Elderberry	Elderberry Liqueur	It's 5 Artisan Distillery, WA
Liqueur, Elderberry	Elderberry Liqueur	Winegarden Estate Ltd., NB Canada

Liqueur, Espresso	Dancing Pines Espresso Liqueur	Dancing Pines Distillery, CO
Liqueur, Figcello	FigCello di Sonoma	HelloCello, CA
Liqueur, Ginger	300 Joules Ginger Infusion	Big Still Liquors LLC, NJ
Liqueur, Ginger	Ginger Liqueur	New Deal Distillery, OR
Liqueur, Ginger	Koval Ginger Liqueur	Koval Distillery, IL
Liqueur, Ginger	broVo+G Ginger Liqueur	broVo Spirits, WA
Liqueur, Ginger	Ginger SweetShine	Bloomery Plantation Distillery, WV
Liqueur, Herbal	Herbal Liqueur	McMenamins Edgefield Distillery, OR
Liqueur, Herbal	Leopold Bros. Three Pins Alpine Herbal Liqueur	Leopold Bros., CO
Liqueur, Honey	Honey Liqueur	Winegarden Estate Ltd., NB Canada
Liqueur, Honey	Old Sugar Factory Honey Liqueur	Old Sugar Distillery, WI
Liqueur, Irish Cream	St. Patrick's Irish Cream	Minhas Micro Distillery, WI
Liqueur, Irish Cream	VanHees' Mean Irish Cream	Tahoe Moonshine Distillery Inc., CA
Liqueur, Jasmine	Koval Jasmine Liqueur	Koval Distillery, IL
Liqueur, Lavender	broVo+L Lavender Liqueur	broVo Spirits, WA
Liqueur, Lavender Rose	Lavender and Wild Rose Liqueur	San Juan Island Distillery, WA
Liqueur, Lemon	300 Joules Lemon Infusion	Big Still Liquors LLC, NJ
Liqueur, Lemon	broVo+LB Lemon Balm Liqueur	broVo Spirits, WA
Liqueur, Lemon	Lemon Ice	Bloomery Plantation Distillery, WV
Liqueur, Lemon	Napa Valley Meyer Lemon Liqueur	Napa Valley Distillery, CA
Liqueur, Lemon	Paula's Texas Lemon	Texacello LLC, TX
Liqueur, Lemon	T & W Lemonela Liqueur	Empire Winery & Distillery, FL
Liqueur, Lemon	Limoncello di Leelanau Lemon Liqueur	Northern Latitudes Distillery, MI
Liqueur, Lemon	Sorbetta Lemon Liqueur	Long Island Spirits, NY
Liqueur, Lemoncella	Cedar Ridge Lemoncella	Cedar Ridge Distillery, IA
Liqueur, Lemoncello	Lemoncella	Yahara Bay Distillers, WI
Liqueur, Lemoncello	Lemoncello	Black Heron Spirits Distillery, WA
Liqueur, Lemoncello	Madison Avenue Lemoncello	45th Parallel Spirits LLC, WI
Liqueur, Lemoncello	Pollyodd Lemoncello	Naoj and Mot Inc., PA
Liqueur, Lemoncream	Pollyodd Lemoncreamcello	Naoj and Mot Inc., PA
Liqueur, Lime Sorbetta	Lime Liqueur	Long Island Spirits, NY
Liqueur, Limecello	Pollyodd Limecello	Naoj and Mot Inc., PA

Liqueur, Limoncello	Demarest Hill Winery Limoncella	Demarest Hill Winery, NY
Liqueur, Limoncello	Fiore Limoncello	Fiore Winery & Distillery, MD
Liqueur, Limoncello	Letterpress Limoncello	Letterpress Distilling, WA
Liqueur, Limoncello	Limoncello	Bloomery Plantation Distillery, WV
Liqueur, Limoncello	Limoncello di Sonoma	HelloCello, CA
Liqueur, Limoncello	Six Mile Creek Limoncella	Six Mile Creek Winery & Distillery, NY
Liqueur, Limoncello	Ventura Limoncello Crema	Ventura Limoncello Company, CA
Liqueur, Limoncello	Ventura Limoncello Originale	Ventura Limoncello Company, CA
Liqueur, Loganberry	Loganberry Liqueur	Clear Creek Distillery, OR
Liqueur, Loganberry	Whidbey Island Distillery Loganberry Liqueur	Whidbey Island Distillery, WA
Liqueur, Mangocello	Pollyodd Mangocello	Naoj and Mot Inc., PA
Liqueur, Maple	Green Mountain Organic Maple Liqueur	Green Mountain Distillers, VT
Liqueur, Maple	Maple Dream liqueur	Winegarden Estate Ltd., NB Canada
Liqueur, Maple	Maple Liqueur	Maple Leaf Spirits Inc., BC Canada
Liqueur, Maple	Maple Smash Liqueur	Sweetgrass Farm Winery & Distillery, ME
Liqueur, Maple	Maplejack Liqueur	Finger Lakes Distilling, NY
Liqueur, Maple	Metcalfe's Vermont Maple Cream Liqueur	Vermont Distillers, VT
Liqueur, Maple	Sapling Vermont Maple Liqueur	Saxtons River Distillery LLC, VT
Liqueur, Maple	Schoharie Mapple Jack	KyMar Farm Distillery, NY
Liqueur, Maple	Tirado Maple Delight	Tirado Distillery, NY
Liqueur, Maple	Tree Spirits Knotted	Maple Tree Spirits, ME
Liqueur, Maple	Vermont Ice Maple Crème	Boyden Valley Winery & Spirits, VT
Liqueur, Nocino	Sidetrack Distillery Nocino	Sidetrack Distillery, WA
Liqueur, Orancella	Demarest Hill Winery Orancella	Demarest Hill Winery, NY
Liqueur, Orange	Paula's Texas Orange	Texacello LLC, TX
Liqueur, Orange	T & W Orangela Liqueur	Empire Winery & Distillery, FL
Liqueur, Orange	Leopold Bros. American Orange Liqueur	Leopold Bros., CO
Liqueur, Orange	Naranjo Orange Liqueur	Rancho de Los Luceros Destilaria, NM
Liqueur, Orange	Sorbetta Orange Liqueur	Long Island Spirits, NY
Liqueur, Orange Blossom	Koval Orange Blossom Liqueur	Koval Distillery, IL
Liqueur, Orangecello	OrangeCello di Sonoma	HelloCello, CA
Liqueur, Orangecello	Pollyodd Orangecello	Naoj and Mot Inc., PA

484

Type	Product	Distillery
Liqueur, Orangecello	Ventura Orangecello Blood Orange	Ventura Limoncello Company, CA
Liqueur, Orangecream	Pollyodd Orangecreamcello	Naoj and Mot Inc., PA
Liqueur, Organic	Bluewater Organic Liqueur	Bluewater Distilling, WA
Liqueur, Organic	FRUITLAB Organic Liqueur	GreenBar Collective, CA
Liqueur, Ouzo	Americanaki Ouzo	Old Sugar Distillery, WI
Liqueur, Ouzo	Eastside Ouzo	Stone Barn Brandyworks, OR
Liqueur, Peaches / Cream	Peaches and Cream	Bloomery Plantation Distillery, WV
Liqueur, Pear	American Fruits™ Bartlett Pear Liqueur	Warwick Valley Distillery, NY
Liqueur, Pear	Pear Liqueur	Clear Creek Distillery, OR
Liqueur, Pear	Pear Liqueur	Magnanini Farm Winery Inc., NY
Liqueur, Pear	Pear Liqueur	Maple Leaf Spirits Inc., BC Canada
Liqueur, Pear	Pear Liqueur	Winegarden Estate Ltd., NB Canada
Liqueur, Pear	Prickly Pear Liqueur	Arizona High Spirits Distillery, AZ
Liqueur, Peppermint Bark	Peppermint Bark Liqueur	Eastside Distilling, OR
Liqueur, Plum Gin	Greenhook Ginsmiths Beach Plum Gin Liqueur	Greenhook Ginsmiths, NY
Liqueur, Plum Gin	Pacific Plum Liqueur	Stringer's Orchard Winery Distillery, OR
Liqueur, Raspberry	Buckeye Distillery Raspberry Liqueur	Buckeye Distillery Inc., OH
Liqueur, Raspberry	Cedar Ridge Lamponcella	Cedar Ridge Distillery, IA
Liqueur, Raspberry	Metcalfe's Raspberry Liqueur	Vermont Distillers, VT
Liqueur, Raspberry	Okanagan Spirits Raspberry Liqueur	Okanagan Spirits, BC Canada
Liqueur, Raspberry	Raspberry Liqueur	Clear Creek Distillery, OR
Liqueur, Raspberry	Raspberry Liqueur	Finger Lakes Distilling, NY
Liqueur, Raspberry	Raspberry Liqueur	Flag Hill Winery & Distillery, NH
Liqueur, Raspberry	Raspberry Liqueur	Hidden Marsh Distillery, NY
Liqueur, Raspberry	Raspberry Liqueur	It's 5 Artisan Distillery, WA
Liqueur, Raspberry	Raspberry Liqueur	Skip Rock Distillers, WA
Liqueur, Raspberry	Raspberry Liqueur	Winegarden Estate Ltd., NB Canada
Liqueur, Raspberry	Sidetrack Distillery Raspberry Liqueur	Sidetrack Distillery, WA
Liqueur, Raspberry	Sorbetta Raspberry Liqueur	Long Island Spirits, NY
Liqueur, Raspberry	Whidbey Island Distillery Raspberry Liqueur	Whidbey Island Distillery, WA
Liqueur, Rasp. Limon.	Raspberry Limoncello	Bloomery Plantation Distillery, WV
Liqueur, Rhubarb	Oregon Blush Rhubarb Liqueur	Stone Barn Brandyworks, OR

Category	Product	Company
Liqueur, Rosebro	Vo+RG Rose Geranium Liqueur	broVo Spirits, WA
Liqueur, Rose	Crispin's Rose Liqueur	Greenway Distillers Inc., CA
Liqueur, Rose Hip	Koval Rose Hip Liqueur	Koval Distillery, IL
Liqueur, Rum	Cacao Prieto Don Daniel Cacao Rum Liqueur	Cacao Prieto LLC, NY
Liqueur, Rum	Cacao Prieto Don Esteban Cacao Rum Liqueur	Cacao Prieto LLC, NY
Liqueur, Sea Buckthorn	Okanagan Spirits Sea Buckthorn Liqueur	Okanagan Spirits, BC Canada
Liqueur, Sea Buckthorn	Seabuckthorn and Wildflower Honey Liqueur	LB Distillers, SK Canada
Liqueur, Spiced	Holiday Spiced Liqueur	Eastside Distilling, OR
Liqueur, Strawberry	Sidetrack Distillery Strawberry Liqueur	Sidetrack Distillery, WA
Liqueur, Strawberry	Sorbetta Strawberry Liqueur	Long Island Spirits, NY
Liqueur, Strawberry	Strawberry Liqueur	Stone Barn Brandyworks, OR
Liqueur, Strawberrycream	Pollyodd Strawberrycreamcello	Naoj and Mot Inc., PA
Liqueur, Sugar Maple	Sugar Maple Liqueur	Flag Hill Winery & Distillery, NH
Liqueur, Tart Cherry	Leopold Bros. Michigan Tart Cherry Liqueur	Leopold Bros., CO
Liqueur, Walnut	Nocino Green Walnut Liqueur	Stone Barn Brandyworks, OR
Liqueur, Walnut	Nocino, Walnut Liqueur	Skip Rock Distillers, WA
Liqueur, Wild Cherry	Wild Cherry Liqueur	Winegarden Estate Ltd., NB Canada
Liqueur, Wild Chokecherry	Montana Wild Chokecherry Liqueur	Willie's Distillery, MT
Liqueur,Chocolatecello	Pollyodd Chocolatecello	Naoj and Mot Inc., PA
Mead	T & W Royal Mead Honey Wine	Empire Winery & Distillery, FL
Moonshine	2bar Moonshine	2bar® Spirits, WA
Moonshine	Apple-achian Shine	Dark Corner Distillery, SC
Moonshine	Arkansas Lightning	Rock Town Distillery Inc., AR
Moonshine	Barrel Aged Onyx Moonshine	Onyx Spirits Company LLC, CT
Moonshine	Bear Creek Sippin' Shine	Georgia Distilling Company, GA
Moonshine	Benj. Prichard's Lincoln County Lightning Whiskey	Prichard's Distillery Inc., TN
Moonshine	Block and Tackle Moonshine Corn Whiskey Un-aged	It's 5 Artisan Distillery, WA
Moonshine	Block and Tackle Sunshine Corn Whiskey Aged	It's 5 Artisan Distillery, WA
Moonshine	Broadslab Legacy Reserve	Broadslab Distillery LLC, NC
Moonshine	Broadslab Legacy Shine	Broadslab Distillery LLC, NC
Moonshine	Butterscotch Shine	Dark Corner Distillery, SC
Moonshine	California Moonshine	Fog's End Distillery, CA

486

Moonshine	Carolina Peach Shine	Dark Corner Distillery, SC
Moonshine	Catdaddy Spiced Moonshine	Piedmont Distillers, NC
Moonshine	Collier and McKeel White Dog	Collier and McKeel, TN
Moonshine	Copper Run Moonshine	Copper Run Distillery, MO
Moonshine	Devil John Moonshine	Barrel House Distilling Co., KY
Moonshine	Devil's Share Moonshine	Ballast Point Spirits, CA
Moonshine	Ezra Cox Moonshine	Ezra Cox Distillery, WA
Moonshine	Fitch's Goat Moonshine	Bone Spirits, TX
Moonshine	Hawaiian Moonshine	Island Distillers Inc., HI
Moonshine	High Proof Onyx Moonshine	Onxy Spirits Company LLC, CT
Moonshine	Honeysuckle Shine	Dark Corner Distillery, SC
Moonshine	House Spirits White Dog	House Spirits Distillery, OR
Moonshine	Junior Johnson's Midnight Moon	Piedmont Distillers, NC
Moonshine	Kings County Moonshine	Kings County Distillery, NY
Moonshine	LBL Most Wanted Moonshine	Silver Trail Distillery, KY
Moonshine	LPR Moonshine	Mastermind Vodka, IL
Moonshine	MBR Kentucky Black Dog	MB Roland Distillery, KY
Moonshine	MBR Kentucky White Dog	MB Roland Distillery, KY
Moonshine	MBR St. Elmo's Fire	MB Roland Distillery, KY
Moonshine	MBR True Kentucky Shine	MB Roland Distillery, KY
Moonshine	Missouri Moonshine	Crown Valley Distilling Company, MO
Moonshine	Montana Honey Moonshine	Willie's Distillery, MT
Moonshine	Montana Moonshine	Willie's Distillery, MT
Moonshine	Moonshine	Flag Hill Winery & Distillery, NH
Moonshine	Moonshine	Dark Corner Distillery, SC
Moonshine	Moonshine Bandits Outlaw Moonshine	Valley Spirits LLC, CA
Moonshine	Moose Shine Pacific Northwest Un-aged Whiskey	Carbon Glacier Distillery, WA
Moonshine	Mount Baker Moonshine	Mount Baker Distillery, WA
Moonshine	Mountain Moonshine Old Oak Recipe	WV Distilling Co. LLC, WV
Moonshine	Mountain Moonshine Spirit Whiskey	WV Distilling Co. LLC, WV
Moonshine	Ole Smoky® Hunch Punch Moonshine™ (seasonal)	Ole Smoky Distillery LLC, TN
Moonshine	Ole Smoky® White Lightnin'™ (Neutral Spirits)	Ole Smoky Distillery LLC, TN

Moonshine	Onyx Moonshine	Onyx Spirits Company LLC, CT
Moonshine	Palmetto Moonshine	Palmetto Moonshine, SC
Moonshine	Popcorn Sutton's Tennessee White Whiskey	Popcorn Sutton's Distillery, TN
Moonshine	Raymond Fairchilds Mountain Moonshine	Howling Moon Distillery, NC
Moonshine	Revenge	Limestone Branch Distillery, KY
Moonshine	Roberson's Tennessee Mellomoon	East Tennessee Distillery, TN
Moonshine	Rocky Mountain Moonshine	Mystic Mountain Distillery LLC, CO
Moonshine	Schoharie Shine	KyMar Farm Distillery, NY
Moonshine	See 7 Stars Moonshine	Batch 206, WA
Moonshine	Shinn Estate Vineyards Shine	Shinn Estate Vineyards Farmhouse, NY
Moonshine	Strait Lightning	Myriad View Artis. Distill. Inc., PE Canada
Moonshine	Strait Shine	Myriad View Artis. Distill. Inc., PE Canada
Moonshine	Sweet Baby Moonshine	Hard Times Distillery LLC, OR
Moonshine	TJ Pottinger Sugar Shine	Limestone Branch Distillery, KY
Moonshine	Virginia Sweetwater Moonshine	Appalachian Mountain Springs LLC, VA
Moonshine	Wagner's White Lightning	Stoutridge Distillery, NY
Moonshine	Whistling Andy Moonshine	Whistling Andy Distillery, MT
Moonshine	White Lightning Moonshine	Firefly Distillery, SC
Moonshine	White Widow	Adam Dalton Distillery, NC
Moonshine	Wildberry Shine	Dark Corner Distillery, SC
Moonshine	XXX Shine White Whiskey	Philadelphia Distilling, PA
Moonshine, Apple	Apple Shine	Hard Times Distillery LLC, OR
Moonshine, Apple Pie	Apple Pie Arkansas Lightning	Rock Town Distillery Inc., AR
Moonshine, Apple Pie	Apple Pie Moonshine	Howling Moon Distillery, NC
Moonshine, Apple Pie	Firefly Apple Pie Moonshine	Firefly Distillery, SC
Moonshine, Apple Pie	MBR Kentucky Apple Pie	MB Roland Distillery, KY
Moonshine, Apple Pie	Ole Smoky® Apple Pie Moonshine™	Ole Smoky Distillery LLC, TN
Moonshine, Apple Pie	Palmetto Apple Pie Moonshine	Palmetto Moonshine, SC
Moonshine, Apple Pie	Pinchgut Hollow Distillery Apple Pie Shine	Pinchgut Hollow Distillery, WV
Moonshine, Blackberry	Palmetto Blackberry Moonshine	Palmetto Moonshine, SC
Moonshine, Blueberry	MBR Kentucky Blueberry Shine	MB Roland Distillery, KY
Moonshine, Buckwheat	Pinchgut Hollow Distillery Buckwheat Moon	Pinchgut Hollow Distillery, WV

Type	Product	Distillery
Moonshine, Caramel	Firefly Caramel Moonshine	Firefly Distillery, SC
Moonshine, Cherries	Ole Smoky® Moonshine Cherries™	Ole Smoky Distillery LLC, TN
Moonshine, Cherry	Firefly Cherry Moonshine	Firefly Distillery, SC
Moonshine, Cinna. Hot	Lightning Hot Cinnamon Arkansas Lightning	Rock Town Distillery Inc., AR
Moonshine, Corn	Ole Smoky® Original Moonshine	Ole Smoky Distillery LLC, TN
Moonshine, Corn	Pinchgut Hollow Distillery Corn Shine	Pinchgut Hollow Distillery, WV
Moonshine, Grape	Ole Smoky® Grape Moonshine™ (seasonal)	Ole Smoky Distillery LLC, TN
Moonshine, Honey Peach	Pinchgut Hollow Distillery Honey Peach Moon	Pinchgut Hollow Distillery, WV
Moonshine, Mint Julep	MBR Kentucky Mint Julep	MB Roland Distillery, KY
Moonshine, Peach	Firefly Peach Moonshine	Firefly Distillery, SC
Moonshine, Peach	Ole Smoky® Peach Moonshine™ (seasonal)	Ole Smoky Distillery LLC, TN
Moonshine, Peach	Palmetto Peach Moonshine	Palmetto Moonshine, SC
Moonshine, Pink Lmnde	MBR Kentucky Pink Lemonade	MB Roland Distillery, KY
Moonshine, Pump. Spice	Corsair Pumpkin Spice Moonshine	Corsair Artisan Distillery, TN
Moonshine, Strawberry	MBR Kentucky Strawberry Shine	MB Roland Distillery, KY
Moonshine, Strawbetty	Firefly Strawberry Moonshine	Firefly Distillery, SC
Pisco	Don Quixote Pisco	Don Quixote Distillery & Winery, NM
Rhum	Shipwreck Spiced Pirate Rhum	Artesian Distillers, MI
Rhum, Spiced	Wit Spiced Rhum	Dogfish Head Craft Brewery, DE
Rock & Rye	Mister Katz's Rock & Rye	New York Distilling, NY
Rum	1492 Cristobal Rum	Artesian Distillers, MI
Rum	Agua Libre Rum	St. George Spirits, CA
Rum	Alchemist Distillery Rum	Alchemist Distilleries Inc., FL
Rum	Alpunto Platinum Rum	Port Morris Distillery, NY
Rum	Backwoods Reserve Straight Rum	Dunc's Mill, VT
Rum	Bardenay Small Batch Rum	Bardenay Inc., ID
Rum	Bluenose Black Rum	Ironworks Distillery, NS Canada
Rum	Braddah Kimo's Extreme 155 Proof Rum	Haleakala Distillers, HI
Rum	Bully Boy Boston Rum	Bully Boy Distillers, MA
Rum	Cacao Prieto Don Rafael Cacao Rum	Cacao Prieto LLC, NY
Rum	Cacao Prieto White Rum	Cacao Prieto LLC, NY
Rum	California Dreamin' Rum	Tahoe Moonshine Distillery Inc., CA

Rum	Cane and Abe Small-Barrel Rum	Old Sugar Distillery, WI
Rum	Carolina Coast Rum	Broadslab Distillery LLC, NC
Rum	Carolina Rum	Muddy River Distillery, NC
Rum	Chamomile Rum	Cacao Prieto LLC, NY
Rum	Chava Rum	Sòlas Distillery, NE
Rum	Chick's Beach Rum	Chesapeake Bay Distillery LLC, VA
Rum	Chocolat Mint Rum	The North Woods Distillery LLC, WI
Rum	Civilized Rum	Northern United Brew. Co. & Distill., MI
Rum	Cypress Creek Reserve Crystal Rum	D.E.W. Distillation LLC, TX
Rum	Dancing Pines Rum	Dancing Pines Distillery, CO
Rum	Deadman's Dark & Spice Rum	Spirits of the USA LLC, FL
Rum	Deadman's Mango Flavored Rum	Spirits of the USA LLC, FL
Rum	Desert Diamond Dist. Gold Miner Barrel Reserve Rum	Desert Diamond Distillery, AZ
Rum	Desert Diamond Dist. Gold Miner Rum	Desert Diamond Distillery, AZ
Rum	Distiller's Workshop Rum	New Deal Distillery, OR
Rum	DiVine Rum	Entente Spirits LLC, MI
Rum	Dry County Rum	Dry County Distillery LLC, WA
Rum	Duck Island Rum	66 Gilead Distillery, ON Canada
Rum	Due North Rum	Van Brunt Stillhouse, NY
Rum	Edgefield Rum	McMenamins Edgefield Distillery, OR
Rum	Eight Bells Rum	New England Distilling, ME
Rum	Esprit de Krewe™ Crystal Rum	Rollins Distillery, FL
Rum	Expedition Rum	StiL 630, MO
Rum	Folly Cove Rum	Ryan & Wood Inc., MA
Rum	Freshwater Superior Single Barrel Rum	New Holland Artisan Spirits, MI
Rum	Heath Rum	The North Woods Distillery LLC, WI
Rum	Holstein Rum	Werner Distilling LLC, IA
Rum	House Spirits Rum	House Spirits Distillery, OR
Rum	Hurricane Rum	Triple Eight Distillery, MA
Rum	Ian's Alley Rum	Mancos Valley Distillery, CO
Rum	Jug Dealer Rum	Tahoe Moonshine Distillery Inc., CA
Rum	Kentucky Honey	Barrel House Distilling Co., KY

Rum	Knock on Wood Rum	LB Distillers, SK Canada
Rum	Mad Bird Rum (aged)	Yahara Bay Distillers, WI
Rum	Maui Platinum Rum	Haleakala Distillers, HI
Rum	Maya Rum Horchata	Minhas Micro Distillery, WI
Rum	Montanya Oro Rum	Montanya Distillers LLC, CO
Rum	Montanya Platino Rum	Montanya Distillers LLC, CO
Rum	Mountain Bum Rum	Spirit Hound Distillers, CO
Rum	Old Ipswich "Tavern Style" Rum	Turkey Shore Distilleries, MA
Rum	Old Ipswich "White Cap" Rum	Turkey Shore Distilleries, MA
Rum	Old New Orleans 10 Year Rum	Celebration Distillation, LA
Rum	Old New Orleans Crystal Rum	Celebration Distillation, LA
Rum	Owney's NYC Rum	The Noble Experiment NYC, NY
Rum	Pacific Rum	Bull Run Distilling Company, OR
Rum	Pecan Street Rum	Spirit of Texas LLC, TX
Rum	Peg Leg Rum	Mile High Spirits LLC, CO
Rum	Pitorro Rum	Port Morris Distillery, NY
Rum	Prichard's Crystal Rum	Prichard's Distillery Inc., TN
Rum	Prichard's Fine Rum	Prichard's Distillery Inc., TN
Rum	Prichard's Private Stock Rum	Prichard's Distillery Inc., TN
Rum	Prichard's Sweet Georgia Bell	Prichard's Distillery Inc., TN
Rum	Prince Edward Merchantman Rum	Prince Edward Distillery, PE Canada
Rum	Privateer True American Rum	Privateer Rum, MA
Rum	Quackenbush Still House Rum	Albany Distilling Company, NY
Rum	Ragged Mountain Rum	Berkshire Mountain Distillers Inc., MA
Rum	Richland Rum	Richland Distilling Company, GA
Rum	Richland Rum – Vennebroeck Velvet Prop. Priv. Res.	Richland Distill. Co., GA
Rum	Riverboat Rum	Rock Town Distillery Inc., AR
Rum	RMD Rum	Artesian Distillers, MI
Rum	Road's End Rum	Journeyman Distillery, MI
Rum	Roaring Dan's Rum	Great Lakes Distillery LLC, WI
Rum	Rum of the Gods	Minhas Micro Distillery, WI
Rum	Six Owls Rum	Six Owls Spirits, NS Canada

Rum	Smugglers' Notch Rum	Smuggler's Notch Distillery, VT
Rum	Sorghum Rum	Dancing Tree Distillery, OH
Rum	Spirit of Texas Rum	Spirit of Texas LLC, TX
Rum	Strait Rum (40%)	Myriad View Artis. Distill. Inc., PE Canada
Rum	Strait Rum (historic 100 proof 57.1%)	Myriad View Artis. Distill. Inc., PE Canada
Rum	Sweet Crude Rum	Rank Wildcat Spirits LLC, LA
Rum	Tesouro Rum	Tesouro Distillery, CO
Rum	Thomas Tew Single Barrel Rum	Newport Distilling Company, RI
Rum	Three Crow Rum	Sweetgrass Farm Winery & Distillery, ME
Rum	Tirado El Pitito Rum	Tirado Distillery, NY
Rum	Treaty Oak Platinum Rum	Treaty Oak Distilling Co., TX
Rum	Turtle Island Rum-style Spirits	Dark Moon Artisan Distillery, WA
Rum	Ugly Dog Rum	Ugly Dog Distillery LLC, MI
Rum	Whistling Andy Hibiscus-Coconut Rum	Whistling Andy Distillery, MT
Rum	White Hat Rum	South Congress Distillery, TX
Rum	Wicked Dolphin Rum	Cape Spirits Inc., FL
Rum	Witherspoon's River Rum	Quentin D. Witherspoon Distillery LLC, TX
Rum	XO Gold Coast Rum	Minhas Micro Distillery, WI
Rum	XO Gold Coast Rum USA	Minhas Micro Distillery, WI
Rum	Yahara Bay Premium Rum	Yahara Bay Distillers, WI
Rum, Agave	Desert Diamond Distillery Gold Miner Agave Rum	Desert Diamond Distillery, AZ
Rum, Aged	State of Jefferson Rum (currently aging)	Immortal Spirits & Distilling Company, OR
Rum, Aged	Treaty Oak Aged Rum	Treaty Oak Distilling Co., TX
Rum, Amber	Amber Rum	Ironworks Distillery, NS Canada
Rum, Amber	Freshwater Michigan Amber Rum	New Holland Artisan Spirits, MI
Rum, Amber	Old New Orleans Amber Rum	Celebration Distillation, LA
Rum, Amber	Sea Hagg Rum (Amber)	Sea Hagg Distillery, NH
Rum, Amber	Spirit of St. Louis Island Time Amber Rum	Square One Brewery and Distillery, MO
Rum, Amber	Sugar Daddy Amber Rum	HelloCello, CA
Rum, Amber	Taildragger Amber Rum	Tailwinds Distilling Company, IL
Rum, Amber	Urban Amber Rum	Urban Distilleries, BC Canada
Rum, Barrel Aged	Downslope Wine Barrel Aged Rum	Downslope Distilling, CO

Rum, Barrel Aged	Three Sheets Barrel Aged Rum	Ballast Point Spirits, CA
Rum, Blueberry	Sea Hagg Blueberry Rum	Sea Hagg Distillery, NH
Rum, Cask	Dancing Pines Cask Rum	Dancing Pines Distillery, CO
Rum, Coffee	Below Deck Coffee Rum	Eastside Distilling, OR
Rum, Cranberry	Prichard's Cranberry Rum	Prichard's Distillery Inc., TN
Rum, Dark	Cedar Ridge Dark Rum	Cedar Ridge Distillery, IA
Rum, Dark	Dark Rum	Spirits of Maine Distillery, ME
Rum, Dark	Desert Diamond Distillery Gold Miner Dark Rum	Desert Diamond Distillery, AZ
Rum, Dark	George Bowman Colonial Era Dark Caribbean Rum	A. Smith Bowman Distillery, VA
Rum, Dark	Kaua`i Dark Rum	Kōloa Rum Company, HI
Rum, Dark	Maui Dark Rum ™	Haleakala Distillers, HI
Rum, Dark	Railean Reserve XO Dark Rum	Railean Distillers, TX
Rum, Dark	Railean Small Cask Single Barrel Dark Rum	Railean Distillers, TX
Rum, Dark	Rogue Dark Rum	Rogue Spirits, OR
Rum, Dark	Rougaroux Full Moon Dark Rum	Donner-Peltier Distillers, LA
Rum, Dark	Sugar Daddy Dark Rum	HelloCello, CA
Rum, Dark Spiced	Dark Spiced Naval Rum	Breckenridge Distillery, CO
Rum, Flav. Elderflower	Dunc's Mill Elderflower Flavored Rum	Dunc's Mill, VT
Rum, Flavored Maple	Dunc's Mill Maple Flavored Rum	Dunc's Mill, VT
Rum, Flavored Pineapple	Maui Pineapple Flavored Rum	Haleakala Distillers, HI
Rum, Flavored Vanilla	Cypress Creek Reserve Vanilla Flavored Rum	D.E.W. Distillation LLC, TX
Rum, Ginger	Below Deck Ginger Rum	Eastside Distilling, OR
Rum, Gold	Aristo Gold Rum	Minhas Micro Distillery, WI
Rum, Gold	Downslope Gold Rum	Downslope Distilling, CO
Rum, Gold	Island Rum Gold	Essential Spirits Alambic Distillery, CA
Rum, Gold	Kaua`i Gold	Kōloa Rum Company, HI
Rum, Gold	Maui Gold Rum	Haleakala Distillers, HI
Rum, Gold	Maui Reserve Gold Rum ™	Haleakala Distillers, HI
Rum, Gold	Sailboat Gold Rum	Minhas Micro Distillery, WI
Rum, Gold	Sea Island Gold Rum	Firefly Distillery, SC
Rum, Gold	Sergeant Classick Hawaiian Gold Rum	Essential Spirits Alambic Distillery, CA
Rum, Gold	Siesta Key Gold Rum	Drum Circle Distilling, FL

493

Rum, Gold	Copper Run Gold Rum	Copper Run Distillery, MO
Rum, Honey	Brown Honey Rum	Dogfish Head Craft Brewery, DE
Rum, Java	Sea Island Java Rum	Firefly Distillery, SC
Rum, Key Lime	Prichard's Key Lime Rum	Prichard's Distillery Inc., TN
Rum, Light	ClearHeart Light Rum	Cedar Ridge Distillery, IA
Rum, Light	Light Rum	Spirits of Maine Distillery, ME
Rum, Light	Sugar Daddy Light Rum	HelloCello, CA
Rum, Organic	CRUSOE Organic Rum	GreenBar Collective, CA
Rum, Peach	Sea Hagg Peach Rum	Sea Hagg Distillery, NH
Rum, Pineapple	Royale Hawaiian Pineapple Rum	Saint James Spirits, CA
Rum, Silver	Below Deck Silver Rum	Eastside Distilling, OR
Rum, Silver	Island Rum Silver	Essential Spirits Alambic Distillery, CA
Rum, Silver	Portside Distillery Silver Rum	Portside Distillery, OH
Rum, Silver	Privateer Silver Reserve Rum	Privateer Rum, MA
Rum, Silver	Sergeant Classick Hawaiian Silver Rum	Essential Spirits Alambic Distillery, CA
Rum, Silver	Seven Brothers Silver Rum	Seven Brothers Distilling Company, OH
Rum, Silver	Siesta Key Silver Rum	Drum Circle Distilling, FL
Rum, Silver	Silver Bayou Rum	Louisiana Spirits LLC, LA
Rum, Silver	Whistling Andy Silver Rum	Whistling Andy Distillery, MT
Rum, Spiced	Aristo Spiced Rum	Minhas Micro Distillery, WI
Rum, Spiced	Corsair Spiced Rum	Corsair Artisan Distillery, TN
Rum, Spiced	Dancing Pines Spice Rum	Dancing Pines Distillery, CO
Rum, Spiced	Downslope Spiced Rum	Downslope Distilling, CO
Rum, Spiced	Esprit de Krewe™ Spiced Rum	Rollins Distillery, FL
Rum, Spiced	Ginger Spiced Rum	Bardenay Inc., ID
Rum, Spiced	Holstein Spiced Rum	Werner Distilling LLC, IA
Rum, Spiced	Humboldt Distillery Spiced Rum	Humboldt Distillery, CA
Rum, Spiced	Ian's Alley Spiced Rum	Mancos Valley Distillery, CO
Rum, Spiced	Kaua'i Spice Rum	Kōloa Rum Company, HI
Rum, Spiced	Old Ipswich "Golden Marsh" Spiced Rum	Turkey Shore Distilleries, MA
Rum, Spiced	Old Ipswich "Greenhead" Spiced Rum	Turkey Shore Distilleries, MA
Rum, Spiced	Old New Orleans Cajun Spice Rum	Celebration Distillation, LA

Type	Product	Distillery
Rum, Spiced	Pieces of Eight Spiced Rum	Arizona High Spirits Distillery, AZ
Rum, Spiced	Railean Spiced Rum	Railean Distillers, TX
Rum, Spiced	Rogue Hazelnut Spice Rum	Rogue Spirits, OR
Rum, Spiced	Sailboat Spiced Rum	Minhas Micro Distillery, WI
Rum, Spiced	Sea Island Spiced Rum	Firefly Distillery, SC
Rum, Spiced	Seven Brothers 100-Proof Spiced Rum	Seven Brothers Distilling Company, OH
Rum, Spiced	Siesta Key Spiced Rum	Drum Circle Distilling, FL
Rum, Spiced	Spiced Bayou Rum	Louisiana Spirits LLC, LA
Rum, Spiced	Stars Spiced Rum	Minhas Micro Distillery, WI
Rum, Spiced	Stingray Spiced Rum	JEM Beverage Company, TX
Rum, Vanilla	Downslope Vanilla Rum	Downslope Distilling, CO
Rum, Vanilla Bean	Charbay Tahitian Vanilla Bean Rum	Charbay Winery & Distillery, CA
Rum, White	Aristo White Rum	Minhas Micro Distillery, WI
Rum, White	Bully Boy Bully Boy White Rum	Bully Boy Distillers, MA
Rum, White	Downslope White Rum	Downslope Distilling, CO
Rum, White	Flag Hill White Rum	Flag Hill Winery & Distillery, NH
Rum, White	Freshwater Huron White Rum	New Holland Artisan Spirits, MI
Rum, White	Kaua'i White	Kōloa Rum Company, HI
Rum, White	Powder™ White Rum	Syntax Spirits LLC, CO
Rum, White	Railean Texas White Rum	Railean Distillers, TX
Rum, White	Sailboat White Rum	Minhas Micro Distillery, WI
Rum, White	Stars White Rum	Minhas Micro Distillery, WI
Rum, White	Taildragger White Rum	Tailwinds Distilling Company, IL
Rum, White	Three Sheets White Rum	Ballast Point Spirits, CA
Rum, White	Urban White Rum	Urban Distilleries, BC Canada
Rum, White Light	White Light Rum	Dogfish Head Craft Brewery, DE
Rumble	Rumble	Balcones Distillery, TX
Rumble	Rumble Cask Reserve	Balcones Distillery, TX
Rumskey	White Rumskey	Las Vegas Distillery, NV
Rye	Bad Rock Rye	Glacier Distilling Company, MT
Rye	Feisty Spirits Rye	Feisty Spirits, CO
Rye	Few Rye	Few Spirits LLC, IL

Rye	Glacier Dew Rye Spirit	Glacier Distilling Company, MT
Rye	Hooker's House General's Reserve	HelloCello, CA
Rye	Hooker's House Rye	HelloCello, CA
Rye	Monterey Rye	Fog's End Distillery, CA
Rye	Nine Square Rye	Elm City Distillery LLC, CT
Rye	Prince Edward Canadian Rye	Prince Edward Distillery, PE Canada
Rye	Widow Jane Rye	Cacao Prieto LLC, NY
Rye	Willett Family Estate Bottled Rye	Willett Distillery, KY
Rye	Smooth Ambler Old Scout Straight Rye	Smooth Ambler Spirits Company, WV
Rye, Organic	Bainbridge Rolling Bay Organic Rye	Bainbridge Organic Distillers, WA
Rye, Organic	Blue Flame Rye	Blue Flame Spirits, WA
Schnapps, Beer	Moylan's Distilling Beer Schnapps	Stillwater Spirits, CA
Spirit	1512 Spirits Signature Poitin	1512 Spirits, CA
Spirit	Black Sam	Black Sam Distillery Co., WA
Spirit	Botanica Spiritvs	Falcon Spirits LLC, CA
Spirit	Civilized Sakura	Northern United Brew. Co. & Distilling, MI
Spirit	Down & Dirty	Black Sam Distillery Co., WA
Spirit	Mamajuana	Cacao Prieto LLC, NY
Spirit	Prairie Moonshine™ Corn & Honey Spirit	Quincy Street Distillery, IL
Spirit	Prairie Sunshine™ Wildflower Honey Spirit	Quincy Street Distillery, IL
Spirit	Prohibition Spirits	Valley Spirits LLC, CA
Spirit	Rex Velvet Sinister Spirit	Freemont Mischief, WA
Spirit	River Baron Artisan Spirit	Mississippi River Distilling Company, IA
Spirit	Sorghum Barrel Aged	Heartland Distillers, IN
Spirit	Sorghum White	Heartland Distillers, IN
Spirit	Spiked Apple Spirits	Panther Distillery, MN
Spirit	Uncle Don's Shining Spirits	Uncle Don's Apple Pie Craft Distillery, MI
Spirit	Whistling Andy Hopshnop	Whistling Andy Distillery, MT
Spirit	White Dragon Shochu	66 Gilead Distillery, ON Canada
Spirit	White Wolf Apple Neutral Spirit	White Wolf Distillery, WI
Spirit	White Wolf Grape Neutral Spirit	White Wolf Distillery, WI
Spirit	Legendary Gold Honey Spirit	Swanson's Mtn. View Apl. Orch.Distill., MT

Spirit, Apple	Still Cellars Apple Cinnamon	Still Cellars, CO
Spirit, Apple	Still Cellars Apple Ginger	Still Cellars, CO
Spirit, Apple	Still Cellars Apple Straightup	Still Cellars, CO
Spirit, Beet	Sidetrack Distillery BETE (a beet spirit)	Sidetrack Distillery, WA
Spirit, Bierbrand	Koval Bierbrand Spirit	Koval Distillery, IL
Spirit, Citrus	Marion Black 106	Fish Hawk Spirits LLC, FL
Spirit, Fig	Mahia	Nahmias et Fils, NY
Spirit, Flavored Pumpkin	Great Lakes Seasonal Pumpkin Spirit	Great Lakes Distillery LLC, WI
Spirit, Herbal	Underground Herbal Spirit	Ogden's Own Distillery, UT
Spirit, Hmong Rice	Yerlo (120 Proof)	Lo Artisan Distillery LLC, WI
Spirit, Hmong Rice	Yerlo Reserve (130 Proof)	Lo Artisan Distillery LLC, WI
Spirit, Hmong Rice	Yerlo X Whisky (90 Proof)	Lo Artisan Distillery LLC, WI
Spirit, Maple Aged	Maple Specialty Spirit	Elm Brook Farm, VT
Spirit, Rice	Vinn Baijiu (pronounced "By-Je-oh")	Vinn Distillery, OR
Spirit, Rice	Vinn Mijiu (pronounced "Mee-Je-oh") Fire	Vinn Distillery, OR
Spirit, Rice	Vinn Mijiu (pronounced "Mee-Je-oh") Ice	Vinn Distillery, OR
Spirit, Rye	Wasmund's Rye Spirit	Copper Fox Distillery, VA
Spirit, Single Malt	Wasmund's Single Malt Spirit	Copper Fox Distillery, VA
Spirit, Sour Mash	Ivy Mountain Georgia Sour Mash Spirits™	Ivy Mountain Distillery LLC, GA
Spirit, Wheat	Myer Farm Strawberry-Mint Wheat Spirit	Myer Farm Distillers, NY
Spirit, Wheat	Myer Farm White Dog Wheat Spirit	Myer Farm Distillers, NY
Sugarshine	Rougaroux Sugarshine	Donner-Peltier Distillers, LA
Tequila Blanco	Charbay Tequila Blanco	Charbay Winery & Distillery, CA
Vodka	18 Vodka	Virtuoso Distillers LLC
Vodka	1911 Vodka	Beak & Skiff Distillery, NY
Vodka	2bar Vodka	2bar® Spirits, WA
Vodka	44° North Magic Valley Vodka	44° North Vodka, ID
Vodka	45th Parallel Vodka	45th Parallel Spirits LLC, WI
Vodka	9 Rocks Vodka	Black Rock Distillery LLC, OR
Vodka	Adirondack ADK Vodka	Adirondack Distilling Company, NY
Vodka	Aeroplano Vodka	Good Spirits Distilling, KS
Vodka	Alchemist Distillery Vodka	Alchemist Distilleries Inc., FL

Vodka	Alpen Glow	Lake Placid Spirits LLC, NY
Vodka	American Vodka	Arizona High Spirits Distillery
Vodka	Aristo Vodka	Minhas Micro Distillery, WI
Vodka	B4 Premium Handcrafted Vodka	Carbon Glacier Distillery, WA
Vodka	Baker Beach San Francisco Vodka	Treasure Island Distillery, CA
Vodka	Bakon Vodka	Black Rock Spirits LLC, WA
Vodka	Bardenay Vodka	Bardenay Inc., ID
Vodka	Barr Hill Vodka	Caledonia Spirits Inc., VT
Vodka	Batch 206 Vodka	Batch 206, WA
Vodka	Beauport Vodka	Ryan & Wood Inc., MA
Vodka	BEE Vodka	Hidden Marsh Distillery, NY
Vodka	Big Gun Vodka	Uncle Don's Apple Pie Craft Distillery, MI
Vodka	Blackstone Vodka USA	Minhas Micro Distillery, WI
Vodka	Blue Flame Ultra Premium Vodka	Blue Flame Spirits, WA
Vodka	Blue Flame Vodka	Blue Flame Spirits, WA
Vodka	Blue Hen Vodka	Dogfish Head Craft Brewery, DE
Vodka	Blue Hen Vodka Infusions	Dogfish Head Craft Brewery, DE
Vodka	Boathouse Vodka	Boathouse Distillery, CO
Vodka	BOHICA Vodka	Mystic Mountain Distillery LLC, CO
Vodka	Bootlegger 21 Vodka	Prohibition Distillery LLC, NY
Vodka	Brandon's Vodka	Rock Town Distillery Inc., AR
Vodka	Buckeye Vodka	Crystal Spirits LLC, OH
Vodka	Bully Boy Vodka	Bully Boy Distillers, MA
Vodka	Canadian Pine Vodka	66 Gilead Distillery, ON Canada
Vodka	Cane Vodka	The Florida Distillery, FL
Vodka	Cardinal Sin Vodka	St. Louis Distillery, MO
Vodka	Cathead Vodka	Cathead Distillery LLC, MS
Vodka	CD Vodka	Mid-Oak Distillery, IL
Vodka	Chambers Bay Craft Distilled Vodka	Port Steilacoom Distillery, WA
Vodka	Charbay Vodka	Charbay Winery & Distillery, CA
Vodka	Chase Nebraska Vodka	Cooper's Chase Distillery LLC, NE
Vodka	Chili Vodka	Arizona High Spirits Distillery

Vodka	China Beach San Francisco Vodka	Treasure Island Distillery, CA
Vodka	Chuckanut Bay Vodka	Chuckanut Bay Distillery, WA
Vodka	Cinco ~ The Five Star Vodka	Azar Distillery, TX
Vodka	Civilized Vodka	Northern United Brew. Co. & Distill., MI
Vodka	Class V™ Vodka	Syntax Spirits LLC, CO
Vodka	CLEAR10 Vodka	Good Spirits Distilling, KS
Vodka	ClearHeart Vodka	Cedar Ridge Distillery, IA
Vodka	Cold House Vodka	Valley Spirits LLC, CA
Vodka	Cold River Classic Vodka	Maine Distilleries LLC, ME
Vodka	Colorado Blue Vodka	Mystic Mountain Distillery LLC, CO
Vodka	Colorado Crystal Vodka	Mystic Mountain Distillery LLC, CO
Vodka	Colorado Gold Premium Vodka	Colorado Gold Distillery, CO
Vodka	COMB Vodka	StilltheOne Distillery LLC, NY
Vodka	Core Vodka	Harvest Spirits LLC, NY
Vodka	Coyote Vodka	Spirits of the USA LLC, FL
Vodka	Crater Lake Reserve Vodka	Bendistillery, OR
Vodka	Crater Lake Vodka	Bendistillery, OR
Vodka	Crown Valley Vodka	Crown Valley Distilling Company, MO
Vodka	Czar	Good Spirits Distilling, KS
Vodka	Dancing Tree Vodka from grains	Dancing Tree Distillery, OH
Vodka	Dancing Tree Vodka from grapes	Dancing Tree Distillery, OH
Vodka	Death's Door Vodka	Death's Door Spirits, WI
Vodka	Deep Run Virginia Vodka	A. Smith Bowman Distillery, VA
Vodka	Deer Camp Vodka	Northern Latitudes Distillery, MI
Vodka	Desert Diamond Distillery Gold Miner Vodka	Desert Diamond Distillery, AZ
Vodka	DiVine Vodka	Entente Spirits LLC, MI
Vodka	Dizzythree Expresso Vodka	Good Spirits Distilling, KS
Vodka	DL Franklin Vodka	Dogwood Distiling, OR
Vodka	Dog Watch Vodka	Ye Ol' Grog Distillery, OR
Vodka	Door County Vodka	Door County Distillery, WI
Vodka	Double Silo (160 Proof)	Project V Distill. Sausage Company, WA
Vodka	Dripping Springs Texas Vodka	San Luis Spirits, TX

499

Type	Product	Distillery
Vodka	Dry County Vodka	Dry County Distillery LLC, WA
Vodka	Dutchess Vodka	New Holland Artisan Spirits, MI
Vodka	Ebb+Flow Vodka	Sound Spirits, WA
Vodka	Elevate Vodka	Mile High Spirits LLC, CO
Vodka	Elk Rider Vodka	Heritage Distilling Company Inc., WA
Vodka	Enchanted Rock Vodka	Rebecca Creek Distillery LLC, TX
Vodka	Esprit de Krewe™ Vodka	Rollins Distillery, FL
Vodka	Finn Huckleberry Vodka	Black Heron Spirits Distillery, WA
Vodka	Fire Puncher Vodka	GrandTen Distilling, MA
Vodka	Firefly Handcrafted Vodka	Firefly Distillery, SC
Vodka	Five Wives Sinful Vodka	Ogden's Own Distillery, UT
Vodka	Five Wives Vodka	Ogden's Own Distillery, UT
Vodka	Flathead Vodka	The Montana Distillery, MT
Vodka	Frizz Vodka	Merridale Ciderworks Corp., BC Canada
Vodka	Frostbite Alaska Vodka	Alaska Distillery, AK
Vodka	Fugu Vodka	Ballast Point Spirits, CA
Vodka	General John Stark Vodka	Flag Hill Winery & Distillery, NH
Vodka	Georgia Vodka	Georgia Distilling Company, GA
Vodka	Glass Vodka	Glass Distillery, WA
Vodka	Goat Artisan Vodka	Peach Street Distillers, CO
Vodka	Grand Teton Vodka	Grand Teton Distillery, ID
Vodka	Great North Vodka	Trailhead Spirits, MT
Vodka	Green Geisha	Hard Times Distillery LLC, OR
Vodka	Grey Heron Vodka	St. Julian Winery, MI
Vodka	Gridiron Vodka	Glass Distillery, WA
Vodka	Hawaiian Vodka	Island Distillers Inc., HI
Vodka	HDC Vodka	Heritage Distilling Company Inc., WA
Vodka	Heartland Distiller's Reserve Vodka	Heartland Distillers, IN
Vodka	Hex Vodka	Honey House Distillery, CO
Vodka	High Ore Vodka	Headframe Spirits, MT
Vodka	High Roller Premium Vodka	High Roller Spirits, CA
Vodka	High West Vodka 7000	High West Distillery, UT

Vodka	High West Vodka 7000 Peach	High West Distillery, UT
Vodka	Humboldt Distillery Vodka	Humboldt Distillery, CA
Vodka	Ice Dunes Vodka	Northern Latitudes Distillery, MI
Vodka	Ice Fox Vodka	Essential Spirits Alambic Distillery, CA
Vodka	Ice Glen Vodka	Berkshire Mountain Distillers Inc., MA
Vodka	Incentive Vodka	Big Cedar Distilling Inc., MI
Vodka	Indiana Infusions	Heartland Distillers, IN
Vodka	Indiana Vodka	Heartland Distillers, IN
Vodka	Industry City Distillery Batch No. 3	Industry City Distillery Inc., NY
Vodka	Industry City Distillery Batch No. 4	Industry City Distillery Inc., NY
Vodka	Ink Vodka	Black Heron Spirits Distillery, WA
Vodka	Ironworks Vodka	Ironworks Distillery, NS Canada
Vodka	Isis Vodka	Mac Donald Distillery, WA
Vodka	Joss Vodka	Sólas Distillery, NE
Vodka	Klondike Vodka	Klondike River Distillery, YT Canada
Vodka	Last Mountain Vodka	Last Mountain Distillery Ltd., SK Canada
Vodka	Letterpress Vodka	Letterpress Distilling, WA
Vodka	Literary Dog Maple Based Premium Sipping Vodka	Elm Brook Farm, VT
Vodka	Literary Dog Premium Sipping Vodka	Elm Brook Farm, VT
Vodka	LiV Vodka	Long Island Spirits, NY
Vodka	Long Table Distillery Texada Vodka	Long Table Distillery Ltd., BC Canada
Vodka	Loyal 9 Vodka	Sons of Liberty Spirits Co., RI
Vodka	Lucky Bastard Vodka	LB Distillers, SK Canada
Vodka	Luminous Vodka	Door County Distillery, WI
Vodka	Mastermind Vodka	Mastermind Vodka, IL
Vodka	Medoyeff Vodka	Bull Run Distilling Company, OR
Vodka	Midwest Vodka	45th Parallel Spirits LLC, WI
Vodka	Miss Kitty's Velvet Vodka	Good Spirits Distilling, KS
Vodka	Mojo Vodka	Saint James Spirits, CA
Vodka	Mount Baker Vodka	Mount Baker Distillery, WA
Vodka	Mount Snow Vodka	Vermont Distillers, VT
Vodka	Myer Farm Blueberry Orange Vodka	Myer Farm Distillers, NY

501

Vodka	Myer Farm Ginger Vodka	Myer Farm Distillers, NY
Vodka	Myer Farm Vodka	Myer Farm Distillers, NY
Vodka	Napa Vodka Vintage Reserve	Napa Valley Distillery, CA
Vodka	Nashoba Vodka	Nashoba Valley Spirits Ltd., MA
Vodka	Nevada Vodka	Churchill Vineyards and Distillery, NV
Vodka	Nevada Vodka	Las Vegas Distillery, NV
Vodka	New Deal Vodka	New Deal Distillery, OR
Vodka	North Shore Vodka	North Shore Distillery, IL
Vodka	Ocean Beach San Francisco Vodka	Treasure Island Distillery, CA
Vodka	Ocean Vodka	Hawaii Sea Spirits, LLC, HI
Vodka	Okanagan Spirits Vodka	Okanagan Spirits, BC Canada
Vodka	Oola Chili Pepper Vodka	Oola Distillery, WA
Vodka	Oola Citrus Vodka	Oola Distillery, WA
Vodka	Oola Rosemary Vodka	Oola Distillery, WA
Vodka	Oola Vodka	Oola Distillery, WA
Vodka	Organic Nation Vodka	Cascade Peak Spirits Distillery, OR
Vodka	Orysa Vodka	Donner-Peltier Distillers, LA
Vodka	OYO Stone Fruit Vodka	Middle West Spirits LLC, OH
Vodka	OYO Vodka	Middle West Spirits LLC, OH
Vodka	P3 Placid Vodka	Lake Placid Spirits LLC, NY
Vodka	Peabody Jones™ Vodka	Woodinville Whiskey Co., WA
Vodka	Peace Vodka	Catskill Distilling Company Ltd., NY
Vodka	Permafrost Alaska Vodka	Alaska Distillery, AK
Vodka	Phrog Premium Vodka	Island Spirits Distillery, BC Canada
Vodka	Pinckney Ben American Vodka	Pinckney Bend Distillery, MO
Vodka	Plantation Vodka	Thirteenth Colony Distilleries, GA
Vodka	Prairie Wolf Vodka	Prairie Wolf Spirits, OK
Vodka	Prince Igor Vodka	Forty Creek Distillery, ON Canada
Vodka	Pure Blue Vodka	Barrel House Distilling Co., KY
Vodka	Quicksilver Vodka	Montgomery Distillery, MT
Vodka	Rain Ciy Vodka	Rain City Spirits, WA
Vodka	RE:FIND Vodka	RE:FIND Distillery, CA

Type	Product	Distillery
Vodka	Real Russian Vodka	Premier Distillery LLC, IL
Vodka	Red Arrow Vodka	Journeyman Distillery, MI
Vodka	Referent Vodka	45th Parallel Spirits LLC, WI
Vodka	Rehorst Premium Milwaukee Vodka	Great Lakes Distillery LLC, WI
Vodka	Rider Vodka	Dark Horse Distillery, KS
Vodka	Rime Organic Vodka	Westford Hill Distillers, CT
Vodka	Ringneck Vodka	Dakota Spirits Distillery LLC, SC
Vodka	River Pilot Vodka	Mississippi River Distilling Company, IA
Vodka	RMD Vodka	Artesian Distillers, MI
Vodka	Rogue Vintage Vodka	Rogue Spirits, OR
Vodka	Rx Vodka	Kill Devil Spirit Company, CA
Vodka	S.D. Strong Vodka	S.D. Strong Distilling, MO
Vodka	SAAVY Vodka	SAVVY Distillers L.P., TX
Vodka	Seven Brothers Vodka	Seven Brothers Distilling Company, OH
Vodka	Silver Tree American Small Batch Vodka	Leopold Bros., CO
Vodka	Singing Whale Vodka	Dark Moon Artisan Distillery, WA
Vodka	Single Silo Chai Infused Vodka	Project V Distillery Sausage Company, WA
Vodka	Single Silo Distiller's Cut Vodka	Project V Distillery Sausage Company, WA
Vodka	Single Silo Ultra Filtered Vodka	Project V Distillery Sausage Company, WA
Vodka	Single Silo Vodka	Project V Distillery Sausage Company, WA
Vodka	Six Mile Creek Vodka	Six Mile Creek Winery & Distillery, NY
Vodka	SlapTail Vodka	4 Spirits Distillery, OR
Vodka	Sloop Betty	Blackwater Distilling Inc., MD
Vodka	Smiths Premium Vodka	Bone Spirits, TX
Vodka	Smooth Ambler Whitewater Vodka	Smooth Ambler Spirits Company, WV
Vodka	Smugglers' Notch Vodka	Smuggler's Notch Distillery, VT
Vodka	Snow Creek Vodka	Collier and McKeel, TN
Vodka	Snowcrest Vodka	Willie's Distillery, MT
Vodka	Snowflake Vodka	Tahoe Moonshine Distillery Inc., CA
Vodka	Soft Tail Vodka	Soft Tail Spirits, WA
Vodka	Solano Vodka	HelloCello, CA
Vodka	Solstice Infused Vodka	Yukon Spirits, YT Canada

Vodka	Southern Son Vodka	JEM Beverage Company, TX
Vodka	Southern Vodka	Thirteenth Colony Distilleries, GA
Vodka	Space City Vodka	Whitmeyer's Distilling Co. LLC, TX
Vodka	Speakeasy Vodka	Meriwether Distilling Co., WA
Vodka	Spike Vodka	Spink Distillery, TX
Vodka	Spirit Bear Espresso Vodka	Urban Distilleries, BC Canada
Vodka	Spirit Bear Vodka	Urban Distilleries, BC Canada
Vodka	Spirit of Santa Fe Vodka	Don Quixote Distillery & Winery, NM
Vodka	Spirits of the Blue Ridge Vodka	Chesapeake Bay Distillery LLC, VA
Vodka	Spring44 Vodka	Spring44 Distilling, CO
Vodka	Starlite Vodka	Treaty Oak Distilling Co., TX
Vodka	Stars Vodka	Minhas Micro Distillery, WI
Vodka	Still Cellars Vodka	Still Cellars, CO
Vodka	Stillwater Spirits Vodka 100°	Stillwater Spirits, CA
Vodka	Stillwater Spirits Vodka 80°	Stillwater Spirits, CA
Vodka	Stoutridge Vodka	Stoutridge Distillery, NY
Vodka	Strait Vodka	Myriad View Artis. Distill. Inc., PE Canada
Vodka	Sun Liquor Unxld Vodka	Sun Liquor Distillery, WA
Vodka	Superfly Vodka	Superfly Distilling Company, OR
Vodka	Tailgater's Vodka	Good Spirits Distilling, KS
Vodka	the Rocket Vodka	Seattle Distilling Company, WA
Vodka	The Vodka	Ransom Spirits, OR
Vodka	Thunderbeast Stampede Vodka	Mad Buffalo Distillery, MO
Vodka	Tito's Handmade Vodka	Tito's Handmade Vodka, TX
Vodka	TOPO Vodka	Top of the Hill Distillery, NC
Vodka	Touch Vodka-Original	Fat Dog Spirits LLC, FL
Vodka	Trail Town Still Colorado Vodka	Trail Town Still, CO
Vodka	Tree Vodka	Celk Distilling, NY
Vodka	Triple Eight Vodka	Triple Eight Distillery, MA
Vodka	Troubador Vodka	The Original Texas Legend Distillery, TX
Vodka	True North Vodka	Grand Traverse Distillery, MI
Vodka	Truuli Peak Vodka	Bare Distillery, AK

Vodka	Twenty 2 True Micro Distilled Vodka	Northern Maine Distill. Co., ME
Vodka	Twister Vodka	Good Spirits Distilling, KS
Vodka	Two James Vodka	Two James Spirits, MI
Vodka	U4RIK Grape based Vodka	Essential Spirits Alambic Distillery, CA
Vodka	Ugly Dog Vodka	Ugly Dog Distillery LLC, MI
Vodka	Ugly Dog Whipped Cream Vodka	Ugly Dog Distillery LLC, MI
Vodka	Valentine Vodka	Valentine Distilling Company, MI
Vodka	Velocipede Vodka	Elm City Distillery LLC, CT
Vodka	Vermont Gold Vodka	Vermont Spirits Distilling Co., VT
Vodka	Vermont Spirits Limited Release Vodka	Vermont Spirits Distilling Co., VT
Vodka	Vermont White Vodka	Vermont Spirits Distilling Co., VT
Vodka	Viezbicke 303 Vodka	Boulder Distillery, CO
Vodka	Vin Vodka	Vinn Distillery, OR
Vodka	Vintner's Vodka	Finger Lakes Distilling, NY
Vodka	Viscova	Double V Distillery, WA
Vodka	Vivacity Fine Vodka	Vivcity Spirits, OR
Vodka	Vodka	It's 5 Artisan Distillery, WA
Vodka	Vodka 14	Altitude Spirits, CO
Vodka	Vodka Morava	Cal-Czech Distillery, CA
Vodka	Vodka Viracocha	Rancho de Los Luceros Destilaria, NM
Vodka	VR Vodka	Rocky Mountain Distilling Co., CO
Vodka	Walla Walla Vodka	Walla Walla Distilling Company, WA
Vodka	Watershed Distillery Vodka	Watershed Distillery, OH
Vodka	WebFoot Vodka	4 Spirits Distillery, OR
Vodka	Western Son Texas Vodka	JEM Beverage Company, TX
Vodka	Whistling Andy Vodka	Whistling Andy Distillery, MT
Vodka	White Owl Vodka	Six Owls Spirits, NS Canada
Vodka	Wishkah River Distillery Vodka Distilled from Grains	Wishkah River Distillery, WA
Vodka	Wishkah River Distillery Vodka Distilled from Honey	Wishkah River Distillery, WA
Vodka	Woodstone Creek Vodka	Woodstone Creek, OH
Vodka	Woody Creek Distillers Reserve Stobrawa Vodka	Woody Creek Distillers, CO
Vodka	Yahara Bay Premium Vodka	Yahara Bay Distillers, WI

Vodka	BelleWood Vodka	Bellewood Distilling, WA
Vodka	Buck 25 Vodka	Atelier Vie, LA
Vodka	Loyal 9 Seasonal Vodkas	Sons of Liberty Spirits Co., RI
Vodka	Portland 88 Vodka	New Deal Distillery, OR
Vodka, Apple	Apple Knocker	Dark Moon Artisan Distillery, WA
Vodka, Bacon	Ugly Dog Bacon Vodka	Ugly Dog Distillery LLC, MI
Vodka, Birch Syrup	Alaska Distillery Birch Syrup Vodka	Alaska Distillery, AK
Vodka, Blueberry	Cane Vodka Buccaneer Blueberry	The Florida Distillery, FL
Vodka, Blueberry	Cold River Blueberry Vodka	Maine Distilleries LLC, ME
Vodka, Cane	Downslope Cane Vodka	Downslope Distilling, CO
Vodka, Chai Tea	Seraphine Chai Tea Vodka	Yahara Bay Distillers, WI
Vodka, Cherry	44° North Rainier Cherry Vodka	44° North Vodka, ID
Vodka, Citrus	Cirrus Vodka	Parched Group LLC, VA
Vodka, Citrus	Dutchess Citrus Vodka	New Holland Artisan Spirits, MI
Vodka, Citrus	Sol Chamomile Citrus Vodka	North Shore Distillery, IL
Vodka, Coconut	Hawaiian Coconut Vodka	Island Distillers Inc., HI
Vodka, Corn	Don Quixote Blue Corn Vodka	Don Quixote Distillery & Winery, NM
Vodka, Flav. Apple	Indigenous Vodka: Fresh Pressed Apple	Tuthilltown Spirits Distillery, NY
Vodka, Flav. Apple	Maple River Distillery Apple Flavored Vodka	Maple River Distillery, ND
Vodka, Flav. Apricot	Maple River Distillery Apricot Flavored Vodka	Maple River Distillery, ND
Vodka, Flav. Cherry	True North Cherry Flavored Vodka	Grand Traverse Distillery, MI
Vodka, Flav. Chocolate.	Mud Puddle Chocolate Vodka	New Deal Distillery, OR
Vodka, Flav. Chocolate	True North Chocolate Flavored Vodka	Grand Traverse Distillery, MI
Vodka, Flav. Chokecherry	Maple River Distillery Chokecherry Flavored Vodka	Maple River Distillery, ND
Vodka, Flav. Citrus Honey	Rehorst Citrus Honey Flavored Vodka	Great Lakes Distillery LLC, WI
Vodka, Flav. Coffee	Glass Kona Coffee Vodka	Glass Distillery, WA
Vodka, Flav. Elderflower	Valentine White Blossom Elderflower Flavored Vodka	Valentine Distilling Company, MI
Vodka, Flav. Garlic	Hot Stinkin' Garlic Vodka	Tahoe Moonshine Distillery Inc., CA
Vodka, Flav. Grape	Maple River Distillery Grape Flavored Vodka	Maple River Distillery, ND
Vodka, Flav. Hazle. Espr.	Crater Lake Hazelnut Espresso Vodka	Bendistillery, OR
Vodka, Flav. Hi. B. Cranb.	Alaska Distillery High Bush Cranberry Vodka	Alaska Distillery, AK
Vodka, Flav. Hunkleberry	Koenig Huckleberry Flavored Vodka	Koenig Distillery, ID

Vodka, Flav. Jalapeño	Coyote Jalapeño Flavored Vodka	Spirits of the USA LLC, FL
Vodka, Flav. Key Lime	Touch Key Lime Flavored Vodka	Fat Dog Spirits LLC, FL
Vodka, Flav. Lemon	Lemon Vodka	Bardenay Inc., ID
Vodka, Flav. Lw. Bu.Blub.	Alaska Distillery Low Bush Blueberry Vodka	Alaska Distillery
Vodka, Flav. Mango	Coyote Mango Flavored Vodka	Spirits of the USA LLC, FL
Vodka, Flav. Oran. Touch	Valencia Orange Flavored Vodka	Fat Dog Spirits LLC, FL
Vodka, Flav. Peach Tea	Firefly Peach Tea Vodka	Firefly Distillery, SC
Vodka, Flav. Pear	Maple River Distillery Pear Flavored Vodka	Maple River Distillery, ND
Vodka, Flav. Pepper	Crater Lake Pepper Vodka	Bendistillery, OR
Vodka, Flav. Pepper	Hot Monkey Pepper Vodka	New Deal Distillery, OR
Vodka, Flav. Pepper	Perky Pepper™ Pepper Flavored Vodka	Syntax Spirits LLC, CO
Vodka, Flav. Peppermint	Coyote Ice Peppermint Flavored Vodka	Spirits of the USA LLC, FL
Vodka, Flav. Red Grapefr.	Touch Red Grapefruit Flavored Vodka	Fat Dog Spirits LLC, FL
Vodka, Flav. Red Rasp.	Alaska Distillery Red Raspberry Vodka	Alaska Distillery, AK
Vodka, Flav. Rhubarb	Alaska Distillery Rhubarb Vodka	Alaska Distillery, AK
Vodka, Flav. Rhubarb	Maple River Distillery Rhubarb Flavored Vodka	Maple River Distillery, ND
Vodka, Flav. Sm. Salmon	Alaska Distillery Smoked Salmon Vodka	Alaska Distillery, AK
Vodka, Flav. Sweet Ginger	Crater Lake Sweet Ginger Vodka	Bendistillery, OR
Vodka, Flav. Sweet Tea	Firefly Skinny Tea	Firefly Distillery, SC
Vodka, Flav. Sweet Tea	Firefly Sweet Tea Flavored Vodka	Firefly Distillery, SC
Vodka, Flav. Texas Tea	Graham's Texas Tea	Treaty Oak Distilling Co., TX
Vodka, Flav. Watermelon	Rocky Ford Watermelon Vodka	Breckenridge Distillery, CO
Vodka, Flav. Wild Blueb.	Alaska Distillery Wild Blackberry Vodka	Alaska Distillery, AK
Vodka, Flav. Wild Plum	Maple River Distillery Wild Plum Flavored Vodka	Maple River Distillery, ND
Vodka, Grain	Downslope Grain Vodka	Downslope Distilling, CO
Vodka, Grain	Seven Grain Vodka	Las Vegas Distillery, NV
Vodka, Grape	Cane Vodka Gator Grape	The Florida Distillery, FL
Vodka, Hemp	Left Coast Hemp Vodka	Victoria Spirits, BC Canada
Vodka, Hemp	Mary Jane's Primo Hemp Vodka	Mary Jane's, ON Canada
Vodka, Hemp Seed	Purgatory Hemp Seed Vodka	Alaska Distillery, AK
Vodka, Honey	Barr Hill Honey Vodka	Caledonia Spirits Inc., VT
Vodka, Honey	Spring44 Honey Vodka	Spring44 Distilling, CO

Vodka, Honeysuckle	Cathead Honeysuckle Vodka	Cathead Distillery LLC, MS
Vodka, Huckleberry	44° North Mountain Huckleberry Vodka	44° North Vodka, ID
Vodka, Infused Cherry	Cherry Infused Flathead Vodka	The Montana Distillery, MT
Vodka, Infused Cherry	Door County Cherry Infused Vodka	Door County Distillery, WI
Vodka, Infused Coffee	Coffee Infused Flathead Vodka	The Montana Distillery, MT
Vodka, Kosher	No. 209 Kosher-for-Passover Vodka	Distillery No. 209, CA
Vodka, Mint	Batch 206 Mad Mint Vodka	Batch 206, WA
Vodka, Orange	Cane Vodka Orlando Orange	The Florida Distillery, FL
Vodka, Organic	Bainbridge Legacy Organic Vodka	Bainbridge Organic Distillers, WA
Vodka, Organic	Bluewater Organic Vodka	Bluewater Distilling, WA
Vodka, Organic	Green Mountain Organic Sunshine Vodka	Green Mountain Distillers, VT
Vodka, Organic	Prairie Organic Vodka	Phillips Distilling Company, MN
Vodka, Organic	TRU Organic Vodka	GreenBar Collective, CA
Vodka, Organic	CapRock® Organic Vodka	Peak Spirits® Farm Distillery, CO
Vodka, Organic Lemon	Green Mountain Organic Lemon Vodka	Green Mountain Distillers, VT
Vodka, Organic Orange	Green Mountain Organic Orange Vodka	Green Mountain Distillers, VT
Vodka, Peanut Butter	Peanut Butter Vodka	Tahoe Moonshine Distillery Inc., CA
Vodka, Pear	Prickly Pear Vodka	Arizona High Spirits Distillery, AZ
Vodka, Pepper	Blue Flame Peppered Vodka	Blue Flame Spirits, WA
Vodka, Pepper	Brushfire Pepper Vodka	Black Heron Spirits Distillery, WA
Vodka, Pepper	Downslope Pepper Vodka	Downslope Distilling, CO
Vodka, Potato	Boyd & Blair Potato Vodka (80 proof)	Pennsylvania Pure Distilleries LLC, PA
Vodka, Potato	Boyd & Blair Professional Proof 151 Potato Vodka	Pennsylvania Pure Distilleries LLC, PA
Vodka, Potato	Koenig Potato Vodka	Koenig Distillery, ID
Vodka, Potato	Portland Potato Vodka	Eastside Distilling, OR
Vodka, Potato	Prince Edward Potato Vodka	Prince Edward Distillery, PE Canada
Vodka, Potato	Schramm Organic Potato Vodka	Pemberton Distillery Inc., BC Canada
Vodka, Potato	Skip Rock Potato Vodka	Skip Rock Distillers, WA
Vodka, Potato	Woody Creek Distillers 100 % Colorado Potato Vodka	Woody Creek Distillers, CO
Vodka, Raspberry	Ugly Dog Raspberry Vodka	Ugly Dog Distillery LLC, MI
Vodka, Rye	Canadian Rye Vodka	66 Gilead Distillery, ON Canada
Vodka, Rye	Penn 1681 Rye Vodka	Philadelphia Distilling, PA

Vodka, Rye	T & W V6 Rye Vodka	Empire Winery & Distillery, FL
Vodka, Saffron	Sub Rosa Saffron Vodka	Sub Rosa Spirits, OR
Vodka, Single Malt	Ezra Cox Single Malt Vodka	Ezra Cox Distillery, WA
Vodka, Single Malt	Still Waters Single Malt Vodka	Still Waters Distillery, ON Canada
Vodka, Strawberry	Cane Vodka Plant City Strawberry	The Florida Distillery, FL
Vodka, Tarragon	Sub Rosa Tarragon Vodka	Sub Rosa Spirits, OR
Vodka, Vanilla	Corsair Vanilla Vodka	Corsair Artisan Distillery, TN
Vodka, Vanilla Bean	OYO Honey Vanilla Bean Vodka	Middle West Spirits LLC, OH
Vodka, Vodka	46 Peaks Potato Vodka	Lake Placid Spirits LLC, NY
Vodka, Wheat	Dry Fly Washington Wheat Vodka	Dry Fly Distilling, WA
Vodka, Wheat	Spirit of St. Louis Midwest Spring Wheat Vodka	Square One Brewery and Distillery, MO
Vodka, Wheat	Wheat Vodka	Grand Traverse Distillery, MI
Vodka, Wheat	Whole Wheat Vodka	66 Gilead Distillery, ON Canada
Vodka, Wild Berry	Vintner's Wild Berry Vodka	Finger Lakes Distilling, NY
Vokda, Wild Blueberry	Prince Edward Wild Blueberry Vodka	Prince Edward Distillery, PE Canada
Whiskey	1816 Cask	Chattanooga Whiskey Company, TN
Whiskey	1816 Reserve	Chattanooga Whiskey Company, TN
Whiskey	291 American Whiskey	Distillery 291, CO
Whiskey	291 Fresh Colorado Whiskey (corn, unaged)	Distillery 291, CO
Whiskey	77 Whiskey	Breuckelen Distilling Company Inc., NY
Whiskey	Abraham Bowman Limited Edition Whiskey	A. Smith Bowman Distillery, VA
Whiskey	Alchemist Distillery Whiskey	Alchemist Distilleries Inc., FL
Whiskey	American Whiskey	StiL 630, MO
Whiskey	Barrel Master	StiL 630, MO
Whiskey	Bear Creek Alaska Whiskey	Alaska Distillery, AK
Whiskey	Belle Meade Manhattan	Nelson's Green Brier Distillery, TN
Whiskey	Belle Meade Mint Julep	Nelson's Green Brier Distillery, TN
Whiskey	Benjamin Prichard's Tennessee Whiskey	Prichard's Distillery Inc., TN
Whiskey	Bighorn Whiskey	Willie's Distillery, MT
Whiskey	Black Canyon Rita	Black Canyon Distillery, CO
Whiskey	Blackjack Aces High Whiskey	Mystic Mountain Distillery LLC, CO
Whiskey	Blended Whiskey	Dakota Spirits Distillery LLC, SC

509

Whiskey	Boathouse Whiskey	Boathouse Distillery, CO
Whiskey	Bourbon Whiskey	Grand Traverse Distillery, MI
Whiskey	Bowen's Whiskey	Bowen's Spirits Inc., CA
Whiskey	Brown Dog Whiskey	AEppelTreow Winery & Distillery, WI
Whiskey	Bully Boy American Straight Whiskey	Bully Boy Distillers, MA
Whiskey	Charbay Whiskey, Release II	Charbay Winery & Distillery, CA
Whiskey	Cherry Bomb Whiskey	Eastside Distilling, OR
Whiskey	Coal Yard New Make Whiskey	Albany Distilling Company, NY
Whiskey	Collier and McKeel Fiery Gizzard Cinnamon Whiskey	Collier and McKeel, TN
Whiskey	Colorado Honey	Honey House Distillery, CO
Whiskey	Copper Run Spirit Whiskey	Copper Run Distillery, MO
Whiskey	Corsair Quinoa Whiskey	Corsair Artisan Distillery, TN
Whiskey	Corsair Rasputin Hopped Whiskey	Corsair Artisan Distillery, TN
Whiskey	Corsair Ryemageddon Whiskey	Corsair Artisan Distillery, TN
Whiskey	Destroying Angel Whiskey	Headframe Spirits, MT
Whiskey	Devil's Share Whiskey	Ballast Point Spirits, CA
Whiskey	Double Down Barley Whiskey	New Holland Artisan Spirits, MI
Whiskey	Downslope Double Diamond Whiskey	Downslope Distilling, CO
Whiskey	Dry Fly Washington Triticale Whiskey	Dry Fly Distilling, WA
Whiskey	Elk Rider Whiskey	Heritage Distilling Company Inc., WA
Whiskey	Estate Rye	Hillrock Estate Distillery, NY
Whiskey	Estate Single Malt	Hillrock Estate Distillery, NY
Whiskey	Feisty Spirits Elementals Whiskey	Feisty Spirits, CO
Whiskey	Few White Whiskey	Few Spirits LLC, IL
Whiskey	Foggy Dog Whiskey	Whiskey Thief Distilling Company, KY
Whiskey	Fortified Belle	Nelson's Green Brier Distillery, TN
Whiskey	Golden Samish Bay Whiskey Reserve	Golden Distillery, WA
Whiskey	Golden White Gold Whiskey	Golden Distillery, WA
Whiskey	Grandaddy Mimm's Whiskey	Georgia Distilling Company, GA
Whiskey	Hardware Distillery Whiskey	The Hardware Distillery Co., WA
Whiskey	Hatter Royale Hopquila	New Holland Artisan Spirits, MI
Whiskey	High West Distillery Barreled Manhattan	High West Distillery, UT

Whiskey	High West Son Of Bourye	High West Distillery, UT
Whiskey	High West Valley Tan	High West Distillery, UT
Whiskey	Hogshead Whiskey	McMenamins Edgefield Distillery, OR
Whiskey	Hoppin' Eights Whiskey	Stone Barn Brandyworks, OR
Whiskey	Hot Mama	Dark Corner Distillery, SC
Whiskey	John Jacob Whiskey	Freemont Mischief, WA
Whiskey	Kinnickinnic Whiskey	Great Lakes Distillery LLC, WI
Whiskey	Kopper Kettle Virginian Whiskey	Belmont Farms Distillery, VA
Whiskey	Legs Diamond Whiskey	Nahmias et Fils, NY
Whiskey	Leopold Bros. American Small Batch Whiskey	Leopold Bros., CO
Whiskey	Lightning Whiskey	Yahara Bay Distillers, WI
Whiskey	Low Gap Clear Whiskey	American Craft Whiskey Distillery, CA
Whiskey	Malthouse Whiskey	New Holland Artisan Spirits, MI
Whiskey	MBR Kentucky Black Patch Whiskey	MB Roland Distillery, KY
Whiskey	McKenzie Pure Potstill Whiskey	Finger Lakes Distilling, NY
Whiskey	McNulty Whiskey	25th Street Spirits, OH
Whiskey	Michigan Spirit Whiskey	Journeyman Distillery, MI
Whiskey	Monkey Puzzle Whiskey	McMenamins Edgefield Distillery, OR
Whiskey	New Age Spirit Whiskey	Tiger Juice Distillery, SC
Whiskey	North Fork Whiskey	Glacier Distilling Company, MT
Whiskey	Old Homicide	Ernest Scarano Distillery, OH
Whiskey	Ole George Whiskey	Grand Traverse Distillery, MI
Whiskey	Oregon Whiskey	Bull Run Distilling Company, OR
Whiskey	Palm Ridge Reserve	Florida Farm Distillers, FL
Whiskey	Pump Trolley Whiskey	Carbon Glacier Distillery, WA
Whiskey	Queen Jennie Sorghum Whiskey	Old Sugar Distillery, WI
Whiskey	Rebecca Creek Fine Texas Whiskey	Rebecca Creek Distillery LLC, TX
Whiskey	Rogue Chipotle Whiskey	Rogue Spirits, OR
Whiskey	Rogue Dead Guy Whiskey	Rogue Spirits, OR
Whiskey	RoughStock Montana Black Label Whiskey	RoughStock Distillery, MT
Whiskey	RoughStock Montana Pure Malt Whiskey	RoughStock Distillery, MT
Whiskey	S.S. Sorghum Whiskey	StiiL 630, MO

Whiskey	Sir Whisquila	StiL 630, MO
Whiskey	Six & Twenty Whiskey "Blue"	Six & Twenty Distillery, SC
Whiskey	Snowflake	Stranahan's CO Whiskey Distillery, CO
Whiskey	Southern Corn Whiskey	Thirteenth Colony Distilleries, GA
Whiskey	Spirit of St. Louis JJ Neukomm Am. Malt Whiskey	Square One Brewery and Distillery, MO
Whiskey	Stocking Stuffer Whiskey	Carbon Glacier Distillery, WA
Whiskey	Stormin' Whiskey	Tahoe Moonshine Distillery Inc., CA
Whiskey	Stranahan's Colorado Whiskey	Stranahan's CO Whiskey Distillery, CO
Whiskey	Tenderfoot Whiskey	Wood's High Mountain Distillery, CO
Whiskey	the Vashon Idle Hour Whiskey	Seattle Distilling Company, WA
Whiskey	Thirteen Corners Virgin Cask American Malt Whiskey	Wishkah River Distillery, WA
Whiskey	Tirado El Caribe Whiskey	Tirado Distillery, NY
Whiskey	Tirado Gold Whiskey	Tirado Distillery, NY
Whiskey	TJ Pottinger Kentucky Whiskey	Limestone Branch Distillery, KY
Whiskey	Tootsie's Apple Pie Whiskey	Georgia Distilling Company, GA
Whiskey	TOPO Carolina Whiskey	Top of the Hill Distillery, NC
Whiskey	Troy & Sons Blonde Whiskey	Asheville Distilling Company, NC
Whiskey	Troy & Sons Oak Reserve Whiskey	Asheville Distilling Company, NC
Whiskey	Troy & Sons Platinum Heirloom Moonshine Whiskey	Asheville Distilling Company, NC
Whiskey	Ty Wolfe Whiskey	Mac Donald Distillery, WA
Whiskey	UPRISING American Whiskey	Sons of Liberty Spirits Co., RI
Whiskey	V Bourbon Whiskey	Yahara Bay Distillers, WI
Whiskey	Valentine Woodward Limited Whiskey	Valentine Distilling Company, MI
Whiskey	Van Brunt Stillhouse Whiskey	Van Brunt Stillhouse, NY
Whiskey	Viezbicke 303 Whiskey	Boulder Distillery, CO
Whiskey	Virginia Gentleman	A. Smith Bowman Distillery, VA
Whiskey	Virginia Lightning Whiskey	Belmont Farms Distillery, VA
Whiskey	War Horn Whiskey	Appalachian Mountain Springs LLC, VA
Whiskey	Washington Select	Double V Distillery, WA
Whiskey	Westchester Whiskey	StilltheOne Distillery LLC, NY
Whiskey	Wheatfish Whiskey	Glacier Distilling Company, MT
Whiskey	Whidbey Island Distillery Whidskey	Whidbey Island Distillery, WA

Whiskey	WhipperSnapper Oregon Spirit Whiskey	Ransom Spirits, OR
Whiskey	Whiskey	Door County Distillery, WI
Whiskey	Whiskey Dick	Ernest Scarano Distillery, OH
Whiskey	Whiskey Is In The Wood	Dancing Tree Distillery, OH
Whiskey	Whistling Andy Harvest Select	Whistling Andy Distillery, MT
Whiskey	White Cat™ Whiskey	Syntax Spirits LLC, CO
Whiskey	White Dog Whiskey	McMenamins Edgefield Distillery, OR
Whiskey	White Owl Whiskey	McMenamins CPR Distillery, OR
Whiskey	White Tiger	Dark Corner Distillery, SC
Whiskey	White Water Whiskey	Panther Distillery, MN
Whiskey	Whitewater Whiskey	Deerhammer Distilling Company, CO
Whiskey	Whitmeyer's Texas Single Barrel	Whitmeyer's Distilling Co. LLC, TX
Whiskey	Wild Buck Whiskey	NJoy Spirits LLC, FL
Whiskey	Witherspoon's Texas Whiskey	Quentin D. Witherspoon Distillery LLC, TX
Whiskey	Wyoming Whiskey	Wyoming Whiskey Distillery, WI
Whiskey	Yahara Bay Whiskey	Yahara Bay Distillers, WI
Whiskey	Zeppelin Bend Straight Whiskey	New Holland Artisan Spirits, MI
Whiskey	4 Spirits Whiskey	4 Spirits Distillery, OR
Whiskey	Charbay Doubled & Twisted Light Whiskey	Charbay Winery & Distillery, CA
Whiskey	Civilized Whiskey	North. Un. Brewing Co. & Distilling, MI
Whiskey	Devils Bit Whiskey	McMenamins Edgefield Distillery, OR
Whiskey	White Pike Whiskey	Finger Lakes Distilling, NY
Whiskey, Aged	291 Colorado Whiskey Aspen Stave Finished (aged)	Distillery 291, CO
Whiskey, Aged	Ironweed	Albany Distilling Company, NY
Whiskey, Aged Bourbon	Koval Bourbon Aged Whiskey	Koval Distillery, IL
Whiskey, Aged Corn	Thunderbeast Spirit Aged Corn Whiskey	Mad Buffalo Distillery, MO
Whiskey, Aged Grain	Koval Four Grain Aged Whiskey	Koval Distillery, IL
Whiskey, Aged Millet	Koval Limit. Ed. Toasted Barrel Millet Aged Whiskey	Koval Distillery, IL
Whiskey, Aged Millet	Koval Millet Aged Whiskey	Koval Distillery, IL
Whiskey, Aged Oat	Koval Limit. Ed. Toasted Barrel Oat Aged Whiskey	Koval Distillery, IL
Whiskey, Aged Oat	Koval Oat Aged Whiskey	Koval Distillery, IL
Whiskey, Aged Rye	Koval Limit. Ed. Toasted Barrel Rye Aged Whiskey	Koval Distillery, IL

Category	Product	Distillery
Whiskey, Aged Rye	Koval Rye Aged Whiskey	Koval Distillery, IL
Whiskey, Aged Spelt	Koval Limit. Ed. Charred Barrel Spelt Aged Whiskey	Koval Distillery, IL
Whiskey, Aged Spelt	Koval Limit. Ed. Toasted Barrel Spelt Aged Whiskey	Koval Distillery, IL
Whiskey, Aged Wheat	Koval Limit. Ed. Charred Barrel Wheat Aged Whiskey	Koval Distillery, IL
Whiskey, Aged Wheat	Koval Limit. Ed. Toasted Barrel Wheat Aged Whiskey	Koval Distillery, IL
Whiskey, Apple	Leopold Bros. New York Apple Whiskey	Leopold Bros., CO
Whiskey, Barley	Still Cellars Whiskey Barley	Still Cellars, CO
Whiskey, Blackberry	Leopold Bros. Rocky Mountain Blackberry Whiskey	Leopold Bros., CO
Whiskey, Blended	Troubadour Blended Whiskey	The Original Texas Legend Distillery, TX
Whiskey, Blended	TX Blended Whiskey	Firestone & Robertson Distilling Co., TX
Whiskey, Bourbon	Arkansas Young Bourbon Whiskey	Rock Town Distillery Inc., AR
Whiskey, Bourbon	Baby Bourbon Whiskey	Tuthilltown Spirits Distillery, NY
Whiskey, Bourbon	Benj. Prichard's Double Barreled Bourbon Whiskey	Prichard's Distillery Inc., TN
Whiskey, Bourbon	Benj. Prichard's Double Chocolate Bourbon Whiskey	Prichard's Distillery Inc., TN
Whiskey, Bourbon	Big Bottom Whiskey Am. Straight Bourbon Whiskey	Big Bottom Whiskey, OR
Whiskey, Bourbon	Big Bottom Whiskey Straight Bourbon Whiskey	Big Bottom Whiskey, OR
Whiskey, Bourbon	Black Reserve Bourbon Whiskey	Cleveland Whiskey LLC, OH
Whiskey, Bourbon	Bloody Butcher Bourbon Whiskey	Cacao Prieto LLC, NY
Whiskey, Bourbon	Bourbon Spring™ Young Rested IL Bourbon Whiskey	Quincy Street Distillery, IL
Whiskey, Bourbon	Bowman Bro. Sm. Batch VA Straight Bourb. Whiskey	A. Smith Bowman Distillery, VA
Whiskey, Bourbon	Cask Strength Straight Bourbon Whiskey	Whitmeyer's Distilling Co. LLC, TX
Whiskey, Bourbon	Cedar Ridge Iowa Bourbon Whiskey	Cedar Ridge Distillery, IA
Whiskey, Bourbon	Charred Oak Bourbon Whiskey	Yahara Bay Distillers, WI
Whiskey, Bourbon	Cody Road Bourbon Whiskey	Mississippi River Distilling Company, IA
Whiskey, Bourbon	Colorado Gold Straight Bourbon Whiskey	Colorado Gold Distillery, CO
Whiskey, Bourbon	Dark Horse Distillery Reserve Bourbon Whiskey	Dark Horse Distillery, KS
Whiskey, Bourbon	Dodge City Distillery Bourbon Whiskey	Good Spirits Distilling, KS
Whiskey, Bourbon	Dry Fly Washington Bourbon Whiskey	Dry Fly Distilling, WA
Whiskey, Bourbon	E.H. Taylor, Jr. Straight KY Bourb. Whiskey	E.H. Taylor, Jr. Old Fash. Copper Dist., KY
Whiskey, Bourbon	Four Grain Bourbon Whiskey	Tuthilltown Spirits Distillery, NY
Whiskey, Bourbon	Garrison Brothers Texas Straight Bourbon Whiskey	Garrison Brothers Distillery, TX
Whiskey, Bourbon	John J. Bowman Sngl. Barl. VA Stra. Bourb. Whiskey	A. Smith Bowman Distillery, VA

Category	Product	Distillery
Whiskey, Bourbon	Lewis Redmond Carolina Bourbon Whiskey	Dark Corner Distillery, SC
Whiskey, Bourbon	MBR Kentucky Bourbon Whiskey	MB Roland Distillery, KY
Whiskey, Bourbon	McKenzie Bourbon Whiskey	Finger Lakes Distilling, NY
Whiskey, Bourbon	Neversweat Bourbon Whiskey	Headframe Spirits, MT
Whiskey, Bourbon	Noah's Mill	Willett Distillery, KY
Whiskey, Bourbon	Oola Waitsburg Bourbon Whiskey	Oola Distillery, WA
Whiskey, Bourbon	Outlaw Bourbon Whiskey	Yellow Road Distilling LLC, TX
Whiskey, Bourbon	Ranger Creek .36 Texas Bourbon Whiskey	Ranger Creek Brewing & Distilling, TX
Whiskey, Bourbon	Red River Texas Bourbon Whiskey	JEM Beverage Company, TX
Whiskey, Bourbon	Rowan's Creek	Willett Distillery, KY
Whiskey, Bourbon	Smooth Ambler Old Scout Straight Bourbon Whiskey	Smooth Ambler Spirits Company, WV
Whiskey, Bourbon	Spring Mill Straight Bourbon Whiskey	Heartland Distillers, IN
Whiskey, Bourbon	Straight Rye Whiskey	Yellow Road Distilling LLC, TX
Whiskey, Bourbon	Temperance Trader Straight Bourbon Whiskey	Bull Run Distilling Company, OR
Whiskey, Bourbon	Widow Jane Bourbon Whiskey	Cacao Prieto LLC, NY
Whiskey, Bourbon	Widow Jane Wapsie Valley Bourbon Whiskey	Cacao Prieto LLC, NY
Whiskey, Bourbon Rye	Smooth Ambler Old Scout	Smooth Ambler Spirits Company, WV
Whiskey, Bourbon Rye	The Microbarreled™ Collection – Bourb. Rye Whiskey	Woodinville Whiskey Co., WA
Whiskey, Bourbon, Aged	Hillrock Soera Aged Bourbon Whiskey	Hillrock Estate Distillery, NY
Whiskey, Chocolate	Kings County Chocolate Whiskey	Kings County Distillery, NY
Whiskey, Corn	Colorado's Own Corn Whiskey	Colorado Gold Distillery, CO
Whiskey, Corn	Dawsonville Moonshine Georgia Corn Whiskey	Dawsonville Moonshine Distillery, GA
Whiskey, Corn	Delaware Phoenix Corn Whiskey	Delaware Phoenix Distillery, NY
Whiskey, Corn	Fitch's Goat 100% Corn Whiskey	Bone Spirits, TX
Whiskey, Corn	Glen Thunder Corn Whiskey	Finger Lakes Distilling, NY
Whiskey, Corn	Hooker's House Corn Whiskey	HelloCello, CA
Whiskey, Corn	Myer Farm White Dog Corn Whiskey	Myer Farm Distillers, NY
Whiskey, COrn	New England Corn Whiskey	Berkshire Mountain Distillers Inc., MA
Whiskey, Corn	New York Corn Whiskey	Tuthilltown Spirits Distillery, NY
Whiskey, Corn	RoughStock Montana Sweet Corn Whiskey	RoughStock Distillery, MT
Whiskey, Corn	Thunderbeast Storm Moonshine Corn Whiskey	Mad Buffalo Distillery, MO
Whiskey, Corn	Tirado NY Corn Whiskey	Tirado Distillery, NY

Category	Product	Distillery
Whiskey, Corn	Two Jays Corn Whiskey	Broadbent Distillery, IA
Whiskey, Corn	Two Jays Corn Whiskey Country Style	Broadbent Distillery, IA
Whiskey, Corn	Water Tower White Lightning™ Unaged IL Whiskey	Quincy Street Distillery, IL
Whiskey, Hickory Smkd.	Arkansas Hickory Smoked Whiskey	Rock Town Distillery Inc., AR
Whiskey, Light	Coyote 100 Light Whiskey	Dakota Spirits Distillery LLC, SC
Whiskey, Light	HDC Light Whiskey	Heritage Distilling Company Inc., WA
Whiskey, Light	Trail Town Still Coyote Light Whiskey	Trail Town Still, CO
Whiskey, Malt	Downslope Malt Whiskey	Downslope Distilling, CO
Whiskey, Malt	Santa Fe Silver Coyote Pure Malt Whiskey	Santa Fe Spirits, NM
Whiskey, Malt	Westward Oregon Straight Malt Whiskey	House Spirits Distillery, OR
Whiskey, Moonshine	Whitmeyer's Texas Moonshine Whiskey	Whitmeyer's Distilling Co. LLC, TX
Whiskey, Oat	Easy Eight Unoaked Oat Whiskey	Stone Barn Brandyworks, OR
Whiskey, Oat	High West Silver Whiskey Western Oat	High West Distillery, UT
Whiskey, Orgainic	Bainbridge 'The Whiskey Forty Saloon' Org. Whiskey	Bainbridge Organic Distillers, WA
Whiskey, Organic	Bainbridge Battle Point Org. Whiskey	Bainbridge Organic Distillers, WA
Whiskey, Peach	Leopold Bros. Rocky Mountain Peach Whiskey	Leopold Bros., CO
Whiskey, Peach	Whitmeyer's Texas Peach Whiskey	Whitmeyer's Distilling Co. LLC, TX
Whiskey, Peach Georgia	Leopold Bros. Georgia Peach Whiskey	Leopold Bros., CO
Whiskey, Peated Sngl. Mlt.	Leviathan American Peated Single Malt Whiskey	Lost Spirits Distillery, CA
Whiskey, Peated Sngl. Mlt.	Paradiso Peated American Single Malt Whiskey	Lost Spirits Distillery, CA
Whiskey, Rye	1512 Barbershop Rye Whiskey	1512 Spirits, CA
Whiskey, Rye	1512 Spirits Aged 100% Rye Whiskey	1512 Spirits, CA
Whiskey, Rye	Benjamin Prichard's Rye Whiskey	Prichard's Distillery Inc., TN
Whiskey, Rye	Catoctin Creek Organic Roundstone Rye™	Catoctin Creek Distilling Co. LLC, VA
Whiskey, Rye	Ceran St. Vrain's Taos Lightning Rye Whiskey	Rancho de Los Luceros Destilaria, NM
Whiskey, Rye	Charred Oak Rye Whiskey	Yahara Bay Distillers, WI
Whiskey, Rye	Cody Road Rye Whiskey	Mississippi River Distilling Company, IA
Whiskey, Rye	Commander's Rye Whiskey	Heritage Distilling Company Inc., WA
Whiskey, Rye	Dad's Hat™ Pennsylvania Rye Whiskey	Mountain Laurel Spirits LLC, PA
Whiskey, Rye	Dark Horse Distillery Reunion Rye Whiskey	Dark Horse Distillery, KS
Whiskey, Rye	Delaware Phoenix Rye Dog	Delaware Phoenix Distillery, NY
Whiskey, Rye	Delaware Phoenix Rye Whiskey	Delaware Phoenix Distillery, NY

516

Whiskey, Rye	Doc Holliday Rye Whiskey	Georgia Distilling Company, GA
Whiskey, Rye	Goldrun Rye Whiskey	Old World Spirits LLC, CA
Whiskey, Rye	Hard Eight Rye Whiskey	Stone Barn Brandyworks, OR
Whiskey, Rye	High West Double Rye	High West Distillery, UT
Whiskey, Rye	High West OMG Pure Rye	High West Distillery, UT
Whiskey, Rye	High West Whiskey Double Rye	High West Distillery, UT
Whiskey, Rye	High West Whiskey Rendezvous Rye	High West Distillery, UT
Whiskey, Rye	John David Albert's Taos Lightning Rye Whiskey	Rancho de Los Luceros Destilaria, NM
Whiskey, Rye	Manhattan Rye Whiskey	Tuthilltown Spirits Distillery, NY
Whiskey, Rye	McKenzie Rye Whiskey	Finger Lakes Distilling, NY
Whiskey, Rye	Myer Farm Rye Whiskey	Myer Farm Distillers, NY
Whiskey, Rye	Old Maysville Club Rye Whiskey	Old Pogue Distillery, KY
Whiskey, Rye	Oldfield Rye Whiskey	Cascade Peak Spirits Distillery, OR
Whiskey, Rye	Organic Aged Rye Whiskey-Small Cask Series	Pittsburgh Distilling Co., PA
Whiskey, Rye	OYO Rye Whiskey (100% Dark Pumpernickel)	Middle West Spirits LLC, OH
Whiskey, Rye	RallyPoint Rye Whiskey	StiLL 630, MO
Whiskey, Rye	Ravenswood Rye	Journeyman Distillery, MI
Whiskey, Rye	Reservoir Rye Whiskey	Reservoir Distillery, VA
Whiskey, Rye	RoughStock Montana Straight Rye Whiskey	RoughStock Distillery, MT
Whiskey, Rye	Ryan & Wood Straight Rye Whiskey	Ryan & Wood Inc., MA
Whiskey, Rye	Rye Whiskey	Skip Rock Distillers, WA
Whiskey, Rye	Spirit Works Rye Whiskey	Spirit Works Distillery, CA
Whiskey, Rye	Staley Rye Whiskey	Indian Creek Distillery, OH
Whiskey, Rye	Templeton Rye Whiskey	Templeton Rye Distillery, IA
Whiskey, Rye	Two James Rye Whiskey	Two James Spirits, MI
Whiskey, Rye	Ugly White Rye Whiskey	Kill Devil Spirit Company, CA
Whiskey, Rye	Walleye Rye Whiskey	New Holland Artisan Spirits, MI
Whiskey, Rye	Wigle Organic White Rye Whiskey	Pittsburgh Distilling Co., PA
Whiskey, Rye	Elias Staley Un-aged Rye Whiskey	Indian Creek Distillery, OH
Whiskey, Rye Un-aged	Corsair Wry Moon Un-aged Rye Whiskey	Corsair Artisan Distillery, TN
Whiskey, Single Malt	Benjamin Prichard's Single Malt Whiskey	Prichard's Distillery Inc., TN
Whiskey, Single Malt	Cedar Ridge Single Malt Whiskey	Cedar Ridge Distillery, IA

Whiskey, Single Malt	Civilized Single Malt Whiskey	Northern Unit. Brewing Co. & Distilling, MI
Whiskey, Single Malt	Corsair Triple Smoke Single Malt Whiskey	Corsair Artisan Distillery, TN
Whiskey, Single Malt	Down Time Single Malt Whiskey	Deerhammer Distiling Company, CO
Whiskey, Single Malt	Ezra Cox Single Malt Whiskey	Ezra Cox Distillery, WA
Whiskey, Single Malt	Golden Samish Bay Single Malt Whiskey	Golden Distillery, WA
Whiskey, Single Malt	Limestone Landing Single Malt Rye Un-aged Whiskey	Old Pogue Distillery, KY
Whiskey, Single Malt	McCarthy's Oregon Single Malt Whiskey	Clear Creek Distillery, OR
Whiskey, Single Malt	Nashoba Single-malt Whiskey	Nashoba Valley Spirits Ltd., MA
Whiskey, Single Malt	Nevada Single Malt Whiskey	Churchill Vineyards and Distillery, NV
Whiskey, Single Malt	Ranger Creek Rimfire Mesq. Sm. TX Sgl. Malt Whsky.	Ranger Creek Brew. & Distill., TX
Whiskey, Single Malt	Rogue Oregon Single Malt Whiskey	Rogue Spirits, OR
Whiskey, Single Malt	Single Malt Whiskey	Tuthilltown Spirits Distillery, NY
Whiskey, Single Malt	St. George Single Malt Whiskey	St. George Spirits, CA
Whiskey, Single Malt	Tatoosh Single Malt Whiskey	Tatoosh Craft Distillery, WA
Whiskey, Single Malt	Three Oaks Single Malt	Journeyman Distillery, MI
Whiskey, Single Malt	Two James "Reserve" Single Malt Whiskey	Two James Spirits, MI
Whiskey, Sour Mash	Collier and McKeel Sour Mash Whiskey	Collier and McKeel, TN
Whiskey, Sour Mash	Copperhead Georgia Sour Mash	Georgia Distilling Company, GA
Whiskey, Sour Mash	Ivy Mountain Georgia Sour Mash Whiskey™	Ivy Mountain Distillery LLC, GA
Whiskey, Sour Mash	Corn Black Canyon Sour Mash Corn Whiskey	Black Canyon Distillery, CO
Whiskey, Un-aged	Catoctin Creek Organic Mosby's Spirit™	Catoctin Creek Distilling Co. LLC, VA
Whiskey, Wheat	1512 Spirits 2nd Chance Wheat Whiskey	1512 Spirits, CA
Whiskey, Wheat	Bill's Michigan Wheat Whiskey	New Holland Artisan Spirits, MI
Whiskey, Wheat	Blue Flame Wheat Whiskey	Blue Flame Spirits, WA
Whiskey, Wheat	Buggy Whip Wheat	Journeyman Distillery, MI
Whiskey, Wheat	Carolina Virgin Wheat Whiskey	Six & Twenty Distillery, SC
Whiskey, Wheat	Dry Fly Washington Wheat Whiskey	Dry Fly Distilling, WA
Whiskey, Wheat	Myer Farm Wheat Whiskey	Myer Farm Distillers, NY
Whiskey, Wheat	Organic Aged Wheat Whiskey – Small Cask Series	Pittsburgh Distilling Co., PA
Whiskey, Wheat	OYO Whiskey (100% Wheat)	Middle West Spirits LLC, OH
Whiskey, Wheat	Reservoir Wheat Whiskey	Reservoir Distillery, VA
Whiskey, Wheat	RoughStock Montana Spring Wheat Whiskey	RoughStock Distillery, MT

Whiskey, Wheat	Ryan & Wood Straight Wheat Whiskey	Ryan & Wood Inc., MA
Whiskey, Wheat	Spirit Works Wheat Whiskey	Spirit Works Distillery, CA
Whiskey, White	Big Jake White Dog Whiskey	StiL 630, MO
Whiskey, White	Bully Boy White Whiskey	Bully Boy Distillers, MA
Whiskey, White	Civilized White Dog	North. United Brew. Co. & Distill., MI
Whiskey, White	Gold Coast White Whiskey	Cathead Distillery LLC, MS
Whiskey, White	Headwaters White Whiskey	Skip Rock Distillers, WA
Whiskey, White	Long Shot White Whiskey	Dark Horse Distillery, KS
Whiskey, White	W.R. Whiskey	Journeyman Distillery, MI
Whiskey, White Millet	Koval Limited Edition White Millet Whiskey	Koval Distillery, IL
Whiskey, White Oat	Koval Limited Edition White Oat Whiskey	Koval Distillery, IL
Whiskey, White Rye	Dad's Hat™ Pennsylvania White Rye	Mountain Laurel Spirits LLC, PA
Whiskey, White Rye	Koval White Rye Whiskey	Koval Distillery, IL
Whiskey, White Spelt	Koval Limited Edition White Spelt Whiskey	Koval Distillery, IL
Whiskey, White Wheat	Koval Limited Edition White Wheat Whiskey	Koval Distillery, IL
Whiskey, White Wheat	Wigle Organic White Wheat Whiskey	Pittsburgh Distilling Co., PA
Whisky	Baby Blue Whisky	Balcones Distillery, TX
Whisky	Big Cat™ Whisky	Syntax Spirits LLC, CO
Whisky	Brimstone Whisky	Balcones Distillery, TX
Whisky	Canada Gold Premium Barrel Aged Canadian Whisky	Forty Creek Distillery, ON Canada
Whisky	Chinook Canadian Whisky	Minhas Micro Distillery, WI
Whisky	Chinook Canadian Whisky USA	Minhas Micro Distillery, WI
Whisky	Coyote Howl Whisky Black	Heron Spirits Distillery, WA
Whisky	Craigdarroch Whisky	Victoria Spirits, BC Canada
Whisky	Forty Creek Carrel Select Whisky	Forty Creek Distillery, ON Canada
Whisky	Forty Creek Confederation Oak Reserve	Forty Creek Distillery, ON Canada
Whisky	Forty Creek Copper Pot Whisky	Forty Creek Distillery, ON Canada
Whisky	Forty Creek Double Barrel Reserve	Forty Creek Distillery, ON Canada
Whisky	Forty Creek John's Private Cask No. 1	Forty Creek Distillery, ON Canada
Whisky	Forty Creek Port Wood Reserve	Forty Creek Distillery, ON Canada
Whisky	Forty Creek Small Batch Reserve	Forty Creek Distillery, ON Canada
Whisky	Ghost Owl Pacific Northwest Whisky	Parliament Distillery, WA

519

Whisky	Glen Scotch Whisky	Artesian Distillers, MI
Whisky	Gold Buckle Club Malt Whisky	The Ellensburg Distillery, WA
Whisky	Okanagan Spirits Whisky	Okanagan Spirits, BC Canada
Whisky	Prince Edward I.C. Shore Whisky	Prince Edward Distillery, PE Canada
Whisky	Stars Rye Whisky	Minhas Micro Distillery, WI
Whisky	True Blue Whisky	Balcones Distillery, TX
Whisky	Walla Walla Whisky	Walla Walla Distilling Company, WA
Whisky	Collier and McKeel Tennessee Whiskey	Collier and McKeel, TN
Whisky	Strait Whisky	Myriad View Artis.Distill. Inc., PE Canada
Whisky, Bourbon	Big Bottom Whiskey Straight Bourb. Whiskey	Big Bottom Whiskey, OR
Whisky, Bourbon	Rough Rider Straight Bourbon Whisky	Long Island Spirits, NY
Whisky, Bourbon	Woodstone Creek 5 Grain Straight Bourbon Whisky	Woodstone Creek, OH
Whisky, Canadian	Special 1+11 Blend Canadian Whisky	Still Waters Distillery, ON Canada
Whisky, Cherry	Moylan's Distilling Cherry Wood Malt Cask Strength	Stillwater Spirits, CA
Whisky, Corn	Desert Lightning Corn Whisky	Black Heron Spirits Distillery, WA
Whisky, Highland Malt	Virginia Highland Malt Whisky	Virginia Distillery Company, VA
Whisky, Light	Walla Walla Light Whisky	Walla Walla Distilling Company, WA
Whisky, Malt	Peregrine Rock – California Pure Malt Whisky	Saint James Spirits, CA
Whisky, Organic Sgl. Malt	Pemberton Distillery Organic Single Malt Whisky	Pemberton Distillery Inc., BC Canada
Whisky, Rye	Aristo Rye Whisky	Minhas Micro Distillery, WI
Whisky, Rye	Copper Fox Rye Whisky	Copper Fox Distillery, VA
Whisky, Rye	Five Fathers Pure Rye Whisky	Old Pogue Distillery, KY
Whisky, Rye	Last Mountain Canadian Rye Whisky	Last Mountain Distillery Ltd., SK Canada
Whisky, Rye	Moylan's Distilling Rye Whisky	Stillwater Spirits, CA
Whisky, Rye	Rough Rider Rye	Long Island Spirits, NY
Whisky, Rye	Royal Crest Rye Whisky	Minhas Micro Distillery, WI
Whisky, Rye	Sailboat Rye Whisky	Minhas Micro Distillery, WI
Whisky, Rye	White Wolf Rye Whisky	White Wolf Distillery, WI
Whisky, Single Malt	'1' Texas Single Malt Whisky	Balcones Distillery, TX
Whisky, Single Malt	Battle of the Glen	Glenora Distillery, NS Canada
Whisky, Single Malt	Defiant Whisky, An American Single Malt	Blue Ridge Distilling Company, NC
Whisky, Single Malt	Glen Breton Canadian Single Malt Whisky	Glenora Distillery, NS Canada

Whisky, Single Malt	Glen Breton Ice	Glenora Distillery, NS Canada
Whisky, Single Malt	Moylan's Distilling American Single Malt Whisky	Stillwater Spirits, CA
Whisky, Single Malt	Notch Single Malt Whisky	Triple Eight Distillery, MA
Whisky, Single Malt	Okanagan Spirits Single Malt Whisky	Okanagan Spirits, BC Canada
Whisky, Single Malt	Pine Barrens Single Malt Whisky	Long Island Spirits, NY
Whisky, Single Malt	Shelter Point Distillery Single Malt Whisky	Shelter Point Distillery, BC Canada
Whisky, Single Malt	Sòlas Single Malt Whisky	Sòlas Distillery, NE
Whisky, Single Malt	Stalk & Barrel Single Malt Whisky	Still Waters Distillery, ON Canada
Whisky, Single Malt	Urban Single Malt Whisky	Urban Distilleries, BC Canada
Whisky, Single Malt	Wasmund's Single Malt Whisky	Copper Fox Distillery, VA
Whisky, Single Malt	Woodstone Creek Sngl. Brl. Peated Sngl. Malt Whisky	Woodstone Creek, OH
Whisky, Single Malt	Moylan's Distilling Am. Single Malt Cask Strength	Stillwater Spirits, CA
Whisky, Single Malt	Single Malt Mesquite Smoked Whisky	Arizona High Spirits Distillery, AZ
Whisky, White	Death's Door White Whisky	Death's Door Spirits, WI
Whisky, White	White Dog Whiskey	Whiskey Thief Distilling Company, KY
Whisky, White	Wildcat White Whisky	The Ellensburg Distillery, WA
White Dog	291 Colorado Rye Whiskey White Dog	Distillery 291, CO
White Dog	White Dog	Fog's End Distillery, CA

David J. Reimer, Sr., has always had an appreciation for fine spirits, however it wasn't until he visited the Caribbean during a work study exchange with the Rotary Club that he became fascinated with the distilling process. Reimer didn't realize it at the time, but this trip would later be the inspiration for the book. Years later, when micro-distilleries started popping up in the U.S., Reimer wanted to learn more about the industry but, when he went looking for a guide to U.S. micro-distilleries, he found nothing. Reimer decided to do his own research, then thought, "If I'm going to do the research, I'm going to write a book." And Micro-Distilleries in the U.S. and Canada was born.

In addition to being a craft spirits connoisseur, Reimer is a freelance journalist, award winning photographer, veteran volunteer firefighter, humanitarian and entrepreneur. Over the past 25 years, he's had scores of articles and dramatic imagery published in professional journals, consumer magazines, and textbooks. When he's not working on upcoming book projects - or traveling and sampling fine spirits - Reimer enjoys woodworking, gardening, and cooking.

www.ingramcontent.com/pod-product-compliance
Lightning Source LLC
Chambersburg PA
CBHW082349270326
41935CB00013B/1560